THE FATE OF THE NEW MAN

# THE FATE OF THE NEW MAN

REPRESENTING & RECONSTRUCTING MASCULINITY

IN SOVIET VISUAL CULTURE, 1945–1965

CLAIRE E. McCALLUM

NIU Press / DeKalb, IL

Northern Illinois University Press, DeKalb 60115
© 2018 by Northern Illinois University Press

27  26  25  24  23  22  21  20  19  18      1  2  3  4  5
978-0-87580-783-6 (case)
978-1-60909-239-9 (e-book)
Book and cover design by Yuni Dorr

Earlier versions of chapters in this book appeared in the following: "The Return: Post-War Masculinity and the Domestic Space in Stalinist Visual Culture, 1945–53," *The Russian Review* 74, no. 1 (2015): 117–43; "Scorched by the Fire of War: Masculinity, War Wounds and Disability in Soviet Visual Culture, 1941–65," *Slavonic and East European Review* 93, no. 2 (2015): 251–85. I thank the journals, Wiley Periodicals, and the Modern Humanities Research Association for permission to reprint materials from these publications.

For links to many of the images referenced in this book, please consult the website fateofthenewman.wordpress.com

Library of Congress Cataloging-in-Publication Data
is available online at http://catalog.loc.gov

For Lizzy, Kathy, and Jenn—for everything

# Contents

# Illustrations

For links to many of the images referenced in this book, please consult the website fateofthenewman.wordpress.com

# Acknowledgments

I have lived with the New Soviet Man for most of my adult life, starting this project at a time when the analysis of both masculinity and visual culture was in its infancy within the context of Slavic studies. Since then I have seen the field develop beyond all recognition and am thrilled that at last I can add my research to the ever-growing body of scholarship. During the decade or so that it has taken to reach this point, I have incurred many debts—personal, professional, and financial—and it is wonderful to finally get the opportunity to publicly acknowledge the support of all those who have helped me along the way.

Firstly, I would like to thank Susan Reid for being the best PhD supervisor any graduate student could hope for, and for her continued support in the years that have followed, not least in the form of writing many references for me while I was on the long, hard path to permanent employment. I would also like to express my gratitude to Miriam Dobson and John Haynes for their advice in the final stages of my PhD work, and to Melanie Ilic, Matthew Stibbe, and Kevin McDermott for their help during my time as a graduate teacher at their institutions. Thanks to the staff of the History and Russian and Slavonic Studies Departments at the University of Sheffield, and particularly to the post-graduate community of the History Department, who helped make my time there so intellectually stimulating. Likewise to all the conference, workshop, and seminar participants too numerous to mention who over the years have encouraged me to think harder, dig deeper, and push further, and have helped shape my work as it evolved through their constructive critiques. I would also like to acknowledge the financial support I received at this stage in my career from the Arts and Humanities Research Council and Joseph Sassoon, without whose scholarship this research would never have got off the ground.

Thanks must also go to the numerous library and archival staff that have aided me in the research process: to those at the School of Slavonic and East European Studies, University College London, who must have dreaded my filling up their office with endless boxes of periodicals; to the staff at the Hoover Institute at Stanford University, California, the British Library in London and Boston Spa, the University of Birmingham, and the National Library of Finland, Helsinki; and to the interlibrary loans team at the University of Exeter, who have had to deal with all kinds of obscure requests over the years and have always proved up to the task. To the fabulous staff of the Slavic Library (as it was back then) at the University of Illinois, Urbana-Champaign, especially Kit Condill and Jan Adamczyk, the latter of whom was literally responsible for putting a roof over my head and food on my table during my month there. To the ladies in the graphic department of the Russian State Library, in particular Svetlana Nikolaevna Artamonova and Iulia Petrovna, who took me under their collective wing and plied me with "English" tea and biscuits while in Moscow, and to the archivist at GARF who let me loose on the institution's neglected poster collection and supplied me with much needed coveralls for the process. I'm also immensely thankful to Olga Kosheleva, who not only let me her apartment but helped with introductions to the archives, arranged for escorts to the market, and helped me negotiate the vagaries of Muscovite life during those first unsettling days.

Since completing the research aspect of this project, I have been very fortunate to work with some incredibly patient and understanding editors, who have helped this neophyte navigate the world of academic publishing. Thanks to Kurt Schultz, Michael Gorham, and Barbara Wyllie for assisting me in my first forays into publication, and of course to Amy Farranto and her colleagues at Northern Illinois University Press for their guidance and support during the whole process of producing this book. I am deeply appreciative of the staff at various galleries, museums, and archives across the former Soviet Union who have helped make the process of tracking down permissions for the images featured here as painless as possible, particularly Liza Zhiradkova at Kommersant, Vera Kessenich of the Russian Museum, Marina Ivanova at the Tretyakov Gallery, and Ralph Gibson at Sputnik. Beyond this practical support, I am hugely grateful to the anonymous reviewers who took the time to read my work and offer their insightful comments and recommendations, and to the Association for Women in Slavic Studies for their recognition of my research, which provided a much-needed boost in the final stages of editing the manuscript.

I count myself very privileged since embarking on my academic career to have worked with some of the most brilliant historians in the UK, who fortunately for me have also turned out to be immensely caring and encouraging colleagues. I am indebted to the whole History Department at the University of Exeter for their support over the past six years, but especially to Freyja Cox Jenson, Laura Sangha, Stacey Hynd, and Helen Birkett for their guidance and friendship, and to Tim Rees and Martin Thomas, whose sage advice has been crucial in helping me manage the pressures of teaching and research as an early career academic. The biggest thanks, though, must go to the wonderful

Matthew Rendle: it is an amazing feeling to know that someone has complete confidence in your abilities at those points when you doubt yourself, and Matt has read more of my work, offered me more support, and bought me more gin than I could reasonably have expected from any colleague, and for this I will always be grateful. A special mention also to my former colleagues Andrew Holt and Emily Manktelow, who shared that tumultuous first year with me, and particularly to Sara Barker, who is not just a fantastic historian and the kind of teacher I aspire to be, but who has also become one of my dearest friends.

Anyone who has worked in academia will know how all-consuming this job can be, especially in the early days when there is often little stability and security, a lot of uncertainty, and a great deal of teaching preparation, job applications, grant proposals, writing, and editing to be done in the hope of becoming employable. I have been guilty of neglecting my friends and family as a consequence of this pressure, and yet despite my self-absorption, they have stood by my side throughout this whole process: I thank you all from the bottom of my heart for your patience and your support. Many years ago, I made a promise to my oldest friends that I would dedicate my first book to them, something that at the start of the PhD process seemed like a complete fantasy: it with immense pleasure, then, that I can make good this promise here. To Lizzy Baker and Kathy Mclusky, both of whom came into my life when I was in the first few weeks of undergraduate study, and nearly twenty years later are still here. Although I may not always have shown it, your friendship and love over this time has meant more than I could ever possibly say, as we've shared heartbreak and hardship, as well as much joy, transitioned from students to (reasonably) responsible adults, and attempted to find our way in the world, often with many miles, and sometimes entire continents, between us. To the indomitable Jenn Schmidt, whom I met during a particularly low point, and who was almost single-handedly responsible for holding me together during this time. More than a decade on, I am still amazed by her fearlessness, her compassion, and her determination to be a force for good, and how this challenges me to emulate these qualities in my own life. I hope to be able to share many more adventures with you in the future, wherever that may lead us. It is to these three outstanding women that I dedicate this book.

To my family—where do I begin? Words cannot possibly hope to express the gratitude I have for a lifetime of unconditional encouragement and love. Huge thanks to my brother, Alastair, for his technical expertise that has saved my work, and consequently my sanity, on more than one occasion; to my aunt and uncle, Margaret and David Robson; to my grandma, Marjorie Palframan; and to all my extended family for their support of both myself and my parents through this whole process. My grandfather, William McCallum, didn't live to see the book completed, but right up until dementia robbed us of this wonderful man, he was immensely proud of what I'd achieved, even though I was living and working in a world that was completely alien to his own, and I carry that with me to this day. Finally to my parents, Susan and Duncan McCallum: never think for one moment that all the worry and sacrifice you have endured to allow me to pursue this path is unrecognized or unappreciated. May this book stand as testament to, and a small token of thanks for, the unwavering and constant support you have given me throughout my life; it quite literally could never have been completed without you.

# Note on Transliteration

Throughout this book the translations of Russian into English and the transliterations from Russian Cyrillic into Latin characters are my own, unless indicated otherwise. The Library of Congress transliteration system has been used, except for when alternative spellings are in common usage, such as for Ilya Repin, the Tretyakov Gallery, and Yuri Gagarin.

# THE FATE OF THE NEW MAN

# INTRODUCTION

More than a decade after its initial censoring, Mikhail Sholokhov's short story "The Fate of a Man" was printed for the first time in the pages of the newspaper *Pravda* in two installments published on the last day of 1956 and the first day of 1957. "The Fate of a Man" was indicative of the emergence of a new kind of postwar hero: it is the tale of Andrei Sokolov, a truck driver from Voronezh who spends the majority of the Great Patriotic War as a prisoner of the Germans, before managing to engineer a daring escape in order to return to the Soviet trenches. It is here at the front that he learns his beloved wife and daughters were killed three years earlier when a stray missile destroyed his house. After the death of his mother and sisters, Andrei's only son, Anatolii, had joined the army, risen quickly through the ranks, and was now a captain and a commander of a battery of "forty-fives." Discovering that they are both on their way to the German capital, the separated father and son arrange to meet in Berlin, only for tragedy to strike on the morning of Victory Day as, just before the reunion, Anatolii is killed by a sniper. In the coming weeks, Sokolov is demobilized, and finding the prospect of returning to Voronezh too painful, he moves to be with friends in Urypinsk. It is there, outside a café, that Sokolov encounters the orphan boy Vania, whose father has died at the front, and who has been living on handouts and sleeping on the streets, since his mother had also been killed. Heartbroken following the loss of his own family and moved by the plight of the small boy, Sokolov decides to tell Vania that he is in fact the boy's father. As the "father" and "son" board a boat to take them to a new life in Kashary, the narrator of Sokolov's sad tale reminds the reader that "not only in their sleep do they weep, these elderly men whose hair grew gray in the years of war. They weep, too, in their waking hours. [...] The really important thing is not to wound a child's heart, not let him see that dry, burning tear on the cheek of a man."[1]

In Andrei Sokolov, Sholokhov presented the reader with a very different vision of the Soviet man from the one they had grown accustomed to since the advent of Socialist Realism. Rather than the confident, self-assured, and optimistic hero of the 1930s, Sholokhov's protagonist was rootless, homeless, searching for a place in society, struggling to rebuild his shattered life, and taking emotional comfort in the new surrogate son he had found, another soul cast adrift as a consequence of war. It was a tale of the aftermath of conflict that was a world away from the images of happy homecomings and loving family reunions that had graced the pages of the popular press back in the 1940s.

Within two years the story had been turned into a film by first-time director Sergei Bondarchuk, had been seen by 39.25 million Soviet viewers, and had been voted film of the year for 1959 by the readers of *Sovetskii ekran* (Soviet Screen Magazine).[2] Stills from the film appeared in the popular magazine *Ogonek* in early 1960, and illustrations for a new edition of the book by L. Petrov and V. Petrova were reproduced in the art journal *Iskusstvo* in June 1965, around the same time as another set of sketches based on the story, this time by the famous graphic artist Petr Pinkisevich, were published over two pages in *Ogonek* as part of the publication's ongoing commemoration of the end of the Great Patriotic War.[3] When the book was reprinted in 1964 by *Khudozhestvennaia literatura*, the new edition featured illustrations by none other than the trio of Porfiri Krylov, Mikhail Kupriianov, and Nikolai Sokolov, known collectively as the Kukryniksy, a group of graphic artists whose work had defined wartime visual culture. The moments of the story that were chosen as the basis for the Kukryniksy's illustrations are telling: the grief of Sokolov and his wife at their separation, the pain caused by the injury he sustains, the moment he comes face-to-face with the bombed-out shell of his former home, the coffin of Anatolii being borne by his comrades, and the emotional "reunion" of father and son were all presented visually.[4] Likewise, writing in *Iskusstvo* about their work on the novella, Petrov and Petrova stated that "we felt it necessary to find the most epic moments that would talk about the main characters and events of the book: the farewell before leaving for the front, the wounded Sokolov in captivity, and Sokolov with his foster son."[5] For these artists the emotional heart of Sholokhov's work was the separation from the family, physical and psychological trauma, and the reconstruction of life around the father-child bond.

In many ways, this book echoes the overarching themes of Sholokhov's short story by focusing on the dual indentities of the Soviet man as a soldier and as a father as it traces the development of the visual representation of the ideal Soviet man over the two decades that separate the end of the War from the reinstatement of Victory Day (May 9) as a public holiday in 1965. It provides the first in-depth study of the use of visual culture to articulate what it meant to be a New Soviet Man during this period, and offers a new assessment of the impact of the War on a model of masculinity that has to date been viewed as constant in its construction and almost entirely removed from the real-life experiences of actual Soviet men.

In order to chart the changes that can be seen in the twenty years under scrutiny here, the full range of official visual culture will be explored, from posters, illustrations, photographs, and cartoons to the great monumental paintings of the day. Rather than confine the focus to what was simply being produced by artists, however, a consideration of how these images circulated in society through the print media will form a crucial part of the study. The aim of this book, therefore, is not only to examine how the vision of the New Soviet Man changed over the course of these turbulent decades, but also how that vision was presented to the vast reading public of the Soviet Union. This approach allows for an investigation that not only explores issues to do with the portrayal of the ideal man in the years following the Great Patriotic War, but that also engages with some of the broader questions raised by the study of Soviet culture during this period: Is it possible to speak of one homogeneous way in which culture responded to the events of the War and its legacies? What impact did the Thaw-time liberalization of culture have on how issues that had been ignored under Stalin were now handled artistically? And how did the emergence of the cult of the Great Patriotic War under Brezhnev shape how those years and their legacy were presented through visual culture?

The analysis offered here is based on an examination of a wide range of print media, from the national press to magazines such as *Ogonek*, which had a yearly circulation of tens of millions, to the thick journals of the art world, most notably the long-running publication *Iskusstvo*. Looking across this spectrum enables us to do a number of things: we can see how the reproduction of certain pieces, in particular fine art, may differ across the professional and popular press; we can gauge what works did or did not find an outlet in print and why this might be the case; and we can see how the other forms of visual material, such as photographs and sketches and cartoons, sat alongside the copies of paintings that were such an important element in magazines of the era. In short, this methodology allows us to not only think about what was being produced across all these genres but what was reproduced and in what context, and subsequently what role these works played in shaping the image of the ideal man in the postwar period.

## WHO WAS THE NEW SOVIET MAN?

Before we can establish the impact that the War had on the Soviet model of masculinity, though, we need to think about what constituted that model prior to 1945. For all that the issue of women under Soviet rule has been a part of scholarship since the birth of gender studies in the 1970s, the experience of men and the state's ideas about what a man should be were largely neglected until the turn of the twenty-first century. In the decade and a half that has followed the emergence of masculinity as a vibrant part of Russian and Slavonic studies, a whole raft of work has been carried out that has brought to light that self-evident but oft-neglected fact that there was no such thing as a universal male experience of Soviet rule.[6] What has been harder to challenge, however, is the notion that there was one consistent idea about who the New Soviet Man was, as if this ideal were utterly impervious to political upheaval and social change. As a consequence the phrase "New Soviet Man" has become an almost unconscious signifier for a range of behaviors and characteristics that we think we are familiar with, with little regard to what actually was encapsulated by this ideal and, crucially, how that ideal may have changed over time.

For all the Bolshevik government wished to create the world anew following the revolution of 1917, it did not enjoy the luxury of an entirely blank slate, and the foundations of the new regime were built upon the ruins of the old. It stands to reason, then, that many of the qualities that were held up as being exemplary of the New Soviet Man were neither new nor Soviet in their origin.[7] Traits that were presented as being central to this Soviet ideal, such as heroic struggle, a readiness for sacrifice, comradeship, and patriotism clearly have roots in both the chivalric code of Western civilization and the pagan warrior model celebrated in Celtic and Slavic cultures. Indeed, as Barbara Evans Clements has pointed out, there was little difference between the cries for courage and glory that proliferated in the Soviet press in the years between 1941 and 1945 and those that were to be found in the twelfth-century epic, *The Lay of Igor's Campaign* (1185–87),[8] a fact that is underlined by the extensive references to the exploits of mythic heroes such as Aleksandr Nevskii and Dmitrii Donskoi in the wartime poster. Similarly, the idea that a man's primary identity was established by his work is one that sociologist R. W. Connell has traced back to at least the nineteenth century with the continued development of industrial capitalism and the emergence of the urban bourgeoisie.[9] The connection between work and masculinity was one that was cemented in the earliest days of the revolution and can be seen as absolutely rooted in the so-called "cult of the machine" that dominated the first wave of Soviet industrialization. Born of a concern with the former empire's industrial backwardness, the overarching aim of this new relationship between worker and machine was ultimately to free the working class from the whims of overseers and to turn them into what Nikolai Bukharin called "qualified, especially disciplined, living labor machines."[10] It was in every way a utopian mission and an integral element in the project of social transformation that underpinned the Bolshevik agenda right from the start of the regime. The new Soviet workforce was to be transformed—in the words of Evgenii Zamiatin—into the "steel heroes of a great epic."[11]

The influence of the theories of Henry Ford and Frederick Taylor, the development of the conveyor-belt system of production, and the increasing mechanization of the workplace was not confined to the new Soviet state, and the impact of these ideas on the conceptualization of the male working-class body was in many respects a pan-European phenomenon. The Nietzschean ideal of hypermasculine bodily construction, as popularized in the culture of the post-1918 period, can be seen as part of this trend: at the time when strength, durability, and consistency were the buzzwords of this new mechanization, so the male body came to be associated with these characteristics.[12] Therefore, as Maurizia Boscagli points out, the modernist agenda was not "simply to emulate and challenge technology but instead to identify with it," leading to a shifting aesthetic appreciation of the male body, which now focused upon its productive uses rather than its physical beauty.[13] In line with the theories of Taylor, which had advocated the rationalization of work through breaking it down into single repeated tasks, by assimilating the machine with the male body it too became a series of moving parts to be kept in good working condition through physical training and away from corrupting influences that could harm its productivity, such as alcohol, religious practice, and illiteracy. It was a radical departure from the Classical ideal of the beautiful and harmonious male form: from the Soviet and modernist perspective, the body was something to be admired, not simply for its beauty and strength, but for what it could achieve and the exertion it could withstand, particularly when a part of a larger labor unit.

This conceptualization of the male body fell out of favor with the decline of the avant-garde movement after 1932 and the move toward Socialist Realism, an aesthetic that had human interaction rather than technology as its central ethos. However, the idea of a physically perfect body, well-tuned to the demands of labor, continued to resonate throughout the 1930s, and the concern with fitness, sporting prowess, and youth during these years can be seen as an offshoot of these early revolutionary ideas.[14] These ideals, of course, were of primary importance at a time when war seemed almost a certainty, as the Soviet workforce now had to be willing not only to fight for the achievement of socialism but to fight against the foreign threats that loomed on the horizon. As the 1930s developed, this militaristic strand that had always been a part of the Soviet masculine model became increasingly prominent, leading to what Thomas Schrand has argued was actually a "new configuration of male hegemony [that] made the male role of soldier a primary element in the new masculine identity."[15] This was a celebration of martial behaviors and qualities that went far beyond just a celebration of the military itself;[16] as it had been since the earliest days of the Revolution, this was a militarism that pervaded almost every aspect of society—everything was a battle and everyone was expected to be willing to fight and sacrifice in order to win the war being waged by both the internal and external enemies of the Soviet state.

The final aspect of what can be seen as a typical part of the ideal masculine model—certainly since the move away from the monastic ideal in the Early Modern period—is paternity, and it is here where we find the most divergence from both contemporary Western and traditional Russian values. The deep patriarchal roots of Russian society were challenged by the Soviet regime on all fronts: practically, through industrialization and the disruption of the family network; ideologically, through Marxist hostility to the family unit; and symbolically, through the range of legislation that was introduced during the early Soviet period that replaced biological fatherhood with the paternalistic state. It was not until the middle of the 1930s that being a good father came to be seen as a relatively important part of being a good Soviet citizen, a rhetorical shift that has been somewhat overlooked in light of the increasing emphasis on mothering and fertility that paralleled this development in the years around 1936. At the same time, the place paternity had as part of this idealized model of manhood was severely restricted by the fact that after 1934 Stalin himself had donned the mantle of ultimate Soviet father, followed by the emergence of what Katerina Clark termed the "Great Family Myth," the idea that one's loyalty to the state and its leadership should always overrule any loyalty one may have to blood kin.[17] This combination of the very public orientation of the male role, the celebration of the mother under Stalinism, and the paternal outlook of the state itself has led to an assumption that fatherhood was always a minor part of what it meant to be a New Soviet Man, if indeed a part of this archetype at all.[18]

The image that we have of the New Soviet Man, then, is one that is highly militarized, based on values of self-sacrifice and loyalty, where dedication to work and the well-being of the collective overrode any personal or private considerations, and demanded physical health and moral fortitude. But as will be shown over the coming chapters, this model of the New Soviet Man created in the 1930s was not a fixed and unchanging constant: as the outlook of society changed, both with the end of the War and then the death of Stalin, so too did ideas about who the ideal man was and how he was represented.

In this respect, this study of the visual representation of the ideal man makes an important contribution to the far more nuanced understanding scholars now have of the late Stalin era and the early years of the Thaw. The postwar period has proved to be one of the most dynamic fields of study in recent years, leading to work that has fundamentally altered perceptions of late Stalinist society—both in terms of its mechanics and policies and in terms of lived experience in the harsh years of reconstruction and officially sanctioned "normalization"—reclaiming it as a distinct period of Soviet development, rather than dismissing it as of lesser importance when viewed alongside the tumult of the 1930s and the verve of the late 1950s and early 1960s. Running in parallel to this new, more complex understanding of the final years of Stalinism came a body of scholarship that began to break down the boundaries between this period and the years traditionally labeled as the "Thaw," as time and again significant continuities were highlighted across the 1953 divide; trends that had to date been seen as a product of the liberalization of the Thaw era were shown to have their roots in the 1940s and early 1950s, and the notion that late-Stalinist society was one that was static and calcified has been repeatedly challenged by research into areas as diverse as official science policy and consumerism.[19] While this emphasis on continuity and the limits of de-Stalinization has raised important questions regarding the perception of the Khrushchev years as a "Thaw" in its own right, when viewed in relation to the preceding regime, scholars have convincingly shown that to speak of one singular "Thaw" in the period between 1954 and the mid-1960s is also problematic. As the work of academics such as Polly Jones, Miriam Dobson, Stephen Bittner, and others has shown, the decade or so that is traditionally seen as a period of liberalization and relaxation can more accurately be viewed as one that was marked by waves of thaw and freeze, as both popular attitudes and official polices fluctuated and society as a whole attempted to deal with the complex legacy of Stalinism.[20]

This book will demonstrate that what can be seen in terms of the visual representation of the New Soviet Man also contests both the perception of 1953 as a great watershed moment in Soviet history and the notion of one unproblematic and consistent process of "thawing" society after 1956. It will be argued here that it was the experience of the War, not the death of Stalin nor the changing gender or cultural policies of the later 1950s, that had the greatest impact on what qualities now constituted the new man and, crucially, how he was portrayed visually, as important shifts in representation occurred after 1945 and equally important continuities remained after 1953. Looking at visual culture it becomes apparent that the heroic-soldier archetype that had previously been so dominant was fundamentally challenged by the actual experience of war, as after 1945 depictions of the military man became softened and romanticized, and over the course of the mid-1950s, an increasing emphasis came to be placed on the heroic nature of labor and the courage and tenacity of those who fought in that arena for the achievement of socialism. Likewise, what is found in visual culture contests the conventional wisdom that there was no place for the New Soviet Man within the family home, as in the aftermath of war the presence of the returned veteran within scenes of homecoming and, later, general everyday life became synonymous with the return to normality. While the roots of this development lay firmly in the postwar period, the inclusion of men in the domestic space, particularly as fathers, only expanded and diversified as the decade progressed, meaning that by the end of the 1950s being a good father and having a real emotional bond with one's children was absolutely integral to how the Soviet man was depicted across a whole range of visual genres. Thus, what will be demonstrated throughout this book is that the way in which the ideal man was represented visually was never the same again once the War was over: it was an experience so profound and so monumental that even the realm of fantasy was shaken by it.

## SOCIALIST REALISM AND SOCIALIST REALITY

After the dynamism and excitement of the years of revolutionary experimentation—which came to a crashing halt in 1932 with the disbandment of the autonomous artistic organizations, followed rapidly by the official introduction of Socialist Realism a couple of years later—the art of the Stalin era has been traditionally viewed as conservative, staid, and repressive; a microcosm of society itself, where strict limits were placed on individual expression, and rhetoric and representation were far removed from the realities of life.[21] Although purporting to be a reflection of the great and heroic transformations taking place within society, Stalinist Socialist Realism is an art form that is rightly seen as disingenuous and blindly optimistic, in which life is presented through the rosiest of lenses.[22] All those aspects that are synonymous with the Soviet Union in the 1930s—famine, hardship, squalid and cramped living conditions, the upheaval of collectivization, arrest, and incarceration—had no place in this version of reality. Socialist Realism was an aesthetic that was geared toward the future, representing society as it was meant to be in its most ideal form, rather than providing Soviet citizens with a way of making sense of the world around them as it really was. By extension, the figures that populated Soviet visual culture were, with a handful of exceptions, paragons—dedicated and hardworking students, heroic workers of industry, smiling and well-fed *kolkhoznitsas*, and the nation's leaders—although the principle that lay behind this representation was *tipichnost'* ("typicalness"). These were meant to be figures drawn straight from life, characters that were understandable and relatable for the average Soviet audience, and while the realist style fueled this pretense, what was presented as being "typical" invariably became a depiction of the ideal.

It is both this varnishing of reality and the environment in which such art was produced that resulted in it being dismissed as a useful tool for exploring Soviet society for most of the twentieth century. Fortunately, as scholars such as Katerina Clark, Susan Reid, and Denise Youngblood have repeatedly demonstrated in the years since the cultural turn of the 1990s, the art, literature, and film produced under the watchful eye of the state may not allow us to access the complexities of lived experience, but they do provide us with an invaluable insight into the ideals and shifting priorities of the regime and, crucially, how those ideals and priorities were articulated to the rest of the Soviet population.[23] What is also becoming apparent as the culture of the post-Stalin period is more thoroughly explored is that this assumption that culture remained largely divorced from reality becomes increasingly shaky once we move beyond 1956. After the stifling atmosphere of the so-called *Zhdanovshchina*— the years immediately proceeding the War that were marked by an intolerance toward any Western influences in Soviet culture and dominated by the theory of conflictlessness—the culture of the Thaw years is often viewed as a breath of fresh air, as the difficulties of life were explored and it was acknowledged by some, such as the author Konstantin Simonov and the artist Gelii Korzhev, that not everyone emerged from the horrors of the Stalin era physically and emotionally unscathed.[24]

In terms of visual culture specifically, this move toward representing a more psychologically complex portrait of the Soviet person and some of the struggles still present in Soviet society—such as family breakdown, the legacy of the War, or the physical toll of labor—is known as the Severe Style, a form of painting that emerged around 1957. Coined by the art critic Aleksandr Kamenskii, the aesthetic of the Severe Style was described by him as "a turning to the everyday and a scrupulously exact, deeply faithful representation of it that rejected any kind of tarting-up and pomp."[25] Typically it is a style that is often accompanied by words such as *dour, harsh, flinty*, and even *bleak*, adjectives that are seemingly incompatible with the heady optimism of Socialist Realism in its original incarnation of the 1930s. Still, the artists that were advocates of this style should not be seen as rejecting or rebelling against the objectives of Socialist Realism, as the art that they produced was often still romantic in its outlook and still populated by heroes. The difference came in that the struggle these people faced in achieving socialism was now shown as one that involved exertion and the overcoming of difficult situations and environments, rather than being carried out by smiling automatons under perpetually blue skies as it was in the canvases of the 1930s. All of this comes with a caveat, however: as discussed above, recent research has complicated our understanding of the relationship between Stalinism and the Thaw and challenged the concept of one singular Thaw itself. This blurring of the distinction between Stalinism and Thaw is critical for what will be examined in this book, as time and again it will be shown that Stalinist visual culture did not completely obfuscate and sidestep difficult subject matter in the way that we might expect and the years of the Thaw did not see the radical visual reconceptualization of the war experience that we imagine it would, especially given how central the memory of the War was in Khrushchev's infamous denunciation of the former leader in February 1956.

What emerges is a far more complex picture of the interaction between Socialist Realism and socialist reality in the years after the War. It would be exceedingly difficult, and probably foolhardy, to argue that the vision of life presented in visual culture during the course of the 1930s bore any resemblance to the lives of the majority of the population; it is, as Jørn Guldberg stated, "a fictitious world" that is depicted in the imagery of the age.[26] There is a case to be made, though, that the War changed this: just as the war years themselves saw the portrayal of real hardship and brutal death alongside the more heroic and resolute representation of the Soviet population, the years after the War did not see all traces of it expunged from the artistic worldview, despite the rhetoric of normalization that was consistently espoused by the state once the initial euphoria of victory had faded: death, grief, injury, and loss can all be found in the art of late Stalinism. These works were not produced in any great quantity and often they are quite emotionally restricted in how they approach these problematic subjects, but such works do exist; what is particularly important in this context is that not only do they exist, but that they were published in magazines that reached millions of people on a weekly basis. As such, the notion that visual culture was the same after the War as before it, or that the move toward grappling more with the realities of Soviet life was solely a product of the Thaw, will be challenged repeatedly by the material under discussion here. Likewise, despite what may have been occurring in other cultural fields, any assumption that the efforts made to reconfigure the memory of the War during the late 1950s and early 1960s had a dramatic impact on how the War and its aftermath were presented artistically will be shown to be equally fallacious: when it came to dealing with the events of the Great Patriotic War and its lasting legacy, visual culture followed a path all of its own.

Across almost every facet of masculinity that is under examination in what follows, it is not the death of Stalin nor the highs of Thaw-time liberalization, nor indeed parallel developments in the world of literature or film, that coincide with important shifts in representation, but the years that surround the twentieth anniversary of victory in 1965. The increased status of the Great Patriotic War in Soviet society in the 1960s and 1970s has always been a part of how the Brezhnev period has been viewed: this was the time when the vast majority of the great war memorial complexes were built and the Tomb of the Unknown Soldier was created outside the walls of the Kremlin, and 1965 saw the reintroduction of Victory Day as a public holiday for the first time since 1947. These were the years during which the War is seen to become mythologized, where the Soviet story from revolution, through the struggles of industrialization and collectivization, to the savior of European civilization was fixed, and although memoirs were no longer banned from publication as they had been in the 1940s and 1950s, strict censorship forced these recollections to comply with this master narrative. Similarly in literature, while during the Thaw years there had been space for an exploration of the more controversial aspects of the war experience, most notably accounts of the horrors and litany of disasters that accompanied the very early months of the conflict, from the mid-1960s these stories were once again silenced.[27] In more material terms, as Mark Edele has highlighted, this renewed focus on the War did not mean that veterans had a new status in society or suddenly found themselves able to access the entitlements and benefits that had been promised to them back in the 1940s.[28] The cult of the War was for many an exercise in rhetoric, bombast, and pomp, designed to reinforce the political legitimacy of the regime, rather than an opportunity for a more honest and full account of those years to finally be told.[29]

And yet, if the way in which the War was represented visually during this period—and by extension the way in which the soldier and the veteran were portrayed—is examined, something very different becomes apparent. Rather than being a time when tired old heroic clichés were resurrected, these years saw some of the most emotionally complex and introspective representations of the War being produced. Disability, bereavement, psychological trauma, fractured interpersonal relationships, and death all found expression in the visual culture of the day, and with a nuance and a frequency that was unprecedented. There is a case to be made, then, that despite the rhetorical posturing associated with the early years of the Brezhnev regime, in terms of visual culture it was at this time that the artistic vision of the War came closer to reality than it had ever done before. This was a development that not only had a profound impact on the way in which the War and its legacies were represented visually but also on how the men who had fought for the Soviet cause were now depicted.

## THE SOVIET ILLUSTRATED MAGAZINE: REPRODUCING VISUAL CULTURE FOR A MASS AUDIENCE

It is one thing for all these shifts and changes to be occurring within the confines of the art world; it is another thing entirely for these developments to
have any bearing on the way life was presented to the Soviet people through
visual culture on a daily basis. Scholars have long recognized the importance
of the print media in the Soviet state's efforts to transform the country's population into ideal socialist citizens. As Lynne Attwood highlighted in her study
of women's magazines of the Stalin period, these publications were a vital link
between the party and the people and a key conduit for the dissemination of
ideology.[30] However, this process of socialization was not simply confined to
the stories these magazines published, the articles they ran, or the letters to the
editors that were commented on; the visual material that was so integral to
many of these publications also had a vital role to play in molding the readers'
outlook and understanding of the world around them, something that has to
date gone largely unexamined.

The number of exhibitions that took place throughout the Soviet Union
on a yearly basis was tremendous; even in the darkest days of the War, art
exhibitions were still being held in places such as Leningrad, Moscow, and
Novosibirsk and were being visited by thousands of citizens. For the vast
majority of the people, though, magazines, such as the weekly *Ogonek*, were
the way through which they encountered fine art most frequently, not to
mention the other visual material that these publications included such as
cartoons, illustrations for stories, reproductions of posters, and, increasingly
as the years went by, photographs. These publications provided a crucial arena
for the best paintings of the day to be shown and discussed and gave people a
frame of reference for interpreting such works. It was also a space for showcasing art from other parts of the union, for offering overviews of current exhibitions, and for providing readers with information both about contemporary
artists and those associated with the late nineteenth-century *Peredvizhniki*
(The Itinerants or Wanderers) movement, whose work continued to prolifer-
ate in print culture throughout the whole of the period under discussion here.
Rather than being ancillary, images were an integral part of these publications,
and their place in print culture only increased as the technology for reproduction improved.

The potential power of such publications lay in their tremendous circulation numbers. In figures released in 1960 to celebrate National Press Day,
the country's most popular publication was the long-standing women's magazine *Rabotnitsa*, which was released each month and had a print run of more

than two million copies per issue (Table 1). However, in terms of circulation, the nation's most widely read magazine was *Ogonek*, issued weekly with an annual print run of almost ninety million; if we assume that more than one person read each issue, then the scale and reach of this publication can begin to be appreciated.[31] Out of the 3,824 journals, magazines, and papers that were produced in the late 1950s, *Ogonek* alone made up around 15 percent of the entirety of this form of print culture in circulation each year.[32] Visual material had played an important part of this magazine since its inception in 1923, although limitations in terms of both technology and materials meant that until 1945 this was largely in the form of simple sketches and photographs, with the occasional poor-quality reproduction of a painting thrown into the mix. By the early 1950s this had moved on considerably, and the publication became even more lavishly illustrated as the decade progressed, a move that was coupled with a significant upturn in the amount of coverage art was receiving in written form in the magazine as well. This visual evolution was echoed in other publications such as *Sovetskaia zhenshchina* and *Rabotnitsa*, albeit on a much smaller scale, and certainly by the end of the Stalin era, visual material was not only an intrinsic part of these magazines but a prominent one as well.

TABLE 1. CIRCULATION FIGURES FOR POPULAR MAGAZINES, 1960

| PUBLICATION | ISSUES PER ANNUM | CIRCULATION PER ISSUE (IN MILLIONS) | YEARLY CIRCULATION TOTAL (IN MILLIONS) |
|---|---|---|---|
| Krokodil | 36 | 1.4 | 50.4 |
| Ogonek | 52 | 1.7 | 88.4 |
| Rabotnitsa | 12 | 2.4 | 28.8 |
| Sovetskaia zhenshchina | 12 | 0.089 | 1.068 |

Taking *Ogonek* as a template, reproductions of paintings in these magazines usually came in two forms.[33] They could be included as part of an article on a particular exhibition or artist, in which case they were more frequently published in black and white and on quite a small scale. Initially, the only exhibition that warranted extensive coverage was the annual All-Union Exhibition that was held at the end of the year and covered by the press the following January. As the coverage devoted to art increased throughout the mid-1950s and into the early 1960s, it became more commonplace for smaller exhibitions to receive attention, and it is also at this point that information about Soviet artists started to appear either in the form of full-length articles for the most prominent—such as Fedor Reshetnikov, Aleksandr Laktionov, and Gelii Korzhev—or in short columns that accompanied a reproduction of a particular work for those of lower standing. Alternatively, paintings could be included in glossy color reproductions that came grouped together in an almost supplemental form at a couple of points in the magazine. What featured here could vary greatly: sometimes works that related to the predominant theme of that particular issue were included, sometimes it was a place to showcase works by newly graduated artists or more works from recent exhibitions, but often work that was published in this format was not privy to the same level of commentary provided for images embedded in actual articles. Frustratingly for the historian, a significant number of the images included in the magazine in this format received no comment or contextualization at all. Sometimes however, a combination of the two can be found, and there are instances of lengthy articles about particular exhibitions—notably the 1965 Soviet Russia Exhibition—and particular artists, where works are then reproduced beautifully and in color over a series of pages.

By far the most common subject matter for this particular format—a lengthy article and then numerous color images—was the art of the late nineteenth century. It is hard to overstate the importance of the work of the nineteenth-century realists in Soviet culture. While they may have been anachronistically cast as proto-revolutionaries in the early days of Socialist Realism, the paintings of the *Peredvizhniki* enjoyed a popularity that went far beyond official rhetoric. Hardly an issue of *Ogonek* was published across the two decades we are concerned with here that did not contain at least a couple of reproductions of works from this era. Even when the number of contemporary works decreased in the late 1960s, as high-quality color photography became the dominant form of image within the publication,[34] the interest in the *Peredvizhniki* did not waver, and in some instances they received even longer appraisals and more lavish reproductions than they had in earlier years. The perennial favorites were the historical paintings of Vasilii Surikov and Viktor Vasnetsov, the battle scenes of Vasilii Vereshchagin, and Valentin Serov's renderings of provincial Russian life,[35] but the artist who received more coverage and whose work was reproduced more frequently than any other— Russian or Soviet—was Ilya Repin. He is still to this day believed by many to be the greatest Russian artist of all time, and the level of affection felt for this artist during the Soviet era can be gauged, not only through the amount of coverage his work received in the popular magazines of the time, but also through the simple fact that despite everything else that was going on in 1944, the hundredth anniversary of his birth was covered by all the major Soviet newspapers in lengthy eulogies to his genius, which for some publications was one of only a handful of substantial articles that dealt with cultural matters across the entire war.[36] At the same time a series of five stamps was released to mark the occasion that were based on two of Repin's works—his self-portrait from 1899 and his masterpiece, *The Zaporozhe Cossacks Writing a Letter to the Turkish Sultan* (*Zaporozhtsy pishut pis'mo turetskomu sultanu*, 1880–91).[37] The influence of the nineteenth century went far beyond simple reproduction; as shall be seen, these realist painters deeply influenced many Soviet artists, and references were made to their works repeatedly in the paintings, posters, and even cartoons of the day. It is no exaggeration to say that the art of the *Peredvizhniki* was a consistent thread that ran throughout the whole fabric of Soviet visual culture.[38]

While reproductions of paintings were an essential element in these magazines, they were not the only form of visual material that readers would encounter on their pages. The covers of the magazines provided a space for photographs, and more infrequently sketches and copies of paintings, with both the back pages and the frontispiece usually given over entirely to visual material of some format, although exactly how this space was used varied considerably from issue to issue. As the years progressed photography played an increasingly important part of the publications, moving from not only illustrating articles but to appearing in the form of photo-essays, a format where the amount of text was minimal and the images took center stage, and by the end of the 1960s the number of paintings had been reduced considerably and the images in *Ogonek* in particular were predominantly photographs. Drawings for short stories, simple cartoons, copies of posters, and even advertisments could also all be found, contributing to publications that were for most of these two decades lavishly illustrated and, as such, vital tools for the dissemination of visual culture to the Soviet public.

Another crucial medium for the circulation of fine art was the thick journal of the professional art world. In contrast to what we find in the magazines, such journals were primarily concerned with painting—with fairly regular features on sculpture and less regular articles on the graphic arts—and, unlike the popular publications, this was also a space for the condemnation of those works that did not meet the exacting standards of the day. Whereas such controversial works had no place in magazines, in journals such as *Iskusstvo* detailed criticism, which was often accompanied by reproductions of the problematic pieces, was a key part of these publications. What becomes apparent by looking across these two types of publication is that developments in the art world in terms of style or content do not always map on to what is then reproduced in a popular format: a number of key works that are discussed here were recognized in the professional press as being of great importance and yet they have no place in popular print, most notably Gelii Korzhev's *Wounded* (1964), which is discussed in detail in chapter 2. The flip side of this is that the popular publications often contain work by "lesser" or more junior artists whose work was not deemed significant enough to warrant serious academic attention, thereby allowing scholars to get a better sense of the whole range of works that were being produced even just within fine art. This interaction between the debates on the pages of these thick journals and the paintings that then appeared in the more mainstream media is one that will be explored throughout the discussion that follows, although the relationship between the two is never wholly straightforward. Of course, while publications such as *Iskusstvo* can tell us a great deal about the reception of paintings both from within the art world and at times from comments provided by visitors to exhibitions, how people responded to the cartoons, photographs, and other types of visual material that filled the pages of the nation's magazines is impossible to discern. Thus, while the reception of these works will form an important part of the analysis offered here, how people responded to the art they encountered will always be secondary to trying to unravel exactly what was being articulated through visual culture in relation to masculinity and the Soviet man's place and function in society.

## OVERVIEW

In his article "Sunday at the Tretyakov Art Gallery," Dmitrii Stonov described the variety of visitors to the famous Moscow gallery on a typical Sunday afternoon in early 1946—Red Army officers on leave in the capital, sixth-form boys who were there with their history teacher, an elderly collective farmer from the central regions, and a group of disabled ex-servicemen: "From all parts of the Soviet Union [. . . these veterans] have come to Moscow for training and rehabilitation. One of them was complaining about the exhibits. 'There is not enough about the war' he said with conviction."[39] This might have been the case for this early postwar exhibition, but there is very little in visual culture that can compare to the number of paintings, sculptures, dioramas, monuments, and photographs produced after 1945 that took the War or its aftermath as their central theme. It was a consistent part of both artistic production and print culture for the whole of the two decades that are examined here and beyond, although of course trends waxed and waned and areas of focus came in and out of fashion. How visual culture dealt with the events of the War and the implications of this for the conceptualization of masculinity will provide the focus for the first part of this book as it examines the representation of three key parts of the military experience—comradeship at the front, the war-damaged body, and issues to do with death and bereavement—in the two decades after 1945.

We begin with the exploration of a theme that is seen to be at the heart of Soviet society, that of comradeship, as the first chapter traces how the experience of war impacted upon the depiction of the Soviet military man. It will show how in the early postwar years the image of soldierly comradeship was presented as highly romanticized, unthreatening, and removed from any insinuation of brutality or violence, a mode of representation that can be seen as intrinsically tied to the prevailing concerns of Stalinist society. As the 1950s progressed, however, and Stalinism gave way to de-Stalinization, we find remarkably little change in how those in the theater of war were presented as saccharine images of military brotherhood continued to dominate, despite the nascent efforts of some artists to explore the war experience with more psychological complexity and depth. What emerges in the place of the traditional warrior-hero during the Thaw is a new type of heroic worker, who was almost exclusively male and who embodied all the traits that had been key components in the highly militarized masculine model of the 1930s. It would not be until the middle of the 1960s that images began to appear that attempted to represent some of the true horrors of conflict, and the sickly sweet image of soldierly life that had been established in the years after 1945 was finally challenged by paintings that showed the blood, death, and violence that was an intrinsic part of this experience. The assertion that it was the period around 1965 that brought about the most radical changes in how the War was depicted will be a continuous strand throughout all the themes that are examined here.

In the second chapter, the representation of the war-damaged body will be the focus as we chart how the issues of injury and disablement were dealt with visually. It will be shown repeatedly that what is found in visual culture does not easily map on to other cultural forms, and the way that the wounded male body was handled across art, literature, and film is demonstrative of the fact that very often visual culture followed its own unique trajectory when it came to exploring particularly problematic or sensitive issues. Again the picture painted here across the 1953 divide is one of remarkable consistency as injury remained something that was predominantly seen as heroic, and the fact that so many men returned home from the War physically disabled was studiously ignored, despite it playing a significant role in Thaw-era cinema and fiction. Likewise, as shall be shown in the following chapter, the fact that so many men failed to return home at all was something that was largely obfuscated by visual culture right until the early 1960s, again despite loss and bereavement being addressed on numerous occasions in other cultural forms. In chapter 3 how the fallen soldier was depicted and the place that male grief had in visual culture will be examined in detail, as magazines around this time started to not only include reproductions of war-themed artwork but also began to chart the construction and use of memorials through photography. Together these three crucial aspects of the war experience present us with a very different image of the Soviet man to the one who had existed prior to 1945. It also challenges the assumptions that can often be made regarding Socialist Realism, as increasingly the emotional and physical cost of victory was explored through visual culture and presented to the public through the magazines of the day.

Intrinsically tied to the legacies of the War, the second part of the book looks in depth at an aspect of traditional male identity that has to date been largely overlooked in a Soviet context, as the impact of the War, de-Stalinization, and Thaw-era domestic policies on the Soviet father and his representation are considered. Although there had been some important developments in how the role of the father in society was conceptualized during the late 1930s, it was really the use of the family in wartime culture that marked the biggest shift as the protection of one's children was used as a motivation to fight. Chapter 4 charts the shifts in the representation of paternity from the prewar period until the end of the Stalin era, focusing specifically on the impact the War had on how the father, his place in the home, and his relationship with his children was presented visually. It will be shown that while almost entirely absent from the visual culture of the 1930s, after 1945 the number of images that depicted the Soviet father increased exponentially, a trend attributed to his ability to act as a barometer for the reestablishment of prewar norms. The portrayal of the Soviet leadership in the guise of the surrogate father will also be discussed, which taken together with the few paintings that seem to hint at paternal absence, seem to suggest that, while issues to do with loss were rarely openly broached during the Stalin years, the impact of the War on the family was a part of some of the most famous and popular works of the day. While the postwar period marked a watershed in the depiction of the Soviet father in visual culture, it was a trend that only flourished after 1953 as across a whole range of genres fathers and their children became a regular feature on the pages of the nation's most popular magazines, providing the perfect motif for the exploration of a variety of Khrushchevite concerns. The final chapter examines this development in detail, tracing how the representation of the Soviet father changed in the light of de-Stalinization and how over the course of the decade from the mid-1950s onward the idea of being a good father came to be presented as an integral part of being a New Soviet Man. Ultimately, through the examination of these two central male identities—that of the soldier and that of the father—what this book will show is that it was not only real Soviet men who were changed by the experiences of war but that not even the ideal man emerged from those years unscathed.

# 1

# THE LIVING

## Representing Military Comradeship and Male Homosociality after the War

In his short story, "A Soldier and a Half," Vsevolod Pavlovskii tells the tale of two comrades brought together by the battle for Stalingrad, one a seasoned lieutenant from Siberia, the other a sixteen-year-old lad, Mitia, from the city. After being seriously wounded trying to hold the shell of a crumbling house, the men are moved to adjoining beds in the field hospital, where the lieutenant gradually improves and regains his sight but where Mitia tragically succumbs to his injuries:

> It was easy for Mitia to die because he knew his comrade would not leave him. [...] I laid my cheek against his. It was cold and hard and sharp, and I dropped his hand. I realised there was no more Mitia. It was as though I had been laid in the grave while still alive; that without Mitia I was no longer a soldier, but just a man who was ill and weak, the worst kind of mutilated husk."[1]

For this man—who as the author makes clear was a real man, a proper soldier who had spent his youth in the wilds of Siberia hunting bears no less—it was not his own severe injuries that devastated him, but the death of his young brother-in-arms.

The ideal of comradeship was at the very heart of Soviet society and had been since the first days of the Revolution. As such, it is a trope that has influenced our understanding of Soviet society and in recent years has been used as a lens by scholars to explore such disparate areas as sexual violence, the literature of the 1920s, motivations for fighting in war, and Soviet relations with its neighbors in the bloc.[2] It is a term that is deployed almost unquestioningly as a form of shorthand for explaining Soviet social interactions—whether actual or imagined—and "comrade" [*tovarishch*] is a label that is synonymous with the Soviet regime in Western culture.[3] Comradeship was a principle that infiltrated Soviet everyday life—fellow workers were not just colleagues but comrades—and could be applicable to citizens of either gender. It was an ideal that went beyond the individualistic notion of friendship and was instead based on a sense of shared experience, of working together to reach a common objective, and of collectively overcoming obstacles.[4] Thus, while this was a concept that was used routinely used in civilian life, its connotations were explicitly martial.

This chapter will trace how the representation of militaristic comradeship evolved in the decades following the end of the War, examining what impact war had on the ideal and how it was portrayed artistically. It will argue that while the notion of comradeship remained central to how the Soviet soldier was presented in visual culture after 1945, the idea of the military band of brothers was fundamentally altered in the aftermath of actual conflict. Rather than victory reaffirming the militarism of the Soviet soldier and his comrades, what can be seen is a stripping away of the elements traditionally associated with the military hero—his courage, his fearlessness, his willingness to perpetrate violent acts in the line of duty—and in its stead we are left with a vision of military comradeship that is good humored, nonthreatening, and which overlooks the horror that in reality such men had just endured. The second half of the chapter will discuss the period after 1953 and will demonstrate that, with very few exceptions, these modes of representation persisted long after the death of Stalin, despite the huge social, political, and cultural shifts that occurred in the years that followed. Rather than look to the soldier, artists during the Thaw instead looked to the worker as a model for heroic masculinity, as the soldier continued to be presented in a highly romanticized fashion. It was only around the twentieth anniversary of victory that visual culture began to broach the emotional and physical toll that war had taken on those on the front line, and the final part of the chapter will chart this development and how it fits with other changes to the memory of the War that were occurring in the early Brezhnev era.

## COMRADESHIP BEFORE 1945

The concept of militarized and collective struggle was central in Soviet rhetoric and had been since the earliest days of Bolshevik power; from revolution to collectivization, from antireligious campaigns to the push for industrialization, everything about the Soviet project was couched in terms of a battle, whether it was against capitalism, kulaks, or quotas.[5] It should not be surprising, then, that this intense militarism imbued visual culture right from the outset, as motifs and themes that had previously been associated with war came to be used to depict the everyday battles of laboring for the achievement of socialism. However, it should not be assumed that just because Soviet life was being couched in terms of a militarized struggle that this led to the depiction of a society that was being built exclusively by bands of heroic men. Posters in particular would often use the figure of a lone man calling his comrades to join him or follow his example, as seen in Viktor Govorkov's *Your Lamp, Comrade Engineer!* (*Vasha lampa, tovarishch inzhener!*, 1933) for example, and some of the seminal paintings of the period, such as Aleksandr Deineka's *The Defense of Petrograd* (*Oborona Petrograda*, 1927), incorporated women into what would have traditionally been an all-male environment. Even with the advent of Socialist Realism and the move away from the anonymous hero representative of the masses, it was the exception rather than the norm for images that depicted groups of Soviet citizens to do so in a manner that completely excluded one or other of the genders. Despite the highly militarized and masculinized nature of Stalinist society, then, scenes of male homosociality were actually a rarity in visual culture in the years prior to the War.

The outbreak of war would change this as scenes of collective action at the front proliferated. However, while the War had a huge influence on the number of canvases that depicted the all-male group, during the years of fighting, images by and large continued to draw on the forms that had been established during the course of the 1930s. Though still espousing the collective nature of the socialist project, Stalinist society after 1932 saw the decline of what Katerina Clark called the Cult of Little Men,[6] a trend that had developed during the First Five-Year Plan and had been heavily influenced by Maxim Gorky's "god-building" theories.[7] This was a form of representation that consciously rejected the celebration of noted individuals, as had been the case under the tsarist regime, and instead celebrated the heroism of the masses, sometimes depicted as a collective, sometimes in the form of a heroic exemplar. In the wake of this decline there emerged a new focus on the achievements of individuals, as seen in the elevation of workers such as Aleksei Stakhanov and Pasha Angelina. In contrast to capitalist societies, these named individuals were drawn from the ranks of the masses rather than the elite and reflected the potential heroism that Soviet individuals contained within themselves rather than being representative of the good fortune and advantage of a lucky few.[8] The mid-1930s may have seen the adoration of the individual, but these men and women were meant to inspire the masses, to be a form of greatness that was attainable to all, and to be indicative of the huge heroic power of the entire Soviet people. It is important to remember, then, that although Stalinist society venerated achievements of the individual, it was what that individual represented on a collective scale that was significant.

This trend of using individual heroism to represent the superior collective flourished in wartime visual culture; the struggle against the Nazi invaders was often presented as something that was deeply personal to each Soviet citizen, whether at home or on the front,[9] but the implication was that this individual action was simply one snapshot of a scene that was being replicated many times over throughout the motherland. Deineka's *The Defense of Sevastopol* (*Oborona Sevastapolia*) encapsulates this trend completely. Started while the city was still under siege, *The Defense of Sevastopol* was shown for the first time just months later at the All-Union Great Patriotic War Exhibition held at the newly repaired Tretyakov Gallery in November 1942, by which time the city had been lost.[10] Despite depicting a defeat, however, Deineka's painting went on to be one of the most popular and enduring wartime works and almost instantaneously became a regular feature in Soviet print culture, warranting numerous color reproductions and whole features in the two decades after 1945, as well as being the image chosen to mark the anniversary of the War on the nation's postage stamps in 1962.[11]

Although Deineka's overall scene was one of collective struggle, the artist chose to convey this through a series of vignettes, each of which had at its heart the struggle of the individual. This personalization of warfare in Deineka's case was achieved through the depiction of hand-to-hand combat, which was in all likelihood far removed from the actual events of July 1942 but which allowed the artist to ground his work in the traditional ideals of knightly heroics and sidestep the depersonalized, mass death that was the far less romantic reality of modern conflict. The central narrative of this epic work is a battle between the injured sailor, who dominates the foreground, and an unseen enemy, whose bayonet ominously penetrates the border of the painting. Because Deineka structured his composition on the diagonal, his protagonist is endowed with a monumentalism that the other figures lack, and as viewers our eyes are immediately drawn to this man despite the chaos of the scene depicted. However, this technique also allowed the artist to depict the events in the background of the canvas with the same level of detail, and so the eye slowly moves from the central hero down through the ranks of sailors, each of whom is performing equally valiant acts. Thus, what appears to be the story of one individual's fight for the freedom of his country is in reality a representation of the collective strength of the Soviet people. The viewer would have been left in no doubt that, while it may have been the sailors of the

Black Sea Fleet whose actions had been immortalized by Deineka, every true Soviet citizen was fighting just as hard for the preservation of the nation and, just like these men, was willing to pay the ultimate price to achieve that goal. In addition to the artist's own skill in its execution, it was undoubtedly this ideal that cemented the painting as a national favorite both during the years of war and in its aftermath.

## "BROTHERS, FRIENDS, AND COUNTRYMEN": MILITARY COMRADESHIP AFTER THE WAR

The emphasis on the collective experience of war endured long after 1945, but found its most popular incarnation during the Stalin years in the form of Iurii Neprintsev's painting *Rest after Battle* (*Otdykh posle boia*, 1951),[12] a scene inspired by Aleksandr Tvardovskii's much-loved wartime poem *Vasilii Terkin: A Book about a Soldier*, and which was awarded a Stalin Prize First Class in 1952. In the intervening period between the end of the War and the production of *Rest after Battle*, representations of the Soviet military had quite understandably presented a triumphalist vision of the Great Patriotic War and, by association, the heroism and comradeship that underpinned the fighting forces. Paintings such as Pavel Krivonogov's *Victory* (*Pobeda*, 1948) that depicted Soviet soldiers rejoicing on the steps of the Reichstag,[13] Valentin Volkov's rendering of the liberation of the Belorussian capital, *Minsk: 3rd July 1944* (*Minsk, 3 iiulia 1944g.*, 1946–53),[14] and Mikhail Khmel'ko's well-known *The Triumph of the Conquering People* (*Triumf pobedivshei rodiny*, 1949)[15] which showed the laying down of the captured German regimental banners on the steps of the Lenin Mausoleum on June 24, 1945, all portrayed the Soviet military en masse, presenting both victory and heroism as a collective achievement. In these early postwar works, the Soviet soldier was simultaneously relegated to a face in the crowd and elevated to the position of hero through his association with the joint effort at the heart of such a victory; in many ways, then, these initial depictions of the triumph were the visual embodiment of Stalin's famous proclamation that victory was due to the cogs in the great machine of the Soviet state, a machine that according to the official history of the War was being operated by just one great man.

However, by 1950 these triumphalist images had all but disappeared from representations of the Great Patriotic War, and along with this decline, the focus once again shifted back to a more individualized portrayal of war. But, unlike Deineka's brave fighters at Sevastopol, the military comrades of the late Stalinist period were not engaged in fighting, but rather shown enjoying each other's company, telling tales, bathing, or feeding the birds in the park. As such, the "military hero" of the early 1950s was far removed from both the guts and the glory of battle and presented in a manner that was distinctly unthreatening and remarkably unmilitaristic. This benign rendering of the military man during this period can be seen as a consequence of a number of prevailing trends in Stalinist society. In cultural terms, these works can be viewed as products of the *Zhdanovshchina*, an era that demanded cultural production be free of conflict and representative of the greatness of social-ist achievement, and which was aggressively anti-Western in its outlook. In broader social terms, these images can be viewed as products of a society in which the state had taken control over the narrative of victory, a process that in turn left the veterans of the War in a rather precarious position. Although it was celebrated in 1946, by the following year Victory Day (May 9) had been stripped of its status as an official holiday. The publication of military mem-oirs was banned, and the senior military officers instrumental in securing the Soviet victory—and who were therefore a threat to Stalin's claims to be the chief architect of Soviet success—were systematically demoted, relocated, or imprisoned. Three years after the end of the War, public commemoration of it was effectively prohibited and would remain so until 1965.[16]

Part of the process of gaining control over the public memory of the War was an attempt to sweep the traumas and dislocation of the war years under the carpet and to reassert what were seen as prewar norms. As Juliane Fürst has summarized:

> Reconstruction only meant the reconstruction of houses, streets and factories. [...] Cripples were viewed as merely physically impaired, orphans were nothing more than children without parents and veterans were just soldiers who had come home. Restoration of the outer trappings of normalcy was to cover and eradicate inner scars and traumas. The difficulties of reintegration of those who had been at the front [...] were studiously ignored.[17]

Thus while some veterans attempted to perpetuate their "trench broth-erhoods" (*okopnoe bratstvo*) by meeting with comrades in student dormi-tories, cafés, and Blue Danube taverns,[18] their efforts were undermined by this official discourse and the reassertion of prewar authority. As Mark Edele so concisely stated, "the goal [of the state] was to unmake veterans as a social group as fast as possible."[19] The dismantling of the veteran as a social identity was tied to normalization and the danger that an organized group of *frontoviki* could potentially pose to the regime, both metaphori-cally as the group with the greatest claim to being the heroes of the Soviet victory and practically as a group that had had extensive military training and exposure to the dangers of the West.

The idea that the veteran presented a possible threat to social stability was not one that was uniquely Soviet, or even uniquely modern. The veteran is by his very nature a liminal character; he straddles the boundaries of war and peace, of violence and civilization; he has lived outside of social norms and is likely to have carried out acts of unspeakable violence in the name of national or self-preservation. In other words, he is "defined and refined by war, [and] stripped of every social superfluity."[20] However, as both Edele and Elena Zubkova discussed in their pioneering works on postwar Soviet society, there were a variety of reasons why this threat never actually developed into a serious challenge to the Soviet establishment, seen to be largely due to the liberating and patriotic nature of the victory. Nevertheless, it is telling that a significant contingent of those arrested under the notorious Article 58 for "anti-Soviet" behavior in the years between 1945 and 1953 were veterans.[21] Beyond the realities of reintegration and the place of the veteran in any given society, the artistic representation of the military man in peacetime presents contemporaries with a rather interesting quandary: Was it even possible to represent these men carrying out acts of violence—however stylized, implied, or justified—when these same individuals are once again meant to be civilized people in a civilized society? Certainly the Soviet images produced during the first decade or so after the War would suggest an inherent tension in celebrating the military hero in an explicitly militaristic manner once the fighting was over, although some of the other broader social and political developments that occurred after 1945, which may also have had a bearing on how the War was handled across culture generally, must be taken into account as well.

Related to this, one final consideration that needs to be made before moving on to look at some of the images produced during this period is that of the Cold War and most significantly the idea of peace. Concern over maintaining the hard-won peace reached a fever pitch in the early 1950s, and proceedings from various domestic and international congresses and conferences dominated the pages of the Soviet popular press, particularly those aimed at a female audience.[22] This obsession with the preservation of peace also gave rise to a new genre in Soviet visual culture, which, although largely associated with the graphic arts, did pique the interests of such renowned artists as Fedor Reshetnikov and Vera Mukhina.[23] The idea that the Soviet people were a peace-loving people was one that permeated Soviet rhetoric and culture during the final years of Stalinism, and while there is a debate to be had regarding how cynical this self-presentation may have been, there can be no doubt that the rhetoric of peace had a significant influence over the visual arts of the early 1950s and that the representation of the military man was very much at the heart of this motif.

Nowhere is this seen more clearly than in Latvian artist Simon Gelbergs's *Friends of Peace (Druz'ia mira*, 1950), a painting that depicts a group of airmen in a generic sun-drenched park, feeding pigeons with a small girl and her mother. The painting was reproduced in color and commented on by both the professional art journal *Iskusstvo* and the women's magazine *Sovetskaia zhenshchina* in February 1951 in articles by the art critic Oleg Sopotsinskii and the sculptor Vera Mukhina respectively; coincidentally, both ran under the title "Soviet Artists in the Fight for Peace." The two commentators also chose to view this work as a comment on the global significance of the Soviet commitment to peace, rather than situating it within the far more problematic context of Latvian/Soviet relations.[24] While for Mukhina, Gelbergs's work was expressive of the "benevolent and peaceful nature of the Soviet people," Sopotsinskii took an altogether more militaristic tone in his assessment of this piece: "The painting takes on special meaning because the heroes are officers of the Soviet army. The artist seems to say that the Soviet soldiers are peaceful people but they will if necessary defend the freedom and independence of the nation [*narod*], [and] protect their children and their happy lives."[25] However, the threatening martial subtext that Sopotsinskii wrote of in his review is not really borne out in the image itself, which is incredibly saccharine in its tone. What is more, although the international context of Gelbergs's painting is significant, particularly given that it was as part of articles related to the theme of peace that this work was first reproduced in the print media, the message that this work could convey to a native viewer should not be overlooked. This was not simply an image aimed at portraying the difference between the peaceable Soviets and the belligerent capitalist West; by placing these uniformed men in a public park, interacting with women and children, Gelbergs's work was a scene of domesticated militarism that, if anything, removed any insinuation of even latent aggression or the sense that these were men who had in any way been barbarized by their recent experience of war, and instead cast them as full participants in Soviet society, a status that was grounded in their roles as husbands, fathers, and providers.

Consequently, after 1945 the specific rhetoric of normalization and the state's firm grip on the collective memory of the War served to divest military comradeship of its potency, both in reality and in terms of its depiction in visual culture. Soviet veterans *as a collective* were reintegrated into the parameters of civilized society, expunged of their explicit militarism, and removed from the brutality of battle. The result of this was the presentation of comradeship devoid of the bitter experiences and the realities of warfare, and left with only the sugar coating of male bonds that had been forged in the most extreme circumstances. If we return to Neprintsev's *Rest after Battle*, we can clearly see how this postwar conceptualization of wartime comradeship was softened and romanticized. Resting in the snow after a successful battle, these comrades gather around Terkin as he regales them with stories of his exploits; this group of men are not presented as battle-hardened, anonymous fighters but as young and charismatic men enjoying each other's company and a good yarn. While this painting has strong visual parallels with that of Ilya Repin's masterpiece *The Zaporozhe Cossacks Writing a Letter to the Turkish Sultan*, the treatment of military homosociality in the two works could not be more different: unlike Repin's evocative presentation of wild and rambunctious ethnic masculinity, Neprintsev's work is tame, controlled, and explicitly nonthreatening.

As was discussed in the Introduction, not only did the work of Repin and his contemporaries garner interest among the Soviet public, but it was also highly influential for Soviet artists. Time and again thematic and compositional references to the work of the *Peredvizhniki* can be seen in contemporary visual culture, across genres that range from wartime posters and the satirical cartoons of *Krokodil* to the huge canvases of Fedor Reshetnikov, Vasilii Iakovlev, and Igor Agapov. It is therefore neither surprising nor unusual that Neprintsev chose to base his own scene of military comradeship on what was probably the most famous painting of that nature, but the artist's decision to do so must be seen as more than a homage to Repin's masterpiece. While the structural parallels between the two works are immediately obvious, it is the thematic parallels that are arguably more significant in this case. Before 1917, the ultimate Russian hero was the Cossack—a man who lived on the edge of civilization, who was free, and who was an exceptional warrior. The Cossack was the subject of interest for such great writers as Nikolai Gogol and Leo Tolstoy, and it was a Cossack, in the form of Koz'ma Kriuchkov, who became the archetypal heroic Russian soldier during the First World War, although the Cossacks' position in the new Soviet society would be far more precarious as a result of their involvement in the Civil War.[26] Repin was not alone in turning to this ethnic group in his efforts to articulate a certain type of Russianness during the years of rampant Slavophilism (although technically both he and his Cossacks were Ukrainian), and even later Soviet commentators were keen to emphasize the qualities of heroism, fearlessness, and love of freedom that were at the heart of the work and, by extension, the people.[27] By choosing to style his own scene on that of Repin's, then, Neprintsev was presenting the Soviet soldiery as nothing less than the modern incarnation of these mythic supermen.

FIGURE 1.1. Iurii Neprintsev, *Rest After Battle*, 1951. Tretyakov Gallery, Moscow.

Although Neprintsev did not acknowledge the debt that he owed to Repin in his account of producing the painting published in *Iskusstvo* in April 1952, he was eager to discuss how Tvardovskii's poem had led him to this subject. According to the artist, it was spending time on the Leningrad front during the harsh winter of 1942 that inspired him to encapsulate the qualities of "courage, genuine patriotism and a high sense of duty, heroism, humanity and confidence in the rightness of their cause and life-affirming power" that he had witnessed firsthand in the troops with whom he had been stationed.[28] For Neprintsev, the folk hero of Vasilii Terkin provided the perfect distillation of these characteristics: "Terkin is not exclusive in nature but contains precisely the common features of the Soviet man ... taken directly from life."[29] By 1945, Terkin had been officially recognized as a quintessential New Soviet Man, "associated with truth, a sense of responsibility for his country, and with high moral standards."[30] And yet, as Katherine Hodgson has argued, there is a case to be made that Terkin was actually more of a Russian hero than a Soviet one; he makes no reference to the Communist Party, to Lenin or Stalin, nor does he use established tropes of Soviet political rhetoric in his speech, and he seems to be innocently unaware of past political upheaval. While the return to national motifs in wartime culture was by no means restricted to this popular tale,[31] Hodgson believes that in this instance the relative lack of a specifically Soviet context was rooted in Tvardovskii's own belief in "front-line universality," the idea that the front was a space impervious to politics.[32] The exclusion of politics from Tvardovskii's poem carried over into Neprintsev's canvas, which presented an extremely egalitarian view of both life at the front and the Soviet victory more generally. Away from the pomp and ceremony so often found in earlier war-themed images, the Soviet leadership was excluded from Neprintsev's scene, which was entirely focused upon the interrelationship between common men.

It was not just the political elite who were absent from Neprintsev's democratic vision of Soviet victory; as Susan Reid has pointed out, *Rest after Battle* also excluded women.[33] However, Neprintsev was not alone in removing any trace of female presence from the front, and visual culture offered a very restricted view of the role women had played during the War; although they were depicted as nurses to wounded soldiers in a handful of images,[34] by and large, women were limited to working on the home front, compelling their menfolk to go and perform heroic deeds, and waiting patiently for their safe return. Yet it would also be unfair to characterize the visual exclusion of women from the theater of war as a trait of Stalinist culture; indeed, it would continue beyond 1965, despite significant changes in the conceptualization of the War and its impact, which now allowed for the representation of experiences that had previously been overlooked or left unexplored.[35] For all intents and purposes, then, artistically the front was an exclusively male domain and depictions of comradeship were a reflection of this. This said, Neprintsev's work did stand apart from other war-themed works in one particular respect, and this is the fact that in addition to being published numerous times in *Ogonek*, it was also reproduced in the two major women's magazines, *Rabotnitsa* and *Sovetskaia zhenshchina*.

Although publications aimed at women did not shy away from coverage of war-related issues after 1945, both the features and the images they published tended to be a reflection of the intended audience of the magazine. Women's participation in the war effort, stories of heroic female partisans, and accounts of homecoming dominated in the immediate postwar years, to be supplemented with the role of women in the fight for peace from 1950 onward, and the choice of posters or paintings that interspersed these features reflected these concerns. Thus, while the publication of images that dealt with the War were relatively common in this era, a trait that almost all of them shared was focus on what could be classed as the female war experience: they were images of nurses, of women partisans helping out the Soviet soldier in need of assistance, joyful family reunions, and, very occasionally, harrowing representations of dead children. In this respect the decision to print Neprintsev's work in both of these magazines is very much an anomaly; there was absolutely nothing in this all-male image that could—at least on the surface—be related to the female experience of war. What makes the inclusion of Neprintsev's work even more interesting is the fact that both magazines renamed the painting; in *Rabotnitsa* it was simply called *Vasilii Terkin*, and in *Sovetskaia zhenshchina* it was *At Rest* (*Na privale*), meaning that in both instances the explicit reference to battle was removed.[36] While this might indicate a certain discomfort with the insinuations made in the title of the image, the fact that the content and tone of the painting were deemed appropriate for an exclusively female audience only serves to underline just how nonthreatening Neprintsev's vision of the Soviet soldier was.

A slightly later painting that can be seen to have much in common with Neprintsev's rendering of military comradeship is Boris Fedorov's *Morning of the Tank Drivers* (1952–54), which depicted a group of young soldiers going through their morning rituals together at an ice hole, and which drew upon the same sentimentalized vision of male relationships. While their comrades watch on, getting dressed, brushing their teeth, or enjoying a morning smoke, one driver douses his bare-chested compatriot with freezing water. As in *Rest after Battle*, in Fedorov's painting, military homosociality was presented as entirely egalitarian, humane, and unaggressive and, in keeping with the ethos of Socialist Realism, was completely stripped of any sexuality. There was no problematic question of the eroticized male gaze or potentially dangerous same-sex friendship; rather, these male relationships were constructed as simple and playfully intimate and, even in Fedorov's canvas that includes men in various states of undress, devoid of any degree of physical tension. What makes this painting particularly interesting in any assessment of the representation of the military man after the end of war is the artist's decision to focus upon personal hygiene—washing, brushing teeth, and pulling on a clean shirt—which only served to highlight the fact that these men had maintained their ties to civilized, "normal" society despite the frontline conditions. As one contemporary critic commented at its display at the First Summer Exhibition of Leningrad Artists in 1954, in this scene of "close-knit camaraderie" it was the "sense of strength and health" that attracted the viewer.[37]

Hygiene and personal grooming had always been an important part of Soviet rhetoric; as the years passed the discourse had shifted from society needing to eradicate the "dirt" of the past and to create a new man who was healthy in body and in spirit, to one that presented hygiene being an essential component in *kul'turnost'*, the living of a life that was cultured and well-suited to both the physical and mental needs of the Soviet citizen.[38] Within a military context, this focus on hygiene had an important precursor in the charitable calls of the First World War prior to 1917, as fundraising for items such as trench baths and showers was deemed important enough to warrant poster campaigns that asked civilians to donate to the cause. Along with calls for book donations,[39] such fundraising efforts presented a clear need for the trappings of civilized society to be transported to the front, as well as suggesting a link between the soldier's physical and mental well-being and his performance in battle. As well as mitigating any insinuation of brutalization through actions in war, the presentation of the well-groomed Russian soldier also served as a foil to the representation of the enemy, who throughout the War was often depicted as ragged and unkempt.[40] This association between military performance and personal hygiene was one that continued in the years of the Civil War, although this was often far less to do with the desire for a cultured soldiery and far more to do with the very real threat that venereal disease and typhus posed to the strength of the Red Army.[41]

Fedorov was not alone in articulating a connection between male grooming and military homosociality in the context of the Second World War. Aleksandr Deineka had, in a characteristically corporeal work, represented soldiers socializing in the showers after battle in 1944.[42] His focus on the naked male body was highly unusual for the time, and the fact that this image was never reproduced in the popular press, despite countless features on his life and work being published in the two decades that followed, perhaps indicates an unease with the physicality of this particular painting. Still, while the voyeuristic perspective of the piece means that it has the potential to be seen as far more sexually charged than works such as those of Fedorov, it is unlikely that this was the artist's intention. Rather, by presenting the Soviet military man as an ideal physical specimen, Deineka was drawing upon the established Classical ideal that equated physical perfection with moral superiority. This was not an image of naked men produced for sensual pleasure but one that was meant to encapsulate the health, spirit, and indefatigability of the Soviet armed forces.[43]

Aleksandr Tvardovskii also wrote at length in *Vasilii Terkin* about the joy soldiers found in ablutions, dedicating a whole chapter of his epic war poem to events in the bathhouse:

> Choice of shower or bath-tub
> And the naked soldiers all
> Give themselves a last rub.
> This one's boiled alive: his mate
> Flops exhausted drooping.
> Number One gives Number Two's
> Back a thorough rubbing . . .[44]

Like the tank drivers, Terkin's comrades engage easily and without hesitation in mutual bathing and simultaneous banter in this intimate homosocial space,[45] and the similarity between Fedorov's canvas and Tvardovskii's poem was one that was seized upon by the critic Shvedova in her review of the piece.[46] The *bania* was turned by Tvardovskii into a space where a Soviet man could really prove his manliness, firstly through the display of scars gained in battle and secondly by withstanding a heat that would render any foreign visitor infertile:

> If some connoisseur and expert
> Drops in—hardy though he be—
> He won't stick it out, or rather
> If he does, he'll be no father
> He'll be seedless presently! . . .
>
> He won't have been, like our soldier,
> (Though he may be strong as most)
> Fried in many a summer heatwave,
> Baked in many a winter frost.[47]

This notion found in Terkin that a true Soviet man was forged in the extreme climates of the motherland was echoed in *Rest after Battle* and *Morning of the Tank Drivers*, as both artists placed their heroes amidst a snowy landscape. For Neprintsev the setting, along with the fact that after battle these men were not exhausted but rather chose to revel in each other's company, served to underline the physical strength and *zakalennost'* (steeliness) of the Soviet fighter, who was capable of withstanding both the harsh conditions of the climate and of combat. Fedorov too drew upon the ideal of *zakalennost'* and expressed the strength of the Soviet man through the cold but in a manner that was more explicitly tied to notions of health and physical strength. The use of cold water in tempering the Soviet body had been a feature of health manuals since the Revolution and was seen to help stave off afflictions such as chills or digestive irregularity and, more importantly, as essential to the concomitant strengthening of the body and the mind.[48] Thus, by drawing so clearly on the ideals of *zakalennost'* and *kul'turnost'*, Fedorov's vision of military life was one that placed these soldiers, not on the periphery as liminal characters, but in the very center of Soviet life.

The immediate postwar years, then, saw a dramatic shift in the conceptualization and representation of militaristic homosociality. While in the first years of peace, triumphalist representations of war had led to the Soviet military man being depicted as part of a victorious collective, by the early 1950s this had been replaced with a far softer image of military fraternity, which was in many cases explicitly devoid of any militaristic overtones, removed from the heat of battle and reassociated with the prevailing rhetorical concerns at the heart of late Stalinist society. Why such a shift occured is the result of the complex interplay between a number of factors that range from the rhetoric of normalization, to the limits placed on cultural production during the *Zhdanovshchina*, to the more philosophical difficulties in representing the military man at war during a time of peace. And yet, it is vital that such limited representation is not attributed to the nature of postwar Stalinism alone for, as will be shown, these limitations lasted far beyond 1953.

## "WE MERRY FEW": COMRADESHIP IN THE THAW

After largely disappearing in the years between the death of Stalin in March 1953 and his denunciation at the Twentieth Party Congress in February 1956, the theme of military comradeship reemerged in the mid-1950s with a frequency that far outstripped that of the immediate postwar era. However, although the Secret Speech marked a watershed moment for the remembrance of the Great Patriotic War and was a huge step toward reclaiming victory for the Soviet people, the War continued to occupy an ambiguous position in the art of the Thaw period. As a number of scholars have demonstrated, it was by no means the case that Soviet society threw off the shackles of Stalinism in a manner that was uniform or universal, and the same held true for cultural production in terms of the style of representation, what was being represented, and how.[49] What will be seen repeatedly throughout this book is that, while the Thaw brought about significant alterations in the presentation of the physical and emotional cost of the War, in many instances it also perpetuated established Stalinist tropes and motifs, particularly when it came to dealing with such tricky subjects as injury, death, and bereavement. This same mix of change and continuity is evident in representations of wartime homosociality, with the Stalinist sentimentalized vision being produced at the same time as what could be deemed more honest portrayals of military brotherhood. To some extent this amalgam between new and established narrative structures can be attributed to the uneven impact of de-Stalinization, both within the art world and society more broadly, but in the case of the representation of military homosociality and comradeship it was the so-called "return to Leninist principles" that had the greatest symbolic impact.

This was a movement that called for, among other things, a renewed commitment to the withering away of the state, the full emancipation of women from their domestic shackles, a fresh attack on religion, a return to the leading role of the party, and a rejection of power converging in the hands of one individual. Most significantly, this new focus upon Leninist ideals saw a revival of the fraternal bonds of the revolutionary years—as opposed to the patriarchal structure that had developed under Stalin—meaning that military homosociality came to be imbued with a new significance, especially around the anniversary years of the Revolution and Civil War. However, despite the notion that there was a return to the true principles of 1917, representations of soldierly fraternity set in the tumultuous years of revolution and civil war were characterized by their syrupy and unquestionably heroic conceptualization of male comradeship, something that set them apart from the more psychologically complex treatments of the subject in a Second World War context that emerged around the same time.

The All-Union Exhibition of 1957 ran from November 5 until March 16, 1958, and was dedicated to the Great October Socialist Revolution and brought together older works that had gained popularity over the preceding years as well as new pieces by both established and graduating artists. Understandably, given its theme, this was the largest exhibition of the 1950s, exhibiting the work of over two thousand artists and warranting extensive comment and numerous reproductions across both the popular and professional press.[50] For the eagle-eyed observer, this would have been an exhibition where the tension between the new direction of Soviet art and the established modes of representation were there for all to see and no more so than in how artists of this period were handling the issue of the Soviet man at war. In his lengthy assessment of war-themed works at the exhibition, published in January of 1958, the critic E. Polishchuk outlined some of the changes that had been instituted since the days of Neprintsev, Fedorov, and their contemporaries. According to Polishchuk, art had moved away from the past rigid categories of either battle scenes or sketches taken from military life, as artists were now capable of seeing "the heroism in the simple, the small, and the everyday." This was not about outward display, but painting with a psychological and emotional depth, concerned with "thoughts, feelings, doubts and hopes": contemporary art was meant to be nothing less than poetry on canvas.[51] While Polishchuk may have been overly optimistic about the new direction that Soviet art was heading in, as will be seen, some of the paintings produced during this era that dealt with the War and its legacy did fulfill this critic's predictions.

When it came to the representation of comradeship, nowhere is this more evident than in Boris Nemenskii's *Scorched Earth* (*Zemlia opalennaia*, 1957), which depicted three men taking refuge in an abandoned trench amidst a desolate landscape of barbed wire and churned earth.[52] What was most striking about Nemenskii's work was the psychological aspect of his characterization, which, as Polishchuk hinted at in his article, had to date been completely lacking from visual representations of the War. Through his three protagonists, Nemenskii presented three differing reactions to battle: the relief of the soldier propped against the trench wall, the almost sexual satisfaction of the man lying on the ground, nonchalantly smoking a cigarette, and the look of utter horror and heartbreak etched upon the face of his central figure. As with Deineka's *The Defense of Sevastopol* before it, Nemenskii used the personal narrative to establish a sense of collective experience, the result of which was a far more complex vision of both the individual reaction to the events of war and the importance of comradeship to those who had witnessed such occurrences. In contrast to the Stalinist interpretation, though, this was not the relentlessly heroic and lighthearted picture of wartime comradeship that was so removed from battle, but one that was grounded in the gritty realism of war and its mental and physical pressures.[53]

Yet at the same time as Nemenskii was beginning to venture into an exploration of the psychological impact of warfare, paintings such as Dmitrii Oboznenko's *Night of the Nightingale* (*Solov'inaia noch'*, 1957) continued to perpetuate the romanticized and domesticated view of wartime brotherhood,

FIGURE 1.2. Boris Nemenskii, *Scorched Earth*, 1957. Tretyakov Gallery, Moscow.

in a manner that is actually reminiscent of one of Nemenskii's earlier works, *The Breath of Spring* (*Dykhanie vesny*, 1955), which depicts a young soldier waking up in wonder at the life stirring in the forest around him and his comrades.[54] Oboznenko's diploma work, which was also exhibited at the All-Union show of 1957 and was reproduced for the first time in the same *Iskusstvo* article as *Scorched Earth*, is an almost cozy and familial scene, depicting a group of soldiers sleeping in the midst of a forest, sharing blankets and using each other's bodies as pillows, while one of the regiment keeps watch. As with *Morning of the Tank Drivers*, this was a scene of chaste intimacy, in which physical closeness was representative of nothing more than the strength of the bond and trust between these men, while the literal covering of their bodies in army-issue blankets masked not only their male form but also their masculine selves, a seemingly contradictory conceptualization of the warrior-hero. The use of the monotone blankets and overcoats in this manner also turned these sleeping soldiers from individuals into a unified mass, lacking in physical distinctiveness or clarity, which again only emphasized their collective identity and codependency. The representation of the soldiers sleeping, while underlining the trust that these men have in one another, is ultimately a representation of the Soviet hero at his most vulnerable.

As can be seen with the case of *Rest after Battle*, it was not unusual for Soviet artists to take their inspiration from earlier artworks—particularly those of the late nineteenth century—and in some cases also from photographs, and it would appear that Oboznenko was one such artist. While it cannot be definitively proven that this was Oboznenko's template, *Nightingales* bears a striking resemblance to an image taken in September 1941 by *Krasnaia zvezda*'s war photographer, Sergei Loskutov, which shows a group of partisans sleeping in a forest and being watched over by a female comrade.[55] Aside from the obvious factors of changing the partisans to regulation soldiers and altering the gender of the night watch, the painting differs from the photograph in a number of other significant ways; for one thing, the soldier in the painting does not appear to be armed, while the young partisan has her rifle in her hand, and while this woman stands resolutely, Oboznenko's soldier somewhat dreamily looks off into the forest, his back half turned from those he is watching over. For all the compositional similarities, then, the tone of the two images is very different—one is tense and fraught with potential danger, the other is more like a pastoral idyll than a war painting—and neatly encapsulates how the visual conceptualization of the Soviet fighter, be it official or partisan, had changed since the days of war. In his assessment of this young artist's work in *Iskusstvo*, Polishchuk echoed this bucolic and romantic tone, completely bypassing the seemingly collective role that the soldier on watch was playing and focusing entirely on his own individual experience: "In the woods, under the birches, soldiers sleep; but one of them, still a young soldier, cannot sleep on this spring night saturated with the smell of grass and flowers. Leaning against the trunk of a birch tree, he listens to the singing of a nightingale, which resonates in his soul and awakens dreams."[56] Given how frequently Oboznenko's work was reproduced in *Ogonek*, this romanticism clearly had an appeal, so much so that in March 1958, around the time the All-Union Exhibition closed its doors, it was used as the back cover of the magazine, a space usually reserved for photographs.[57] Nemenskii's *Scorched Earth*, on the other hand, was not reproduced at all beyond the pages of the professional art press.

Like Polishchuk before them, modern critics such as Matthew Cullerne Bown who have commented on Oboznenko's work have tended to give most weight to the relationship between man and his environment in their assessment, placing it firmly within a much broader trend in Thaw-era art.[58] However, given the wartime context of the piece, it is also useful to view this painting as a continuation of the tendency established earlier in the decade to remove the soldier from the battlefield and place him in a position of relative peace and safety, although there are important distinctions that need to be made between these paintings and those of the late Stalin period. While earlier works may have used the same device of physical distance from the battle-field as a means of negating the violence and brutality of war, the attempt by some artists in the middle of the 1950s to incorporate a more psychological dimension into their canvases led to a series of works characterized by inac-tivity and a sense of the internalization of thought. While they are two very different representations of war, it is clear to see that both Nemenskii's and Oboznenko's images convey much more emotional sophistication than either Neprintsev's Terkin or Fedorov's tank drivers. In a wartime context this was a device used by other artists, such as A. Konstantinopol'skii in his *At Dawn* (*Na rassvete*, 1960–61) and V. Knyzhov, whose painting of an exhausted group of fighters at Sevastopol, resting in the brief respite from battle, was in stark contrast to the earlier action-packed and highly physical work of Deineka.[59] More generally, these pieces can be placed alongside some of the other pop-ular works of the period, such as Iurii Anokhin's *Spring Is Coming: A Village Is Being Built* (*Vesna idet. Derevna stroitsia*, 1959) or Anatolii Levitin's *Warm Day* (*Teplyi den'*, 1957), as being characteristic of the Thaw-time concern for the New Soviet Person's inner life.[60]

While the Second World War continued to be an issue that concerned Soviet artists during the late 1950s, with the proclaimed return to Leninist val-ues after the Stalinist "deviation" and the fortieth anniversary of the October Revolution, there was a renewed artistic focus on the early revolutionary years and particularly on the Civil War. Although it reached its peak in 1957, the theme of revolutionary struggle and success would continue for the rest of the Khrushchev period and beyond, and it is in this context that the most romanticized visions of war and its associated homosociality are seen, something that sets representations of the revolutionary era apart from the slowly changing presentation of the Great Patriotic War. This romanticization can be seen as taking one of two forms: there was the conceptualization of wartime comradeship epitomized by Evsei Moiseenko's *The Reds Have Arrived* (*Krasnye prishli*, 1961), which is full of heroic vitality as the cavalry of the Red Army sweep through a village,[61] and then there was a more expressively lyrical idealization, seen in works such as Lev Kotliarov's *To the Front* (*Na front*, 1957) and the Tkachev brothers' *Between Battles* (*Mezhdu boiami*, 1957–60). In images such as these, a range of Thaw-period artistic concerns are evident, not least the rhapsodic treatment of rest and the removal of the comrades from the heat of battle, which are presented within the framework of Leninist ideals, as exemplified by the literate and cultured soldiers of the Tkachevs, who spend their time away from battle reading and writing letters.[62] For Kotliarov, this lyricism took a more clichéd form: a steam train plowing through the Russian countryside at sundown, a young recruit playing his guitar, another with his face illuminated by a lit cigarette, while others listen and watch as the scenery rolls by.[63] Despite the dynamism of the title—the excitement, fear, and thrill of going to join the battle—Kotliarov's canvas is remarkably still and sedate. As we find in other works from this era, such as Pavel Nikonov's *October* (*Oktiabr'*, 1956),[64] through the artist's use of light and shade—the smoking soldier, the light-colored uniforms, and the bright red banners adorning the train—the drama of the events was displaced, taking place in the imagined, shaded distance of the canvas, leaving the protagonists, and the viewer, in a state of anticipation.[65]

Thus, the representation of the Revolution and Civil War can be seen as broadly falling into two main styles: the work of Moiseenko, along with those of artists such as Indulis Zarin, Viktor Shatalin, and Gelii Korzhev and his much-celebrated *Communists* triptych,[66] focused on the exhilaration and verve of the revolutionary struggle, while those of Kotliarov and the Tkachevs continued the strange trend found in depictions of the Great Patriotic War and produced peaceful portrayals of a wartime subject. In these pieces in particular one can see a great deal of similarity to the construction of male homosociality immediately after the Great Patriotic War, in which the actual events of war and the heroics of military engagement were undercut by the focus on rest, relaxation, and comfortable intimacy. However, what both approaches to this formative period in Soviet history share is a distinct lack of violence. As A. Kantor commented in his assessment of the 1957 exhibition in the (relatively) liberal art journal *Tvorchestvo*, contemporary representations of the revolutionary era were a "genre of 'romantic memoirs' of what artists have not seen or at least cannot remember," and blood, mud, and death had no place in the Thaw-time memory of their crucible.[67]

Could there be more to this highly romanticized vision of the Soviet past than a simple case of rose-tinted glasses and selective remembrance, though? In order to really get to grips with why one sees this type of representation of war during the early Khrushchev era, it is imperative to think beyond what was happening within the art world and look at how the place of the man had changed within society more broadly over the last decade or so. The male social role had altered dramatically in the forty years since the Revolution and often in parallel to shifting ideas about the role of the family within Soviet life. The masculinity, and some would even say hypermasculinity, of the early revolutionary era, was explicitly martial in its characterization. In the struggle for a Soviet utopia, only the New Soviet Man was guaranteed success; beyond the Red victory everything, from the mechanization of the workplace and industrialization, the eradication of illiteracy and the rationalization of society, to the ideals of international revolution and the destruction of the bourgeoisie, was couched in clear military terms. This mobilization of society can be seen in parallel to the Soviet attacks on the family unit; as one literary scholar has surmised, "With the family and femininity in disgrace [due to their association with the intelligentsia and bourgeoisie], the building of the new world was implicitly a task for men" in which the focus was on "production rather than reproduction."[68]

The social dynamics of the family, and particularly the man's place within it, is something that will be looked at in much more detail in chapters 4 and 5, but while thinking about the issue of comradeship, it is important to recognize how the rhetoric of the revolutionary era shaped the notion of the ideal man and his relationships at the time. Both rhetorically and practically, through legislation such as the new Family Code of 1918, the Revolution was styled as the destroyer of patriarchy: the strict vertical ties between the state and people were torn asunder and replaced with the ideal of the proletarian society of equals, a society of brothers, not the old imperial or capitalist model of fathers and sons. In his work *The World, the Text and the Critic*, Edward Said brought to light a similar trend in Western literature that emerged around the fin de siècle, in which traditional family (filiative) ties were eroded by the pressures of modernity only to be replaced by bonds that transcended the biological (affiliative):

> If a filial relationship was held together by natural bonds and natural forms of authority [...] the new affiliative relationship changes these bonds into what seems to be transpersonal forms—such as guild consciousness, consensus, collegiality, professional respect, class and the hegemony of a dominant culture. The filiative scheme belongs to the realms of nature and of "life," whereas affiliation belongs exclusively to culture and society.[69]

Although not a part of his discussion, Said's framework for the replacement of the filial with the affilial has particular significance in the Soviet case, in which the destruction of the traditional family was not simply due to the demands of modern life but an actively pursued state policy. It is within this context, then, that we can begin to appreciate the centrality of the fraternal bonds of comradeship and the interplay between masculine ideals and the assault upon the family in the early Soviet period.

But for all they may have been representing this era in their work, artists of the 1950s were not living in a society that espoused the same gendered dynamics as the 1920s; instead, they were a part of a society that, if not necessarily less masculinized than its predecessor, was certainly less militaristic in its outlook. Given the so-called "arms race" during the Cold War, this may seem like an odd statement to make; the case is not being made here that the Soviet Union was in any way less concerned with displaying national strength than it had been in the past, and in that respect militarism remained a key part of the social topography, but, unlike in the revolutionary era, militarism was no longer being used as the structural trope of the entire society. Changing attitudes toward the family are also a part of this context, as the interrelationship between men, masculinity, and the family was impacted upon massively by such intervening developments as the recriminalization of abortion and other changes to family policy in 1936,[70] the 1944 Family Code, and of course the trauma of the War itself. By the mid-1950s official rhetoric had shifted once again, and now the focus was on regeneration and family life, and Leninist ideals were retrospectively reconfigured to fit this more domestic vision of Soviet society.

Thus, although it is tempting to view these representations of wartime comradeship in isolation as a genre in their own right, it must be remembered that such images were being created at the same time as a huge range of other paintings and posters that presented a far more domesticated and family-centric view of Soviet masculinity. This stands in contrast to works that were produced during the actual Revolution or Civil War, which were grounded upon the epic struggle at hand and thus explicitly martial in their tone and their vision of social relationships. The modification of the masculine ideal to accommodate an active domestic role for men that occurred during the Khrushchev era can perhaps then go some way to accounting for this continued romanticization of wartime brotherhood, despite there now being some freedom to explore themes that had previously been prohibited. The militaristic man who had provided the heroic staple of the previous four decades was now out of step with the outlook and concerns of post-Stalinist society.

## MEN OF GRANITE: MASCULINITY AND COMRADESHIP ON THE NEW FRONTIER.

While the Thaw saw the softening of military masculinity, a new masculine archetype emerged to fill the void that the military man had left. With the renewed focus on the regeneration of society, the influx of funding into science and technology, and the inauguration of the Virgin Lands Scheme in 1954, an alternative vision of masculinity came to be presented, which was in many ways a reversion to the representation of the anonymous and fraternal proletarian heroes of the early revolutionary years who were giants, subjugators of nature, and denizens of an almost exclusively homosocial world. These depictions of a new hypermasculinity appeared at the same time as a very domesticated form of masculinity was emerging, and these two paradoxical trends ran in parallel from the late 1950s until the end of the Khrushchev era. However, although they offered two very different visions of Soviet masculinity, both of these models were predicated upon the same basis, and that was the rejection of the military ideal of the past.

The idea of the self-sufficient, rugged man of the frontier, battling nature for his very survival, was by no means a Soviet invention, nor were the Soviets alone in turning to this model in the years following the end of the Second World War. With the "conquest" of Everest in late May 1953 and the coronation of a young monarch a few days later, new life was breathed into the British imperial adventure hero, particularly in film. British imperial identity had been threatened in the decade after 1945, due in part to Indian independence and the more general questioning of the relationship between colonizers and colonized, which had been brought to the fore by colonial involvement on the battlefields of Europe. This trend continued into the period of decolonization, which saw a reinvigoration of the classic imperial heroic model, as epitomized by Peter O'Toole's *Lawrence of Arabia* (1962) and the defenders of Rorke's Drift in the film *Zulu* (1964).[71] In Germany, after initial condemnation by authorities in both the East and West as being responsible for the Americanization of German culture and the rise in youth crime, the Western genre film during the course of the 1950s came to be seen as a vehicle for offering an acceptable nonmilitaristic model of masculinity, particularly in light of the rearming of the Federal Republic. As Uta Poiger argued, the authorities believed that "by consuming western films, German men no longer need to physically join any front(ier)s [...] instead they could take care of their healthy desires in the realm of the movie theatre and the psyche."[72] And in the ultimate incarnation of the frontier man, the American cowboy, the movies of John Wayne offered the Western audience an "undomesticated, pure, red-blooded example of prime American masculinity."[73] Although their reception and their mode of representation differed from case to case, the man on the edge of society, unfettered by domestic shackles, was a regular feature of postwar Western culture, harking back to an imagined simpler time when men were men, when women knew their place, and where adventure was not negated by modern technologies. While the Soviet model can be situated to some extent within this broader trend, the idea of pioneer manhood was, of course, based upon a very different set of precepts to those found in the West, offering a vision of frontier masculinity that could be rooted in a bona fide frontier and true Soviet-style adventure: the cultivation of the Virgin Lands, the exploration of the mineral wealth of Siberia, and the building of hydro-electric power stations.

The Siberian expanse provided a malleable backdrop to the new feats of the postwar hero, demonstrative of technological progression, the engagement of the Soviet youth with the socialist project, and a vehicle for the representation of the true working might of the Soviet people. However, the interest in Siberia, especially around 1961, can also be seen as part of the larger process of de-Stalinization, in which the space and the people of the periphery were brought back to the bosom of the new political regime. Despite the massive influx of volunteers into Siberia and the Virgin Lands of Kazakhstan—somewhere in the region of 1.23 million between 1955 and 1960—the population of the area actually fell due to the return of political prisoners and exiled nationalities after 1956, with an estimated two million people leaving over the same period.[74] In his article examining the changing nature of the Siberian workforce, S. G. Pociuk encapsulated this multifarious reimagining of the Soviet space when he wrote, "We [foreign observers] can sincerely admire the courage of the Soviet explorers in Siberia and appreciate the many young people who are unafraid of physical hardship in the fight for the *rehabilitation* of Siberian lands for human habitation and civilization."[75] In a few short years, Siberia was transformed from a liminal territory to one that was at the heart of the Soviet vision of socialism under Khrushchev.[76]

In terms of artistic production, the activity in Siberia and the Virgin Lands provided the perfect genre for the implementation of Georgii Malenkov's plea at the Nineteenth Party Congress to represent conflict and struggle in Socialist Realism.[77] What is more, by depicting the men involved in these projects, the space was provided for an exploration of those ideals that had in the past been articulated through the military trope—strength, courage, resilience, resourcefulness, dedication to the well-being of the collective, and so on—and brought about a reconceptualization of the very idea of Soviet comradeship, which was freed from association with armed service. This shift in representation also created an arena for the establishment of a non-*frontovik* model of heroism, allowing those who had been too young to fight in the War to actively participate in the socialist project. In the visual culture of the Thaw, then, the epitome of Soviet (hyper)masculinity was to be found in these men and not in the representation of the heroes of the Second World War.

In a speech given to the Conference of Leading Agricultural Workers of the Virgin Land Territory in March 1961, Khrushchev urged those involved in cultural production to pay closer attention to the work going on in Kazakhstan: "I would like to express the wish that workers in literature and the arts create a greater number of good books, films, plays and compositions about the working people of the Virgin Lands—remarkable heroes of our times."[78] The cultivation of the wild land of Siberia and Kazakhstan, instigated in 1954, was to be the great heroic project of the age, turning the unproductive steppe into an agricultural region that was to supply the empire with much-needed grain. While the campaign would have serious environmental consequences, introduce a large, alien population into Kazakhstan, and have little real long-term impact in terms of agricultural output, the scheme remained a staple theme in Soviet film and art for around the next decade. As with the Stalinist campaigns for Far East resettlement during the 1930s,[79] much of the propaganda concerning movement to the Virgin Lands was aimed at young women as well as Soviet men, and this cross-gender appeal was reflected in visual representations of the project; the task at hand was to not only get the youth to go, but also to stay, and for this to be successful both sexes would have to participate in the scheme.

Broadly speaking, the art of the Virgin Lands was divided into two distinct genres—the physical task of working the land and the domestication of the land—and this in turn led to the presentation of two distinct visions of life on the Virgin Lands. Artists such as Boris Vaks and Dmitrii Mochal'skii, who devoted most of his working life to the subject, focused their attention on representations of domestic life in the new lands, producing works that featured the tents and outdoor living—complete with a sense of adventure and lack of creature comforts—of the early days of settlement. Later the focus shifted to young couples, and to a lesser extent families, in their new homes, with a particular emphasis on the communal way of life on the periphery.[80] In contrast, other artists chose to concentrate on representing the task at hand, but even then continued to depict the taming of the Virgin Lands as an endeavor undertaken by the youth of both sexes. The work of Michaela Pohl would suggest that the primary role foreseen for the "girls" of the Virgin Lands was that of wife and homemaker.[81] This did not directly correspond, however, to the image projected artistically, which continued to place women in the fields as well as the home, although admittedly frequently in a subsidiary role.[82] Nor were the men of the Virgin Lands visually excluded from the domestication and civilization of the region and presented singly as workers, as works such as Raisa Galitskii's endearing *Love Is Not a Potato* (*Liubov'—ne kartoshka*, 1954) and Igor Kabanov's *Young Life* (*Zhizn' molodaia*, [1955–59?]) show.[83]

Running alongside these depictions of domestic life on the periphery, the most common conceptualization of the heroic nature of the work in Kazakhstan was that of the individual worker on the land. These works were characterized by a distinctive use of light, especially the crepuscular light of late afternoon, and of a lowered horizon that both bestowed a monumentalism upon the protagonist and underlined the expanse of the steppe. Works such as V. Basov's *In New Spaces* (*Na Novykh prostorakh*, [1960?])[84] and Viktor Oreshnikov's *Student-Virgin Lander* (*Student-Tselinnik*, [1959?]), both of which were exhibited at major shows at the same time as their inclusion in the popular press, were typical of this imagining.[85]

In many ways, then, the work on the Virgin Lands was representative of Thaw art in general: optimistic, focused on new life, expressive of joy in both labor and rest, and increasingly concerned with activities within the domestic sphere. And yet, although these canvases were romantic and heroic, the kind of masculinity projected in them was one of youthful enthusiasm and indicative of a vitality for life, and stood in stark contrast to some of the other major paintings of this period by artists such as Igor Agapov and Pavel Nikonov that depicted the tough, epic heroes of Siberia. This differing presentation of frontier masculinity can be linked to the task at hand; as the Virgin Lands Scheme was as much about resettlement as it was cultivation, there was a domestic aspect to these works that was not relevant to those focused on exploration or construction. What is more, as an agricultural project, the Virgin Lands Scheme was about a symbiotic relationship between the worker and the land, about toil and nurture in equal measure, while shaping the natural world to harness its power or uncovering its mineral wealth was an inherently more violent process, lending itself more readily to macho men and hypermasculine heroics.

The sweat and muscle found in Thaw-time representations of the subjugation of nature through labor was very different from how artists depicted the triumph of humanity over the elements during the Stalin era. The elimination of connotations of hardship or strenuous labor that typified such works is encapsulated in a poster produced by Boris Berezovskii, Mikhail Solov'ev, and Ivan Shagin, an image that was reproduced in poster form half a million times and that was also chosen to mark the new year in 1951 in a double-page spread in *Sovetskaia zhenshchina*.[86] In this poster Stalin is shown standing on a podium, arm aloft in a gesture reminiscent of his predecessor, in front of a huge map of the Soviet Union, while workers of differing nationalities gaze up adoringly at their great leader, and behind them thousands of anonymous citizens gradually morph into an indistinguishable mass. There is nothing particularly extraordinary in this postwar conceptualization of Stalin's leadership or his paternalistic relationship with his people, but what is striking is the backdrop used for this scene. On the horizon to the left is one of the Seven Sisters of Moscow; adjacent, a series of pylons fade into the far distance, while the map itself depicts nothing but the new canals and hydroelectric power stations in the southern regions of the empire. The message of the poster was clear: that the Soviet achievement of Communism was linked to technological development, achievable only under the leadership of Stalin and dependent on the shaping of the natural world to the will of the *vozhd'*. To paraphrase Lenin, Communism was Stalinism plus the harnessing of nature.[87]

While obviously it would never be acknowledged that labor on projects such as canal construction had in the past been drawn from the prison population and had claimed the lives of many thousands, by choosing to articulate the message of technological advancement through labels on a map, *all* connotations of labor were eradicated. The harsh conditions in which people had been forced to work, and ultimately their triumph in success, were eliminated completely from this vision of progress, and all collective achievements were redirected unto Stalin himself. This notion was to be repeated in the 1951 brigade work *At the Great Stalinist Construction Site (Na velikoi Stalinskoi stroike [Kuibyshevskaia GES])*,[88] which depicted the early days in the construction of the Kuibyshev hydroelectric power station. The bright sunshine and fixed smiles of the workers in the painting undercut any insinuation of intense labor, and, as the title suggested, the work was carried out joyfully for and in the name of the great Soviet leader. The achievements of these construction workers, as well as the real-life polar heroes and aviators who had also won their battle with the elements,[89] was refracted by the cult of personality to shine glory onto Stalin. In contrast, during the Thaw, the representation of the subjugation of the natural world became far more egalitarian in its outlook and, what is more, emphasized the collective nature of such work.

It was this genre of collective labor in the extremes of the Soviet expanse more than any other in the late 1950s and 1960s that inspired the production of works that marked genuine watersheds in the development of Socialist Realism and encapsulated the concerns surrounding what came to be known as the Severe Style [*surovyi stil'*] during the years of de-Stalinization. A movement that can be seen to parallel Khrushchev's calls for a return to Leninist values, the exponents of the Severe Style drew inspiration from the revolutionary artists of the 1920s, particularly the Russian Cézannists and the members of the OSt [*Obshchestvo stankovistov*] and their leading light, Aleksandr Deineka. The work of these young artists could be characterized by, among other features, the monumentality of their canvases, the rejection of the Stalinist lacquering of reality [*lakirovka*], a reorientation of perspective so that the events of the canvas confronted the viewer square-on, strong lines, and a specific use of color.[90] However, it would be inaccurate to think of these artists as turning their backs on either the dogma of the state or Socialist Realism entirely for, as Aleksandr Sidorov surmised, "Their canvases, however dour in content and flinty in execution, were nonetheless life-affirming and attuned to the heroic in a way which seems [...] to link them umbilically to the official utopian outlook."[91]

The theme of exploration and the full exploitation of the natural wealth of the Soviet Union would be a consistent feature of art during the Thaw period; consequently, the geologist would emerge as one of the unlikely heroic role models of the era, and by 1963 this group of workers even warranted a specific mention in the slogans published to commemorate the anniversary of the October Revolution, as they were urged by the state to "discover the inestimable riches of the motherland more quickly."[92] Building upon this interest, one of the most iconic works in the Severe Style oeuvre was Pavel Nikonov's *Geologists* (*Geologi*, 1962), produced toward what has traditionally been seen as the end of the movement and which represented a group of men, pausing amidst the bleak and barren Siberian landscape.[93] This was not the purposeful progression of the New Soviet Man that people had come to expect but rather a canvas that was evocative of doubt and a lack of direction, as epitomized by the fragmented and undulating horizon and absence of a unified gaze on the part of the protagonists. Nor were these men the masterful conquerors of the elements, as the physical frailty of the human body in the extreme conditions of the frozen wilderness was expressed through the man seated on the ground, wrapping a bast-like dressing around his frostbitten foot. The tonal uniformity and one-dimensionality of the composition complements the air of gloominess inherent in the scenario, but it can also be seen as indicative of the interest in medieval icon painting that arose in the early years of the 1960s and strongly influenced the work of Nikonov and Dmitrii Zhilinskii among others.[94] However, while the painting would come to be viewed as a turning point in Soviet art in the years to come,[95] the pessimistic vision of Soviet life that the artist presented along with its modernist style was strongly criticized at the time. Commenting at the infamous Thirty Years of Moscow Art Exhibition at the Manezh Gallery in December 1962, Khrushchev denounced Nikonov's work:

> We're going to take these blotches into communism, are we? If government funds have paid for this picture, the person who authorized it will have the sum deducted from his salary. [...] This painting should not have been hung in the exhibition. Pictures should arouse us to perform great deeds. They should inspire a person. But what kind of picture is this? One jackass riding on another...[96]

*Iskusstvo*'s editorial on the exhibition and its fallout a few months later was no less cutting in its assessment of this young artist's work:

> "Geologists," apparently, is dedicated to the heroic labor of the discoverers of the riches of our land. But [...] on the canvas in front of the viewer is presented a group of exhausted, gloomy-minded people lost in the sand and cut off from the world. Not even people but disembodied ghosts... A cold spirit of hopelessness [and] pessimism emanates from the painting. Such a product, where there are ugly masks only vaguely reminiscent of people, cannot, of course, call a man to heroic deeds...[97]

Although Nikonov received criticism for the execution of his painting, as the commentary in *Iskusstvo* implied, it was also the tone of the piece that was highly problematic. This is underlined by the fact that plenty of other works from this era—including those that took geologists as their subject matter— examined the hardships of exploration and the physical struggle inherent in the achievement of socialism.[98] By and large, though, such works espoused an optimism that was lacking in Nikonov's canvas and as such managed to avoid the vitriolic condemnation of his *Geologists*. Given its reception, it is not surprising, then, that this painting can only be found in reproduction on the pages of the professional press, an arena where works that were both celebrated and condemned found an outlet, as such an abomination was clearly deemed unsuitable for widespread public consumption. However, while such controversial works had no place in popular print culture, their legacy, and that of the Manezh exhibition, cast a long shadow, and satirical cartoons condemning art that did not conform to the Socialist Realist aesthetic proliferated on the pages of both popular magazines and newspapers for most of 1963.[99]

Alongside geologists, the construction workers of large hydroelectric (*gidroelektrostantsiia*, hereafter cited as GES) projects also regularly appeared in paintings during the late 1950s and early 1960s, depicted as heroic workers who were wrestling with the landscape and elements of the Soviet empire to improve the lives of their fellow citizens. Focus fell on the construction of the construction of Bratsk GES—which was completed in 1961 and at the time was the largest in the world—and with it the relationship between the Soviet man and the Siberian taiga. The obsession with GES projects, and Bratsk in particular, was not just confined to the fine arts, as in the early 1960s numerous published features detailed life in and around the stations, often accompanied by lavish color photo spreads that ran over several pages.[100] It is ironic, then, that one of the great projects of the age and one that was covered with such enthusiasm in print culture should be the inspiration behind some of the most controversial works of the early 1960s, although with hindsight we should also recognize these works as some of the greatest of the era. While they may have provoked intense discussion among professional critics, these are paintings of huge significance in any assessment of Khrushchevite models of masculinity, and although several were only reproduced in the art press, all of them (bar one) were shown at major exhibitions. What such works seem to suggest about notions of heroic masculinity in the early 1960s cannot be overlooked.

One such painting is Igor Agapov's *The Subjugators of Siberia* (*Pokoriteli Sibiri*, 1961), which was shown at the Sixth Moscow Youth Exhibition. It depicts three powerfully built men with exaggeratedly large, phallic drills penetrating the frozen Siberian earth and was the distillation of virile masculinity, Soviet work ethic, and homosocial cooperation.[101] The contemporary critic Vladislav Zimenko likened Agapov's canvas to a modern reinterpretation of the much-loved work of Viktor Vasnetsov, *Bogatyri* (1898),[102] in which the "great public sense of the everyday heroics of the labor of the collective Soviet people" was encapsulated.[103] Zimenko had particular praise for the "strong-willed man with an intelligent, beautiful face" in the red sweater closest to the viewer; yet, as Susan Reid has argued, the evidence presented on the canvas itself hardly supports Zimenko's own analysis, as the emphasis of Agapov's work is on the physicality of the male body, with explicit connotations of conquest and penetration that have little to do with intellect. However, it was the established matrix that equated beauty with moral superiority that allowed

Zimenko to reach this conclusion; as the characters were such fine physical specimens, they had to be, by extension, in possession of equally fine minds and a sense of civic duty.[104] Given how warmly Agapov's work was received critically, and the power and zeal of the canvas, it is perhaps surprising that no reproduction of this work can be found beyond the coverage in *Iskusstvo*—clearly positive critical reception was no guarantee of a popular platform. This was in contrast to G. Kharitonov's *At the Bratsk GES* (*Na Bratskoi GES*, 1959) and Vilen Chekaniuk's *Morning in Siberia* (*Utro Sibiri*, 1963),[105] which were compositionally and thematically very similar to Agapov's subjugators, but had the exposure in the popular press that was never afforded to the young artist.

There were a handful of other artists that also concerned themselves with the construction of GES stations around this time but who moved away from the dominant trend of presenting these construction sites as a homosocial environment and introduced women into their paintings. However, to say that women were significant in these scenes would be an overstatement, and in each case it was the male workers who were the center of the narrative, with the female form serving as little more than a foil for the hulking masculine bodies around her. Viktor Popkov's *The Builders of Bratsk* (*Stroiteli Bratska*, 1961) is probably the best-known example of this; the central male figure, who is presented legs astride, his enormous hands on his hips, and with his jacket thrown over his shoulders as if to resemble the cape of some proletarian superhero, is made even more physically domineering by the presence of the petite woman next to him.[106] While the female reviewer in *Literatura i zhizn'*, I. Shevtsova, dismissed the work as "boyish" and lacking in both craftsmanship and inspiration, Zimenko was more appreciative of the piece, seeing it as representative of the "agonizing quest" of artists to truly encapsulate the greatness of the Soviet people and their achievements.[107]

A piece that is similar to Popkov's in its treatment of women is *Our Working Days* (*Nashi budni*, 1960) by the controversial Pavel Nikonov, which depicts a group of workers traveling to a construction site in the back of a truck. In this scene the lone woman worker is physically diminished by both the bulk of the men traveling with her and the palette of the work that blends the color of her skirt with that of the truck and her jacket with the coils of wire around her, making her seem more like a part of the backdrop of the painting than a protagonist in it.[108] Unlike Agapov's *Subjugators of Siberia*, which for Zimenko captured the collective nature of Soviet labor, *Our Working Days* was criticized for being too individualistic in its outlook, underlining the importance of the notion of comradeship through labor during this era. "The fundamental mistake was made by the artist when he decided to show the characters in the picture as isolated individuals, casual travelers, each with his or her own thoughts and concerns. And then they were appointed to represent the labor collective!" Zimenko exclaimed in his review.[109] Nikonov had received the commission from the Ministry of Culture to produce a painting for the Soviet Russia exhibition on the theme of the journey to work, but such was the controversy surrounding Nikonov's piece, both in terms of its representation of the Soviet person and its execution, that the painting was excluded from the exhibition and the artist received absolutely no payment, including the expenses incurred during a lengthy stay in Siberia researching the subject.[110] As would be the case a few years later with *Geologists*, there would be no reproduction of this maligned work outside the publications of the art world.

Popkov's *Builders of Bratsk* was not only indicative of a certain trend in representing women involved in heavy construction work—something that was of contemporary concern—but was also far less dynamic than most of the other works that dealt with the theme of heroic labor in the wilds of the Soviet empire, a trait it shared with Tair Salakhov's *Maintenance Men* (*Remontniki*, 1960).[111] Out of all the artists whose work is discussed here, it was Salakhov who gained the most exposure in the popular press, enjoying a couple of features exclusively on his work as well as being mentioned in several others in the same breath as contemporary artists of the caliber of Korzhev.[112] It is hard to pin down from the coverage of his works exactly what it was about this Azeri artist that made his work more appealing than that of others dealing with the same subject matter or painting in the same "severe" style, but there was certainly a consensus that his work managed to convey the complexities of the human character without compromising "integrity, [or] monumentality, without resorting to [the depiction of] every social detail in depth, [and] without reducing the significance of the image."[113] Or as Cullerne Bown surmised, "The grim view of things does not leave a grim impression; rather it tends to reinforce the familiar rousing spirit of socialist realism: it is essentially, conventional heroism with a gritty Khrushchevian texture,"[114] and this seems to have been the key.

For all that motion is implied in *Maintenance Men*, as the boat plows through the water carrying these workers out across the Caspian Sea to the oil rig in need of repair, the geometric nature of the canvas with its flat parallel horizon of sea, land, and sky, gives the piece a static quality, a quality that is underlined by the strong, fixed gaze and planted feet of the central protagonist (who, like Popkov's hero, wears his jacket as if he were a superhero). Unlike the depictions of Siberia or of Bratsk where the harshness of the natural world was explicit in the scene, the only indications the viewer has of the bitter conditions these men are enduring are the ruffled hair of one worker who has, like his coworker, pulled his jacket across his body; we are left in no doubt that it would take far more than the inclement environment of the Caspian Sea to deter these men from their task or challenge them physically. As if Salakhov's work was not manly enough, the order of the composition, its strong lines, thinly applied paint, and lack of texture eliminated what could be deemed the "feminine" sensuality of the canvas;[115] thus Salakhov's image was entirely masculine not only in its subject matter but also in its execution.

In contrast to the solid resolve of both Popkov's and Salakhov's work, another critically acclaimed painting of the period, Latvian artist Edgar Iltner's *Masters of the Earth* (*Khoziaeva zemli*, 1960), explored the theme of heroic labor and the trope of progress through the determined striding of men across the Soviet landscape.[116] Because the heroes of Iltner's canvas are all discrete characters, differently dressed with differently directed gazes, their diverse appearances allowed them to act as a universal standard for all Soviet workers—or at least all the male ones—as no one occupation was privileged over another. Yet, all this individuality was just on the surface, as the workers' synchronized striding and forward momentum unifies the group, giving their progress a common objective—they are a collective. Iltner's use of the foreshortened background presents these men as being of the same monumental scale as the landscape they march through, underlining the fact that however epic the Soviet land may be, it was populated by citizens who were more than capable of bending it to their will: these men were "masters of the earth" in terms of their mastery over nature and their moral superiority as socialist beings, and both ideals were rooted in labor and collectivity.

In her detailed examination of many of these works in 1999, Susan Reid situated the emergence of the hypermasculine worker within the context of the Third Party Program, which was formally adopted at the Twenty-Second Party Congress in October 1961 and would, it was believed, see the final transition from Socialism to Communism. According to Reid, the prevalence of the Soviet superman was the artistic manifestation of Khrushchev's vision of communist society, a society that would be populated by people who "harmoniously combine[d] spiritual wealth, moral purity and a perfect physique."[117] Not only this, but works like Salakhov's *Maintenance Men* were demonstrative of a shift away from the Stalinist norm of a feminine viewer back to that of the male viewer of the 1920s. In Salakhov's painting, this is achieved by placing the viewer on the boat alongside the heroes; the fixed stare of the central character out toward the viewer is challenging, seeming to question whether the observer is "man enough" to join them on this mission, not only of fixing the rig but of achieving Communism. In Reid's analysis of these works, she argued that it was only by embodying the masculine values inherent in such heroes that one would be deemed fit to enter into the new communist utopia.[118]

The framework and context laid out by Reid in this article is extremely valuable in helping us to evaluate how and why the representation of both masculinity and femininity changed following the death of Stalin. She was certainly correct in identifying the central theme of the struggle for the accomplishment of Communism in such paintings, at the heart of which were the ideals of collective labor and comradeship. However, it is also useful to look beyond the immediate context of the aims and ambitions of the Third Party Program as a motivating factor behind the production of such images and to view these works through the lens of the War. It has been argued here that the traditional masculine ideal of the military hero was challenged by the bloody reality of war and that, in the aftermath of such death and destruction, the image of the military man was softened and romanticized and presented as removed from the violence of battle—a trend that far outlived Stalin and perpetuated throughout the Thaw. Thus the hypermasculine worker-hero can be seen as filling the vacuum that the destruction of the military archetype left; all the qualities that were valued in the military man—courage, dedication to the cause, a willingness to put one's body on the line for the achievement of victory, and so on—could now be found in the worker. Crucially, then, the paintings of Iltner, Agapov, Salakhov, et al., offered a vision of heroic manliness that was egalitarian, that was not intrinsically linked to military service, and that provided a model for patriotism and service to one's country open to those too young to have fought in the War; instead, the youth could fight for the achievement of Communism.

The idea that the Soviet man was the master of nature, a theme so prevalent in representations of civilian life, can be juxtaposed with those works that depicted the Soviet soldier during this period, as in these images the relationship between man and land was far more symbiotic, and in some cases almost spiritual. In contrast to the Stalin-era paintings of Neprintsev and Fedorov, who used the landscape to underline the strength of the Soviet soldier, in the works of the late 1950s and early 1960s the landscape was used as a balm or shelter and man was depicted as being a part of this natural world, not its subjugator. This chapter has already shown how Oboznenko's *Night of the Nightingales* can be viewed as an ode to nature, in which the richness of the natural environment transported the watchman away from the man-made horrors of war, and it is a scene that has striking parallels with one of Nemenskii's earlier works in which a young soldier wakes in the forest to be entranced by the beauty around him. In his later piece, *Scorched Earth*, however, Nemenskii uses the landscape to articulate the violence of war as he shows it churned, burnt, and scarred from the ravages of battle, as much a victim of war as the men who shelter in the muddy trench. In his 1958 review of the military-themed pieces from the previous year's All-Union show, Polishchuk elaborated on the narrative Nemenskii presents: the protagonist of the piece is a farmer, who holds in his hand a few grains he has found from spikelets still growing amidst the carnage, and as he does so he grieves for the ruined harvest back home and for his native land, which is now "blood-soaked, scorched [...] naked [and] tortured."[119] However, just as Nemenskii's work was a rarity at this time in its depiction of the psychological impact of war in a retrospective setting, it was also unusual for the landscape to be presented as traumatized; it was far more common for it to be shown as an unchanging constant, somehow unmarred by human action of any kind.

This is revealed most clearly in the images of homecoming that also started to appear again after 1956. The theme of the returning soldier had been a popular one in the art of the late 1940s and early 1950s and had focused very much on the human element of this return with images that were centered on the domestic space and the veteran's relationship with his wife, children, and in some cases parents, a development we will examine in detail in chapter 4. With the reemergence of the homecoming genre in the late 1950s, though, the focus shifted away from the home and out to the fields.[120] In many ways parallels can be drawn between these representations of the return home and the conceptualization of the landscape in the works of the *Peredvizhniki*, which were characterized not only by their sweeping vistas, but also by the depiction of pristine landscapes untouched by human activity. In the masterpieces of artists such as Isaak Levitan, Arkhip Kuindzhi, and particularly Ivan Shishkin, the landscape of the Russian Empire was depicted as timeless and eternal, unchanged by agriculture or urbanization, and above the social and political turmoil of the late nineteenth century.[121] In a similar vein, Andrei Lysenko's *Homecoming* (*Vozvrashchenie domoi*, 1958),[122] T. Kotov's *Return to the Land* (*K zemle*, 1958),[123] and the works of V. K. Dmitrievskii [1958?] and E. Lesin [1961?], both of which were entitled *In Native Places* (*V rodnye mesta*),[124] presented the Soviet soldier returning to a locale that was—at least on the surface—identical to the one he had left a few years before; the sun still shines, the rye still grows in the fields, and the river holds the same course.[125] The arrival back home was not simply a return to normality but a reinstatement of peace, as the veteran was divested of any connotations of brutalization or violence and returned to a place that, like himself, was unchanged by war.

What these images of homecoming and those of homosocial comradeship share is the centrality of the relationship between man and the motherland, although clearly this was expressed in very different ways across the two genres. The idea of Mother Russia had been around for centuries prior to the Soviet regime, and the notion that the feminine nation was a linchpin in the creation of bonds between men is not one that is exclusively Soviet either; as Afsaneh Najmabadi restated in her examination of Iranian identity, "In nationalist discourse representing the homeland as a female body has often been used to construct a national identity based on male bonding among a nation of brothers."[126] Still, while the theme of mastery over nature was very much a part of Stalinist discourse, in terms of visual culture the relationship between the land and the people was predominantly expressed through the *kolkhoznitsa*, and during collectivization in particular visual culture was saturated with images of women working together to ensure the success of the venture, although there is an important context here of female-led riots and acts of resistance to the process that undoubtedly influenced how the project was depicted, particularly in the poster art of the day.[127] However, in Thaw-era visual culture something rather different can be seen, and although representations of women working the land did not disappear, the coding of the landscape as both feminine and intrinsically tied to ideas of nationhood was repeatedly used to reassert the bonds between the men that lived and worked on it, enabling the representation of heroic labor and soldierly life to be expressed almost exclusively in masculine terms.

It is probably not surprising that one sees a difference in the role landscape played in the art of the Thaw across the genres of heroic labor and wartime retrospectives; after all, the themes that were articulated through the battle with the elements and terrain could be explored in far more human terms in a time of conflict. What is noteworthy for our purposes is the difference in the representation of the soldier when compared to that of the worker: while there seems to have been no hesitation in depicting the Soviet man as aggressive, physically dominant, and resolute in his capacity as a worker, this stands in complete opposition to either the romanticized or angst-ridden portrayals of the Soviet soldier. This, then, was not about a certain squeamishness in showing the Soviet man to be hard or tenacious, but in the Thaw these were no longer qualities that were being articulated through the traditional military model.

## "WE BAND OF BROTHERS": MILITARY FRATERNITY TWO DECADES ON

Like the history of any other country, there is a tendency to divide the Soviet past into convenient chunks, which more often than not correspond to the leadership of the day or are based around seismic events that impacted upon the nation in some way. Reality is obviously not this clear-cut; the problems created by war were not magically solved on May 9, 1945; Soviet society was not radically different on March 6, 1953, to what it had been the day before; and de-Stalinization was not one consistent linear progression from repression to liberalization through the period we neatly label as the Thaw. It is for this reason, then, that this examination of the representation of the war experience in visual culture ends in 1965 not in 1964, the year that Khrushchev was ousted from office. While the late 1950s and early 1960s had witnessed some important shifts in how the War was depicted in relation to the themes of comradeship and collectivity—most notably in the work of artists such as Nemenskii who had attempted to bring psychological depth to his exploration of the military experience—for the most part portrayals of the Soviet soldier perpetuated the tropes that had been established earlier in the decade. The motivation behind the representation and the execution of it may have differed from works produced under Stalin, but time and again an artificial distinction between the soldier and the events of war was created in the paintings; they were removed from danger, they were placed in beautiful natural environments, and they were cultured men rather than battle-hardened warriors. This would change dramatically in 1965.

Although the development of a war cult had been occurring by stealth since the death of Stalin, the reinstatement of Victory Day as a public holiday in 1965 appears to have let the genie out of the bottle. In parallel to the memorial building, the lighting of eternal flames, and the elevation of an unknown soldier to a holy relic that also occurred around this time, visual culture witnessed a dramatic upsurge in both the number of images produced generally that dealt with the War in some way and the number of images that now attempted to grapple with aspects of the experience that had to date been largely swept under the collective carpet. As we will see in the following chapters, after 1964 the themes of trauma, bereavement, physical injury, suffering, and death were examined with a frequency and depth that was unprecedented; a development that seems to go against the bombast and grandiloquence usually associated with the early war cult and a development that also seems to go against what was happening in other cultural genres, especially literature and film. Rather than being the domain of a few pioneers, as had been the case in the late 1950s, the physical and emotional scars inflicted by the events of 1941–45 became a concern for most artists who turned their attention to a war-themed genre from the mid-1960s onward, and even though there were still some who continued to present the War effort as relentlessly heroic, it was generally a far grittier vision of heroism than had been presented previously.[128] Indeed, as Cullerne Bown summarized, "Paintings of wartime subjects are perhaps the one area of socialist realism in which the demands of the severe style artists for a more honest scrutiny of life were realised during the sixties."[129] This new, more emotionally honest, way of depicting the War was seen most clearly in works that confronted some of the lasting legacies of those traumatic times— the strain it placed upon marriages, the generational gap between veterans and their children and grandchildren, and acts of remembrance, for example—but it also impacted upon how the years of the War were presented retrospective-ly.[130] In the case of the representation of comradeship, the serene and cozy scenes of the late Stalinist and Thaw period gave way to a new visual discourse as the Soviet soldier was returned to the field of action and once again placed in the line of fire.

In a spate of images produced in the decade after 1965, one can see the rise of a new conceptualization of military fraternity, which was grounded in the dichotomy between death and survival and which was conveyed through the intimate relationships between men. If any single painting captures this transi-tion from lyricism to candor, it is Dmitrii Oboznenko's *Compatriots* (*Zemliaki*, 1969);[131] in a startling contrast to his earlier *Night of the Nightingale*, which was demonstrative of the saccharine formulation of comradeship typical in the decade after the War, in this canvas Oboznenko presented the unvarnished brutality of war and its psychological impact upon those involved. Against the bleak background of a bullet-riddled wall, surrounded by heaps of rubble, one man looks away in anguish as he cradles the body of his comrade, whose life he has clearly struggled to save given the bloody cloth he still clutches in his hand. This was not the death of the heroic last stand or the beautiful death of youth, but a vision of war replete with dirt, blood, and grief. The juxtaposi-tion between death and survival that forms the narrative core of Oboznenko's painting was echoed in several other works from this period, most notably in Anatolii Nikich's *War Correspondents* (*Voennye korrespondenty*, 1965), Viktor Safronov's *The Banner of the Guard* (*Gvardeiskoe znamia*, 1974), and V. V. Ianke's *Attack Repelled* (*Ataka otbita*, 1976).[132] Another example, Evgenii Samsonov's monumental *For Every Inch* (*Za kazhduiu piad'*, 1966), was exhib-ited at the Defenders of Moscow Exhibition in 1966 and was dedicated to his father, I. V. Samsonov, a regimental commander who died during the breaking of the Leningrad Blockade in 1944, and whose likeness was used for the por-trait of the fallen hero.[133]

However, alongside images such as those by Oboznenko and Iltner's more allegorical *Immortality* (*Bessmertie*, 1968),[134] there also emerged a far less pos-itive interpretation of wartime brotherhood. Although the explicit violence inherent in this work sets it apart from the vast majority of other works from this period, which tended to be more contemplative in tone, a mention must be made of Belorussian artist Mikhail Savitskii's highly evocative *A Field* (*Pole*) from 1972.[135] Using a palette of burnt yellows and oranges, with the sky an apocalyptic mix of red and black, in this painting Savitskii presented a bloody clash between Soviet and enemy troops in a style that parodied the pastoral idyll so often found in both Russian and Soviet realism. This dark image, in which waves of black-helmeted enemy soldiers move through the field to the melee in the center of the canvas, was one of the few works of this era that dealt with the War on a more collective level. Unlike earlier works, such as Deineka's *The Defense of Sevastopol* where the violence was not only restrained but also individual, in Savitskii's image there is no singular heroic

FIGURE 1.3. Dmitrii Oboznenko, *Compatriots*, 1969.

feat as the men, as if with one mind, ruthlessly attack their opponents, carrying on relentlessly despite the accumulation of bodies at their feet. The animalistic ferocity of the killing and the synchronized movement of the soldiers in Savitskii's vision of battle reduced both wartime heroics and comradeship to little more than a simple fight for survival and was a far cry from the scenes of unmitigated glory that had adorned the gallery walls in the immediate postwar period.

## SUMMARY

In 1973 Iurii Neprintsev produced a painting that depicted a band of soldiers marching disconsolately through a scorched landscape, the sky illuminated by the flames of battle; it was an image that was a world away from the scene of wartime fraternity he had created a little over twenty years previously.[136] How this transformation could have come about is rooted in the social, political, and cultural changes that the Soviet Union had endured since 1945 as even something that was so central to the Soviet ethos—the idea of military comradeship and collectivity—could not remain unaffected by the sea changes wrought by the experience of total war. In the years of the War itself, the trope of the band of brothers had taken on a new significance and was presented visually with a greater frequency than at any point since the end of the Civil War, but in its aftermath the depiction of the close-knit group of military comrades was shaped by the distinct dynamics of postwar Stalinist society with its focus on normalization and conflictlessness, and its concerns over the potential power of a victorious veteran class. Stripped of its essential militarism and removed from the battlefield, military comradeship after 1945 was left impotent, founded upon a camaraderie that was explicitly nonthreatening and cloyingly good-natured.

As we have seen, this conceptualization of military brotherhood would largely persist for the years of the Thaw, despite efforts by some artists to bring more psychological depth to the soldier-hero. During these years, the hypermasculinity that had once been the domain of the military man was usurped by a new type of laboring hero, one who battled nature rather than the Nazi hordes, and whose success was dependent upon the strength of the collective. Thus, the most significant change in the conceptualization of military masculinity after the death of Stalin came, not in the Thaw as might be expected, but with the beginnings of a systematic war cult in the mid-1960s. For the first time since 1945 extensive memorial building and public ceremonies of remembrance took place, paving the way for a reassessment of the war experience and its meaning for contemporary society, and visual culture was very much a part of this new discourse. Although the number of images that dealt with the issue of military comradeship is modest in comparison with some of the other themes that came to the fore at this time, the changes that one sees in the space of a few short years are profound. Gone were the images of good-natured banter, of morning ablutions, and of wonder at the beauty of the Soviet motherland, and in their stead came a series of works that emphasized both the physical and emotional toil that combat took, where men were placed in real danger, and where it was not only the enemy who lost their lives.

The visual evolution of military comradeship across these two decades takes us from the collective heroic mass and sickly sweet peaceniks of the last years of Stalinism, through the benign band of brothers of the Thaw, to the howling and mutilated men of the late 1960s. The great irony is that what this transition seems to show is that victory in the Great Patriotic War had rendered the military hero problematic as a model for the ideal Soviet Man.

# 2

# THE DAMAGED

## Representing the Wounded and Disabled Soviet Man

Returning home from fighting in the Civil War, Gleb Chumalov, the protagonist in Fedor Gladkov's seminal novel of the 1920s, *Cement*, finds the factory where he used to work a crumbling wreck. Determined to restore the cement works to its former productivity, Chumalov confronts his former coworkers, whom he accuses of being work-shy, revealing his war-damaged body as a visible indication of his commitment to the Soviet cause: "With his fingers he tapped his chest, neck and side. And wherever he tapped scars showed purple and pallid [...] his naked body, all knotted and scarred."[1] For Chumalov, his patriotism, heroism, and strength were quite literally inscribed upon his body. Two decades later another quintessential fictional Soviet hero, Vasilii Terkin, would prove his wartime heroics through the exposure of his damaged body in the *bania*:

> On the naked skin, a star
> Flaming bright and livid
> Like a medal that he's won.
> And he always wears it [...]
> Like a hieroglyph, each scar
> Tells a different story ...[2]

In a society that was founded upon a cult of youth, in which physical beauty was equated with moral superiority, and in which the heroic ideal was embodied by those who had made the most significant contribution to the collective, the damaged body is seemingly incongruous with the Soviet paradigm of the New Soviet Man. And yet, as it has been demonstrated repeatedly in scholarship of recent years, the disabled body has a complex and often con-tradictory place in Soviet discourse.[3] This was particularly the case during the 1930s and 1940s, when the transgressive and liminal aspects of the violated male form were coupled with a rhetoric, especially prominent in the literature and film of the period, in which the wounded soldier was actually the most perfect embodiment of idealized masculinity, representative of a uniquely Soviet form of heroism and strength of character.[4]

However, as this chapter will demonstrate, despite the pedagogical merit and popularity of such literary and cinematic characters, this was not rhetoric found in visual culture either in the Stalin era or beyond. In contrast to liter-ature and film, in art after 1945, the damaged man was never presented as an ideal nor was he ever cast as a figure symbolic of the Soviet war experience. Instead, until the mid-1960s bodily damaged inflicted by war was consistently presented as a temporary state of being, and as something confined to the combat zone that would have absolutely no impact on the life of the soldier or his loved ones once the fighting was over. While other cultural genres grap-pled with the complexities of the disabled experience after 1945, for the most part, visual culture continued to utilize frameworks that had been established during the war years, in which war wounds were symbolic of heroism rather than a graphic reminder of the cost of victory. Indeed, it was not until the years surrounding the reinstatement of Victory Day as a public holiday in 1965 that art began to approach the legacies of the War with a more brutal realism— culminating in the production of the *Scorched by the Fire of War* (*Opalennye ognem voiny*) series by the Muscovite artist Gelii Korzhev in 1967—a develop-ment that can be seen as one strand in a far more extensive reassessment of the significance of the War experience for contemporary Soviet society.

This disjunction between how issues to do with injury and disability were handled across the various genres can be seen as rooted in the media them-selves as, unlike the temporal forms of literature and film, visual culture could not easily present the complexity of the standard tale of injury and despair to ultimate triumph, and thus frame bodily damage or disability in a way that was ideologically appropriate. In order to fully appreciate the nuances of both Soviet cultural production and the significance of the damaged man for the masculine ideal after the Great Patriotic War, then, is vital that we acknowl-edge the fact that visual culture followed a unique trajectory when it came to grappling with some of the more problematic aspects of the Soviet victory. Yet, as will be demonstrated, after 1941 the damaged Soviet man was a consistent presence in both the images that were being created and those that were being reproduced in the Soviet press, although the fact remains that for the majority of the period under review here the mode of representation lacked the range and nuance found in other cultural forms. Thus, while it is valid to see the damaged man as a staple element in the artistic construction of Soviet military masculinity from the outbreak of War onward, at the same time it must be remembered that what was presented in visual culture was often very different from what was to be found in fiction or on the silver screen.

## REPRESENTING THE DAMAGED BODY BEFORE 1941

In contrast to its almost total absence from Soviet visual culture prior to 1941, the wounded male body played a surprisingly prominent role in the propaganda generated by the tsarist regime during the early years of the First World War. Within months of the outbreak of hostilities, posters were being produced that explicitly articulated the toll of the War on the bodies of those fighting and mobilized the wounded soldier as a call for charity. The most iconic of these was the lithograph *Help the War Victims* (*Na pomoshch' zhertvam voiny*, 1914) by Leonid Pasternak, which shows an exhausted and bleeding soldier wrestling with mental distress, reflecting with a remarkable honesty the consequences of industrial warfare on the body and psyche of the Russian soldier.[5] This image would be reproduced tens of thousands of times on postcards, labels, stickers, and even on wrappers of confectionary, despite Nicholas II being less than satisfied with this portrayal of his soldiery. According to Pasternak, the tsar commented that "*his* soldiers behaved bravely and not in such a manner."[6] Whatever Nicholas's objections may have been to this characterization of the injured Russian soldier, Pasternak's image provided the template for other representations of the wounded man between 1914 and 1918 as he appeared time and again across a whole range of posters. Whether being used as a vehicle for raising funds, for demonstrating the exceptional ministrations of Russian field nurses, or for highlighting the heroism of the Russian soldier who valued the life of his injured comrade more than his own, the wounded soldier of the First World War was consistently depicted as a rather pathetic creature in need of rescuing or charity.[7]

After 1917, following the Bolshevik seizure of power and the subsequent outbreak of civil war, there was a sharp decline in the representation of injury and disability as attention turned from the imperialist war to the task of creating and consolidating the new state. Even during the course of the bloody Civil War, by and large, the wounded soldier did not make a reappearance on the ubiquitous Soviet poster; Aleksandr Apsit's two posters created to mark the Day of the Wounded Red Army Man (*Den' ranenogo krasnoarmeitsa* and *Vpered k pobede*), held on November 2, 1919, are two rare exceptions.[8]

In the mid-1920s, though, a very limited number of representations of the wounded First World War veteran started being produced. By far the most harrowing of these works was Iurii Pimenov's *War Invalids* (*Invalidy voiny*, 1926), which was presented at the second Society of Easel Painters (OSt) exhibition later that year to a not entirely warm reception.[9] Depicted staggering through a bleak, post-apocalyptic landscape, these two veterans are presented by Pimenov as fragments of their former selves. With fingers shot off, teeth missing, and limbs encased in bandages, these men stare out of the canvas at the viewer with opalescent eyes blinded by gas. But these are not the pitiful men in need of charity that graced the prerevolutionary poster, as the upright pose and determined forward motion of the composition endows these men with a heroism that was often lacking from earlier representations of the war wounded.[10]

At the OSt exhibition, critic D. Aranovich condemned Pimenov's painting for being too much like those presented at a recent German exhibition,[11] and indeed the aesthetic similarities between this work and that of Otto Dix and George Grosz, both of whom drew upon the similar subject matter, is evident. While Dix's paintings are on the whole underpinned by a morbid humor that is absent from Pimenov's work, as seen in paintings such as *Skat Players* (*Skatlub*, 1920), there is the same unflinching brutality in representing the impact of war on the human body.[12] Grosz, on the other hand, employed the figure of the disabled/wounded veteran as a means of social commentary, presenting the heroes of the First World War as isolated in German society and ignored by the Weimar government. Although Pimenov's canvas did not contain an explicit condemnation of the imperial government, the same simplified painting style, desolate setting, and cadaverous presentation of the central characters can also be found in Grosz's *A Gray Day* (*Grauer Tag*, 1921). However, while the soldier in Grosz's work is presented as an ignored and uncared-for individual—underlined by the ironic preliminary title of the work, *Municipal Officer for Disabled War Veterans*, the job title of the bourgeois figure in the foreground who passes the former soldier oblivious to his hardship—Pimenov's protagonists at least have the comfort of comradeship to help ease the physical and emotional pain.

While more famous for paintings such as *You Give Heavy Industry* (*Daesh' tiazheluiu industriiu*, 1927) and later *New Moscow* (*Novaia Moskva*, 1937), Pimenov produced works with a more macabre and decidedly less optimistic outlook on several occasions in the decade between the end of the Civil War and the disbandment of the autonomous artistic groups in 1932, as seen for example in his *On the Northern Front: Seizure of an English Blockhouse* (*Vziatie angliiskogo blokgauza (Severnyi front)*, 1928), which depicted the storming of a British stronghold during the Civil War and the grim death of one of the Red Army soldiers involved. It is Pimenov's 1933 canvas, *Soldiers Come over to the Side of Revolution (Soldaty perekhodiat na storonu revoliutsii)*, though, that is the most astounding in this context, as it is the only work this research has uncovered that addresses the issue of war-inflicted injury and death produced after 1932 and the move toward Socialist Realism. In this rather extraordinary image, Pimenov depicts the celebration of Bolshevik triumph taking place amidst corpses of the victims of the Civil War, and with the victorious soldiers shown in various states of bodily distress. This painting encapsulates the beliefs of Pimenov's former master, Vladimir Favorksii, that art should be both multi-temporal and multi-spatial, a trait that allows Pimenov to present a more complex narrative in his work—one that moves from the carnage and horror of war to the victory of revolution. The work of Pimenov, however, stands alone—with the exception of perhaps Kuz'ma Petrov-Vodkin, who also broached the theme of death in his paintings—and these few pieces represent both the beginning and the end of the representation of the damaged man in early Stalinist art, even in a retrospective context, as the artistic output of the Soviet Union became even more relentlessly optimistic in tone.

While the wounded male body disappeared from Soviet visual culture with the advent of Socialist Realism, the ideal of a physically mutilated hero emerged as a key trope in the literature of the period. This ideal was embodied most completely and popularly in the figure of Pavka Korchagin in Nikolai Ostrovskii's classic novel, *How the Steel Was Tempered* (1932), which presented a disabled veteran of the Civil War overcoming his incapacities to serve the state and the party until the end of his life. In her research, Beate Fieseler has linked the emergence of heroes such as Pavka Korchagin to a changing attitude toward social welfare that developed over the course of the 1930s. This placed an increasing emphasis on a return to work as the optimum way of supporting an individual, representing a shift "from material support to mobilization," which in turn led to a recategorization of invalidity, with those who were now deemed capable of work being stripped of their benefit entitlement.[13] This new discourse of overcoming, which was idealized during the struggles of collectivization and industrialization, has led some scholars to suggest that the disabled male body was in fact the *ultimate* incarnation of Stalinist masculinity. Lilya Kaganovsky's work on male subjectivity under Stalin asserts that "blind or paralyzed, limping, one-legged, or wearing prostheses—the world of the Stalinist novel and Stalinist film is filled with damaged male bodies. [...] Together these texts construct a Stalinist fantasy of masculinity, turning the New Soviet Man into a heroic invalid."[14] For Kaganovsky, in the years of Stalinism there existed two paradoxical but equally idealized models of

masculinity: that of the physically perfect man, the square-jawed and mus-
cle-bound Stakhanovite, and the mutilated man whose physical imperfections
were overcome in an effort to rejoin the revolutionary ranks.

However, for all they may have been cast as the ultimate Stalinist hero in
the novels and films of the era, these damaged men were never presented as
an ideal in art, a discrepancy arguably grounded in the differing qualities of
the media themselves. The impact of visual culture must be immediate and
its narrative hermetically contained and understandable from what is in front
of the viewer. It does not have the luxury of time, as film does, to construct a
narrative arc, and so only cinema and literature had the scope to develop the
complexities of the standard heroic disabled narrative fully, which ran from
injury and psychological struggle, to eventual triumph and reintegration into
either the home or work environment. While this narrative of progression
could easily be expressed on the page, it was far harder to render such inspirational tales effectively onto canvas. During this period, despite the plurality
of models found in literature, Socialist Realist art continued to draw on the
tenets of the Classical world in which the ideal inner and outer self were a
harmonized whole. In visual culture prior to 1941, then, heroes continued to
be physically—and by extension morally—perfect.

## THE WOUNDED MAN IN THE GREAT PATRIOTIC WAR

This would all change with the outbreak of war in 1941, when the previous disparity between literary/cinematic and artistic representations of the
wounded male dissipated and the injured soldier was cast as the apotheosis
of Soviet masculinity, patriotism, and strength. During the war years, a small
but noteworthy number of sketches, paintings, and sculptures were produced
that tacitly acknowledged the bodily toll that the War was taking as seen, for
example, in Vera Mukhina's bust of the one-eyed and scarred Colonel Iusupov
(1942) or I. A. Lukomskii's portrait of a wounded defender of Stalingrad
(*Uchastnik oborony Stalingrada*, 1943).[15] Crucially, though, it would seem that
such works only found an outlet in print on the pages of the thick art journals *Iskusstvo*, *Tvorchestvo* (founded in 1947), and, much later, in *Khudozhnik*
(founded in 1958). However, as *Iskusstvo* was suspended from July 1941 until
the beginning of 1946 and the other two prominent art journals were founded
in the postwar period, these were not images that were in circulation in print,
even in the professional art world, at the time at which they were produced,
although Mukhina's bust of the recently injured general would go on to
become one of her most famous pieces, winning the sculptor a Stalin Prize

Second Class in 1943. Thus during the War itself it was in the wartime poster that the wounded soldier found his most frequent incarnation, in images that were obviously intended to both reach and inspire a mass audience.[16]

Produced by the prolific graphic artist Viktor Ivanov in 1942, the poster *Every Border Is Decisive* (*Kazhdyi rubezh—reshaiushchii*) was indicative of a shift toward using injury as a marker of heroism in visual culture,[17] mirroring what had been the case for several decades in Soviet literature. Against a backdrop of entrenched fighting and the falling bodies of the German infantry, Ivanov's warrior appeared helmetless and carrying a head wound. While his steely blue eyes and furrowed brow were established modes of representing the steadfastness and determination of the Soviet soldier, the bloodstained bandage around this man's head, placed in almost the exact center of the poster, added a new element to the depiction of the Soviet hero: the fact that this soldier has sustained such an injury does not in any way compromise his military prowess, but rather only serves to enhance his courage and resilience as he carries on fighting without consideration for his own bodily welfare.

This ideal was taken to the extreme in Aleksei Kokorekin's *For the Motherland!* (*Za rodinu!*, 1942) which, like Deineka's *The Defense of Sevastopol* (*Oborona Sevastapolia*), produced in the same year, turned to the heroic exploits of the sailors of the Black Sea Fleet and depicted the already wounded central character carrying out an act of suicidal heroism. Kokorekin drew his inspiration from the real-life heroics of Commander Stepan Ermolenko, who in this poster is pictured on his knees, blood pouring over the hand he has clasped to a chest wound, about to lob a grenade toward an unseen enemy. Yet despite the mortal injury that he has sustained, Ermolenko is shown as physically undiminished—his bulging biceps, enormous thighs, and resolute demeanor are presented as stoic markers of both his physical and moral superiority—and his heroism is only heightened by his wounds and the act of self-sacrifice he is willing to commit for the motherland. In such instances, the wounded male body superseded the physically intact body as the paradigm of Soviet heroic masculinity, as injuries were cast as indicators of valiant achievement, duty, and a willingness to die for the cause, rather than being tainted by any association with inability, incompetence, or the superior strength of the enemy. By representing the wounded soldier on posters rather than on canvas, the focus was on mass dissemination, and the acts of (real-life) heroism that such posters depicted were intended not only to inspire confidence in the civilian population and to reiterate the certainty of eventual victory, but also to emphasize the collective nature of the war effort and the sacrifices that victory would entail. In this context, then, the injured male body was transformed from being transgressive and problematic to being the very epitome of Soviet subjectivity.

It was also in the years of the Great Patriotic War that the maimed body of the enemy emerged as a metaphor for military defeat. While posters of the First World War had shown the kaiser in various states of undress, as mad, or even as having a body full of cockroaches (a play on words between *prusak* meaning cockroach and *prussak* meaning Prussian),[18] his physicality was never equated with Russian military success. During the Civil War, visual culture had frequently turned to the grotesque or emasculated body as a means of articulating the moral corruption of hated figures such as the tsar, the pope, or the various White generals, but again such images had never correlated events on the battlefield with the body of the enemy. It would appear, then, that this use of disfiguration was a new iconographical trope, a device generally reserved for posters containing top-ranking Nazi officials and providing an amusing contrast to the countless, often horrific, images that cast these same men as barbarians, cannibals, and the bestial murderers of women and children.[19] This visual correlation between military defeat and physical disrepair was highly effective. For example, in the poster produced by *Okna Tass* in 1941, *Criss-Cross* (*Krest na krest*), Hitler is shown in one panel proudly straightening his Iron Cross, while in the next panel he has been reduced to a limping wreck, forced to hobble around on crutches, as the result of Red Army victories.[20] In a 1943 poster by the renowned graphic artist Viktor Deni, each wound on Hitler's comically disfigured face is representative of a Red Army "correction."[21] Deni would return to this motif a year later in the poster *The German "guests" will soon be at the graveyard!* (*Khodil nemets „v gosti"! Skoro budet na pogoste!*), in which the injuries on Hitler's face are equated with the strength of the natural resources of the Soviet Union—Ukrainian bread, Caucasian oil, and Donbass coal.[22] Nor was this a mode of representation that was just confined to posters, as the motif of the wounded Hitler was repeatedly used in cartoons published in the press, such as the one by the Kukryniksy published in *Pravda* in February 1944 that paralleled Hitler's injuries with successful Red Army campaigns.[23]

These two contrasting models of the injured Red Army soldier and the mutilated enemy that we find in the iconography of the War are in fact part of the same process of the Soviet state's articulation of power and military prowess. Through the body of their own soldiery, Soviet artists articulated not only a rhetoric of the physical superiority, bravery, and resilience of the collective force of the Soviet people, but the strength of the political superstructure of which these extraordinary beings were a part. In this context, the wounded body of the military man and his/the state's ability to withstand the blows

inflicted by the enemy and remain fighting until victory had been assured
was a symbol of greater potency than his physically unscathed counterparts.
Meanwhile, the decrepit and decaying bodies of the Nazi leadership presented
the ideal vehicle for emphasizing the comparative health of the Soviet body
politic as well as Soviet military might.

## OVERCOMING THE DAMAGED BODY, 1945–53

Any positive connotations that the wounded male body may have gained
during the war years were largely lost after 1945 and were a completely alien
notion by 1950. Now the wounded or disabled body was representative of
the cost of victory and its terrible legacy. In his inventory of Soviet casualties
during the Great Patriotic War, G. F. Krivosheev determined that, according
to official reports, out of the 3.7 million servicemen who were sent home on
sick leave during the War, 2.5 million were left permanently disabled by their
injuries.[24] Due to the difficulties in defining categories of disability, and the
state's reluctance to do so, in reality the number of those left permanently inca-
pacitated by the War is likely to be far higher. As would be expected, it was the
rank and file that made up the vast majority of military losses, accounting for
somewhere in the region of 75 percent of all casualties.[25] Catherine Merridale
has proposed that the demography of those who had borne the brunt of the
War accounts for the absence of injured/disabled men in postwar Soviet society; as many would be lacking in "education, cash and influence," they were
more likely to be seen as an embarrassment than as heroes.[26] Since the mid-
1940s it has been believed by citizens and academics alike that, instead of
receiving the adulation that they had rightfully earned with their bodily sacrifice, many disabled veterans were rounded up by the authorities and died in
exile on the shores of Lake Ladoga, a postwar myth that has been challenged
most recently by Robert Dale.[27] However, whatever the real story is behind
places such as the "invalid's home" at Varlaam, what is undisputable is that
the inability to work, a shortage of wheelchairs, and poor-quality prosthetics
often condemned the disabled veteran to a life of practical hardship and marginalization. The difficulties of the situation were exacerbated in 1947, when
Stalin ordered that the streets of Moscow be cleared of beggars—the majority
of whom were war amputees—a move that was followed by a decree in July
1951 against "anti-social parasitic elements" that, while not specifically aimed
at beggar war veterans, undoubtedly contributed to their declining visual
presence in the big cities.[28] As was shown in chapter 1, the end of the War
and the focus on normalization left every veteran in a potentially ambiguous

place within the postwar social order, but this was particularly acute for those who had not returned from the front physically unscathed. The clearing of the streets of Moscow and other major cities,[29] the anti-parasite legislation, and the privations of the immediate postwar period, as well as the more nebulous impact of the renarrativization of the War to recast Stalin as the prime hero of the entire venture, placed the disabled veteran in a precarious position: after all, what role could such men have in a society that was built upon collective ideals and labor, when they themselves could no longer work and found that the rewards promised for their sacrifice never materialized?

Despite, or possibly even because of, the liminal status of the disabled veteran, official rhetoric from this early postwar period repeatedly emphasized what measures the state was enacting to bring these men back into the fold of Soviet society, and again participation in the workforce was seen as the miracle cure for all physiological difficulties. A report by the Minister of Social Maintenance in May 1946 claimed that, among many other achievements, the government had given out over thirty million rubles in pensions to the war-disabled in the first year of peace, that there were over fifty thousand men no longer capable of working in their old profession in training centers, and that over ninety million rubles had been spent on artificial limbs to date.[30] The sacrifice of the disabled soldier also warranted special mention in the May Day and October Revolution Anniversary slogans, which in 1946 hoped for "the employment and rehabilitation of the disabled of the Patriotic War."[31] While the press hailed the treatment of disabled veterans as a hallmark of the progressive, inclusive, and technologically advanced nature of the Soviet society, as Beate Fieseler has demonstrated, the reality of the situation was far less positive: pensions and compensations were insignificant (and it would seem were deliberately so to force veterans back to work), the majority of disabled veterans did not receive any retraining and were left to find suitable employment on their own, and employers openly admitted to preferring to hire former prisoners than "cripples."[32] For many, even having being fortunate enough to have received prosthetics from the state did not mean that they could then fully participate in the workforce, as this one letter to the editor of *Pravda* written by a couple of disabled veterans from the Kostroma Province highlights: "We lost our legs in battles for the fatherland. Despite our disabilities we are burning with desire to work for the good of the Soviet people. However we are prevented from carrying out our wishes by the lack of good artificial legs. [...] We received artificial legs [...] but they chafe and cause pain. They are useless."[33]

In the immediate postwar years, then, there emerged two parallel discourses concerning the disabled veteran and his place in Soviet society: one that stressed the benevolent nature of the Soviet state in helping care for these men and one that treated disability as something that could be surmounted by a return to labor and the unique physical and psychological strength of the Soviet man. In the space of just a few years, the damaged body had shifted from being the ultimate marker of heroism and patriotic duty to an impediment that needed to be overcome in order to reclaim one's masculine virility. To this effect, the postwar press was full of headlines proclaiming the remarkable achievements of the disabled veteran: men with no hands surpassing production quotas, amputees driving tractors, and veterans using the convalescing period to learn new skills. These men were not to be pitied for the misfortune of their injuries but emulated in their exceptional achievement, courage, and determination.[34]

However frequently these concurrent narratives were articulated in the press, though, neither the discursive trope of support nor superhuman overcoming impacted upon artistic representations of injury or disability. While the damaged soldier did not vanish completely from the visual culture of the late Stalinist period, he was always cast in a retrospective context and confined to the front rather than being shown as a figure in postwar society. In contrast to the heroic depictions of the wartime era, between 1945 and when these images disappeared around 1948,[35] instead of being the heroic figure himself, the wounded soldier became a vehicle for the presentation of the heroism of others. Such images found their way onto the pages of popular magazines and professional journals alike as, for example, in V. Khimachin's sketched image of the nurse Motia Nechiporchkova tending to the wounded (1946) or Vera Orlova's painting, *Counterintelligence* (*V razvedke*, 1947), which depicts a young partisan woman helping a wounded soldier through the forest, published in *Ogonek* and *Sovetskaia zhenshchina* respectively.[36] Nor was it the case that the wounded soldier was exclusively a tool for celebrating the actions of women during the War; former partisan N. Obryn'ba's painting *First Heroic Deed* (*Pervyi podvig*, 1947) shows a young boy leading two wounded soldiers through the woods to safety,[37] while the 1948 work *Stalin in the Dugout* (*I. V. Stalin v blindazhe*) by K. Finogenov completely circumvented the heroism of the injured soldier being greeted by the *vozhd'* by placing him in the shadows and presenting Stalin as sturdy and physically superior to those around him.[38]

One of the most celebrated paintings of the era—and indeed of the entire war-themed oeuvre—Aleksandr Laktionov's *A Letter from the Front* (*Pis'mo s fronta*, 1947) presents a slightly different use of the wounded soldier. In this case, rather than being a means of emphasizing the courageous actions of others around him, the injury portrayed in Laktionov's work served as a narrative device in which absence from the front was legitimized. According to the artist's own, highly stylized recollections on the origins of the painting, it was an encounter with a real-life disabled veteran that first gave him inspiration:

> I saw a soldier coming along the dusty road, limping, with one hand in a bandage and a letter in the other. [...] I talked with him. He was just out of hospital, where he had been with a comrade who had not written home for many years and was considered missing without a trace. He had asked him to pass on a letter to his relatives. Meeting this soldier gave me a theme for my work ...[39]

This soldier would go on to provide Laktionov with his protagonist for a painting he produced the following year, *Defender of the Motherland* (*Zashchitnik rodiny*, 1948), and the injuries that this soldier has suffered bear a close resemblance to that of the soldier in *Letter*.[40] Although *Defender* is a little-known work, Laktionov's representation of injury in portraiture was unique for this period, and indeed would not be repeated again until the work of Gelii Korzhev in 1964.

Later regarded as a Socialist Realist classic, in its early years *Letter* had quite a checkered history; it was initially criticized for its photorealism, and the painting was hung in a dark and dingy corridor in the Tretyakov Gallery upon its first showing at the 1947 All-Union Exhibition. Within days, however, following rhapsodic praise in the visitors' book and the small corridor being jammed with viewers, the painting was moved to a more suitable location.[41] The contrast between the work's popularity and the reaction of the professional art world to the young painter's war-themed canvas was reflected on the pages of the popular press, as *Letter* was reproduced for the first time not in a professional journal but in the women's magazine *Sovetskaia zhenshchina* in April 1948. Later that same month Laktionov was awarded the Stalin Prize First Class.[42] Thus cemented as a favorite piece among the public and the authorities alike, *Letter* became a staple image in Soviet print culture for many years to come, being reproduced for a mass market in the form of postcards, and even appearing as a stamp in 1973 as part of a series celebrating Soviet painting,[43] as well as frequently gracing the pages of popular publications, particularly around significant anniversaries.

In this scene of the personal and domesticated impact of war on the Soviet family, the wounded soldier plays a crucial part in the story of the canvas, cast as the bringer of the joyful news that the father and husband who they thought was lost is actually alive. In addition to his unique use of the injured soldier for narrative purposes, Laktionov is also distinct in placing him in a domestic setting, but when one looks specifically at how the artist has rendered this man's injuries, one sees the same degree of understatement and obfuscation that characterized visual representations of the damaged male body in this period and beyond. By the very act of delivering the precious letter, Laktionov presents this man as one who is on the road to complete recovery, and perhaps even back to the front; the bandaged arm and the cane appear as transitory and to some extent inconsequential as the soldier notably stands, rather than sits, while the letter is read aloud.

As had been the case in the 1930s, the absence from visual culture of men who had been left forever scarred and changed by their injuries was in marked contrast to the characters that populated literature and film of the late Stalin era. Although there was a continued emphasis on the restorative power of labor in overcoming disability, the severity of the injuries that these men had suffered—and it was always men despite the participation of women in a wide variety of roles at the front[44]—found no parallel in visual culture. As with the prewar heroes of Chumalov and Korchagin, who had had to prevail over significant physical difficulties in order to reclaim their place in the Soviet collective, so in the postwar era we find characters such as Colonel Voropaev in Petr Pavlenko's Stalin Prize–winning novel *Happiness* (1947) who, despite having being injured four times, suffering from pulmonary tuberculosis, and having a prosthetic leg, commits himself fully to his labor, creating a new heroic identity for himself that is then emulated by others.[45]

In an early foray into the field of literature and disability, Vera Dunham suggested that rather than providing a reflection of reality with regard to the status of the disabled veteran, the presentation of these men in postwar literature was bound up with issues of "compassion for suffering, responsibility for it, and guilt—all of it frequently blending with the apocalyptic memory of the war [that kept . . .] evolving and reshaping itself with curious tenacity."[46] However, recent scholarship has moved away from this idea of the disabled soldier as representative of the suffering of Soviet society to a focus upon the rhetoric of resilience, in which the invalided veteran became the embodiment of the need to return to prewar norms, particularly with regard to work and family life. In her discussion of Soviet literature spanning the period from the Ten Stalinist Blows of 1944 to the first year of peace, Anna Krylova argued that Soviet literature after 1943 offered a new version of the Socialist Realist hero; "with limbs missing and faces mutilated, minds depressed or hysterical, men in the new Soviet novel cried in their hospital beds from helplessness, self-disgust, and the seeming impossibility of ever imagining themselves as part of normal family life."[47] In this manner, the author became not the engineer but the healer of the damaged Soviet soul, and as Krylova notes, it would often be through the character of the wife or mother that this healing process would begin as she stood, complete and unscathed, to welcome her wounded hero home: "Women were to recognize in the deformed, mutilated men their former masculine selves, to see in them their former strength and beauty, and to provide of their own healthy body parts substitutes for those missing or dysfunctional."[48] Through the woman in his life, then, the mutilated or traumatized man was restored and capable of taking up his former position within the family.

In relation to a different literary genre, Katherine Hodgson has pointed out that while "Soviet poetry was eloquent on the subject of the inner transformation which war brought about, it had little to say about the physical or mental damage inflicted upon soldiers."[49] The notion of the restorative power of home was, however, also found in contemporary Soviet verse. For example, the much-loved and oft-repeated words of Mikhail Lukonin's *I'll Come to You* (1944) expressed a soldier's desire to return home and to labor, concluding that it was "yet better to come [home] with an empty sleeve / Than with an empty soul."[50] Conversely, the sentiments expressed by Sergei Orlov—a former tank commander who had himself been burnt and scarred—on how being wounded had robbed him of his self-esteem, self-recognition, and his ability to work was very much a rarity.[51]

Above and beyond such fictional characters, however, the disabled hero soon came to be epitomized by the fighter pilot and amputee Aleksei Meres'ev, who lost both his feet after being shot down but eventually retook to the skies despite his disability. Through Boris Polevoi's "biography" *A Story about A Real Man* (1946) and the subsequent 1948 film by Aleksandr Stolper, Meres'ev was elevated to the position of the ideal Soviet man, whose resilience and dedication to the cause surpassed any obstacle. And yet the treatment of Meres'ev and his story across the various genres provides a succinct distillation of the discrepancies we find in how problematic issues such as injury and trauma were dealt with in late Stalinist culture. Although ultimately a tale of heroism and triumph, Polevoi's biography did not shy away from the psychological damage that physical injury could inflict: as the author recognizes, in the world of the "severely wounded man, the thing on which all his thoughts are concentrated is his wound, which had torn him out of the ranks of the fighters, out of the strenuous life of war and flung him on to this soft and comfortable bed."[52] This was not the idealized wounded body of the wartime poster, representative of either a dogged determination to continue fighting or of a suicidal heroism, but was a stark reminder of the effort that was required for these men to quite literally get back on their feet and leave the comfort of their emasculating hospital beds behind them.

The wounded airman's liberation from his hospital bed and his doctor's amazement at his achievement were the themes of two watercolor illustrations produced by N. N. Zhukov based on Polevoi's biography, reproduced in *Ogonek* in early 1951 as part of a retrospective of the 1950 All-Union Art Exhibition.[53] However, it is telling that both of these images, while including injured men, painted a far rosier picture of hospital life and overcoming injury than was found in the book. Perhaps the most illuminating aspect of these pictures, though, especially when taken in conjunction with how Meres'ev is presented in both the film and in Polevoi's book, is the fact that in his illustrations Zhukov conveniently bypasses the severity of Meres'ev's injury by only showing the airman from the knees up. In comparison, in a lengthy article about the film that was featured in *Ogonek* in December 1948, the central image of the whole piece was a still of Meres'ev attempting to walk on his new feet for the first time with the help of his doctor, which, while a moment of triumph, is an acknowledgment of difficulty and struggle and did at least feature the prosthetics, even though they are indistinguishable from "real" feet.[54] However, in a photograph published in *Soviet Union: Illustrated Monthly* in July 1950, which was taken outside his home with his wife, Olga, and their son, Meres'ev is shown again with his feet missing (the photograph starts at the pilot's ankles), with no other outward indication of his disability such as a cane, and, more importantly, as a participant in normal family life; both his body and his life are entirely unhindered by his disability, which has been completely surmounted.[55] This depiction of Meres'ev again stands in contrast to the treatment of his story in Polevoi's novel that, as Kaganovsky highlights, constantly reminds the reader of Meres'ev's lost feet by repeated references to his prostheses or his haunted thoughts of the "strong, tanned legs" of Olga.[56] Even though it is a photograph, then, by having his prosthetic feet compositionally amputated in this image, the real-life Meres'ev is brought into line with artistic modes of representation in which injury was never so severe.

During the Stalin era—with the exception of the wartime work of Mukhina and the rather limited depictions of Meres'ev in the 1950s—it is practically impossible to talk of visual representations of the disabled man. While the wounded man appeared on the pages of the nation's popular and professional publications with some degree of frequency after 1945, and the damaged body of both the enemy and the hero had appeared on the wartime poster prior to this, such injuries were invariably presented as temporary, largely superficial, and of a type that would have no impact on the individual once he returned to civilian life after the War was over. It would appear that this was not simply a case of there being a reluctance to reproduce images of the permanently disabled in such a public forum or that somehow the strictures of Stalinism or the prevailing rhetoric of normalization prevented their broader circulation. Rather, it would appear that, in contrast to contemporary film and literature, visual portrayals of the disabled veteran were just not produced in the first place. Why this was the case is difficult to ascertain, but it certainly cannot be wholly ascribed to the conservatism of the late 1940s and early 1950s given that all cultural production was constrained by the same ideological shackles. Again, then, we return to the question of genre and, more broadly, the role that Soviet culture was seen to play. Culture in the late Stalin era was not designed to provoke discussion or to wrestle with the problems facing contemporary society but to educate, inspire, and radiate optimism about the nation's future. When the issue of disability was broached, it needed to be packaged in a way that fitted into these broad criteria—the trauma needed to be overcome, the family needed to be a balm for the "wounded soul," and work needed to offer salvation—a complex task that even the most gifted artist would struggle to convey with simply oil and canvas. It would appear that none even attempted such a feat.

## DEPICTING THE DAMAGED MAN AFTER STALIN

Khrushchev's denunciation of the cult of personality in his Secret Speech to the Twentieth Party Congress in February 1956 profoundly changed the collective and official memory of the War: credit for the triumph was wrested from the hands of the political elite, and the Soviet people were reinstated as the true heroes and instruments of victory. However, as was discussed in the previous chapter, this radical reconceptualization of the events of 1941–45 did not lead to a radical reconsideration of how the War was portrayed in art, as many of the pre-1953 tropes of representation persisted, and this included how issues relating to injury and disability were handled. Yet at the same time, it is important to recognize the fact that while scenes of heroic action and a generally romanticized vision of soldierly life continued to be produced, a new pathos did emerge in some Thaw-era representations of the War, which for the first time began to explore themes such as the emotional impact of separation, homecoming, and the disruption to the normal life course that war had caused. This was just one part of a wider trend in Thaw-time art that rejected the Stalinist varnishing of reality (*lakirovka*) and instead attempted to inject psychological depth and emotional complexity into Socialist Realism, a trend that is commonly referred to as Severe Style (*surovyi stil'*). But while this was a move that brought about significant changes in how the everyday life of the Soviet person was portrayed in general, it was one that had a very limited impact on the representation of the War and its legacy.

The handful of works that brought this new emotional honesty to the war
genre include Boris Nemenskii's *Scorched Earth* (*Zemlia opalennaia*, 1957) and
Edgar Iltner's *The Husbands Return* (*Muzh'ia vozvrashchaiutsia*, 1957)—both
of which are set during the War—and Gelii Korzhev's *Lovers* (*Vliublennye*)
from 1959, one of the earliest paintings to explore the lasting psychological
impact of such trauma. A work that had been reproduced in both the popular
and the professional press by the end of the year,[57] Korzhev's painting depicts
a middle-aged couple sitting on a pebble beach looking out to the horizon
and is founded upon the dichotomy between the physical closeness of these
two people and their emotional distance, at the heart of which is the man's
experience at the front.[58] Although not entirely uncritical of the piece, in her
lengthy review of Korzhev's work accompanying its reproduction in *Iskusstvo*,
D. Bezrukova concluded by stating that "the positive attitude of the majority
of viewers toward *Lovers* shows how our people appreciate truthful art," suggesting that for many this more profound treatment of the War experience
was a welcome development.[59] Yet, this new psychologism we find in Thaw-
era art did not lead to a more honest portrayal of the bodily cost of victory.

Although the reemergence of the wounded soldier in visual culture
occurred around the same time as the rise of the Severe Style, rather than
being linked to these developments in the art world, this reappearance was
actually a consequence of the fortieth anniversary of the October Revolution.
Between 1957 and 1960 in particular, the Soviet art world was consumed with
celebrating the victories of the Revolution and Civil War, with the jewel in
the crown being the All-Union Exhibition of 1957, the exhibition where the
works by artists Nemenskii, Oboznenko, and Kotliarov, which were examined
in chapter 1, were presented for the first time. One of the other artists whose
work was displayed at this showcase was Vladmir Serov, a conservative voice
in the Thaw-era art world who would go on to become the president of the
Academy of Arts in 1962. Serov was one of many artists whose work in the
mid-1950s was predominantly concerned with the revolutionary era, and the
1957 exhibition marked the first display of three of his best-known pieces—
*The Decree on Peace* (*Dekret o mire*), *The Decree on Land* (*Dekret o zemle*),
and *Waiting for the Signal* (*Zhdut signal*) (all from 1957).[60] While Serov was
by no means alone in choosing to focus on revolutionary themes, what makes
these works particularly significant in this context is that in each of these
paintings he included a wounded soldier—a seemingly bold move for such a
traditionalist.[61]

Serov's series contained what could be classed as incidental portrayals of
injury and can be placed within a wider trend in which the wounded soldier was located in a Revolutionary or Civil War setting, seen perhaps most

famously in Vilen Chekaniuk's *The First Komsomol in the Village* (*Pervaia kom-somol'skaia iacheika na sele*) from the following year.[62] Rather than being confined to a hospital bed or in need of rescuing by others, the wounded soldier in this context was depicted as a man still carrying out his revolutionary tasks and as someone who was intimately involved in the creation of the new Soviet state.[63] Still, such injury never exceeded a bandaged arm or a slightly game leg. This relatively minor change in how the wounded man was represented was confined to this distant and quasi-mythical setting of the revolutionary era, though. As with their Stalinist antecedents, the handful of contemporaneous works that presented the wounded soldier of the Great Patriotic War continued to depict injury as a marker of Soviet valor and place the damaged hero in a variety of extraordinary situations that demanded extraordinary acts of bravery.

The work of the artist Petr Krivonogov either side of the 1953 divide is demonstrative of just how resilient the visual lexicon surrounding injury was, despite the significant social and cultural shifts that had recently occurred. During the last years of Stalinism, Krivonogov was one of just a handful of artists who produced "realistic" battle panoramas, as seen in his *On Kursk Arc* (*Na Kurskoi duge*, 1949), which depicted the greatest tank battle of the Second World War,[64] and his *Defenders of the Brest Fortress* (*Zashchitniki Brestskoi kreposti*, 1951).[65] In keeping with the trend of equating physical injury with heroic deeds, Krivonogov's defenders are shown as battered and bloodied, several with wounded limbs and with three of the group sporting bandaged head wounds, as they fearlessly charge toward an advancing enemy across land strewn with the bodies of both their fallen comrades and German adversaries. A highly popular work, this huge battle scene would be published numerous times during the mid-1950s, and indeed a detail from the painting focusing on the group of injured but resolute defenders was singled out for pride of place in Boris Polevoi's piece in *Ogonek* celebrating the twentieth anniversary of the Grekov Studio in November 1955, with this same section of the work going on to become a stamp in 1961.[66] In his work after the death of Stalin, Krivonogov would return to the defense of the Brest Fortress several times but continued to equate exceptional heroism with the damaged male body. In a departure from his earlier paintings, his *Brest Fortress 1941* (*Brestskaia krepost,' 1941 g.*, 1958),[67] along with N. P. Tolkunov's *Immortality* (*Bessmertie*, 1959–60),[68] reduced the collective struggle to defend the fortress to that of a heroic last stand of a lone, wounded warrior. In both Krivonogov's and Tolkunov's canvases, the viewer is confronted by the physicality of the Soviet soldier who, like Stepan Ermolenko before him, aside from his injuries was presented as an archetypal male specimen—tall, athletic, imposing—and who encapsulated a Sovietized version of the Classical ideal of "masculine beauty caught in a hopeless struggle to the death."[69] As it had been in the art of the war years, both the heroism and masculinity of these men were founded upon their utter devotion to the cause, and the magnitude of their heroic actions was amplified through their already mutilated bodies.

For the first time, though, there appears to be a disconnection between work that was being produced and work that was being reproduced when it came to representations of the damaged body in print culture. In the late 1950s two significant pieces of sculpture that depicted the disabled Soviet man were created and exhibited—Ernst Neizvestnyi's *Invalid* (*Invalid*, also known as *Man with Artificial Limb*, 1957) and Dmitrii Shakhovskoi's *People Be Vigilant!* (1958)—and yet neither work graced the pages of either the professional or the popular press at the time, despite the fact that it would appear that these pieces represent the first depictions of Soviet Great Patriotic War amputees in any medium. In the years after 1955, Neizvestnyi produced a series of works entitled *War Is . . .* that dealt explicitly with issues surrounding death and disablement and which drew on his own experience of being left for dead behind German lines. While his sculptures *Soldier Being Bayoneted* (1955) and *Dead Soldier* (1957) were demonstrative of the abstract and avant-garde style that would cause him so much trouble in the coming years, his *Invalid*—which shows a double amputee reaching out to touch the prosthetic leg that lies in front of him—was more realistic in execution. The body of the man in this bronze is reminiscent of the Belvedere Torso (first century BCE, Hellenistic), a sculpture amputated by the vicissitudes of time. In Neizvestnyi's work, though, it is not time but war that has left the body broken.

The Belvedere Torso is believed to represent Hercules after death, "his now beautiful body purged of the marks of the violent struggle in which he realized himself a hero,"[70] and similarly Neizvestnyi transformed this man into a Herculean figure through his battle with his disability. In his 1969 essay on Neizvestnyi's work, the influential art historian John Berger dismissed *Invalid* as an unsuccessful piece, although tellingly he acknowledged that Neizvestnyi intended to articulate the fact that "this mutilated man is a Prometheus because he is alive; his mutilation adds to his Promethean character by allowing him to show the extent of human [some may say Soviet] adaptability, and the strength of will to survive."[71] Similarly, in his more recent biography of the sculptor, Albert Leong concluded that "his men are powerfully masculine. [. . .] As we see in *War Is . . .* even the amputees and bayonetted men he depicted were, and remain, strong men who exhibit strength of will and power of resistance in the face of death and mutilation."[72] The *War Is . . .* collection was exhibited in late 1959 and was the subject of a discussion at the general meeting of the Moscow Section of the Union of Artists in December of that year, the tone of which was remarkably encouraging despite the artist's subject matter and style. Although expressing concern regarding the "very pessimistic" outlook of the works, critics such as S. S. Valerius were forced to concede that "what Ernst gives in his series *War Is* ... [...] is a talented depiction of the physiological side of human suffering in war."[73] The fact that Neizvestnyi's work was not reproduced or even discussed in the professional art press, given its groundbreaking subject matter and its generally positive critical reception, is perhaps a little puzzling. However, it is not at all surprising that Neizvestnyi did not find an outlet in more popular publications given both the tone and manner in which he broached the issue of the war-damaged body, which was starkly divergent to the images of the wounded man that did populate print culture.[74]

While Neizvestnyi's work was generally positively received, Dmitrii Shakhovskoi's brutally realist work presented in 1958 at the Fourth Moscow Youth Conference was roundly condemned by the critics. Depicting a legless man, sitting on a *telezhka* and clutching the blocks he uses to wheel himself through the city streets, Shakhovskoi's sculpture provoked strong criticism for its bleak narrative, which according to some had neither educational nor inspirational merit.[75] Such youth exhibitions were a new development of the Thaw and, as Susan Reid has demonstrated, represented the "avant-garde of the official art system," and although such events were eventually quashed by conservative forces in 1963 (albeit temporarily), among the reformists they were welcomed as an opportunity for innovation and reinvigoration.[76] It is perhaps even more significant, then, that Shakhovskoi should come in for such sharp criticism in this context, but as Reid states, "Even committed reformers equated 'authenticity' and 'contemporaneity' with a fundamental optimism, however 'severely' it was expressed,"[77] and there was nothing optimistic about this young artist's depiction of disability.

The treatment of disability by both Neizvestnyi and Shakhovskoi in terms of its realism and its psychological edge is in many respects closer to how contemporary cinema dealt with these problematic issues. While the complexities of Thaw-era cinema are not a main concern here and have been well addressed elsewhere,[78] the gulf between art and cinema in how themes such as disability and psychological suffering were depicted—as had been the case between art and literature in the immediate postwar period—once again highlights the complicated and often contradictory nature of both Soviet cultural production itself and how the legacy of the War was broached in particular. A brief look at two of the most acclaimed films of the Thaw, Mikhail Kalatozov's *The Cranes Are Flying* (1957) and Grigorii Chukhrai's *Ballad of a*

*Soldier* (1959), demonstrates this disjunction all too clearly, as in both these movies the wounded soldier is presented as a complex man, grappling with a variety of psychological issues and coming to terms with an injury that goes far beyond the bandaged limbs and bleeding heads of Thaw-time art. In Kalatozov's *Cranes*, the wounded soldier plays a series of roles in the development of the plot; he is both the cause of the death of the hero, Boris—who is shot by a sniper during a reconnaissance mission while trying to save his injured comrade—and also the vehicle for his former sweetheart Veronika's heroic self-redemption at a hospital in the depths of Siberia, where she and her father-in-law care for the wounded of Stalingrad. However, unlike what is found in other forms of visual culture, the presentation of the wounded soldier in this film is far more than a simple narrative device. From the character of Vorobev, who despite his injuries tries to retain his manly pride by refusing to ask for a bedpan, to Zakharov, whose physical pain is cast as insignificant in comparison to finding out that his sweetheart has married someone else, to the numerous wounded men who are greeted by their families in the closing sequence of the homecoming parade, Kalatozov time and again presents injury and its effect on the male body and psyche as complex—both emasculating and heroic, life-threatening and life-affirming, a marker of bravery and a source of self-doubt.

A similarly nuanced depiction of injury can be found in *Ballad of a Soldier*. In his attempt to return home during a week's leave granted for an act of heroism, the protagonist Alesha Skvortsov encounters an amputee, Vasia, on the platform of a railway station, attempting to get home to his wife. Racked with doubt at the chances of a happy reunion and filled with self-loathing, Vasia is presented as torn between the desire to go home, the fear of rejection, and the longing for his wife to be happy, something he believes can only happen if he never returns. After trying to write a telegram to his wife explaining his decision, Vasia only decides to board the train home after being berated by the female telegraph operator, who condemns his cowardice in leaving his wife after she has waited so long for him. Yet the decision to go home does not ease his mind, a torment visually symbolized by a lingering shot in which Vasia's crutches become bars, underlining the isolation that this soldier feels now he is on the periphery of "normal" society, a place where he believes happiness and a conventional family life are unattainable. It is only when he is reminded by another stranger—this time an elderly man in the carriage—that he should be grateful to be alive and returning home despite what he has gone through, that Vasia's mind is eased somewhat. At the moment when it looks as if his worst fears would be confirmed, Vasia's wife arrives and passionately greets him, exclaiming, "You're back! You're alive!" seemingly ignoring his injury and proceeding to worry about her own appearance and explain her slightly wounded finger, a subtle nod to the trivialities of domestic life to which he has now returned. Although this homecoming is immediately portrayed as a happy one, the difficulties of reintegration are handled beautifully in the final scene of Vasia and his wife: as they walk to the car waiting to take them home she tries to hold on to his arm, which in turn impedes his ability to maneuver his crutches, and so, despite their enduring love, they depart the station in a state of uncertainty, unsure as to what his disability may now mean for their life together.

Of course, even though the modes of representation were very different, it is inaccurate to see art and film as being completely divorced from one another. In her thoughts on Korzhev's *Lovers* accompanying its first reproduction in *Iskusstvo*, Bezrukova highlighted the fact that some observers had drawn parallels between this work, trends in postwar Italian cinema, and, closer to home, Sergei Bondarchuk's film adaptation of Mikhail Sholokhov's 1946 short story, "The Fate of a Man" (first published in 1957). Later, Korzhev himself would acknowledge the cinematic influence on his painting style and treatment of his subjects, seen in his tendency for what Aleksandr Sidorov described as "expanded scale and dramatic cropping."[79] Bezrukova was, however, rather dismissive of those who drew too close an equivalency between Korzhev's paintings and film, declaring that "it is possible that one form of art influences another but this kind of art should never lose its specificity. Film can tell you a lot in two hours, a painting must provide everything all at once. The artist can also say [a lot], but only insomuch as he can do without sacrificing artistry and poetic [expression] (*poetichnost'*)."[80]

Here Bezrukova pinpoints a potential reason why one sees such a disjuncture between even the most psychologically complex and nuanced work—as Korzhev's was at this stage—and cinema: not only were there restrictions inherent in the nature of the media themselves in terms of the distinction between temporality and spatiality, but painting was also meant to fulfill a purpose beyond simple narrative; it needed to do more than tell a story, it had to remain *art*. What is more, official cultural bodies still advocated that art should be optimistic in its outlook, despite the high-gloss coating of reality that had characterized Stalinist visual culture having been to some extent stripped away. As Vladimir Serov declaimed:

> The task of Soviet art is to depict the beauty of our life. [...] A demand for so-called harsh truth has emerged. One may ask: Why should truth be harsh only? Why should truth not be joyous, optimistic and appealing? ... The meaning

of our work consists in seeing the great truth, the truth about the beauty of the
Soviet man, who is fighting for peace, for social progress, for communism.[81]

   As such, the representation of the more profound aspects of the War experience in general remained highly problematic throughout the 1950s and
into the 1960s, despite the significant changes that had occurred in other
areas of Soviet culture. It is this combination of the intrinsic characteristics
of the respective medium and the prevailing atmosphere of the Thaw that
arguably offers the best explanation as to why this disparity in dealing with
what Krylova termed "inappropriate themes" persisted well after the death of
Stalin.[82] However, there is no escaping the fact that, even taking these constraints into account, artistic representations of the impact of the War—physically, psychologically, and materially—continued to be very limited.
   More than anything, the representation of the damaged military man
during the Khrushchev era demonstrates the remarkable resilience of the
established Soviet tropes for dealing with such issues. While cinema forged
ahead with increasingly colored depictions of these men, with very few exceptions, on the pages of the nation's major publications the same old type of
image continued to be churned out. Injury was still portrayed as something
that marked men as real heroes rather than something that left individuals
scarred, and it was certainly not something that had to be dealt with by either
the men or their families once the fighting was over. The work of artists such
as Korzhev, though, are demonstrative of how the terrible legacies of the War
were now beginning to be broached in the visual arts, with such images finding both a place in the press and, it would seem, a broadly supportive public.
Yet what the examples of Neizvestnyi and Shakhovskoi demonstrate is that,
while some artists were now being inspired to produce works of this nature—
and received a public platform to show such pieces—there was a limit to what
was deemed acceptable when it came to depicting the physical cost of war, and
this did not include such bleak depictions of shattered lives.


## SCORCHED BY THE FIRE OF WAR: THE DAMAGED MAN TWENTY YEARS ON

Rather than during the Thaw, it is not until the mid-1960s and the twentieth
anniversary of the War's end that we begin to see a noticeable shift in the
artistic presentation of the wounded or disabled soldier. As discussed in the
previous chapter, this was not a unique development but one strand in a much
broader visual reconceptualization of the War experience that at last began to
incorporate consistent reference to issues such as bereavement, trauma, and

death. It cannot be coincidental that works of this nature should emerge in the years surrounding the reinstatement of Victory Day as a public holiday (1965), which marked the emergence of the war cult in the Soviet Union and witnessed the first wave of concerted memorial building within the USSR, both of which brought the memory of the War experience legitimately into the public arena. Nina Tumarkin in her survey of the development of cult of the Great Patriotic War is quick to point out the political upside of its reinvigoration for Brezhnev and his administration: "The idealized war experience was a reservoir of national suffering to be tapped and tapped again to mobilize loyalty [and] maintain order ... [as] from 1965 on, the Great Patriotic War continued its transformation from a national trauma of monumental proportions into a sacrosanct cluster of heroic exploits."[83] Polly Jones, in her work on literature and the trauma of the Stalinist past, recounts in great detail how authors who attempted to publish works that broached the harrowing experiences of terror or of the catastrophic early days of the War repeatedly found their works banned by the authorities in an era that was characterized by a renewed commitment to a heroic narrative of the Soviet—and Stalinist—past.[84] However, it is undeniable that this same period also saw a profound change in the visual representation of the War, which seems to stand in contrast to the disingenuous motives of the regime described by Tumarkin and the marginalization of traumatic memories that Jones finds in literary circles. Again, then, it would seem that visual culture was following its own trajectory when it came to dealing with the War and its terrible legacies, a trajectory that perhaps calls into question some of the assumptions about the nature of the early Brezhnev era as one that typically saw "the edginess and contentiousness of Khrushchev-era war culture ... [fade] into stable bombast at the level of public ritual."[85]

The watershed painting in this new, more realistic treatment of the damaged male body was Korzhev's *Wounded* (also known as *Traces of War*; *Sledy voiny*, 1964);[86] everything about this work distinguished it from what had gone before. No longer simply an incidental figure in a crowd, or a lone man in a heroic duel with an unseen enemy, Korzhev's use of portraiture to represent the disabled soldier was unique and unprecedented. Offering the viewer no place to escape the unvarnished reality of his injuries, Korzhev's soldier stares confrontationally out of the canvas, his bright blue eye providing the focal point of the composition, creating an uneasy intimacy between the man and his observer. Embodying the struggle of self-recognition that was so often found in literature, this man is presented as two halves of a former whole: his left side intact and handsome; his right side burnt, scarred, and blinded. The injuries that this soldier has suffered are great—his hair is burnt away, his nose

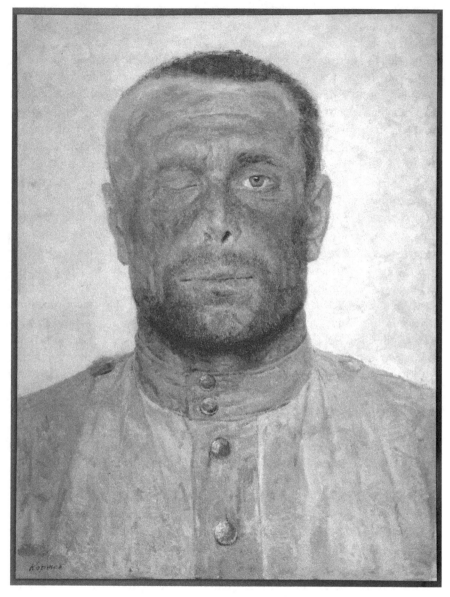

FIGURE 2.1. Gelii Korzhev, Wounded, 1964. The Russian Museum, St Petersburg.

is almost collapsed, his ear is damaged, his cheeks scarred, and his eye gone—
and this lack of bodily integrity is enhanced by daubed background paint that
encroaches onto the soldier's head and ear, creating an indistinct silhouette.

Altogether, this was a clear departure from the Classical ideal of the concrete male body that had influenced Soviet representations to date.

*Wounded* was one of a series of works that formed Korzhev's *Scorched by the Fire of War* collection, and several of the paintings that are part of this set can be seen as Socialist Realist masterpieces; certainly the series as a whole marked a defining moment in the visual representation of the impact of the Great Patriotic War on the Soviet population. Said to have invoked "strong passions" at its first display in its original format at the Moscow Regional Exhibition in 1965, contemporary critics, while not universally praising Korzhev's artistic style, recognized the thematic importance of this young artist's work, calling it an "aesthetic refraction of the conscience of the time,"[87] "strong and inflexible in its truth," and demonstrative of a "severe simplicity, a bluntness that expresses the immensity of suffering during the war years," an experience that itself was called "an oozing wound in the heart of literally every family."[88] In his review of the final series in *Khudozhnik* in May 1968, V. Gavrilov concluded that "an artist who has found in himself the courage [*muzhestvo*] and strength to perform such a great work, deserves great respect and gratitude.[89]

As acknowledged by the critics, the defining feature of these paintings is the treatment of psychological suffering as a consequence of the War, most poignantly rendered in the piece *Old Wounds* (*Starye rany*, 1967),[90] the visual parallel of an untitled poem by Aleksandr Tvardovskii from 1965 in which he describes how "All wounds hurt more at night" and the feeling of isolation that this continual physical and mental pain can cause.[91] Using the same protagonists as in his earlier piece *Lovers*, in this painting Korzhev returns to the emotional distance that the War has created between a husband and wife; while he lies awake, she sleeps soundly, her back turned, unaware of—or simply accustomed to—her husband's psychological struggle. *Old Wounds*, along with *The Farewell* (*Provody*) and *The Human Shield* (*Zaslon*), were added to the *Scorched* series in 1967, which had originally been presented as a triptych in 1965 comprised of the paintings *Mother*, *Wounded*, and *Street Singer*. While the first two paintings would remain as part of the collection, the image of the street singer was eventually dropped when Korzhev decided to introduce his later, and much more powerful, works. In *Street Singer* (*Ulichnyi pevets*, 1962),[92] Korzhev again tackles the issue of disability and its impact upon the life of the individual concerned, depicting a former soldier who has been blinded in the War now being forced to play his accordion for money on the street. This is not a particularly successful work: it is melodramatic and lacks the emotional depth found in his other paintings from this period, and tellingly the soldier's disability is hidden from the viewer's gaze by his dark glasses, making it hard for the viewer to establish an emotional connection with this individual. Despite the failings of this painting, it is interesting to note that, in its original composition, two out of the three pieces in the series took the disabled veteran as their central theme.[93]

As might be expected, the critical art press discussed Korzhev's series extensively over the coming years, and the final collection of five works was published several times in its entirety and in color in *Iskusstvo* between 1967 and 1970 and at least once in *Khudozhnik* over the same period, as well as single pieces being reproduced individually on other occasions. The paintings, in their varying configurations, were also publicly displayed at least twice at major exhibitions after the original showing in Moscow—at the Soviet Russia Exhibition of 1965 and the Fiftieth Anniversary of the Great October All-Union Exhibition in 1967. The latter prompted the first (and this research would suggest only) reproduction in a popular magazine of pieces from the series, when *Rabotnitsa* published *The Farewell* and *Old Wounds* and a brief but glowing feature on Korzhev to mark the exhibition.[94] While the selection of these two works seems logical given the resonance that the images would have had with *Rabotnitsa*'s female readership, at the same time it is telling that no reproduction of *Wounded* in a popular medium has been found, despite the professional art world acknowledging the importance of the work.

What has been found, though, are numerous articles that mention the work of this young artist, and even a few features that discuss his work exclusively. It was the triptych *Communists* (1960) that secured Korzhev's place as one of the most popular artists of the period,[95] and the column inches dedicated to him, particularly in *Ogonek*, also made him one of the most written-about Soviet artists of the era, despite the controversial nature of some of his work.[96] While extensive articles on a particular artist—particularly those associated with the late nineteenth-century *Peredvizhniki* movement—were a regular feature of *Ogonek* by the 1960s, it was not commonplace to have lengthy discussions of a specific exhibition beyond the annual All-Union show; images from a particularly significant event may be reproduced over several issues, but the commentary that was provided to accompany these images was usually quite limited, if it was provided at all.[97] The Soviet Russia Exhibition of 1965 was an exception to this rule, as it was the subject of a long article that featured in a March issue of *Ogonek*, in which Korzhev's original trio of paintings were examined in turn. Despite the fact that the commentator, Vladimir Voronov, did not offer the most incisive or detailed analysis of these works—just two or three lines on each—it is significant that, although no copy of *Wounded* has been found in the popular press, it was a painting that was at least discussed in a public forum.[98] Still, while it is correct to see this painting as a landmark in the Socialist Realist treatment of the damaged Soviet body, how many ordinary citizens would have been aware of its existence given its limited circulation is impossible to judge.

Although the work of Korzhev may stand alone in many respects, other artists across a variety of war-themed genres also offered a closer examination of the damaged male body at this time. Works such as Samsonov's *For Every Inch* (*Za kazhduiu piad'*, 1966), Orlovskii's *For the Land, For Freedom* (*Za zemliu, za voliu*), Khmelnitskii's *In the Name of Life* (*Vo imia zhizni*), and Khaertdinov's *After the War* (*Posle voiny*) (all from 1967) are indicative of an increased willingness to explore death, bereavement, and even psychological trauma through art by the late 1960s. Though some artists, such as Petr Krivonogov and Nikolai But, continued to emphasize the extraordinary heroism of the Soviet military man, it was generally now a far grittier vision of heroism that was being portrayed, and notions of bodily sacrifice were still key even in works of this nature.[99] Yet despite this new more brutal representation of the bodily cost of conflict, artists continued to confine their exploration of such themes to the theater of war; there was no artistic equivalent of Chukhrai's Vasia, as the reality of the man who returned home from the War physically altered continued to be almost entirely absent from visual culture.

The only representation of the physically damaged man in the domestic space that this research has uncovered is Nikolai Solomin's *He Came from the War* (*Prishel s voiny*) from 1967, which was published as a double-page color reproduction in *Ogonek* in December that year,[100] and which depicts a soldier still in uniform, with his crutches hung on the back of his chair, seated at the kitchen table surrounded by his extended family. Unfortunately, while it is noteworthy that Solomin's painting appeared in *Ogonek*, and was reproduced so prominently and so quickly following its completion (suggesting that it had been a part of an exhibition at some point that year), the fact that we have no commentary on the image either in this context or—as far as can be ascertained—in a professional one, means that we have no way of gauging the response to the work and its content. This should not necessarily be taken as automatically indicating an unease with the subject matter, though, as Solomin's work was by no means alone in being reproduced without comment, and generally by the late 1960s, commentaries on individual images, which had always been brief and rather intermittent, were becoming even more of a rarity. However, the fact that this is the only reproduction of the work that has been found, and that it stands alone in its placement of the damaged man in the domestic sphere, does serve to underline just how artistically marginal this subject continued to be, something that stands in stark contrast to how crucial the home and family had been for the wounded veteran in literature and film for the previous two decades.

The disparity between the conspicuous inclusion of Solomin's work and the absence of Korzhev's astonishing painting is particularly intriguing and at the very least underlines the fact that what was included in the printed media was not based on artistic merit alone. Again, we come back to this issue of disability having to be correctly packaged to make it fit for public consumption. Like Meres'ev before him, surrounded by family, Solomin's protagonist is shown as a participant in normal society, there is no indication of any psychological trauma, and his physical disability is untroubling and hidden from view; Korzhev's soldier by contrast is both explicitly wounded and alone, suffering an anguish that is almost palpable. However lauded this young man's work was, however popular his earlier vision of revolutionary triumph may have been, and however willing publications such as *Ogonek* now were to publish scenes of bodily sacrifice that resulted in a heroic death, it would seem that, even two decades on, the unvarnished truth of the disabled body still had no place in popular print.

The absence of the disabled veteran from popular print culture would persist into the 1970s, with the first photograph appearing in the women's magazine *Rabotnitsa* in May 1970, as part of the publication's commemoration

FIGURE 2.2. Nikolai Solomin, *He Came from the War*, 1967.

of the end of the War. In a feature on the Battle of Stalingrad, and the subsequent construction of the memorial complex in the city, the magazine published four photographs taken by Nikolai Surovtsev and V. Titaev over the double-page spread – one of the Panorama, one containing both sculptures from the Square of Heroes and the famous *Motherland Calls!*, one a close-up shot of visitors' faces, and in the top lefthand corner, an image of an amputee, standing in the Panorma, his head bowed and resting against the top of his crutch.[101] For all there had been hesitancy in publishing images of the disabled Soviet soldier, disabled soldiers from other nations had appeared in magazines from the early 1950s. A sketch by Petr Pinkisevich of a West German double amputee begging on the street, which had been shown at the 1952 All-Union Exhibition, appeared in *Ogonek* in early 1953,[102] and disabled veterans of other nations were also included in a number of antiwar paintings from the early 1950s, such as the brigade work by Poliakov, Radoman, and Shats, *Song of Peace* (*Pesni mira*, 1950), which featured the American singer Paul Robeson; Popov and Snatkin's *We Demand Peace* (*My trebuem mira*, [1952?]); and Iraklii Toidze's *We Need Peace* (*Nam nuzhen mir*, [1954?]), all of which were published in *Sovetskaia zhenshchina* and were a part of that magazine's fervent advocacy of peace in the early postwar period.[103] Photographs of a German veteran amputee on an antiwar march and a Japanese man who had lost his leg in Hiroshima, along with a cartoon by M. Abramov entitled *The Winners and the Losers*, which showed two military officers striding past a double amputee on a trolley opposite the Palace of Westminster, appeared in *Ogonek* in the early 1960s.[104] As had been the case with the handful of images of the disabled soldier from the First World War, by and large these damaged men were used as a political cudgel with which to bash the cold and uncaring West, rather than a straightforward comment on the physical cost of war itself.[105] The image featured in 1970 was different: here was a photograph in which the disability of the veteran was in plain sight, and more than this, it was a photograph that depicted the emotional anguish still felt by this man more than twenty-five years later.[106]

Just over a year later, *Ogonek* published its first photograph, taken in a setting that was very similar to the earlier *Rabotnitsa* image and that, like so many earlier representations, confined the damaged Soviet man to a militaristic context. In this shot, the disabled veteran appeared as a part of a crowd of veterans gathered together to mark the opening of the Brest Fortress memorial, and this image was just one of several by Mikhail Savin—himself a former war photographer—that constituted the spread on this event. While nowhere near as explicit in its representation of disability as Surovtsev's photograph, the disability of Savin's veteran is hinted at only through his crutches, although his placement in the foreground of the photograph makes him an unmissable figure amidst a sea of faces. As understated as this was, it would appear that this man was the first published photographic evidence in the mainstream popular press that the War had indeed taken a bodily toll on those Soviet men who had fought and lived through the ordeal.[107]

This leads us into the final genre that grappled with the issue of the damaged body and which had a place in the print culture of the 1960s, that of memorials, and most significantly the new memorial site that was opened at Volgograd (formally Stalingrad) in October 1967. With plans having been drawn up in 1958, the complex at Volgograd was the most extensive memorial to be constructed during these early days of rehabilitation and, with the possible exception of the one in Leningrad, was the site most closely tied to the mythology of the War. As will be discussed in the next chapter, an understandable focus has fallen on the statue by Evgenii Vuchetich, which has immortalized the Volgograd complex—the sword-wielding, avenging Motherland that stands atop Mamaev Kurgan—but in reality, the memorial complex offers a far more diverse vision of the Soviet war experience. In addition to Vuchetich's other major piece—the grieving mother shown cradling the body of her fallen son beside the Lake of Tears—there is an area known as the Square of Heroes, which is edged by an artificial lake symbolic of the Volga and in which stands six paired sculptures. Designed between 1961 and 1963 by Vuchetich—who had himself been severely injured during the War[108]—five out of the six sculptures include a wounded soldier and went on to feature prominently in the coverage of the complex given in *Ogonek* in October 1965, two years prior to its official opening.[109]

In a way, Vuchetich's sculptures perfectly summarize the continuing ambiguity surrounding the representation of the war-damaged man. While acknowledging that the War had taken both an emotional and a physical toll was absolutely at the heart of this memorial—something that can be seen as being broadly in line with other developments in visual culture—the fact remains that the design of the statues continued to draw on those motifs that had been so firmly established during the War itself, in which injury was either a personal badge of ultimate bravery or a vehicle for expressing the bravery of others. Also, like works that came before them, such as Kokorekin's *For the Motherland*, these sculptures offer a distinctly corporeal vision of the wounded Soviet man, as the injuries sustained (which are not explicit) are tempered by the fact that in each instance they are inflicted on an otherwise perfect physique, once again transforming the damaged body into a marker of both valiant achievement and the moral superiority of the Soviet man. Still, we should not overlook the fact that when photographs of the memorial were published on the front page of *Komsomol'skaia pravda* in October 1967 to celebrate the site's official opening, or when images from the complex were published in *Ogonek* just a month later as part of the commemoration of the fiftieth anniversary of the Revolution, it was the combination of both the avenging Motherland and the wounded soldier that was deemed worthy of marking these historic occasions.[110]

## SUMMARY

Despite the seismic changes that the Soviet Union had endured in the years since 1941, the visual representation of the damaged male body reveals remarkable consistency. Although the processes associated with de-Stalinization had changed the memory of the War and had had a significant impact on cultural production, for the most part neither the changing social context nor the liberalization of the art world influenced how the wounded male body was depicted. With very few exceptions, up until the mid-1960s the wounded man continued to be presented in the manner established by the wartime poster, as injury remained a marker of real conviction and patriotism. This is not to say that the equating of injury and heroism was a creation of the Soviet state—it is an ideal we find in Homer and in Shakespeare among many other places—but the connection between the body and unshakeable conviction was recalibrated to become symbolic of a uniquely Soviet form of heroism and superiority. For all that the wounded body was a consistent aspect in the visual representation of the Soviet man at war, then, such representation remained very limited: injury was either relatively superficial or demonstrative of a willingness to die for the cause, and it was predominantly confined to an explicitly militarized context. Prior to 1964, it is almost impossible to talk of visual depictions of disability.

The shift in the visual presentation of the damaged male body came not in the Thaw, as one might expect, but in the mid-1960s at the height of the war cult. For all that the revivification of the War may be seen as a politically calculated move on the part of the Brezhnev administration, the fact is that from 1964 onward visual culture at last began to turn its attention to the wounds that the War had inflicted on the Soviet people—both physically and psychologically—with a consistency and nuance that had to date been lacking. Works examined here, along with those such as Viktor Popkov's 1966 series of paintings on the widows of Mezen and Dmitrii Oboznenko's *Compatriots* (1969), are evidence of a greater degree of emotional realism being injected into works that dealt with the War experience, and by a far greater number of artists. As discussed in chapter 1, as issues of commemoration and recognition were legitimately brought into the public sphere on a large scale for the first time since 1945, finally the plurality of discourses surrounding the War experience found an outlet. Thus, while artistic portrayals of the effects of 1941–45 on the Soviet populace may have lagged behind other cultural media in many ways, the changes that appear in the visual construction of the War and its impact around 1965 were one part of the more extensive reappraisal of the Great Patriotic War taking place in contemporary Soviet society. Yet, it is crucial to remember that in the vast majority of cases this shift toward the profound did not include a reconceptualization of how injury and disability were presented visually: in this respect, the work of Korzhev is peerless.

Ultimately, then, what the material discussed here demonstrates is that the Great Patriotic War brought with it a new component in the visual construction of Soviet masculinity, as the wounded man was regularly featured in war-themed art from 1941 onward. At the same time, we also need to recognize both the limitations of the visual representation of the damaged man and how this differs from the trends that have been identified in other cultural forms, particularly in relation to postwar Stalinism. Even in this era alone, the treatment of the damaged man in visual culture differed significantly from what was presented in literature and film, as he was neither an exemplar of Soviet manhood nor a conduit for dealing with the horrific legacy of the War, and this disparity would only become more marked during the years of de-Stalinization. The fact that in so many ways Korzhev's vision of the damaged man stands alone, despite the art world's increasing willingness to deal with the issues of grief and death after 1964, highlights the fact that even twenty years after the end of the War, the visual narratives surrounding injury were still largely confined to the heroic and did not include the representation of the mutilated bodies, shattered psyches, and destroyed lives that were the painful reality for so many Soviet men.

# 3
# THE DEAD

## Representing and Remembering the Fallen Soviet Soldier

Outside the walls of the Kremlin, edged by a series of caskets bearing soil from the twelve "hero cities" of the Soviet Union and under a permanent armed guard, is the Tomb of the Unknown Soldier. It was unveiled on May 8, 1967, following the interment of a soldier's body that had been removed from one of the mass graves on the outskirts of Moscow, and marked the full rehabilitation of the Great Patriotic War by the Soviet authorities. Composed of a simple slab of red granite, topped with a bronze helmet and Soviet flag and engraved with the maxim "Your name is unknown, Your deed is immortal," its lack of figurative design signals its purpose: this shrine represents the Soviet Ivan, the everyman who fought for the motherland and paid the ultimate price. Writing in *Pravda* the day after the inauguration, Soviet Minister of Defense Andrei Grechko called this new memorial "a place sacred to every Soviet person" and stated that the eternal flame taken from Leningrad's Field of Mars was "as if wrung from the heart of the people," reiterating the by now familiar rhetoric of the profound significance of the Great Patriotic War for the entire nation.[1] Even today, as it was in Soviet times, it is customary for a newly married couple to go and lay flowers on the memorial, a solemn reminder at the height of a joyous occasion of the debt still owed to those who fought and died to secure the freedom of the Soviet people from the fascist yoke.

The issues of death, remembrance, and trauma in a Soviet context are contentious ones. Up until very recently, popular wisdom and even academic opinion had attested to a uniquely Russian way of dealing with such difficulties, due to a temperament forged in the hardness of life in the Russian Empire and the stoic endurance of the people living under such oppression.[2] Practically, the Revolution had also brought with it many changes to the disposal of and

the grieving for the deceased, most notably with the introduction of crema-
tion, a practice that went against Orthodox beliefs that in order for the soul to
reach heaven the body had to decompose naturally. Overcrowded cemeteries,
new secular burial sites that for many lacked the dignity and solemnity they
desired at that time, and the disruption to many traditional grieving practices
were serious problems for those who had lost loved ones in ordinary circumstances; the treatment of the dead at times of crises, such as during the famine
in 1932–33, was often viewed by local authorities as simply a practical issue
that needed to be dealt with quickly and efficiently, with little to no consideration for those relatives left behind.[3]

For all the catastrophes that had befallen the Soviet people since 1917,
nothing compared to the mass death of the War. The issues surrounding how
the War was remembered and how individuals, groups, and society processed
what they had lived through are complex to say the least. The fact that official
commemoration of these years marginalized the narratives of many to present a vision of the War that was predominantly white, Russian, and male can
hardly be disputed; when it comes to the notion that during the Soviet era
the War was always presented in such commemorative spaces as triumphalist,
there is arguably a need for greater nuance. In her research on memory and
death during the Soviet period, Catherine Merridale found that, even fifty
years on, recollections of trauma and loss were still largely omitted from private accounts of the war experience, leading her to conclude that grief was
something that "Russians do not wish to find encoded in their memorials
of concrete, bronze and stone."[4] Yet, repeatedly in the memorials that were
built during the Soviet period—and particularly those constructed during the
course of the 1960s—this is exactly what is found . What is more, as seen from
the photographs that magazines such as *Ogonek* published of such sites, these
were not only spaces where people came to grieve, but that the grieving process was frequently a part of the visual representations of these sites.

Starting with how death was treated in the visual culture of the war years,
then, this chapter will go on to examine how the Soviet war dead and those
who were left behind were depicted in the years that followed. It will explore
what role death and bereavement played in early memorials, largely in Eastern
and Central Europe, before thinking more specifically about how emotions
such as grief were gendered, and how the way this was handled visually differed from what is found in other forms of culture. The final section brings
us back to the war memorial by looking at how the newly constructed memorials were presented through photography in the popular press and what role
the dead and bereaved Soviet man played in this official narrative of the war
years. What will be shown is that the trends one sees in the representation

of the dead and the bereaved largely map on to the trends that have been identified in relation to other war-themed works, in that the Stalin period did not completely whitewash the emotional impact of the War and the Thaw did not bring about a dramatic reassessment of its cost, either for those who fell or for those who were left behind. Instead it was at a time that is most commonly associated with bombast and pomp that the issues of bereavement and mourning became integral to the artistic vision of the legacy of victory.

## IMAGES OF DEATH DURING THE WAR

Given what is known about the strictures that were placed on Stalinist visual culture by intertwining constraints of the Socialist Realist aesthetic and political outlook of the period, it is perhaps surprising how prominent the representation of death and hardship was during the years of the War. While the Allies presented a largely sanitized vision of the Second World War to its reading public, in the Soviet Union the pages of mainstream and military papers alike covered the atrocities being carried out against the nation's civilian population in gruesome detail, while artists repeatedly depicted scenes of horror—firing squads, hanged partisans, and dead children. Of course, the context was very different; after all, these were difficulties and deaths that could unequivocally be attributed to the ruthless fascist barbarians, regardless of what the role of domestic policy might have been in causing or exacerbating such things. But while such images undoubtedly had a great deal of propagandistic power, the War placed human tragedy in the center of Soviet art and photography on a scale that, like the War itself, was entirely unprecedented.

The use of atrocity photographs in the Soviet press was part of a much wider campaign to highlight the villainous nature of the enemy: reports about the treatment of prisoners of war, extracts from diaries and letters seized from German soldiers, and official orders were all printed that detailed the barbarism experienced by those at the front, while countless articles recounted the rape, murder, and starvation of the Soviet population who had come under Nazi occupation.[5] The photographs that often accompanied such articles tended to be used in groups in order to maximize the sense of the magnitude of the suffering, with little distinction made between what was suitable for a military audience and what was to be circulated more widely. Indeed, there was frequently no difference in the images that were printed across the various papers, as seen for example with the coverage of the atrocities carried out against the people of the village of Vertiachiy (near Stalingrad), published in *Pravda* on December 21, 1942, and in *Krasnaia zvezda* on December 22, which used exactly the same photographs presented exactly the same way on the page.[6] Similarly, the coverage of the aftermath of the seven-month Nazi occupation of Rostov-on-Don in March 1943 was covered in both *Izvestiia* and *Pravda* by an identical article released by the Soviet Information Bureau and the same harrowing photographs, which were clustered in the center of the page, detailing at close quarters the human and material destruction that had been rained down upon the city.[7] Such images were not just restricted to the press, as during the War even magazines like *Ogonek* frequently published images of atrocities and later recounted the horror of the camps to its significant readership. In fact, it was on the pages of *Ogonek* that Dmitrii Baltermants's photographs of the murdered Jewish population of Kerch on the Black Sea were first published; photographs that were some of the earliest to document the mass extermination of Soviet Jews at the hands of the *Einsatzgruppen* and which, as will be seen, by the 1960s had become representative of the universal grief and suffering caused by the War.[8]

While the circulation of such photographs through the medium of the press and other forms of print culture, like *Ogonek* or Okna TASS, is there for all to see, it is much harder to gauge how fine art that portrayed the horrors of war circulated at the time. Publication of *Iskusstvo* was suspended for the entire duration of the War, and while magazines such as *Ogonek* kept publishing—and publishing images—they did not have the capability, either technologically or in terms of resources, to be printing copies of fine art with any regularity or in decent quality. Still, despite everything that was going on, the Stalin Prize was still awarded and exhibitions were still held, as seen in the 1942 show *Leningrad in the Days of the Patriotic War* and the Tretyakov's All-Union Exhibition *The Heroic Front and Rear*, which ran from November 1943 until October 1944. Between late 1941 and the autumn of 1944, around twenty exhibitions were held—not just in Moscow and Leningrad but also in cities such as Novosibirsk, where many of the Tretyakov's treasures were in store—and visited by an estimated half a million people.[9] Although there were concerns about depressing Soviet patriotism through overly pessimistic representations of the War,[10] and there were undoubtedly artists that continued to toe the Socialist Realist line of focusing on essentially positive or inspirational scenes of heroism and resistance—as seen in the Kukryniksy's painting of the execution of Zoia Kosmodem'ianskaia (Tania) or Sergei Gerasimov's *Mother of a Partisan*, for example—at the same time some artists did depict death as being callous and senseless.[11] Vladimir Serov's *Execution* (*Rasstrel*, 1943), which showed the death of a group of civilians at the hands of a German firing squad,[12] Arkadii Plastov's depiction of the death of a young shepherd boy in the fields in his *A Fascist Flew Over* (*Fashist proletel*, 1942),[13] T. G. Abakeliia's sculpture of a young woman carrying the body of her dead child, entitled *Vengeance!* (*Otomstim!*, 1945),[14] and Taras Gaponenko's *After the Expulsion of the Fascist Invaders* (*Posle izgnaniia nemtsev*, 1943–46) that portrayed hanged civilians being mourned by their surviving relatives, are just some of the works from the war years that presented a thoroughly unheroic vision of death.[15] While we may not be able to gauge how many people saw these works in person, it is telling that a number of them were reproduced in some of the earliest postwar issues of both *Iskusstvo* and *Sovetskaia zhenshchina*, while others, such as Plastov's work, went on to be a staple image in retrospective features on the art of the war for years to come. Yet, such representations of civilian death would disappear completely from works created after the end of the War, as dying for the Soviet cause was reconceptualized to become almost exclusively male and militaristic. No longer representative of the barbarity of the enemy, the Soviet dead now became symbolic of the price of freedom—a price that, according to official rhetoric, was absolutely worth paying—and the debt that was owed by the living.[16]

## EARLY MEMORIES: REPRESENTING BEREAVEMENT IN THE POSTWAR YEARS

On May 9, 1965, *Ogonek* published correspondence from one Raisa Kanaeva from Khabarovsk in the far east of the country, in which she recounted her trip to Rozhmital' (Rožmitál pod Třemšínem) in Czechoslovakia in 1963 to visit the grave of her father. Her letter is worth quoting in full:

> War. A sinister, black word. Not that you realize this when you're two years old. On 25 June 1941 my father went to the front. [During] those dark years of war, mother told constant stories about him [and we had] his letters and postcards—first from the territory of our own country and then from Hungary, Romania and Czechoslovakia. In his letters father said: "the fascists will soon be crushed, soon there will be victory, soon we will meet." And finally, Victory! I will never forget this day. It was like it was everyone's birthday—we all congratulated each other [with] hugging and kissing. And my mother, with such happiness [said] "The war is over, your father is alive, your father will be back soon."
>
> But suddenly. No, this cannot be, because the war is over—it's a misunderstanding. A small piece of paper screams "Your husband Kolomin, Dmitrii Ivanovich ... died on 9 May 1945." It is hard to read any further. "[He is] buried in Rozhmital'." So, I no longer have a father? Instead of answering, my mother cried.

After came school, [and then] the institute, but I constantly thought about going to Czechoslovakia, to visit Rozhmital' and see my father's grave and those places for which he gave his life.

In the summer of 1963, I went to Czechoslovakia. Prague, Golden Prague. The days were overcast but Prague struck me with its beauty.... And now the car is speeding along the concrete highway to Rozhmital' and a sacred place for me—the grave of my father.

The cemetery. My heartbeat is loud, pounding in my temples. An obelisk of gray granite, with a bas-relief of a tank driver, and the names of those who liberated Rozhmital' and died here on the last day of the war, the first day of peace, Victory Day. My eyes run through the letters. And suddenly "Kolomin, Dmitrii Ivanovich." I have no strength to hold back the tears.

—Hello father!

The car returns to Prague and I look at those places where my father drove his tank and in my memory are the red roses on the memorial, a grateful tribute from liberated Rozhmital'.[17]

Kanaeva's personal tale of loss, memory, and the need to commemorate the life of her father is a fascinating one for anyone wishing to explore how issues to do with grief and remembrance were expressed in the postwar period. What is arguably even more significant is the fact that this account of a childhood haunted by the thoughts of a lost parent and the need to seek out his final resting place was published in *Ogonek* on the anniversary of Victory Day, a day that had first and foremost been a celebration of Soviet achievements, rather than a meditation on of the cost of war. At its most basic level, though, while suffused with Soviet rhetoric regarding noble sacrifice and liberation, Kanaeva's pilgrimage to Czechoslovakia is a reminder that, while the Great Patriotic War was conceived as one of defense of the motherland, countless thousands of those who died did so beyond the boundaries of the Soviet Union.

It was these soldiers who fell during the fight to "liberate" the various parts of Central and Eastern Europe who were among the very first to be commemorated once the War was over, as memorials sprang up like mushrooms across many of the major towns and cities in what would become the Soviet bloc. Removed from the families who would find catharsis or solace from the act of visiting and tending such sites, it would be easy to dismiss these early

Stalinist memorials as little more than an expression of power—the triumph of socialism over fascism, and the much less metaphorical new Soviet authority in the region—and an educative tool designed to remind the local population to whom they owed their freedom. Certainly the memorial that was completed in August 1945 and that still stands in the center of Vienna seems to attest to this motivation, with its towering victorious soldier and impressive neoclassical colonnades. Other monuments such as Karl Pokorny's sculpture *Brotherhood* (*Bratanie*, 1947–50), which was originally situated outside the main train station in Prague but is now somewhat hidden away in the dusty scrubland behind it,[18] and the controversial Monument to the Soviet Tank Crews (erected July 1945), which used to stand in the city's Štefánik Square, were similarly triumphalist in their tone, although unlike the Vienna memorial were never sites of burial. However, none of these monuments and memorials can compete with the one that was erected in Berlin's Treptower (Treptov) Park and which was unveiled on May 8, 1949, to commemorate those eighty thousand soldiers who gave their lives during the Battle of Berlin.

The Treptower Park memorial was one of three that were built in Berlin in the immediate aftermath of the War, all of which still survive to this day: the memorial in the famous Tiergarten right in the heart of the city opened in 1945 and is very similar in design to its Austrian counterpart in using classical motifs to articulate the greatness of the Soviet victory, while the Schönholzer Heide in Pankow is the largest of the Soviet cemeteries (around thirteen thousand Soviet dead are interned here) and is made up of a range of sculptures and monuments, at the center of which is a defiant Motherland standing over the body of one of her fallen sons. It was the Treptower site, though, that would become a Soviet icon. While today, when we think of Soviet memorials, our minds perhaps automatically conjure up the image of the strident Motherland of Stalingrad, prior to the Mamaev Kurgan complex opening in 1967, it was the figure of Evgenii Vuchetich's Soldier-Liberator of Treptower that was the most celebrated monument to victory. It was an image that appeared with great frequency in contemporary print culture, being referenced in posters, paintings, and cartoons as well as appearing in photographic form on numerous occasions.[19] It was Vuchetich's sculpture that was chosen as the front cover of the first volume of the new *History of the Great Patriotic War of the Soviet Union*, published in 1960 (advertised in *Ogonek* in late 1959), and it was this image that *Ogonek* would go on to use, like an historiated initial, throughout 1965 to signify articles related to the War.[20] The statue was also turned into a stamp in the Soviet Union on no fewer than nine occasions between 1951 and 1981,[21] as well as being used multiple times in at least two other bloc countries, and even featured on a celebratory stamp marking forty years since the defeat of fascism released in Cuba in 1985.[22] Interestingly, the use of the monument in this way was not just to commemorate significant war anniversaries; when Vuchetich's sculpture was featured on the sixty-kopek stamp in 1957, it did so as part of a series to mark the two hundredth anniversary of the Academy of Arts, appearing alongside one of Repin's self-portraits and Mukhina's *Worker and Kolkhoznitsa*. Its moment of widest circulation came in 1965, though, when it was used on the one-ruble coin issued to mark the twentieth anniversary of victory, placing the Soldier-Liberator literally in the hands of the entire nation. Indeed, this monument was so popular that a replica was even suggested as the centerpiece for Moscow's proposed Poklonnoia Hill Memorial in March 1963, where it was going to tower over the complex at eighty-five meters high (the original is around thirteen meters).[23] Moscow's memorial site was not completed until the 1990s, and in the end the designers chose an obelisk over Vuchetich's statue; however, in 2003 it did become the focal point of the mosaic by Zurab Tsereteli commissioned to adorn the new Park Pobedy metro station.[24] This is quite a legacy for a monument that was not even in the Soviet Union!

While the focus may fall on the handsome Soldier-Liberator, cradling a rescued child in one arm while using his other arm to cut through the swastika he has crushed underfoot, there is far more to this memorial site than this sculpture, and indeed the attention that falls on this centerpiece actually masks a far more moderated view of the Soviet victory, in which grief for the dead plays a pivotal role. Any visitor to the Treptower site enters between the lowered banners of the Soviet Union, at the side of which two soldiers kneel reverentially before the row of mass graves in the center of the grounds. Flanking these graves along both the left and right sides are a series of panels—one side with German inscriptions and the other with Russian—that show a number of scenes that range from the actions of courageous partisans and the great Red Army, to the human and material destruction caused by German bombing raids and the heroic death of men and women fighting for the Soviet cause. At the far end of the complex is Vuchetich's iconic sculpture, and facing the Soldier-Liberator at the entrance to the whole site is a figure of a woman, the grieving Mother(land).[25] The magazine *Soviet Union: Illustrated Monthly* captured the scene on its pages in May 1950:

> Following the leafy avenue which leads in from the park entrance, the visitor comes upon the grey granite figure of a woman seated, with head bowed—her pose and expression eloquent of poignant grief for her fallen sons and at the same time of pride in her sons' great deeds and victories. This figure symbolizes the Russian mothers who in the days of the great war of liberation sent their

sons forth to battle for the Motherland and for the liberation of the peoples of Europe from fascist bondage.[26]

This, then, was not a site of unmitigated triumphalism, but one in which the sacrifice of those buried in the ground and the grief of those who were left behind was an integral part of how the War was commemorated. As well as appearing in the form of this sculpture and on a number of the stelae lining the graves, the grieving Mother(land) was also actually a part of the complex's most famous monument. The pedestal on which the soldier stands is a mausoleum containing a book listing the details of every soldier buried in the grounds, the walls of which are covered by a mosaic created by Anatolii Gorpenko: depicting a range of different ethnic and national groups, the centerpiece of the mosaic is a group of men laying a wreath at the encased book of remembrance in front of them, overlooked by a woman clad in black and wrapped in the Soviet flag. Thus at Treptower as it would be across the Soviet Union in the years that followed, the sense of loss as a result of the War was articulated through the figure of the mother—both the biological *mat'* and the allegorical *Rodina*.

Even in the Stalin era, though, the use of the mother to express grief and loss was not just confined to the monuments built beyond its boundaries. Of course, the use of women as symbols of bereavement and mourning is not a uniquely Soviet phenomenon: as Julia Kristeva wrote, women "spread out of the flesh of suffering, of which men are the skeleton,"[27] and women traversing the line between mother and nation frequently adorn cenotaphs and memorials, seen perhaps most poignantly in Käthe Kollwitz's *Mother with Her Dead Son* (1937–38) in the Neue Wache, Berlin, now dedicated to the victims of war and dictatorship. However, the fact that the Motherland summoning her sons to service had become such a staple feature of Soviet wartime visual culture made her the ideal motif for expressing the nation's grief at the loss of those who had heeded her call. In many cultures where the nation is characterized as female, representations of the Motherland tend to draw upon classical allegory and present the nation as a virginal young woman, as in the case of Britannia or the French Republic's Marianne, for example: in contrast, in 1941 *Rodina* was a buxom, middle-aged peasant matron.[28] This shift was a product of the 1940s as the Motherland moved away from the maiden-knight of the First World War era, as seen in the classic poster *Russia—For Truth* (*Rossiia—za pravdu*, 1914), and toward the image that would become cemented in the public's consciousness largely thanks to Iraklii Toidze's stirring *The Motherland Calls!* (*Rodina-mat' zovet!*, 1941). The transformation of the *Rodina* into the older, sturdier Motherland of the Great Patriotic War opened up a new visual lexicon for the presentation of notions of loyalty, duty, and sacrifice, which could now be couched in filial terms. These two strands—the traditional female association with grief and the feminized representation of the nation—merged in the aftermath of the War to form a potent symbol of loss and articulated a vision of the emotional cost of the War that was at one and the same time individual and collective.

From Fedor Bogorodskii's almost Davidesque 1945 canvas *Glory to the Fallen Heroes* (*Slava pavshim geroiam,* also known as *Rekviem*) to the sculptor V. V. Lishev's *Mother* (*Mat',* 1946), the image of the bereaved mother became an instant icon in the later years of the War and the early years of peace.[29] While, as we might expect, these works hardly represent an outpouring of raw emotion—these are after all sons deemed to have died in the most glorious and noblest of fashions—at the same time, it is important to recognize that grief and bereavement were a part of visual culture at this time, albeit in a rather limited fashion. Nor were these minor works as the status of Bogorodskii's painting attests: awarded the Stalin Prize in 1945, Bogorodskii's work went on to be reproduced many times in the popular press over the next two decades, even appearing as a color pullout poster-sized supplement in the January 1947 issue of *Tvorchestvo*.[30] Along with other such celebrated images as Toidze's *Rodina-Mat'*, Gerasimov's *Mother of a Partisan*, and Neprintsev's *Rest after Battle, Glory to the Fallen Heroes* was turned into a stamp in 1965 to commemorate the twentieth anniversary of victory.[31] Drawing upon the neoclassical, republican conventions of heroic death that had been established by the work of French revolutionary artist Jacques-Louis David, Bogorodskii presents his fallen hero as undiminished, his body seemingly untouched and his handsome features unravaged by either war or death itself. Swathed in huge lengths of fabric, the sailor is flanked by armed comrades and his mother, whose pain and sorrow are etched on her lined face. Compositionally, the work draws strong parallels with David's *Andromache's Grief* (1783) and his seminal *The Lictors Returning to Brutus the Bodies of His Sons* (1789), which both contrasted the controlled emotion of the male protagonist with the hysterical reaction of the women to the death of their menfolk, and recounted the father's sacrifice of his own sons for the higher cause of his country. The faded palette of the canvas along with its highly allegorical setting transcends time and place, making very little use of Soviet-specific iconography, and thus succeeds in equating the death of this twentieth-century hero with those in the heroic pantheons of Rome, Troy, and Revolutionary France. However, as with the work of David, it was through the figure of the woman (and more specifically mother) that Bogorodskii explored the emotional and personal impact of this death, a particularly poignant motif in this instance given that the painting was dedicated to the artist's own son, Vasilii, who had died at the front.[32]

While the most popular of such works, Bogorodskii's painting is characteristic of many of the canvases from this era that deployed the mother icon in their representation of the fallen soldier in creating a distance between bereavement at the front and family life back home. As we will see in the next chapter, out of all the images we have of the bereaved—either male or female—there was only one that associated loss with the domestic space, Tikhon Semenov's 1948 painting *Sad News (A Letter from the Front)* (*Vesti s fronta*), which depicted a family being informed of the death of their loved one while having breakfast.[33] All the others, whether through Bogorodskii's technique of situating death and grief in a setting removed from reality or V. V. Lishev's presentation of a mother encountering her son's body still on the battlefield, display a striking reticence to shatter the myth of the home as a safe and sacred space removed from the horrors of war. This was not unique to just representations of the bereaved; as is evident in images of the wounded and disabled soldier, there was a tendency to situate these men within an explicitly militaristic setting, creating an artificial boundary between the events at the front and the home that was clearly incongruous with the experience of countless Soviet citizens. Like so many of the themes examined here, it would not be until the mid-1960s that the impact of the war on home and family life was explicitly articulated, and even then such works remained few and far between.

While the depiction of the fallen soldier would largely disappear after 1948, the image of the grief-stricken mother would prove to be a persistent image that perhaps found its most harrowing incarnation in Gelii Korzhev's *Mother* (*Mat'*) from 1964, which was one of the original three paintings that made up his *Scorched by the Fire of War* series, and along with *Wounded* was the only other work from this collection not to find an outlet in the popular press.[34] Described by contemporary critic Vladislav Zimenko as being representative of a woman "crushed by grief [and] overwhelmed by loneliness,"[35] as with his portrait of the blinded soldier, Korzhev also painted his mother against a stark background, which was surely designed to allow the viewer to focus solely on the heartbreak of the figure in front of them, but inadvertently maintained the separation of grief from the home that had been instituted two decades earlier. Yet, while by far the most powerful and evocative representation of war-inflicted grief, in this work even the usually nuanced Korzhev perpetuates the idea that was repeatedly articulated in postwar visual culture—it was men's duty to sacrifice themselves for the Soviet cause, and it was the women's role to grieve for them. After 1945, the fact that women gave their lives fighting on the front lines or in the forests of the borderlands or died at the hands of the enemy was entirely absent from the artistic vision of the war years. As far as postwar visual culture was concerned, women's suffering in the conflict was caused by the loss of husbands, sons, and brothers: their grief and trauma were entirely defined by their interpersonal relationships with men.

## MASCULINITY AND MOURNING

In June 1948, the International Exhibition of Women Artists was held in Paris, an event that was covered in *Sovetskaia zhenshchina* later that year. Interestingly, in the spread published in the magazine one particular painting appears twice—once as the backdrop in a photograph of the group of Soviet female artists who exhibited in Paris and also as the only image from the Soviet works on display to be reproduced in color. That painting is M. I. Maksimova's *At the Grave of a Warrior* (*U mogily voina*, 1948), which depicts a young girl laying flowers at the tombstone of (presumably) her father, set rather improbably among lush green fields, rolling hills, and a meandering river.[36] While there is absolutely nothing special about the quality of the work—it is rather crude in its execution—there is something special about its subject matter as it is the only work from this immediate postwar era that portrayed that act of going to a gravesite and, along with Semenov's *Sad News*, is one of just a couple of works that examined the loss caused by the war through relationships other than that between a mother and her son. Still, even in Maksimova's work, although the focus is not on the mother, it is female grief that is presented; in contrast, works that dealt with the issue of the bereavement of men are conspicuous by their complete absence.

As was seen in chapter 1, it was only in the mid-1960s that visual culture began to address the grief caused to men by the death of a comrade in a spate of works that explored both the bodily and the emotional toll of war. But when it came to representing the sorrow of men at the loss of a family member, it was a very different matter. Across the whole of the twenty years under examination here, this research has uncovered just one image that deals with the issue of paternal grief, the Georgian artist Bezhan Shvelidze's *In Memory of a Lost Son* (*Vospominanie o pogibshem syne*, 1964), a striking painting that portrays an elderly man surrounded by younger men in uniform raising a toast to the son, brother, and comrade lost as a consequence of war.[37] Discussed in *Iskusstvo* a few years after its production, Shvelidze's work was described as "pioneering" and referred to by the critic G. Pletneva as a work of "living memory," a meditation on the depths of human emotion provoked by such loss that could

FIGURE 3.1. Bezhan Shvelidze, *In Memory of a Lost Son*, 1964.

only be hinted at through the artist's taciturn figures.[38] Pletneva was right to
hail this work as groundbreaking: while the psychological struggle as a consequence of war had found an outlet in earlier works such as Boris Nemenskii's
*Scorched Earth* (1957) or Korzhev's *Lovers* (1959), Shvelidze stands alone in

exploring such themes through the figure of a bereaved father. Yet, even now, there was no place for this representation of bereavement within the home as the men are shown outside, the artist seemingly contrasting the healed and rejuvenated landscape with the scarred psyche of this grief-stricken father.[39]

It was around the same time as Shvelidze's painting that some of the other topics that had been studiously avoided since the end of the War began to find representations, albeit in very small numbers. It was not until Aleksandr Romanychev's *The Paternal Home* (*Otchii dom*, 1964) that the scene of a man returning to a deserted house was portrayed—a scene that in reality must have played out thousands of times in the years that followed 1945. A preliminary sketch was reproduced in *Khudozhnik* in 1963, and in the few lines of commentary that accompany the image, the commentator echoes the concerns of the viewer: "What happened here? Where are the family? Are they still alive?" The critic, like the painting itself, offers no answers to these troubling questions.[40] This reticence to associate the domestic space with the War will be examined in much more detail in the next chapter, but the fact that even in the 1960s Shvelidze's and Romanychev's work is so anomalous raises all kinds of issues when thinking about how grief and bereavement were dealt with in Soviet visual culture: if loss as a result of war was an acceptable topic for Socialist Realism to tackle—which would seem to be the case even before 1945, provided that such death was presented as glorious—why was it that so few artists chose to do so through the eyes of fathers, husbands, and sons? It would be far too easy to dismiss this dearth as being indicative of an established cultural norm that coded grief as a female domain, or of an idealized model of masculinity grounded in stoicism and emotional control, or even as a consequence of the Socialist Realist ethos, which so often shied away from reality and the honest representation of the human experience in whatever form for, as we have already seen on a number of occasions when it came to the treatment of the War, what was happening in visual culture was very different from what was being tackled in other cultural arenas.

Even before the War had ended, literature, and especially poetry, was exploring the grief caused by the loss of a son in battle from the male perspective. Pavel Antokolskii's *Son* of 1943 was a personal reaction to the death of the poet's own son in June 1942, and runs the gauntlet of human emotion from recalling his son's happy childhood to expressing a desire for vengeance; for the poet his son's supposedly heroic death in the service of his country was cold comfort as he wrote "A Soldier? . . . That will never help us / To understand the page rubbed bare and dry."[41] Similarly, Mikhail Sholokhov in his short story "The Fate of a Man," which was written in 1946 although censored until 1957, wrote poignantly about the impact of the death of a son on his protagonist, Andrei Sokolov:

> Right on the ninth of May, on the morning of Victory Day, my Anatolii was killed by a German sniper. [...] The lieutenant-colonel came up to me and said "Bear up, father. Your son, Captain Sokolov, was killed today at his battery." [...] I reckon the tears dried up in my heart. Perhaps that's why it still hurts so much. I buried my last joy and hope in the foreign German soil.[42]

Likewise, the soldier who returned home to discover his family had been killed also found expression in contemporary literature. Although also censored until after 1953, Mikhail Isakovskii's poem *The Enemies Burnt His Family Home* (1945) tells the story of a soldier returning home from liberating Budapest to discover his house in ashes and his family murdered.[43] Even the relentlessly jolly *Vasilii Terkin* contained a chapter entitled "The Bereaved Soldier," which recounted the tale of one of Terkin's comrades who, passing through his hometown, found that he "Has no window, has no cottage / Has no housewife, though he's married / Has no son, although there was one."[44] Although the circumstances surrounding their production and the fact that some of these works were subject to censorship must be taken into consideration, what the writing of Antokolskii et al. demonstrates is that the expression of male grief across a range of scenarios was something that was a part of postwar literary culture in a way that simply was not the case in the art world. Even when Sholokhov's novella was eventually published and then turned into one of the highest-grossing Soviet films ever in the late 1950s, visual culture was still several years away from broaching the theme of paternal loss.

The fact that some of these poems and stories were not in the public domain until after the death of Stalin clearly suggests deep misgivings about the expression of such negative emotions, but they were still created and eventually came to light: that no image whatsoever has been found dating to this period that deals with male grief would suggest that it was not a subject that was explored visually, and that the absence of such imagery from print culture was not simply due to Stalinist censorship. While it might be possible to attribute this dearth to the peculiarities of the period—its conservatism, its focus on normalization, and its straitjacketing of the memory of the War— this rationale begins to look increasingly shaky as we approach the end of the 1950s. And yet, this lack of representation of issues such as bereavement from a male perspective during the so-called Thaw is congruent to what one sees with the treatment of other problematic aspects of the war experience: the lack of images of the disabled, the persistent treatment of injury as superficial, and the consistently romantic portrayal of soldierly comradeship all point to an astounding degree of continuity when it came to how the War was presented artistically across the 1953 divide. While there were changes and some artists did demonstrate a real willingness to deal with the grittier and more problematic aspects of contemporary life, for the most part—with one or two notable exceptions—this did not extend to a visual reconceptualization of what the Soviet people had endured in the War.[45] In relation to the themes examined here, for nearly twenty years this amounted to an almost complete absence of works that dealt with grief and mourning for any sector of society other than the mothers of fallen soldiers.

Again, then, we must look to the years surrounding the twentieth anniversary of the War's end to find works that tackled the issue of male bereavement: although the grieving father, husband, and son were still largely lacking visual representation, the development of how comradeship was portrayed runs in tandem with the emergence of images of the grieving man, as it was on the battlefield and in the relationship between brothers-in-arms that the issue of loss from a male perspective was finally broached. In addition to analyzing these paintings for what they can tell us about male homosociality, many of the works from the 1960s that were examined in chapter 1 can also be explored from the perspective of grief and mourning. Oboznenko's *Compatriots*, and later works such as Viktor Safronov's *The Banner of the Guard* and V. V. Ianke's *Attack Repelled*, centered on the knife-edge between life and death that separated men during war, and portrayed war as taking an emotional as well as physical toll. As such, these works contributed to a far harsher artistic vision of the Great Patriotic War; while the deaths of the soldiers in all these works were undeniably heroic, what is striking is not only the capturing of the moment of death on canvas—in itself a new development to which we will return shortly—but the emphasis that was placed on the impact of these deaths on those serving alongside the fallen individual. In *Compatriots*, for example, the narrative focus of the canvas is the grieving soldier, cradling the body of his comrade, his dirty, sunburnt face contorted with pain, the bleak emotion of the protagonist complemented by the equally bleak setting. Neither the classically glorious death of youth nor the characteristically stoic and proud model of reaction to loss that had been established in the early years after the War, Oboznenko's painting is truly heartrending.

Other works were less successful in stirring the emotions of the viewer: it was also around the midpoint of the 1960s that a spate of works was produced that took the funeral of a comrade as the central theme. The motif of the military funeral had appeared in the very early postwar period, as seen in the paintings of Bogorodskii and Zaitsev, for example, but these images had depicted the burial of a Soviet soldier and had focused on the grief of the mother, while the later works centered on the grief of comrades and portrayed partisan losses rather than those of the official military. The model for such paintings was Sergei Gerasimov's Civil War–inspired *Oath of the Siberian Partisans* (*Kliatva sibirskikh partizany*, 1933), and the motif of a group of fighters standing around the body or freshly dug grave of a fallen comrade was recalibrated for a Second World War context by a number of artists, such as I. Stasevich in his *The Oath* (*Kliatva*, 1965–67) and in *Earth* (*Zemlia*, 1967) by L. Stil'.[46] Others stayed with Gerasimov's original setting and portrayed the Civil War funeral—symbolized by the inclusion of the distinctive *budenovka* hat—as seen in I. Broido's *Farewell to a Comrade* (*Proshchanie s tovarishchem*, 1965) and the Turkmen artist Chari Amangel'dyev's *The Funeral of a Warrior* (*Pokhorony boitsa*, 1966).[47] Although the settings of the paintings differ, it is interesting to note that in all of them it is the grief of the men that features most prominently, despite a number including women in the scene: some are bowed by the graveside resolved and determined, while others bury their heads in their hands. There is nothing exceptional about any of these works, either in the quality of their execution or in terms of their emotional impact, but they are representative of a body of work that, at the very least, acknowledged that loss in war was not just about heroic death and sacrifice but also about the conseqeunces of that loss for those left behind.

One final type of image also began to emerge around this point, and in some ways these images are the most interesting as they straddle the boundary between depicting grief and what could tentatively be called trauma. These are the paintings that presented a contemporary perspective on the War and showed a lasting emotional and psychological struggle, rather than depicting grief as something confined to the immediacy of battle. The term "post-traumatic stress disorder" (PTSD) is one that is used widely in modern parlance, and in historical terms this has led to some incredibly influential work on the legacy of the Holocaust and some very problematic attempts to apply this term retrospectively to whole societies in the aftermath of the Second World War.[48] As has been pointed out by a number of scholars, so many social and cultural factors come into play when trying to assess and analyze the psychological state of an individual or population in the aftermath of such horrific events, one must not assume that because those events were in themselves traumatic that those who lived through them are all in some way traumatized.[49] In addition to these general considerations, the issue of trauma in a Soviet context is one that is particularly fraught with difficulties: as Catherine Merridale highlights, the taboo of mental illness, the persistent idea that trauma was not a Russian way of thinking, the pressures of material survival, and the Soviet legacy of silence all shape how people today talk about what they lived through, how they color what they are willing to share, and what they omit altogether.[50] Yet there is a case to be made that a number of paintings from the mid-1960s depict what we might think of as traumatized men. Some of the symptoms of PTSD include "persistent re-experiencing, for example [through] dreams [and] intrusive recollections [...] feeling of detachment or estrangement from other [... and] persistent symptoms of increased arousal, for example difficulty falling or staying asleep":[51] all these symptoms seem to be manifest in the protagonist of Korzhev's *Old Wounds* (1967).

The previous chapter showed just how radical Korzhev's *Scorched by the Fire of War* series was; for this reason, these paintings are often anomalous rather than representative of the contemporary art world, and Korzhev was certainly the only artist from this period to tackle the psychological legacy of war so explicitly. *Old Wounds* is a powerful painting in its own right—the scene of the elderly man lying awake at night, consumed with his own thoughts, emotionally isolated from those who are physically closest to him—but the pathos of the work is arguably heightened when we consider the series as a whole, as it is believed that the protagonist of this painting is the same man who is lovingly saying goodbye to his wife in the first picture from the collection, *The Farewell*.[52] Viewers, then, are left to speculate as to what this man may have witnessed during his time at the front to cause such lasting mental turmoil and to fracture his interpersonal relationships so irreparably. While Korzhev's work stands alone in terms of its power and emotional impact, it does not stand alone in representing a generation of Soviet men as haunted by their war experience: M. Khaertdinov's *After the War* (*Posle voiny*, 1967), A. P. Kholmogorov's *Veterans of the Great Patriotic War* (*Veterany Velikoi Otechestvennoi voiny*, 1969), and Engels Kozlov's slightly earlier work *Native Land* (*Rodnaia zemlia*, 1964), which was displayed at the Soviet Russia Exhibition of 1965 along with Korzhev's first iteration of the *Scorched* series, all centered on the lingering memories of war and the emotional toll this was still taking on veterans decades after the event.[53] These works can be seen alongside others from this period such as Viktor Popkov's 1966 series of paintings on the widows of Mezen or the continual pain of bereavement found in Evsei Moiseenko's *Mothers and Sisters* (*Materi-sestry*, 1967), and of course Korzhev's own *Mother*, which while treading the more familiar path of depicting female grief, also examined the continuing presence of the War in contemporary society. Whether these paintings are indicative of trauma is open to interpretation; what is indisputable is the fact that by the mid-1960s the grief, mourning, and emotional pain suffered by both women *and* men were key elements in the visual representation of the war experience.[54]

FIGURE 3.2. Gelii Korzhev, *Old Wounds*, 1967.

## DULCE ET DECORUM: THE MASCULINITY OF DEATH

The creation of the Tomb of the Unknown Soldier outside the walls of the Kremlin in May 1967 marked the zenith of the war cult in the Soviet Union. As with other such memorials across the world, Moscow's monument was symbolic of the deindividualization and universalization of the fallen soldier: its simple form, its nationally significant motifs, and its placement in the heart of the capital were designed to be representative of a shared grief and glory. Prior to Brezhnev lighting the eternal flame, which had been taken from Leningrad's Field of Mars, the resting place of hundreds of heroes of the Revolution, N. G. Egorichev, the first secretary of the Moscow CPSU, proclaimed, "It is as if the soldiers of the Revolution and the soldiers of the Great Patriotic War have closed ranks into one immortal rank, illuminated

by the Eternal flame of glory, lit by the living in honor of the fallen who will
always live." He continued, "Heroes do not die. They were victorious, they
have achieved immortality."[55] Those who had sacrificed their lives to assure
Soviet victory were at the heart of the official rhetoric concerning the War—a
rhetoric that Nina Tumarkin has attributed to the need to shame the current
generation of youth, to maintain order, and to mobilize support.[56] But before
this process of memorialization had begun in earnest, the place of the fallen
soldier in visual culture was rather ambiguous: it was one thing to represent
heroic actions that would lead to certain death, it was another thing entirely
to portray the aftermath of such encounters.

Dying the right kind of death is a key component in cementing the reputation of many heroes, and the final moments of such figures have provided
inspiration for some of the world's finest art—from the Laocoön (first century
BCE, Hellenistic) to the scenes of martyrdom that proliferated in medieval
icon painting, to Jacques-Louis David's *Marat at His Last Breath* (1793).[57] As
a long-standing component in the construction of heroic masculinity, it is
hardly surprising that men laying their lives on the line for the Soviet cause
was a key part in depictions of the front, particularly during the War and its
immediate aftermath. We only need to refer back to some of the works already
examined in the previous chapters, such as Aleksandr Deineka's *The Defense
of Sevastopol* (1942) or Aleksei Kokorekin's poster *For the Motherland!*, which
also focused on the heroic, if ultimately futile, efforts of the Black Sea sailors,
or the work of Petr Krivonogov and his iconic *Defenders of the Brest Fortress*,
another scene of heroic but unsuccessful defense, to see how potent the notion
of dying for the nation was. It was an ideal that was emphasized even further
following the introduction of the infamous Order 227 (July 28, 1942) when
"Not One Step Back" and the demand to defend Soviet lands until "the last
drop of blood" became official policy. It was a mode of representation that
proved tenacious, particularly with regard to those episodes of the War that
were associated with Soviet resistance—even if the eventual outcome was a
Nazi victory—as can be seen in Krivonogov's later work along with the paintings of Nikolai Tolkunov and Nikolai But' on the defense of Brest, and P. T.
Mal'tsev's series of works that depicted the attack on Mount Sapun, Sevastopol
(1958), that went on to form the basis of the memorial diorama he completed
on the site a year later.[58]

What all of these highly popular works have in common, though, is that
they do not actually represent the Soviet dead, but represent the Soviet man
facing certain death. In contrast to these fairly common scenes of heroism and
sacrifice, works that focused upon the soldier or sailor who had given his all
in fighting for his country were much more of a rarity; Viktor Ivanov's stark

lithograph from 1943, published in *Ogonek* in 1947, which shows the body of a young sailor, still clutching his gun, blood trickling down the steps on which he lies, is one of only a handful of works from the war era and beyond in which the fallen formed the focus of the work rather than being an incidental figure in the background.[59] Commenting on the relationship between the soldier and death in his personalized exploration of the pressures faced by men in battle, first published in 1959, John Glenn Gray wrote:

> There are soldiers in the Anglo-Saxon world and perhaps many more in the Teutonic and Slavic lands [...] for whom death is a fulfilment. [...] Thus it is for a soldier who, for example, sacrifices his life willingly out of love for his country or glorified leader or for an ideal like fascism or communism. [...] He uses death as a means by which to prove his love and devotion to something beyond himself. Death is not welcomed for itself but as a sign of his utter faithfulness.[60]

While we should certainly ignore some of the essentialist and even racist clichés concerning the "Slavic man" that Glenn Gray espoused in his analysis, there is some value to his identification of an association between attitudes toward death and ideology. Whether this was really enacted on the front line, whether soldiers really ran into battle screaming the name of Stalin, is not the issue here; the fact remains that the Soviet state demanded and expected that its military personnel be willing to pay the utmost price to defend the motherland. Given this, it could be expected that the fallen hero would emerge as the epitome of Soviet masculinity in the postwar era, a symbol of those whose dedication to the nation and state was unquestionable; instead, with the focus on normalization and restoration rather than reconstruction, the image of the dead soldier faded from view.

The lack of representation of the war dead would, for the most part, continue for much of the Thaw period, despite Tumarkin's assertion that A. P. Krasnov's *For His Native Land* (*Za zemliu rodnuiu*, 1958), which portrayed the dead body of a soldier, gun still in hand, upon the churned earth of the battlefield, was "represent[ative of] the new face of the war in the Thaw period; the fundamental truth about the Great Patriotic War was not that soldiers tore into battle for Stalin and the Motherland but that millions of young men with large, strong hands died, their faces nestled in the pungent Russian land."[61] There were a handful of exceptions, however, most commonly in the form of the representation of the dead partisan by non-Russian artists,[62] and one particularly notable piece by Boris Nemenskii, entitled *A Nameless Height* (*Bezymiannaia vysota*, 1961–62; reworked under the title *"Eto my, Gospodi!"* [*Bezymiannaia vysota*], 1961–95). In an interview given February 2015,

Nemenskii recalls how he came to produce this work and how its subject matter still resonates for him today:

> As I was walking to Velikiye Luki, I sat down to rest and munch on a piece of
> dried bread on what I thought was a tree stump protruding from the ground,
> but it turned out to be the shoulder of a dead German soldier, not yet frozen in
> the snow. I turned the body over; I was stunned to see a young man of my own
> age [Nemenskii was around twenty at this time] who somehow looked quite a
> bit like me, only with red hair. It was the first Fascist soldier with whom I had
> come "face to face." My enemy? This boy? Later I saw many dead soldiers, both
> German and our own. Often they would be lying on the ground, sometimes
> next to one another. It could have been me lying there . . .
>
>     As the years went by, this incident made me contemplate the causes of war
> and the origin of Fascism that led to what was effectively fratricide. What hap-
> pened that day moved me to draw many sketches of two dead soldiers, first
> on a beautiful flowering spring meadow, and later various other versions of
> the same composition. These versions are now in Aachen, Tokyo, Omsk and
> Moscow. The latest version of "It Is Us, Lord!" poses the question to everyone
> concerned—when will this stop happening?[63]

As Nemenskii himself admits, this was a painting that caused a great deal of
controversy when it was first displayed, but it was apparently put forward by
some as an example of how conflict in art should be presented, as "the moral
superiority of the Soviet soldier was revealed, even in death."[64] According to
the artist, the painting caused such a stir that Konstantin Simonov organized
a showing of the work at the Central House of Writers in order to facilitate a
discussion of the issues raised by it among others involved in cultural production.[65] Controversial and inspirational it may have been, but Nemenskii's work
does not appear to have been reproduced in the professional or popular press
either at the time or in the decade that followed.

With the production of the paintings discussed above that examined the
relationship between the living and the dead comrade, the fallen Soviet soldier
began to feature in visual culture with a regularity that was unprecedented,
although the number of works still remained relatively small at this stage. In
a departure from his usual style, Latvian artist Edgar Iltner produced one of
the most evocative images on this theme in his 1968 painting *Immortality*
(*Bessmertie*): in this recasting of the pietà, against a backdrop of a vivid dawn
sky, four soldiers hold the body of their fallen comrade aloft, the uniformity of
their physical appearance creating a sense of the interchangeability between
each man and serving to emphasize the strength of their communal bond,

which is unsevered even by death.[66] The elevated position of the deceased soldier speaks of not only the persistence of memory and comradeship but also the burden of living up to this sacrifice, as the living are shown literally carrying the weight of the dead with them. As had been the case in his earlier, and thematically very different, *Masters of the Earth*, Iltner again presents his protagonists as representative of the Soviet everyman, this time through the use of simple figures that lack any individual features—this could be any soldier, this could be every soldier.

Yet, as it had been since the end of the War, the depiction of the lone Soviet soldier remained a rarity as the focus continued to be placed on his interpersonal relationships, whether this was with his family members, as seen in very early representations of the war dead, or in these later works that emphasized the bond between those who served. Indeed, Aleksandr Khmelnitskii's 1967 work *In the Name of Life* (*Vo imia zhizni*), which was displayed at the All-Union Exhibition celebrating fifty years of the Soviet Armed Forces, is the only one from this period of the mid-1960s that portrayed the fallen soldier without including any other figure. Drawing upon a similar compositional style to Nemenskii's earlier work, which presented the dead, but physically perfect, Soviet soldier, along with the three German soldiers he had vanquished, on a high and featureless plateau, Khmelnitskii's hero is lying prone upon a deserted, bloodred battlefield, with his gun by his side.[67] The soldier is young, and there is an undeniable air of vulnerability in the fact that he lies alone, which is only heightened by his boyishly smooth skin, long eyelashes, and slim physique: this is not a representation of a violent death, as his body carries no indication of wounds and his face does not contort with pain, but rather it is as if one has simply caught this young man sleeping. In this instance, death is simultaneously tragic, sacrificial, and beautiful. Reviewing the painting in *Iskusstvo* a few years later, the artist and general major Evgenii Vostokov turned to the words of the poet Sergei Orlov when he stated that for Khmelnitskii's fallen hero "the earth became his mausoleum";[68] words that would, along with the poetry of Aleksandr Tvardovskii, go on to provide the basis for the Polish composer Mieczysław Weinberg's Eighteenth Symphony: *War—There Is No Word More Cruel* (1982–84), written in memory of those lost in the Great Patriotic War.

As is evident, then, for all the dead were at the heart of the rhetoric about the War, they were not a particularly prominent part of its visual representation and very much a rarity when it came to images that focused on the fallen soldier alone. The willingness to lay one's life on the line for the cause was articulated time and again and was a critical part in how the heroism of the Soviet soldier was constructed, as defeat was turned into resistance and certain death became a noble sacrifice for the sake of the Soviet people. On the other hand, works that depicted the soldier once his fighting was over tended to stress his interpersonal relationships, suggesting that there was much more to these paintings than the straightforward celebration of ultimate bravery and loyalty—they were also there to serve as a reminder of the cost of victory: after all, what was this sacrifice worth if there was nobody there to grieve, remember, and take pride in such actions?

## MONUMENTS AND MEMORIES: THE WAR MEMORIAL IN VISUAL CULTURE

Trying to get a sense of how issues to do with the war dead and the grief associated with this loss were presented to the Soviet public through print culture is rather hard to do. For all that a range of works were produced that tackled these aspects of the war experience, very few appeared on the pages of the popular press, with the vast majority being consigned to discussion and reproduction within the confines of the art world alone. Some, such as the work of Oboznenko and Ianke, were published in contemporary exhibition catalogues and art books on the War, while others like the representations of the fallen soldier by Krasnov and Nemenskii, though exhibited at the time, do not appear to have been circulated in print until years after their production. However, while fine art that dealt with the negative and potentially problematic issues of grief, loss, and death was largely absent from magazines such as *Ogonek*, there was one genre that grappled with these issues in a way that was more immediate and arguably more relevant than any other, as over the course of the 1960s photographs of newly constructed war memorials became regular features of such publications.

In a much-cited article written in 1984, Michael Ignatieff called Soviet war memorials "icons in a cunning, but also self-deceiving process of choosing the past one can bear to remember and consigning the rest—the undignified sorrow, the shameful suffering—to oblivion."[69] While there is no doubt that the narrative of the War that is presented in such places is one that excludes any insinuation of excessive casualties or official incompetence, and often marginalizes the experience of those who were not Russian, male, and in the armed forces, it is certainly not the case that sorrow and suffering are completely ignored. More often than not, memorial sites are attempting to walk the tightrope between mourning loss and celebrating victory, a victory that in the end justifies the cost at which it came. With the focus usually falling on iconic sculptures such as Vuchetich's Soldier-Liberator or his later Rodina-Mat' at Volgograd, it is too easy to overlook the often more emotionally charged aspects of these memorial sites; just as the grieving mother was an integral part of the Treptower Park in the late 1940s, so too is the representation of death, mourning, and injury a part of the complexes developed over the course of the 1950s and 1960s. What is more, not only were they a part of the sites themselves but they were also a part of how these sites were presented to the Soviet public through print culture.

The memorial at what was Stalingrad is the only one that comes close to challenging the status of Treptower and played a central role in the creation of the War myth: it is also the one that featured most prominently in the popular press throughout the 1960s, separating it from other iconic sites such as the Piskarevskoe Memorial Cemetery in Leningrad, which, although opened in 1960, only seems to have appeared in such publications twice, once in *Ogonek* in January 1964 in the form of a photograph of a weeping woman at the side of one of the grave markers, and a few years later in *Rabotnitsa* as part of a photo-essay on the city.[70] The evolution of the Volgograd memorial provides an interesting insight into how the treatment of grief and the representation of emotionally complex issues developed over the course of the mid-1950s to around the time the memorial actually opened in October 1967. Although the idea of building a large-scale memorial at Mamaev Kurgan had first been mooted in 1951, due to the limits placed on commemoration after 1947, it was not until after the death of Stalin that plans began to make any progress with an open design competition for the memorial launching in March 1954.[71] A few years later *Iskusstvo* published an overview of the winning plan, designed by none other than Evgenii Vuchetich, along with Anatolii Gorpenko and Iakov Belopol'skii, both of whom had also been heavily involved in the creation of the Treptower site. In this original incarnation, the memorial was to feature three main sculptures, a mother carrying the body of her dead child and calling for vengeance, a soldier launching a grenade at an unseen enemy, and a warrior laying down his sword and kneeling at the feet of the Motherland, designed to represent "the peaceful aspirations of the people."[72] The twenty-two-meter statue of the Motherland was to sit atop a mound that would house the Panorama, the central point of the whole complex and the location of the eternal flame.[73] The opening date for the site was set at this stage as February 2, 1963, although the changing and increasingly ambitious plans for the project meant that this was never really going to be achievable. Still, in February 1963, readers of *Ogonek* got their first glimpse of this new memorial, when the sculpture *Stand to the Death* (*Stoiat' nasmert'*) appeared, along with a group of Soviet schoolchildren, on the magazine's front cover.[74] Unveiled in July 1962, the eagle-eyed observer may have noticed that, while still resolute and determined, the finished sculpture was far less militant than in the original design, with the grenade now being held by the soldier's side, in anticipation of attack.

The next parts of the memorial to be unveiled in print were the "Wall-Ruins" [*Steny-ruiny*] and some of the statues that lined the Square of Heroes, which, as was seen in the previous chapter, all featured a wounded soldier, both of which appeared in an *Ogonek* article in late 1965.[75] It was also in this spread entitled "They Were All Mere Mortals"—words that were inscribed on the Wall-Ruins themselves—that Soviet readers first saw one of the new additions to the Stalingrad complex: added in Vuchetich's 1959 overhaul of his plans for the site,[76] a sculpture of a grieving mother cradling the body of her dead son (*Skorb' materi*, 1965), edged by the Lake of Tears, now stood at one end of the Square of Heroes. Of course, this was a motif that was by now very familiar to the public and has been described by Scott Palmer in his analysis of the construction of the site as demonstrative of Vuchetich "recycling an idea earlier used in the Treptower Park,"[77] although in actuality this later incarnation of the Soviet Pietà is both more prominent and arguably more emotionally stirring than its German counterpart. Writing about the effectiveness of the sculpture for *Iskusstvo* in 1967, A. Fedorov stated that "Every mother feels that she is bent over her son. Her feelings are clear to mothers from all over the world who come here and stop in front of the monument [...] immense suffering is traced on the beautiful face of the Motherland. In her eyes, [we see] sorrow and love and tenderness and maternal pride in her hero-son."[78] Also, in contrast to the grieving mother of Berlin, the sculpture was to feature in print culture on numerous occasions over the coming years, appearing not only in *Ogonek* but also in the expatriate magazine *Rodina* and the art journals *Iskusstvo* and *Tvorchestvo* between 1965 and 1968, and in 1973 it featured alongside *Stand to the Death* and *The Motherland Calls!* in a series of stamps released to commemorate the thirtieth anniversary of the battle.[79] It may be the avenging Motherland that is the most iconic today, but in those early years, the grieving Mother(land) was just as prominent in the coverage the memorial complex received in the popular and professional press.[80]

Photographs of memorials and eternal flames from across the Soviet Union would appear with a degree of regularity throughout the 1960s, although none compared to the coverage that the Volgograd complex received. While the official inclusion of grief and mourning in such sites are enough to raise questions regarding some of the long-standing Western preconceptions about how the War was memorialized in the USSR, what is even more interesting is the way the popular press depicted the Soviet people interacting with such monuments. Probably most common were the photographs that showed children at the memorial—often in the act of laying down flowers—as can be

FIGURE 3.3. The two faces of the motherland, Volgograd. Reproduced courtesy of Sputnik.

seen on the front cover of *Ogonek* in November 1963, which showed a small boy crouching by an eternal flame with a flower in his hand, and the scene of a group of girls tending the memorial at Kursk, which had appeared on the magazine's back cover a few weeks earlier.[81] But the images published did not simply reassert the glory of victory or the need for the next generation to be aware of the Soviet achievements during the War, as repeatedly grieving individuals were included in the photographs of these sacred sites. While some commentators have dismissed such spaces as little more than an attempt to enshrine the narrative of the Soviet Union as the savior of Europe and a rightful world superpower in granite and concrete, others have highlighted the far more complex interplay between official and personal memory in how these memorials were utilized after their construction.[82] Arguably, then, the

photographs of these grieving individuals offer an insight into the personal
memories of the War in a space that espoused the master narrative of the conflict, and through a medium that was geared toward articulating the desires of
the state. The photographs of individuals for whom the grief inflicted by their
experience was still so raw two decades later fundamentally challenge the
notion that loss and suffering was a part of these sites as a way of demonstrating what had been overcome or the strength of the nation now: the grieving
women at the Wall-Ruins and at the eternal flame at Volgograd, the weeping
woman at Piskarevskoe Memorial Cemetery, the elderly man on his knees
besides Moscow's newly constructed Tomb of the Unknown Soldier—notably
a photograph that was printed without comment over two pages in *Ogonek* in
1966[83]—the veteran who stands with his head resting on a memorial plaque,

FIGURE 3.4. Grieving Man at the Tomb of the Unknown Soldier, *Ogonek* 50, 1966. Reproduced
courtesy of Kommersant.

flowers in hand, at the opening of the memorial at Brest, along with the first photograph of the disabled veteran discussed in the previous chapter, all seem to demonstrate that such sites did offer catharsis for some individuals, a place to mourn and remember both individually and collectively.[84] What is more, the emotional pain such remembrance brought to both men and women was a part of how these spaces were visually represented.

In addition to the photographs of the newly constructed memorials, during the 1960s retrospective accounts of various episodes from the War and photographs taken during the conflict were also published; photographs that along with fine art contributed to the consistent presence of the War in print culture throughout the decade. Some features were concerned with civilian suffering, as in the coverage of the massacre of 6,700 people in the Ukrainian village of

Right side of FIGURE 3.4

Kuriukivka (Koriukorka) in March 1943, which was the subject of an *Ogonek* article in January 1962, complete with photographs of grieving women and a lone man standing by the village's memorial to the atrocity.[85] Others focused on the commemoration of military success, although even here the visual representation was rarely wholly triumphant: the central photograph of *Ogonek's* commemoration of the feats of the twenty-eight guardsmen of the Panfilov Division, for example, was of survivor Grigorii Shemiakin, who sat gazing down at his feet, "remembering his comrades and that painful [*tiazhkiye*] but glorious day—16 November 1941."[86] As the decade progressed, photo-essays were published to coincide with significant anniversaries and included contemporary images, some of which were being circulated publicly for the first time since 1945 and which captured moments of introspection or explicit emotional turmoil, as can be seen in *Ogonek's* 1965 and 1970 coverage of the Battle of Kursk, both of which featured the same photograph of an exhausted soldier, head in hands, sitting on the remnants of his machine gun, with the body of a fallen comrade beside him.[87]

In January 1965, Dmitrii Baltermants's photograph of the aftermath of the massacre of Kerch was republished for the first time since the War, an image by now simply known as *Grief*. It was presented as a double-page spread in *Ogonek* under the title "We Will Never Forget" and was accompanied by a caption that stated: "January 1942, Kerch. As they were withdrawing, fascist troops shot thousands of peaceful Soviet citizens, tossing their corpses in a nearby antitank trench. 'Women on the battlefield searching amongst the dead for their loved ones. Their crying ceases to be personal, it becomes the cry of humanity,' said Heinrich Böll [the German writer] of this photograph."[88] Baltermants's 1965 image was markedly different from those that had appeared in the magazine in March 1942: in the earlier photograph, the focus was on P. I. Ivanova's search for her murdered husband, which was itself just one image among more than half a dozen that detailed the aftermath of the violence, whereas in 1965 the whole panorama of the scene is included in the published photograph, as the grief of Ivanova is situated among the grief of others who have also discovered the bodies of their loved ones.[89] Baltermants's not only expanded the scale of the image but also made aesthetic changes, most notably darkening the sky, which gave the photograph a more ominous and heavy atmosphere; as David Shneer writes, "The sky itself became a subject, and the woman figured as a representative of grief, one of many mourners, as the image leads off into infinity on the left side."[90] With its republication, Baltermants's image, which had started out as a representation of the extermination of a Jewish community in the Crimea, had become a universal representation of the grief of the Soviet people.[91]

## SUMMARY

The issues surrounding the visual representation of the physical and emotional cost of the War in the two decades between its end and the reinstatement of Victory Day are complex to say the least. While grief found an outlet in the few memorial sites constructed during the 1940s and in fine art of the late Stalin period, it was an emotion that was consistently expressed as being feminine as the mourning Mother(land) was cast as the sole symbol of a nation's sorrow. It was a mode of representation that would prove enduring, as is evident by the fact that the Mother(land) watching over the bodies of her fallen sons would feature again and again in the hundreds of memorials constructed in the years after 1953. The consequence of this powerful visual conceptualization of grief that served to be both collective and highly individualized was that there was no place for the bereaved man: the reality that fathers also lost sons at the front, to say nothing of the loss of those behind the lines, was entirely absent from visual culture until the middle of the 1960s, despite the fact that both film and literature had repeatedly broached the subject in the intervening years. Yet again the shift came at the time that we associate most closely with the mythologization of the war experience, not as we might expect with the liberalization of the Thaw, as for the first-time grief, mourning, and the lasting emotional cost of war found expression through the Soviet man, as the stoic onlooker of the Stalin years was replaced by men who cried in the face of death and lay awake at night troubled by what they had experienced.

The photographic portrayal of the memorial site in print culture, which parallels these developments in the fine arts, adds yet another complication as it provides windows into not only how these sites tackled the issue of loss and grief and what place those emotions had within the master narrative of victory, but also how the Soviet public interacted with these sites. Photographs of these memorials and other commemorative moments, along with republished images from the 1940s, repeatedly showed the Soviet man expressing emotion as a consequence of loss. In their work on the politics of commemoration, T. G. Ashplant, Graham Dawson, and Michael Roper argued that "the politics of war memory and commemoration *always* has to engage with mourning and with attempts to make good the psychological and physical damage of war; and wherever people undertake the tasks of mourning and reparation, a politics is *always* at work."[92] Of course, if this politicization of memory is true of anywhere, it is true of the Soviet Union, but while the inclusion of grief and mourning in memorial sites may be seen as a way to "make good" the damage inflicted by the War, this does not provide a particularly satisfactory explanation as to why the less allegorical grief of survivors featured in both photographs of these spaces and many war-themed paintings of the era. While the broader issues to do with the memory of the War, how it relates to Soviet identity, and the political motivations that may have stood behind its reinvigoration are for the most part beyond the scope of this work,[93] even the very specific body of evidence discussed here would seem to suggest that death, trauma, and loss were not just used as a politically calculated barometer by which to measure the country's progress and strength, but were actually part of a much more fundamental shift in the way the War and its legacy was both conceptualized and represented in official visual culture in the years around 1965.

# 4

# HOMECOMINGS

## Representing Paternal Return, Reintegration, and Replacement before 1953

In the summer of 1947, John Steinbeck and Robert Capa traveled through the Soviet Union, sponsored by the *New York Herald Tribune*, with the aim of relating to the American public what life was really like behind the Iron Curtain. After being wined and dined at the American Embassy in Moscow, Steinbeck and Capa set out for Stalingrad. One afternoon the visitors were taken on a tour through the ruins of the city and came across a park near the town square:

> There, under a large obelisk of stone, was a garden of red flowers, and under the flowers were buried a great number of the defenders of Stalingrad. Few people were in the park, but one woman sat on a bench and a little boy about five or six stood against the fence, looking at the flowers. He stood there so long that we asked Chmarsky [the guide] to speak to him.
>
> Chmarsky asked him in Russian, "What are you doing here?"
>
> And the little boy, without sentimentality, in a matter of fact voice said "I am visiting my father. I come to see him every night."
>
> It was not pathos, it was not sentimentality. It was simply a statement of fact, and the woman on the bench looked up, and nodded to us, and smiled. And after a while she and the little boy walked away through the park, back to the ruined city.[1]

The human and material cost of the Great Patriotic War for the Soviet Union is by now familiar, if no less startling; according to official sources 1,710 towns, 70,000 villages, and six million other buildings were destroyed, leaving an estimated twenty-five million people homeless. The task of calculating the human cost of the War, on the other hand, has largely been left to the historian, and while there is still no consensus on this figure, the most recent estimates put the death toll at around 26.6 million people, three quarters of whom were male and most of whom were from the 1901 to 1931 cohort.[2] The immediate consequences of this demographic crisis were realized in the workplace and on the collective farm, but were most keenly felt in the homes of families across the Soviet Union, who were left dealing with the realities of single parenthood, fatherlessness, and bereavement.

This chapter will chart the attempts to both articulate and obfuscate the impact of this loss on the family by examining the shifting representation of the father in postwar visual culture. It will be argued that the War represented a fundamental shift in the imagining and portrayal of fatherhood, as the use of the family as a motivational tool in fighting the fascists had intrinsically tied masculinity to paternity and patriotism, and this new focus on the Soviet man as a family man would be carried into the postwar period. Running alongside this development, though, it will be shown that in contrast to the images of returning soldiers and family reunions, the demographic reality of postwar society was also acknowledged in numerous works during the last years of Stalinism, through both the representation of the single mother with her children and the introduction into the home of the ultimate surrogate father, Stalin himself.

The impact of the October Revolution on the Soviet family, particularly with regard to the position women were seen to now occupy in the new society, has long been an area of interest for Slavic scholars and has generated a vast and varied historiography.[3] However, in both contemporary discourse and, until recently, the historiography on the family, the figure of the father was conspicuously absent; while women, right from the earliest days of the Revolution, were readily cast as political activists, workers, and mothers, the male role in the creation of a Soviet society was largely limited to that of proletarian-hero, a person too consumed with the task at hand to be hindered by personal relationships or a private life of any sort. Indeed, in his analysis of Soviet patriarchy, Sergei Kukhterin argues that the family policies of the 1920s were founded upon an alliance between the state and the mother and child, in which the father was actively excluded in an attempt to socialize the family unit, something that was only achievable with the destruction of traditional patriarchy.[4]

There was a perceivable shift in the rhetoric of the male social role around the years of industrialization and collectivization, though, which can be viewed within the complex framework of the rise of the paternalistic cult of

Stalin, pronatalist policy,[5] the development of what Katerina Clark termed "the Great Family Myth,"[6] and the emphasis on *kul'turnost'*, in which the home was seen as the crucible wherein ideal Soviet citizens were forged.[7] The emergence of the Great Family Myth—in which allegiance to the state overrode loyalty to biological kin—was, according to Clark, linked to the preoccupation of 1930s society with enemies, both internal and external.[8] In this formulation, interpersonal relationships were restructured, and the horizontal ties between actual family members were superseded by the vertical bond between individual and leader. Nevertheless, this new relationship between the Soviet citizen and the paternalistic *vozhd'* was not designed to completely replace the family unit, which was now cast as a microcosm of the state itself and viewed as a key element in maintaining the stability of the Soviet system. The confluence of these factors manifested itself culturally in a reappraisal of what constituted the ideal New Soviet Man, leading to—among other things—a move away from the revolutionary notion of the mass heroism of the proletariat to the singling out of exemplary heroes, such as Aleksei Stakhanov and Valerii Chkalov, whose names were known throughout the empire.

This new heroic pantheon was a hierarchy of fathers, heroes of "a truly extraordinary caliber," and the "less-than-absolutely-extraordinary" sons.[9] The position of father was generally reserved for the party elite but with Stalin as its ultimate living incarnation, casting him as a leader who was dedicating his life to the protection and education of his people. In addition to the paternal rhetoric of heroism and emulation, after 1934 Stalin's role as father-in-chief took on a new dimension with the development of a strand of his personality cult that was specifically aimed at the Soviet child,[10] explicitly expounding the paternalism of the state while concurrently undermining the role of biological paternity. Posters proliferated emblazoned with *Thank You Dear Stalin for Our Happy Childhood!* (*Spasibo liubimomu Stalinu za schastlivoe detstvo!*)—a maxim that adorned classrooms across the Soviet Union—and the press carried photographs and stories of the lucky child who had had the chance to meet with their benevolent leader. The role of son was taken up by a plethora of archetypal male models, first Stakhanovites, and then "border guards, long-distance skiers, violinists, mountain climbers, parachutists and above all, aviation heroes."[11] And at the top of the pile of heroic aviators was Chkalov, whose 1937 flight across the North Pole was seen as a testament to both Soviet technology and the subjugation of nature to the might of the Soviet man.

As Jay Bergman has demonstrated, the rhetoric that surrounded Chkalov, his feats, his reputation, and his relationship with Stalin, was a complex interplay of heroic and masculine ideals, in which he was simultaneously a loving father, naïve son, and Stalinist Prometheus.[12] Writing in *Literaturnaia gazeta* in December 1938 after the death of Chkalov, Vladimir Kokkinaki encapsulated the essence the aviator's myth: "Fearless in battle but modest with his comrades, severe with his enemies but kind-hearted towards his friends, strict in his work but affectionate with children, an indefatigable warrior in the skies and an inspired artist of the art of aviation—all of these traits characterized Chkalov."[13] Similarly, his wife described him as "a devoted father and husband [... who] enjoyed puppet shows, Russian baths, funny stories, Volga boat songs and dominoes."[14] The heroic pilot in return referred to Stalin as "the embodiment of one word, the most tender and human word of all—father."[15] In his famous tribute published in *Izvestiia* in August 1938, Chkalov went on to state that "He [Stalin] is our father. He teaches us and rears us. We are as dear to his heart as his own children. [...] We Soviet pilots all feel his loving, attentive, fatherly eyes upon us."[16]

Whether as the supreme figure of authority in the Soviet collective or as a figure for emulation, the father was *symbolically* at the heart of Soviet manhood during the early 1930s. However, this was not a model of fatherhood that was rooted in the domestic space or the activity of everyday family life, but one that was based on the extraordinary. This ambivalence toward both the private sphere and the role of the real-life father was reflected in the extremely small number of artistic works that depicted the father as part of the family unit. Because fatherhood was the subject of so few works during this period— this research has uncovered just four paintings—it is difficult to extrapolate any clear picture of the use of visual culture to present a model of idealized paternity. We can, however, take this paucity as indicative of the persistence of the idea that a present and proactive father was not a necessary component in the Soviet family, especially now that mothers and their children had Father Stalin to look after their every need. Even in the couple of paintings produced in these years that did include the father in a family scene, there was a tendency to place him on the periphery of the family unit, and in every instance, it was the bond between the mother and child that was given priority.

If any one picture encapsulates the deeply ambiguous place of the father in Soviet society, it was Taras Gaponenko's *To Mother for the Next Feed* (*Na obed k materiam*, 1935).[17] Taking a break from their work in the fields, a group of young mothers and their coworkers lay down their tools to attend to their children who have been brought into the fresh air to be fed. Amidst this group of broody women, there is one man, who joyfully raises his small, bare-bottomed child to the sky as his wife anxiously watches on. While it is intriguing that this father should even be present in an otherwise all-female scene in the first place, what is even more telling is that in carrying out the act of raising his child above his head, the man's features are completely obscured by his own arms. This, in combination with the placement of the father and his child on the edge of the canvas and away from the main body of action in its center, makes this man a quintessential Soviet father of the early 1930s: a dispensable figure on the periphery of family life. Similarly, in Kuz'ma Petrov-Vodkin's *The Year 1919: Anxiety (1919 goda. Trevoga*, 1934–35), it is the relationship between the mother and her child that forms the focal point of the painting, as the father, with his back turned, was again physically distanced from his family. It could even be argued that he was presented as completely superfluous to the scene, as the anxiety exhibited by the mother strips her husband of his primary masculine function as the protector of his family. Therefore, while it is significant that the father began to appear, albeit with great infrequency, in the visual culture of the early 1930s, these works can hardly be seen to mark a watershed in the presentation of paternity.[18]

The mid-1930s witnessed a shift in official attitudes toward the family, leading to a well-documented sentimentalization of motherhood;[19] but this period also saw a shift in attitude toward the role of the father in the family, with his function now increasingly seen as more than financial. This more polyvalent view of fatherhood would develop during the years of the Cultural Revolution, as the traditional economically based model of fatherhood began to be combined with the emerging view that the father was a crucial element in child-raising, which itself became explicitly tied to both the strength of the Soviet state and the qualities of the individual: good fatherhood became synonymous with good citizenship. This duality was demonstrated by the constitutional reform that was introduced in 1936–37; while the new constitution and the changing divorce laws brought about a clampdown on fathers who were seen to be shirking their fiscal obligations to their family, the public discussion surrounding this legislation conveyed a far broader conceptualization of fatherhood. Amidst the public debate concerning the amendment of the abortion laws, in June 1936 *Pravda* published an article discussing the role of the father in Soviet society. Couched in terms of both financial support and social obligation, the traditional paternal role of provider was now combined with a duty to inculcate a suitable socialist morality:

> A father who cannot feed his children, give them an elementary education, provide for their future and bring them up, loses not only his "rights" but also all the pride and happiness of fatherhood. [...] In the Soviet land, "father" is a respected calling, it does not mean "master" in the old sense of the word. It designates a Soviet citizen, the builder of a new life, the raiser of a new generation. [...] Under Soviet conditions the father is the social educator. He has to prepare good Soviet citizens: that is his duty, that is also his pride. [...] A man

who cowardly and basely abandons his children, shuns his responsibility, hides in corners and puts all the paternal duties on the mother's shoulders, shames the name of a Soviet citizen. [...] A Soviet child has a right to a real father, an educator and a friend.[20]

Similarly, in his contribution to the father question, V. Svetlov wrote that "a good production worker, a good Stakhanovite, a good social worker must organize his family in such a fashion that he has time both for family and for cultural leisure and the education of his child."[21] Being a good father by the late 1930s, then, was no longer simply about financial provision but now demanded an active and participatory role in the lives of one's children: by extension the ideal man was not that purely public animal of the revolutionary period, but a man who now spent time in the domestic space ensuring a secure Soviet future through the socialization of his children as well as through his labor.

This development of the paternal role found an outlet in a couple of paintings produced just after the introduction of the new family legislation: Samuil Adlivankin's *The Prize*, also known as *A Family on Excursion* (*Premiia*, 1937), and Vladimir Vasil'ev, *A Commanding Officer's Family* (*Sem'ia komandira*, 1938). Both of these canvases are demonstrative of a change in the portrayal of the father; no longer a figure on the periphery of family life, in these works the Soviet man is shown to have an emotional bond with his children. What is telling, though, is the fact that both works show the family in exceptional circumstances: the prize won by the father in Adlivankin's painting took the family on a special trip, and the very presence of the father, on leave from the army, in Vasil'ev's image transforms what appears to be a simple family scene into something extraordinary. Despite the rhetoric, then, the visual inclusion of the father in family scenes appears to have been reserved only for special occasions.

Thus one can see that for all its supposed one-dimensionality, the issue of fatherhood and paternity was an incredibly complex and often contradictory formulation throughout the 1930s and into the war years. The paternal personality cult of the leader ran alongside an increased focus on the importance of the father in child rearing, meaning that the authority of the biological father was simultaneously reinforced and undermined by official state rhetoric and, after 1936, the private enacting of fatherhood became enmeshed with civic responsibility and public persona. By the end of the 1930s, the father was seen to have a crucial role to play in shaping the next generation of Soviet citizens, and for the first time men were, at least ideologically, in the position that women had been in since 1917 in having to be simultaneously an effective worker and parent, which by extension made them model Soviet citizens. This intermingling of the private and the public was not something that was confined to the Soviet father, but it was the blurring of these boundaries and the creation of the symbiotic relationship between good citizenship and fatherhood that enabled the family to be used to such great effect during the war years, as the protection of loved ones became synonymous with the protection of the state.

## PATERNITY AND PATRIOTISM: FATHERHOOD DURING THE WAR

With the outbreak of total war in 1941, every aspect of Soviet society was mobilized to aid the War effort, and the family was no exception. In the indistinct boundaries between the home and the front, familial relations were cast as a motivation for fighting for those in the forces, and as part of a rhetoric of support and of waiting for those who were left behind the lines, and it was through the poster that this relationship between the family unit and the nation-state was most evocatively portrayed. The revival of the figure of the motherland, epitomized by Iraklii Toidze's *The Motherland Calls! (Rodina-mat' zovet!*, 1941), became one of the instantly recognizable icons of Soviet poster art and represented a shift in the conceptualization of patriotic duty from being based on an ideological affinity with the principles of Marxist-Leninism to being grounded in nationalistic sentiment. As was discussed in chapter 3, the transition in visual representation of the motherland from the young warrior-maiden of the First World War to the middle-aged, homely woman of the Second World War allowed for participation in the War to be couched in terms of filial obligation and is illustrative of how the lines between the public and the private, the biological and the metaphorical family, were further entangled during the war years: as Lisa Kirschenbaum has written, "Mothers functioned [...] both as national symbols and as the constantly reworked and reimagined nexus between home and nation, between love for the family and devotion to the State."[22] Beyond Toidze's *Rodina-mat'*, the image of the mother proliferated in both the wartime poster and in the press, urging her sons to heroic deeds and calling for their protection.[23] While the guarantee of victory at Stalingrad after January 1943 has frequently been seen as a turning point in the iconography and rhetoric of the war effort,[24] this supposed reversion to the grand master narrative of fighting for Stalin and the Soviet state was actually coupled with a continuation of the family trope, both in terms of the icon of the motherland/mother and in the use of familial motifs more generally.[25] Thus the parallel conceptualizations of motivation for fighting and the seemingly incongruous loyalties of the parochial and state perpetuated until the end of the War, and the Soviet father was very much a part of this discourse. This potent mix of the most intimate personal relationships with national security and the blend between family and patriotic obligation was one of the defining characteristics of wartime visual culture.

While the sentimentalization of the mother-son relationship was the most frequently utilized trope that spanned the private/public division, the link between the family and masculine duty was also directly invoked through the figure of the heroic father and husband. Posters such as Leonid Golovanov's *For the Sake of My Wife, For My Children's Lives* (*Za chest' zheny, za zhizn' detei*, 1942) and Viktor Koretskii's *Red Army Warrior—Save!* (*Voin Krasnoi Armii, spasi!*, 1942),[26] both of which presented the German threat to the lives of women and children, coupled individual performance at the front with the integrity of the family that remained at home. In this way, soldiers were compelled to do their duty at the front, not only out of filial devotion, but as part of their role as husbands and, more crucially, as fathers. Golovanov's later work, *My Daddy Is a Hero! And You?* (*Moi papa geroi! A ty?*, 1943),[27] which depicted a small girl holding a picture of her father and pointing to the male viewer in a Kitcheneresque manner, went even further and explicitly linked paternal duty, the protection of the family, and masculine imperative.[28] Thus, the extensive use of the mother and the wife and infant can be seen as part of the same framework, in which idealized masculinity, soldierly conduct, and heroism were intrinsically tied to notions concerning the inherent defenselessness of women and children and the role of the male to provide protection.

In contrast to the mother figure, whose vulnerability and dependence upon the actions of her heroic sons provided the basis of both written and visual propaganda, the father-son relationship was not conceived of in terms of protection but rather emulation. It was a common device in the wartime poster to present two, and sometimes more, temporal planes, in which the contemporary struggles and fighters were shadowed by those of the past. This trend was particularly common in 1942—which both marked the 130th anniversary of the Napoleonic retreat from Moscow and the defeat of the Teutonic Knights in 1242 at Lake Peipus—and numerous posters were produced that invoked the heroics of General Suvorov and the legendary Aleksandr Nevskii in particular.[29] Many works drew more generally upon the idea of the mythical *bogatyr*, with some explicitly referencing Viktor Vasnetsov's 1898 painting.[30] Others looked to the more recent Soviet past for their heroes, finding their ideal incarnation in the anonymous fighters of the Civil War, and it was in this context of the Revolution and Civil War that the father-son relationship was directly invoked in Solomon Boim's simple sketched poster of 1941.[31] The invocation of the events of the Civil War was not confined only to the poster, and, as Kirschenbaum has demonstrated, the written propaganda of the time was also explicitly couched in terms of paternalism, as "the heroes of the Civil War appeared in the wartime press not only as dedicated revolutionaries but as exemplary fathers" and by extension a "sons' loyalty to Soviet power was in turn represented as a very personal obligation to their fathers."[32]

Even beyond the context of the Civil War, it is possible to view the use of diachronic planes in the wartime poster as drawing upon this same sense of filial duty, not in a strict biological sense but generationally as, by representing the heroism of the forefather, the current generation of sons were to be inspired to similar greatness. Thus while representations of actual fathers and sons were rare—Govorkov's *I Am Proud, Son!* (*Gorzhus' synom!*) from 1941 being one exception—symbolically this was a relationship that was at the heart of how Soviet heroism was constructed during the war years.[33] The use of the mother/motherland icon during the Great Patriotic War has been well documented, and it is of course important to think about the implications of this feminine imagery for notions of contemporary masculinity and idealized manly performance. However, we should not lose sight of the fact that in the world of the wartime poster, the Soviet soldier was not simply his mother's son but a family man in the fullest sense of the word, as relationships between men and their children and men and their own (fore)fathers were also used to great effect and would have an enormous influence in how fatherhood was represented once the fighting was over.

Amidst the discursive mobilization of the family, in 1944 the state turned to the real concerns of family life after the end of the War, introducing a new family code that was an interesting blend of pragmatism and idealism. Taking into account the expected rise in the number of unmarried mothers and the demographic crisis that was expected to follow the end of the War, a range of measures was introduced to boost the birth rate. The status of Heroine Mother was created for women with more than seven children, and taxes were levied for citizens with no children (and every unmarried man was now classed as legally childless) and for married couples with less than three children. And yet amidst these new financial incentives for childbearing, Article Twenty of the new code removed a woman's right to sue for paternity and alimony from a man to whom she was not married. By the end of the War, then, paternity was not simply a case of biology but was defined by law, and as such a man was no longer legally obliged to provide for his illegitimate children financially, nor could he use his illegitimate offspring to avoid the new "bachelor" tax. This provided a rather paradoxical view of fatherhood, as the new code seemingly reinforced the traditional family unit, encouraging fecund marriage, while at the same time it financially rewarded unmarried mothers and removed some of the financial burdens for men that were associated with having children outside of wedlock. Thus, specifically in terms of unmarried fathers, if paternity was reduced to its most basic social element—that of financial provision—the Family Code of 1944 shifted the responsibility for this from the biological father to the paternal state. With this, fatherhood was now limited by law to being exclusively something that occurred within the institution of marriage. Both practically and symbolically, then, the War was a watershed for the conceptualization of paternity and, with it, Soviet masculinity as a whole.

## RETURNING FATHERS

In July 1945, *Pravda* commented on the ongoing process of demobilization: "Everywhere the frontline soldiers are welcomed with excitement and joy, with open arms [...] they are returning home to peaceful labor, to their own families, with their sense of patriotic duty fulfilled."[34] In officially organized parades and welcoming committees, the demobilized soldier was greeted by his relatives and grateful compatriots and promised a wealth of benefits and a special standing within postwar society. This theme of homecoming would resonate throughout the years of demobilization, the last wave of which ended in March 1948; it encapsulated the promise of postwar society, which in itself was firmly rooted in the notion of the Soviet soldier as a family man, and especially as a father. Needless to say, neither the horrific conditions that many had had to endure just to arrive back home nor the limitations of the state benefits to which they were now entitled were part of the official rhetoric of homecoming.[35] The reality of the many soldiers who found they had no home or no family to return to, either due to death or evacuation, was likewise glossed over: in official discourses the Soviet soldier always returned home to find his wife and children waiting for him. As popular magazines of the time were festooned with both photographs and tales of happy homecomings, so homecoming gained attention in other artistic media, attention that persisted beyond the suppression of the commemoration of the War instigated in 1947. Like both the rhetoric and the photographs of homecoming, these works were also devoid of any indication of trauma or tension, but crucially they demonstrate a vastly different familial hierarchy to those presented before 1941, as the focus was now placed on the bond between the returning father and his child. Thus, in the paintings and sculptures produced in the last decade of Stalinism that explored the theme of homecoming, it was the child that was presented as the linchpin in the relationship between the Soviet man and the domestic space.

One of the most commonly reproduced representations of homecoming, both in the years immediately after the War and beyond, was Vladimir

FIGURE 4.1. Vladimir Kostetskii, *The Return*, 1945–1947. National Art Museum of Ukraine, Kiev.

Kostetskii's *The Return* (*Vozvrashchenie*, 1945–47),[36] a painting inspired by a much earlier scene of homecoming, Rembrandt's *The Return of the Prodigal Son* (c. 1669).[37] In the communal area outside their apartment, husband and wife are reunited, shown locked in a heartfelt embrace, while their young son clutches on to his father's overcoat and gazes up adoringly at his all-conquering hero. With the grandmother standing in the darkness of the doorway, the focus of the work is on the nuclear family unit in the center of the canvas. Although it is the clinch between husband and wife that physically dominates the piece, Kostetskii presents them as completely consumed in their reunion, and as such they in turn obscure each other's features; the bulk of the man, who has his back turned from the viewer, hides the woman's petite frame, whose face is buried into her husband's chest. The only figure not obscured by the shadows or the embrace, the happy face of the young boy—reinforced by his light clothing against the generally dark palette—provides the locus of the canvas and is the distillation of the homecoming narrative: now Father was home, normal life could once again resume. However, although it appears as such a positive interpretation of the joy of victory and reunion, the more pessimistic aspects of Kostetskii's work did not pass unnoticed by contemporary commentators. After its first showing at the All-Union Art Exhibition in 1947, one critic wrote that Kostetskii had truthfully represented the hardships endured by the Soviet people, encapsulated in the thin arms and hands of the wife and the "haggard face" of the young boy.[38] A later discussion of Kostetskii's work also questioned whether the "thin pale boy in worn sandals" was a suitable embodiment of the optimism of the War's end.[39] Yet, in neither instance did the physical appearance of the wife and child lead to a condemnation of Kostetskii's work; rather, they were highlighted as contributory factors to the overall success of the composition.

The artistic tradition for representations of homecoming did not only come from masterpieces produced in the West: Ilya Repin's *They Did Not Expect Him* (*Ne zhdali*, 1884–88), which showed the return of an emaciated political prisoner to his family home, provided a template for the exploration of homecoming in a Russian context. In spite of the differing circumstances of the return from exile and the return home after victory in war, Repin's work would be frequently reproduced throughout the late 1940s and 1950s,[40] suggesting that the image continued to resonate with a modern Soviet audience, a contrast to the lukewarm reception that the painting had received from Repin's contemporaries.[41] However, unlike the narratively simple Soviet images, Repin's painting is riddled with uncertainty: What are the relationships being presented here? Is the returning man to be welcomed home or rejected by his family? Is this a scene of impending domestic happiness or will the reunion be a brief one? Leaving this ambiguity to one side, though, one can see several important trends that are also found in the later representations of wartime homecomings. It is particularly interesting that amidst the range of reactions that are portrayed by Repin, it is only the young boy who is visibly pleased to see his father, a man he instantaneously recognizes despite his disheveled state and the years that have passed. Perhaps more significantly, Repin's work offered what David Jackson called "a statement on personal suffering, the price that both exile and family pay for upholding political ideals."[42] While the setting and political context may have been different, the notion that the act of homecoming was also representative of the sacrifices that had been made in the name of the nation-state—sacrifices that had had a deep impact upon the family—was clearly pertinent after 1945 and perhaps goes some way to explaining why this painting was repeatedly reproduced in the years following the War.

Kostetskii was not alone in prioritizing the father-child relationship above all others when dealing with the subject of homecoming. Dementii Shmarinov, whose poster work during the war years had drawn heavily on the vulnerability of the mother and child as a spur for heroic action, continued to focus upon the family in his painting *Reunion on Liberated Land* (*Vstrecha na osvobozhdennoi zemle*, 1946).[43] Like Kostetskii, Shmarinov showed the reunited nuclear family in his canvas, and again portrayed the emotion of reunion through the reconnection between father and son. This was also the case in Viktor Kiselev's *He's Back* (*Vernulsia*, 1947), which depicted a young peasant father being embraced by his daughter upon his return to the family home,[44] and in both B. Karadzha's sculpture *Reunion* (*Vstrecha*, [1945–50?]) and V. L. Kostetskii's bronze *The Return* (*Vozvrashchenie*, 1946).[45] Nor was the prioritization of the father-child relationship something that was unique to fine art, as the sketches accompanying short stories such as "Faith, Hope, Love" by A. Avdeenko and the homecoming-themed posters of Maria Nesterova-Berzina and Nina Vatolina show, all of which focus on the relationship between father and child in their representation of this happy occasion.[46] Tellingly, in the commemorative edition of *Ogonek* from May 9, 1970, a selection of paintings was reproduced in a glossy supplement in the middle of the magazine, and of the eight images featured three dealt with the theme of the returning father—Kostetskii's *Return*, Sergei Grigorev's *In the Family Home* (*V rodnoi sem'e*, 1947), which depicted a newly returned father singing and playing the accordion for his small children, one of whom is sitting on his suitcase, and Laktionov's *Letter from the Front*. Decades after victory, these images of homecoming were still to be found on the pages of magazines, giving some indication of just how popular, and in some cases powerful, these works were.

Laktionov's *Letter from the Front* was without a doubt the most well-loved representation of the promise of imminent return. Overlooking a communal courtyard with the merest glimpse of the village church in the background, a family stands on the ramshackle porch of their apartment block, listening attentively to the young boy as he reads aloud a letter from his father, which has been brought to them by a wounded comrade; the sky is blue, summer is in the air, and soon this father will return home. This is not the war of the master narrative of the state; rather, this is a highly personal insight into the impact of war on one provincial family (the village being modeled on Zagorsk) and the importance of the impending victory on their future happiness. As the title would suggest, the focal point of Laktionov's canvas is the letter itself—bright light reflects off its surface, bestowing it with an aura of sanctity—and through it, the small boy is transformed into an emissary, the only one deemed worthy to read its precious contents. The authority invested in the boy is mirrored in the larger compositional structure of the piece through the placement of the child in the center of the canvas and the fact that he is the only one seated, while his female relatives all gather around him to hear him read. What is more, by having the boy read the letter, as opposed to his mother, who is the natural figure of authority in the piece, a direct link between the absent soldier and his son is established, and the relationship between father and child is prioritized above all others.

Given the mobilization of the family in wartime visual culture, it is perhaps unsurprising that artists in the years after the War chose to present the Soviet soldier as a family man: after all, what could better symbolize the value of victory and the hope for a better future than a child? However, the shift in dynamic between these depictions of family life and those that were produced in the years before 1941 is not explained satisfactorily by the simple desire to tug on the viewer's heartstrings. What is more, beyond any emotional motivation that may have existed in the creation of such images, it is both the fact that the demobilized Soviet soldier came to be represented first and foremost as a father, and the impact this had on the portrayal of the Soviet family, that arguably had the greatest consequences for the conceptualization of Soviet idealized masculinity. As was discussed above, the introduction of the father into the family unit was a development of the mid-1930s, a trend that was cemented by the extensive use of the familial motif during the war years. Yet, in every work that this research has uncovered from the prewar period, the father's relationship with his child is mediated through the figure of the mother, whether as an explicit physical barrier between the father and child or as an ever-watchful guardian. This would change after 1945 as the bond between a father and his child took on a more direct quality, seen in the first instance in representations of homecoming.

The visual representation of father-child interaction would diversify after the immediate postwar period, but what was consistent across this range of images was a continual reference to the father's military service. This was seen, for example, in Arkadii Plastov's *Threshing on the Collective Farm* (*Kolkhoznyi tok,* 1949), which juxtaposed the father's return to work with the presence of his young son, who is shown wearing his old army cap,[47] or Aleksei Shirokov's *In the Family* (*V sem'e,* [1947–53?]), which depicted a chess game between a father and son, both of whom are in uniform.[48] It can also be seen in illustrations for short stories that, while tellingly had titles such as "Father," represent these men as soldiers within the domestic space, and even in photo-essays from the maternity home, which show the new father holding his child for the first time while in uniform.[49] This link between the military experience of the father and his relationship with his children was most explicitly articulated in another oft-published work of the era, Nikolai Ponomarev's *A New Uniform* (*Novyi mundir,* 1952).[50] Following its first display at the All-Union Exhibition of 1952, Ponomarev's work was hailed by critics as the epitome of Soviet genre painting of the early 1950s, and while much praise was lavished on the artist's ability to capture the "special power of the domestic genre," little attention was actually paid to the content of the painting, which is in of itself noteworthy.[51] The central interaction in Ponomarev's canvas at first appears to be that between the hero and his wife, shown dutifully pinning his hard-earned medals onto his new jacket. However, it is the link between the father and son—who is playfully trying on his father's new army cap, standing on a dining room chair so that he is able to see in the mirror—that forms the primary narrative strand of this work. One can see the connection between father and son here operating on two levels. There is what one might think of as the national-symbolic connection that is created by the representation of the small boy in his father's military garb, a not-so-subtle indicator of the perpetuity of the Red Army and the inherent heroism of the Soviet people. Second, there is a more personal and intimate connection between the father and his son, which is constructed through the use of the mirror, a device that establishes a direct and unmediated connection between the males in the painting to the exclusion of the female family members. What is more, as if to underline the primacy of the bond between the father and his son, the placement of the boy on the chair both physically and symbolically puts him above his older sister in the family hierarchy.

This new, more complex conceptualization of both the place of the father within the domestic space and his relationship with his children found expression in media other than painting as, in the last years of Stalinism, popular magazines began to publish photographs of the Soviet father. Featuring both known and "average" men, such publications showed fathers enjoying the company of their children, teaching them to play the piano, to showing them how to ski, or doing the gardening together, offering a vision of fatherhood that was far more interactive than was ever presented on canvas. However, the frequency with which such images were reproduced in the press should not be overstated, and had they not been a new development, they would have paled into insignificance when compared with the equivalent representation of the mother-child bond. Although a consistent feature throughout the 1945 to 1953 period, it is worth noting that the focus upon the father-child relationship reached its peak in the months following the death of Stalin, indicative perhaps of the impact the paternal cult of the leader had on the representation of biological paternity. In *Ogonek*, for example, between May 1945 and March 1953, twenty-five photographs were published that featured *direct* father-child interaction; in the following nine months alone, a further eighteen were printed, almost 42 percent of the total published across the eight years between the end of the War and Stalin's demise.[52] Thus in the years between 1945 and 1953, there are two parallel developments with regard to representations of the Soviet family; first, the father became a palpable presence in the domestic space, and second, his relationship with his children began to emerge from under the shadow of the omnipresent mother. The different presentation of fatherhood across the various media should be remembered, however; the more active father figure of the published photographs did not have an equivalent incarnation in fine art, which continued to emphasize the legacy of the Great Patriotic War in its depiction of the man within the family home. Furthermore, with the specter of war looming large over these works, it should not be surprising that time and again it was the father-son relationship that was the focus, while such gender bias did not exist in contemporary photography as the War was less frequently a subtext.

That the War marked a watershed in the conceptualization of the parent-child relationship can be seen beyond artistic production of postwar Stalinism. As Vera Dunham highlighted in her seminal work on the literature of this period: "[After 1946] the family theme began to overshadow all others. None brought the mass reader to the literary town hall with such effectiveness. Within the family domain, it was neither sex nor love nor the nexus of marital problems or even promiscuity which most fascinated the regime. What held everyone's attention was the new relationship between parents and children."[53] For Dunham, the rise of what had been traditionally viewed as *meshchanstvo* (petty bourgeois) values in postwar literature was explicitly tied to the

War itself and parental desire to give their children a better life, free from the hardships that the youngest generations had been forced to endure in the recent past. This notion of betterment was reinforced by the various decrees that were passed between 1943 and 1945, which offered a range of concessions to the Soviet family, such as the changes in the inheritance laws and the reinstatement of the concept of private property.[54] The tolerance and, in some cases, the legal reinforcement of what had typically been seen as middle-class or bourgeois values was in Dunham's analysis central to what she termed the postwar "Big Deal," the regime's attempt to prevent dissent within a "bereaved and exhausted population [that] was prone to disaffection."[55]

Dunham's concept of the Big Deal, the "embourgeoisment" of Soviet society and the transplantation of the private into the realm of the public, is one that is particularly resonant in any assessment of the visual culture of the postwar period. It provides a satisfactorily neat explanation for why the presentation of the family proliferated in the last decade of Stalinism. It also accounts for why, despite constant references to the War through the persistence of military iconography, in so many cases (Laktionov's *Letter* being one of the rare exceptions) this interest in the family was coupled with domestic comfort and material well-being, in a manner that was a radical departure from the asceticism of the prewar era. Yet Dunham's framework only gets us so far as it does not adequately account for why, after decades of neglect, the father was now cast as an intrinsic element within the Soviet family. Instead, more than just being about interpersonal relationships, this new artistic focus on the father in the home can be seen as a barometer by which the restoration of prewar norms was gauged, even if this form of representation had very few prewar antecedents. As home life became a crucial element in the reconstruction of Soviet society, nothing could symbolize the return to normality more succinctly than the presence of those who had left to secure the Soviet victory.

## LOST FATHERS

Of course not every father returned from the War, and issues surrounding homecoming and reintegration were incongruent with the experience of many Soviet families. As one would expect, with the prevailing mood of the *Zhdanovshchina*—an era of cultural production based on the philosophy of "conflictlessness"—and the emphasis on normalization, the representation of the long-term impact of the War, in either emotional or material terms, had no place in postwar visual culture. And yet, there were a number of works produced in the late 1940s and early 1950s that omitted the father from domestic scenes and which seemed to hint at a restructuring of the family hierarchy in line with this absence. In addition to these works, this period saw a significant number of images—paintings and photographs alike—that not only lacked the presence of the biological father but included the presence of the national father in the guise of Stalin or, less frequently, Lenin. Both of these developments would seem to suggest that, at the very least, the demographic impact of the War was an inherent part of visual culture during the final years of Stalinism.

Aside from political and aesthetic constraints, one of the most problematic factors in deciphering whether one is in fact dealing with a permanent paternal absence in these images lies in the nature of fatherhood itself; after all, the ideal father who provides for his family must be by extension often away from

FIGURE 4.2. Tikhon Semenov, *Sad News (A Letter from the Front)*, 1948.

the home. However, there is no such problem of interpretation in Tikhon Semenov's 1948 painting *Sad News (A Letter from the Front)* (*Vesti s fronta*),[56] which was deemed "particularly noteworthy" by the authors of a brief survey of recent art from the RSFSR published in *Ogonek* in April 1949.[57] In retrospect, Semenov's painting was much more than noteworthy, it was entirely unique: it was one of only a handful of works that dealt openly with the issue of loss in the years before 1953 and was the only one from this period that placed the bereaved within the domestic space. Highlighting the indiscriminate nature of death, the family is depicted receiving the news of their loss at the breakfast table; among the trappings of a normal morning, the letter from the front in the young woman's hand is transformed into an alien object, out of kilter with the domesticity of the scene. Reminiscent of the device used by Kostetskii to highlight the father-child bond in his work, the wife of the fallen soldier in Semenov's canvas is shown with her face covered by a handkerchief. Through this, it is the man's children who provide the focus of the piece, in particular the young woman, letter in hand, whose body fills the foreground and whose black dress contrasts greatly with the lightness of the domestic interior. The son, who is himself in uniform, is presented as in a state of reserved shock but is compositionally overshadowed by his mother and sister, thus reinforcing the premise that grieving was predominantly a female occupation, an association that was not a Soviet invention but, as seen in the previous chapter, one that gained particular significance after 1941 as the bereaved mother became a central trope in both wartime and postwar visual culture. The explicit emotion and clear narrative of Semenov's painting were exceptional for this period, and it is telling that other works examined here contain such ambiguity that it is impossible to say with any degree of certainty whether we are indeed dealing with a permanent paternal absence.

In the years after the War, renowned artist Fedor Reshetnikov produced a number of well-received works that focused on the everyday lives of children. The Stalin Prize–winning *Home for the Holidays* (*Pribyl na kanikuly*, 1948) explored adult-child interaction, inspired by what one contemporary commentator called the "new, friendly relationship between the different generations,"[58] from which the father was significantly omitted. An immensely popular painting at the time, *Home* was reproduced on numerous occasions in the Soviet press over the next few years, even gracing the front cover of *Ogonek* in January 1949—the only painting in this era to do so—as well as appearing on postcards, being referenced in other images, and even being reproduced as a sewing pattern.[59] Bedecked in his cadet uniform, saluting his grandfather, the young boy in *Home* was the embodiment of the patriotism, heroism, and self-renewing nature of the Red Army. Yet despite the sense of

FIGURE 4.3. Fedor Reshetnikov, Home for the Holidays, 1948. Tretyakov Gallery, Moscow.

optimism and festive cheer that the painting exudes, the boy's father is a notable absence. There are several indications that this absence was a permanent
one, rather than being a straightforward scene concerning the relationship
between grandfather and grandchild, not least of all the fact that it was the
grandfather who was privy to this welcome. While the chair at the head of the
dining table occupied by the family cat may be a rather tenuous allusion to a

paternal absence, it is the portrait hanging above the young boy's head that provides the viewer with the most substantial clue that this family had suffered a loss during the War. This photograph is of a man in uniform, presumably the boy's father, and it hangs on the wall alongside a copy of Vasnetsov's 1898 much-loved painting *Bogatyri*. Compositionally this is very significant, as these two images and the boy form a pyramid, creating an unbroken genealogy of tradition and heroism, which leads from the knights of the mythical Russian past, to the heroes of the Great Patriotic War to the potential heroism of the young cadet. It is also telling that of the three generations of heroes, it is the (fallen) hero of the recent war who sits at the apex.

In *Low Marks Again!* (*Opiat' dvoika!*, 1952), Reshetnikov seemed to continue to explore this sense of inconspicuous loss,[60] although in this work there is no clear indication that the absence of the father from the scene was a permanent one. Arriving home from school with a battered briefcase, with a telltale edge of a skate poking through the top, and in an overcoat that swamps his small frame, this young boy stands dejected in the presence of his disappointed mother. While his brother plays and his sister studies, the boy appears as the world-weary master of the household and is greeted in such a manner by his faithful dog. *Low Marks* was exemplary of the indolent schoolboy whose extra-curricular activities had compromised his academic attainment. This painting, and a slightly earlier work by Adolf Gugel' and Raisa Kudrevich entitled *A Big Surprise* (*Bol'shoi siurpriz*, 1951), which depicts a young boy caught smoking by his mother, have been seen by some as representative of the traditional structure of Soviet family life in which the father was the disciplinarian: in these works where the father is absent, the mother is portrayed as a somewhat ineffectual figure, capable of little more than a censorious look when it comes to disciplining her son.[61]

While the absence of a male disciplinarian was at the heart of both of these paintings, and may even have been understood by the contemporary viewer as the reason behind these boys' wayward behavior, there is nothing definitive in either image to prove that the father was permanently absent. Likewise, contemporary criticism was striking in its avoidance of the issue of the father. Writing for *Iskusstvo* in February 1953 about its display and reception at the latest All-Union Art Exhibition, Nina Dmitrieva called *Low Marks* "undoubtedly one of the best works at the exhibition" as visitors could not help but "genuinely love this sweet, simple family." In two separate instances in this article, Dmitrieva discussed Reshetnikov's representation of the mother of the family, writing that the viewer could "clearly see that the mother puts her whole soul into ensuring her children learn and grow into decent, educated people."[62] At no point in her analysis of this "charming" family scene was the father so much as hinted at, let alone his absence, or even potential return, discussed. One sees a similar obfuscation in an earlier critical analysis of *Home*, dating from February 1949, in which the author places Reshetnikov's work, not in the context of the War, but in that of the latest Five Year Plan.[63] Beyond *Iskusstvo*, on the pages of the popular press, Reshetnikov's works, while reproduced with relative frequency, garnered little written attention: for all they were lavishly illustrated, magazines such as *Ogonek* rarely included any detailed analysis of artworks, and the majority of paintings in this period were presented as a series of color reproductions separated from the main body of the magazine in an almost supplemental fashion. The exception to this would be the annual survey of works displayed at the All-Union Exhibition, which generally ran over several pages and would include upward of a dozen images. In January 1953, *Ogonek* published its overview of the offering from 1952, stating simply that *Low Marks* was a "touching" piece characteristic of the genre works that typified Socialist Realism without providing any comment on the content, context, or subtext of the painting.[64]

The seeming ambiguity surrounding the absence of the father in Reshetnikov's work in particular is even more striking when one considers the lengths that the state went to in order to establish "one-meaningness" [*odnoznachnost'*]. As Jan Plamper highlighted in his work on censorship in Karelia during the 1930s, there was an obsessive effort to eliminate ambiguity and polysemy from Soviet culture during this time, which led to images being withdrawn from newspapers and magazines for a wide variety of reasons that ranged from looking too much like Trotsky to inadvertently containing swastikas.[65] Thus, Reshetnikov's work presents us with a rather curious problem in terms of ambiguity and interpretation. It could be the case that the family dynamics presented in these works were so commonplace in the late 1940s and early 1950s that the father being missing from the domestic scene was not even worthy of comment, but it is rather hard to believe that contemporary audiences viewed these paintings completely in line with the interpretation espoused in the critical press—that these were scenes of happy domesticity in which the absence of the father was either unnoted or entirely insignificant. Did the Soviet populace really not see the shadow of the War in the tone, composition, or subject matter of these works? Or was it the very subtext of the War and the pertinence of absent fathers and a longing for a happy childhood that made these pieces so appealing to the Soviet public?

When thinking about such issues, it is important to note that for all the attempts to control the interpretation of images through the 1930s, Reshetnikov was not alone in presenting the Soviet viewer with a portrait of life that could be read in multiple ways during the early postwar era. As

Matthew Cullerne Bown points out in his survey of Socialist Realist paintings, works such as Laktionov's *Letter from the Front* and Arkadii Plastov's *They Are Going to the Elections*, both from 1947, are open to interpretations that are independent of the communist ethos that on first appearances they seem to espouse. Employing the framework of dual belief [*dvoreverie*], Cullerne Bown sees these images as being indicative of the persistence of traditional Russian values lurking under the facade of Soviet iconography. For example, the markers of Sovietness in Laktionov's canvas—the uniform and medals of the soldier, the young woman's red fire warden's armband, the Pioneer neckerchief of the small boy—are arguably secondary to the more traditionally Russian features of Laktionov's much-loved work: the sleepy provincial setting, the onion-domed cupola of the church in the background, and the rickety floorboards and peeling plaster of the family home all point at a way of life that has been unchanged by the Soviet project.[66] Similarly, in his comments on Plastov's work, Cullerne Bown contrasts the "official" reading of the painting that these citizens are exuberant at the prospect of participating in the nation's political future and the "unofficial" reading that, title aside, this could simply be a scene of a group of friends enjoying a traditional Russian pastime of taking a troika ride through the snow.[67] Cullerne Bown thus draws the conclusion that "such ambivalent narratives are a widespread feature of socialist realist painting from the 1940s onwards."[68] It is debatable how "widespread" this phenomenon really was, certainly during the Stalin years, but such duality does open the door to legitimate multifarious readings of images such as those by Reshetnikov, despite the prevailing conservatism of the art institutions at this time and the fact that this was not a part of the critical reception of such works. Thus, beneath the veneer of school days and holiday celebrations, one can see Reshetnikov's works as acknowledging the losses inflicted by the War—a factor that arguably played no small role in the popularity of these paintings, which, as visitors to the 1952 exhibition commented, offered a rare truthful glimpse into everyday life, a life that was populated by real people, not the tedious paragons they had previously had to endure.[69]

Ultimately, though, whatever pathos may be stirred by paintings like Reshetnikov's, and others such as Laktionov's *Into the New Apartment* (*V novuiu kvartiru*, 1952)—which is examined in more detail below—the emotional impact of these works is severely restrained by the rendering of the comfortable domestic setting. These are not images of destroyed lives, of fragmented families, or of individuals struggling to come to terms with the horrors that the war years have inflicted upon them; rather, these are optimistic future-oriented scenes of a happy everyday life, taking place in a space of material and emotional security. Indeed, the cozy domestic interior can be seen as compensating for the absence of the biological father by underlining the paternalism of the state as the provider of new apartments, free education, and employment; despite their (potential) loss, these families are, after all, still able to enjoy the material benefits of life in the Soviet Union. If we accept the premise first espoused by Dunham that the reconceptualization of the domestic space from the asceticism of the 1920s and 1930s to the doilies, floral throws, and lace tablecloths of the postwar years was part of a concerted effort to minimize the legacy of the War—both in terms of the disaffection of the population and in terms of its physical impact[70]—we should also see the combination of material well-being with the absent father as particularly significant. Yet, however emotionally limited they may be, the crucial point should not be overlooked that, despite the lack of acknowledgment in the professional art world, the loss suffered during the War appears to be an intrinsic part of the narratives of these works.

The works of Reshetnikov and Laktionov are also indicative of how both the destruction and shortage of housing was entirely glossed over in postwar visual culture. Given that around twenty-five million people were left homeless by the events of 1941–45, and even taking into account the huge construction projects that followed the end of the War, as Lynne Attwood reminds us, "The reality was that thousands of people [...] had to live in whatever makeshift shelter they could find."[71] What is more, given that official policy was that a tenant was no longer entitled to accommodation after an absence of six months and nonpayment of rent for three, those who had been evacuated or carried out essential work in the east, and even those who had served at the front, frequently returned home to find their previous dwelling occupied by others, with no legal standing for recompense;[72] home was at the same time a very precious and a very precarious concept after 1945. Attwood draws a direct line between the construction projects of the postwar period and the representation of the beautiful home in women's magazines of the era: "The interest in the construction of homes logically led to an interest in home life ... A typical photograph in *Sovetskaia zhenshchina,* a glossy new post-war women's magazine, showed a family 'spending Sunday together' seated cozily around a large dining table in the center of the room surrounded by homely decorative touches."[73] Undoubtedly there is a connection between building houses and concern with interior design, but when one looks at the relationship between the War and the home through the prism of emotion rather than materiality, there is perhaps a more compelling reason as to why one sees such a prevalence of images of the beautiful family home—both in terms of photographs and reproductions of artworks—on the pages of the popular press after 1945.

Given the massive destruction of housing that had occurred during the War, it is not surprising that the home became a key element in the restoration of normality, and the joint venture of rebuilding and recalibrating Soviet life only served to reinforce the symbiotic relationship between the family and the Soviet state, as once again private and public concerns meshed. Beyond this ideal of a comfortable family home, though, paintings such as those by Reshetnikov and Laktionov are symptomatic of a much broader reluctance to visually link loss and the domestic space, something that holds true even in works where loss is the central narrative, and the ambiguity we encounter in paintings such as *Home* is not an issue. As was demonstrated in the previous chapter, in the very early days of peace, a small space was carved out for the visual representation of bereavement, which was most commonly associated with the mother, as seen in works such as Fedor Bogorodskii's *Glory to the Fallen Heroes* (*Slava pavshim geroiam*, also known as *Rekviem*) and V. V. Lishev's *Mother* (*Mat'*). Yet despite the use of familial relationships to articulate the range of sentiments—pride, glory, honor, and, of course, grief—felt over the fallen soldier, there was at no point either an explicit connection made between the deceased and his home life or, with the exception of Semenov's rather extraordinary work, between the domestic space and the grief of those left behind. The transference of grieving to a setting removed from reality (Bogorodskii) or the trope of the discovery of the son's body still on the battlefield (Lishev) preserved the domestic space, allowing it to be cast as a place of healing and a sanctuary away from both war and its aftermath.

Conversely, the reality of the soldier who came home to ruins or the destruction of his family seems to have been completely unrepresented visually until the mid-1960s, with the publication of a preliminary sketch for Aleksandr Romanychev's *The Family Home* (*Otchii dom*, 1964) in *Khudozhnik*.[74] Standing on what used to be his parents' doorstep, this soldier returning from the War finds the house in disrepair, grass growing wildly, and the front door boarded; an image that is in stark contrast to the earlier photographs of homecoming in which the soldier returned to both his family and a lovely home and garden. The publication of Romanychev's draft work was closely followed by the publication of Boris Shcherbakov's *The Invincible Soldier* (*Nepobedimyi riadovoi*, 1965) as a color double-page space in *Ogonek* in July 1966,[75] which depicted an exhausted and emotional soldier seated among the ruins of a house.[76] The two decades between the end of the War and the emergence of artistic representations that linked loss with the domicile suggests that one should look beyond the political constraints of Stalinism for an explanation of the dearth of images that explored the War/home nexus. Instead, we could view the lack of such works as a statement about the restorative power and sacrality of the domestic space; a view that was by no means uniquely Soviet and one that would resonate across Europe in the aftermath of 1945.[77]

Why this reluctance to associate the home with the legacy of the War was so pronounced in visual culture is highly debatable: certainly both the prevailing atmosphere of the *Zhdanovshchina* and the conservative nature of fine art production in the immediate postwar period—as typified by the creation of the All-Union Academy of Arts in 1947—could go some way to explaining why such potentially problematic or divisive themes found no outlet in the last years of Stalinism, but this fails to explain why there is such a divergence across cultural production, when all media were subject to the same ideological constraints and why, for the most part, this reluctance persisted throughout the Thaw.[78] Rather than look at the machinations of the various institutions governing cultural production, it is perhaps more fruitful to think about these differences as related to the inherent qualities of the media themselves. What one sees time and again in literary and cinematic handling of subject matter such as bereavement or trauma is the centrality of overcoming: the way that Sholokhov's hero in "The Fate of a Man" channels his grief at the loss of his entire family to become a father to little orphaned Vania, or how the fighter pilot Aleksei Meres'ev overcomes having his feet amputated to once again take to the skies. The complexity of these tales of service, through despair to ultimate triumph or recovery, is simply better suited to the temporal rather than spatial arts, as this narrative of progression is almost impossible to represent on canvas.

However we may conceptualize the different handling of similar themes across the genres, though, what is clear is that it is impossible to speak of one homogeneous way in which the War and its legacy was dealt with in Soviet culture even during the Stalinist years, let alone in the plurality that was increasingly possible during de-Stalinization. It is vital to acknowledge that the bereavement caused by the War was a part of Soviet culture across a multitude of genres, but of equal import is the recognition of the vast differences that existed in the way its legacy was dealt with. In the case of visual culture, although one sees explicit grief being expressed through the figure of the mother, what we do not see in this period is any acknowledgment of the impact of the War on either children or the domestic space more generally—something that sets it apart from other contemporaneous media. Specifically in terms of the lost father, we are left with a very ambiguous picture and an apparent disjunction between the narrative of the paintings themselves and the critical reception of them on the pages of both the popular and professional press; a disjunction that aptly demonstrates the limits of official discourse on issues of postwar social reality.

## PATERNITY BY PROXY: NATIONAL LEADERS AS SURROGATE FATHERS

At the All-Union Exhibition in 1952, Aleksandr Laktionov's *Into the New Apartment* was displayed for the first time and garnered a mixed reception. Criticized for its varnishing of reality, for showing the wrong kind of paper on the walls and for having the audacity to place artificial flowers in a modern apartment,[79] Laktionov's canvas nonetheless emerged as a staple image in the Soviet popular press.[80] Standing on the parquet floor of her newly built, spacious apartment, Laktionov's heroine, hands on hips, proudly surveys her domain, surrounded by the accoutrements of life. Behind her, her eldest son stashes his bike in another room, and her daughter holds the family cat, also taking in the wonder before them; standing next to this woman is her younger son, who looks questioningly at her as if to ask, "Where are we going to put Stalin's picture, Mother?" Thus the dynamic of this family was established, with the woman placed in the middle of the canvas, her feet firmly planted, forming the solid, central vertical axis of the painting,[81] a literal presentation of her role as the support that holds the family together, and at her side, not a husband, but a portrait of the *vozhd'*. While this woman was in many ways the center of the narrative in Laktionov's work, the portrait of Stalin was not just there as a replacement spouse, but through its close proximity to the young boy, it also functioned as a surrogate father, as the natural male authority figure, the elder son, is relegated to a position of insignificance. Hence, Laktionov presented Stalin as far more than the figurative paternal leader of the nation, or the bestower of the gift of a new apartment on this family: as Jørn Guldberg states, "Via his picture, Stalin [...] completes the family and by replacing the absent 'real' father, he reestablishes the family's harmony and order."[82]

The idea of Stalin as the father of the nation was clearly not a product of the postwar period; it had been a significant trope in literature, film, and the visual arts throughout the 1930s, as detailed by scholars such as Katerina Clark, Hans Günther, Catriona Kelly, and Jan Plamper.[83] Nor was the idea of Stalin making up for a lack—particularly a parental one—a new conceptualization. The figure of the orphan had played a prominent role in early Socialist Realist cinema, particularly in the rags-to-riches plots of musical comedies, and the frequency of the motif prompted Maria Enzensberger to proclaim as early as 1993 that "the absent family of the Soviet cinema of the 1930s and 1940s is a subject worthy of separate investigation."[84] But what was new—certainly as far as non-cinematic visual culture was concerned—was the transference of this surrogate paternalism into the domestic space in the years after 1945. After being largely dormant for the first years of the War, the paternal cult of Stalin was revived with a vengeance after 1943. As part of this postwar resurgence, genre paintings of this era consistently included Stalin in the home, leading to a domestication of the personality cult that set it apart from its prewar counterpart. What is more, building upon the established link between Stalin and the Soviet child, his inclusion in the domestic space was almost exclusively confined to works that had children as their primary focus.

In his painting *The First of September* (*Pervoe sentiabria*) from 1950, Andrei Volkov showed a young girl preparing to return to school, adjusting her Pioneer neckerchief in her light and spacious bedroom, all under the loving gaze of Stalin, whose portrait hangs over her bookcase.[85] Likewise, Elena Kostenko in *Future Builders* (1952) depicted a group of small children at play, again in a well-appointed apartment and with an abundance of toys, while being watched over by Stalin from a photograph–also featuring the young Buryat girl Engelsina Markizova (Gelia)-hanging conspicuously on the wall.[86] However, the introduction of Stalin into these domestic settings was positively deft when compared to that presented by Grigorii Pavliuk in his painting, also from 1950, *To Dear Stalin*, which combined the domestic scene of a group of children writing a letter to their leader with an improbably large bust of Stalin himself overlooking proceedings from the corner of the room.[87] Due to the absence of a flesh-and-blood father in these works, Stalin is transformed into the alpha male of this family, fulfilling a range of traditional paternal functions as he is portrayed as their source of inspiration, their adviser, the focus of their love and devotion, and the generous provider of their spacious private home.

In addition to being used in scenarios that included no parental presence, Soviet leaders also appeared in scenes in which the father was markedly absent, thus strengthening the premise that this domestication of the paternal personality cult was the result of the demographic impact of the War. This was seen, for example, on a number of front covers of *Ogonek*, which appear to have been doctored to introduce Lenin and Stalin into the domestic space, as in the case of the magically floating portrait of Lenin as a child that hangs above the heads of several women of one family and a young boy attempting to do his studies on the front cover of *Ogonek* in January 1952 or on the New Year's edition of *Ogonek* in 1951, which showed a mother gazing adoringly down at her baby in its crib with a curiously clear photograph of Stalin on top of the piano behind her.[88] It was also seen in an interesting poster created by N. N. Zhukov, *We Will Surround Orphans with Maternal Kindness and Love!* (*Okruzhim sirot materinskoi laskoi i liubov'iu!*, 1947), in which the impact of the War loomed even larger as the maternal care for orphaned children is juxtaposed with a portrait of Stalin with Gelia, herself a famous orphan, which hangs on the wall behind the child's bed.[89]

There was also a handful of paintings that depicted the Soviet family and included both the father and the Soviet leadership. Devoid of a war-themed subtext, works such as Akhmed Kitaev's *The First Time in the First Class* (*Pervyi raz v pervyi klass*, [1945–51?]) and Vladimir Vasil'ev's *A Young Family* (*Molodaia sem'ia*, 1953)—both of which were published in *Rabotnitsa*— returned to the familiar trope of the 1930s in which the mother-child relationship is prioritized and the father is more of an onlooker than participant in what is going on.[90] Vasil'ev's work, which had been shown at the recent Spring Exhibition of Moscow Artists, featured a portrait of Maxim Gorky, while in the far cruder image by Kitaev, the family is being watched over by an image of Stalin, who is again shown with Gelia as if to underline his paternal credentials. Intriguingly, in February 1951, *Ogonek* published an early draft version of Ponomarev's *A New Uniform*, as part of a brief review of this young artist's work, which featured an unwieldy sketched portrait of Stalin hanging on the wall behind the hero.[91] In the final version, Ponomarev removed the portrait, placing a dresser along the wall instead, but as no explanation has been found as to why the artist may have made this change, we can only speculate on the reasons behind this decision.

From oil paintings to low-quality illustrations, from posters to the front covers of *Ogonek*, the presence of Stalin in the domestic space is one of the defining features of early postwar works that depicted family life. With the exception of Pavliuk and Kostenko, whose works have only been found in modern collections of Socialist Realist painting, all of these images were reproduced on the pages of the popular press, some very prominently, as with the New Year's front cover of *Ogonek* in 1951. As Plamper has demonstrated in incredible depth in his survey of the Stalin cult in visual culture, any manifestation of the cult could not happen without sanction from above;[92] therefore, the domestication of the cult in the manner one sees after 1945 could not be accidental given the control that Stalin, or those in his inner circle, had on what images of all genres were deemed suitable for publication. In the climate of the early Cold War period and the potential for disillusionment that existed at home, this shift could be representative of a need for the Soviet political elite to associate itself with the current young generation. However, it is surely not coincidental that both Stalin and, to a lesser extent, Lenin were introduced into the domicile in the aftermath of such great male loss, at a time when millions of children were left fatherless and a further 8.7 million were born to unmarried mothers in the decade after the end of the War.[93]

Accompanying the domestication of the leader cult through the use of busts, photographs, or portraiture in the home, there continued to be many works across a range of media that presented the close connection that both the "real" Lenin and Stalin enjoyed with the Soviet child.[94] But in 1947 one sees a new, and seemingly unique, aspect of this ubiquitous association—Stalin as a biological father. In his survey of *Pravda*, Plamper selects 1947 for detailed consideration, labeling it "a typical, most ordinary postwar year of the cult,"[95] and yet it is during this most run-of-the-mill year that Vasilii Efanov completed his painting *I. V. Stalin and V. M. Molotov with Their Children (I. V. Stalin i V. M. Molotov s det'mi)*, an image that was reproduced in *Iskusstvo* in a full-color plate early the following year and that in 1952 would grace the cover of the women's magazine *Rabotnitsa*.[96] Stalin was very rarely shown with his biological children in photographic form—just once in *Pravda* between 1929 and 1953[97]—and never in any other medium prior to 1947, but in Efanov's strangely unsettling pastoral scene, Stalin and Molotov are shown walking through a field accompanied by their small children. Although all of Stalin's and Molotov's children would have been at least in their mid-twenties when the artist produced this painting, the unadorned military uniform and jackboots that Stalin wears suggest that this was in fact a retrospective work, set sometime in the early 1930s. This makes the image even more jarring in its conceptualization, as the setting for the painting would appear to be around the time that Stalin's second wife, Nadia, committed suicide, and by the time that it was reproduced in *Rabotnitsa*, Molotov's wife would be in exile facing criminal charges—hardly the traditional underpinnings of a happy family scene! Despite the rather strange contexts in which the painting was both set and reproduced, it is telling that Efanov, who was himself no stranger to the portrayal of Stalin in all his pomp and glory, chose this mode of representation for the two statesmen, and it is indicative of the new postwar status of fatherhood. No longer just the father of the nation, or the surrogate father of the fatherless, by 1947 the paternal role of Stalin was also grounded in biology.

## SUMMARY

The Great Patriotic War marked a watershed moment in the representation of the Soviet man: though tentatively and incredibly infrequently a presence in the domestic space during the 1930s, the blending of the personal with the public in wartime visual culture signified a shift that would perpetuate for the rest of the Soviet period as, for the first time with any regularity, the Soviet man was visually associated with the private sphere. The full fruition of this development would not occur until the late 1950s, as will be explored in the next chapter, but what one sees in the aftermath of the War is the emergence of the Soviet father as a figure in his own right, first in the guise of the returning veteran and, by the end of the 1940s, in a more diverse range of scenarios, although predominantly still with a military subtext. Though the significance of this development should not be underestimated, what must be noted is that despite the War looming large in the majority of such images, there was at no point any indication of strained relationships, material hardship, or physical or emotional trauma. Visually, homecoming was nothing less than happily-ev-er-after, as there was always a home and a family for the soldier to return to; an aphorism that would remain true until the mid-1960s.

While the years after 1945 brought about a positive visual reconceptual-ization of the place of the man in the home, in contrast the representation of the lost father is indicative of a very different shift in visual culture as a consequence of the War. In Stalinist portrayals of the absent father, one finds some small space that allowed for the expression of sentiments that did not usually sit comfortably within the Socialist Realist ethos and, along with other earlier works that centered on the bereaved mother, allowed for a very limited acknowledgment of the bodily and emotional cost of victory, as for the first time one sees the treatment of death, bereavement, and loss in Soviet art. Such representations of the consequences of war not only further complicate our perception of Soviet visual culture during this period, but also underline the complexities of Soviet culture more generally when it came to dealing with what Anna Krylova termed "inappropriate themes."[98]

Unlike the emotional rawness found in literature and later in film, what one sees in visual culture is intimation. While the father may be absent from post-war scenes of family life, the reason behind this absence, or the psychological or material consequences of this absence, were never articulated, either in the paintings themselves or in the official comment made about them. As such, we are left to read between the lines and to interpret oblique references made in the canvases of artists like Reshetnikov and Laktionov in a manner that was never part of the contemporary discussion of these works but was surely a way in which they were intended to be—and were—viewed. Still, despite their constraints, the fact remains that even under Stalin works that dealt with both the implicit and explicit legacy of the War were not only produced but were also reproduced on the pages of the popular press, and the figure of the father played a crucial part in this small acknowledgment of the toll that the War had taken on the Soviet people.

# 5

# FATHERHOOD AFTER FATHER STALIN

## Representing Paternity and Domesticity in the Khrushchev Era

As a response to letters from its readers that expressed concern about family life, in December 1960 the newspaper *Izvestiia* launched a new feature entitled "*Izvestiia* in the Family Circle" with the aim of exchanging news and views on "morality, ethics and various questions on public life. [...] The world outlook of the Soviet man. His ethical principles, production and the family, labor and rest, the rearing of children in the family—the cell of Communist society."[1] The issue of domesticity and home life was at the center of Khrushchevist concerns. The processes of de-Stalinization, the massive housing project, and the rapidly advancing world of science and technology all combined to revitalize interest in Soviet citizens' private lives, how they spent their time away from work, how their homes were furnished, and how their families functioned. As Victor Buchli surmised, "If the Stalinist state was poised at the threshold of the 'hearth,' the Khrushchevist state walked straight in and began to do battle."[2]

Homes and housing have been of particular interest for scholars of the Khrushchev era in recent years, something that is not surprising given the scale of the Khrushchevite housing project and the subsequent infamous reputations of the *Khrushchoba*, the five-story apartment blocks that sprang up around the Soviet Union's major cities in the late 1950s.[3] As such, it has become well-established that, as in the high Stalin era, the home was a vital space when it came to shaping the ideal Soviet citizen, and that the technological and progressive dimensions of the Soviet home were tangible evidence of the continued march toward communism. The biggest difference was now that the home was also a key battlefield in the program of de-Stalinization, as taste and home decoration became increasing wrapped up in issues to do with morality and the correct worldview.[4] Although much of the literature that discussed decoration and creating a comfortable and cozy space for one's family was aimed at a female audience, the state's interest in the home and the family was not something that only had implications for women.[5] This was also a period that revolutionized how men were represented, as the seeds that had been sown in the aftermath of the War came to fruition, and for the first time in the whole of the Soviet period, the role of father became absolutely integral to the visual representation of the New Soviet Man.

This chapter will explore how the depiction of paternity in print culture continued to develop after 1953. As we have already seen, the War had an enormous impact on how men were depicted both within the home and in their relationship with their children, and while the events of the early 1940s may have been the spark that caused this shift, it was by no means a trend that ceased with the death of Stalin; in fact, the changes seen in the representation of paternity after 1953 were arguably even more radical than those that came before. It was in the years of the Thaw that the portrayal of fatherhood finally shook off the remnants of the military subtext that had previously dominated and became more varied in its presentation of the paternal role, both in terms of actual behaviors and in terms of the genres of visual culture that examined the interaction between the Soviet man and his children. Men were seen to have a role to play in the lives of their offspring right from birth and, rather than being the staid figure of the Stalin era, were shown to be actively and emotionally engaged in raising their children. Just as the War had fundamentally changed how the father was presented in the 1940s and early 1950s, so it would seem that the death of Stalin and the destruction of the symbolic paternity of the personality cult would profoundly alter the portrayal of fatherhood in the decade that followed.

## SOVIET MEN AND THE DOMESTIC SPACE

The housing policy launched by Khrushchev in 1957 transformed Soviet dwellings, creating 230 million new apartments by the end of the Brezhnev era and doubling the amount of living space for each Soviet citizen over the same period.[6] New settlement and housewarming became, at least theoretically, a rite of passage for the postwar generation. This discourse of the new— new beginnings, new living, new society, new morality—permeated the visual culture of the period, most evocatively captured by Iurii Pimenov's *Wedding on Tomorrow Street* (*Svad'ba na zavtrashnei ulitse*, 1962), which depicted a newly married couple walking along a makeshift path through a construction site for new apartments.[7] The watery blue sky, blurred forms, and unfinished, impressionistic style of Pimenov's work, along with the scene itself that was one of explicit progression toward a brighter future, embodied the spirit of a society in the process of being made anew. The theme of construction and house building would become a dominant motif in the visual culture of the Thaw and can be seen as tied to both de-Stalinization and the resettlement of young families as part of the Virgin Lands Scheme. But while men may have been presented as the builders and inhabitors of homes, as far as visual culture was concerned, there was no active role for them in the homes' furnishing, decoration, or upkeep.[8]

There is no doubt that ever since the Revolution, the Soviet man had been an awkward presence in the domestic space: largely absent for most of the 1920s and a very infrequent presence in the 1930s, by the time he found a place in the home through the visual culture of the late 1940s, it was intimately tied to his position as a father and wrapped up with issues to do with postwar normalization and the restoration of society. If the domestic space was generally problematic for the Soviet state, then the role of the man within that space, and how that related to the ongoing problem of total female liberation, was a particularly thorny issue. The development of domestic technologies during the course of the 1950s complicated the matter even further as the home and homemaking stopped being a feminine domain and instead became associated with professionalism, science, and modernity. The nexus of this struggle between the private and the public within the home itself was the kitchen, as the burgeoning debate on microbes, technology, and kitchen design transformed this space into one that could showcase the latest Soviet technological achievements.[9] The introduction of shiny new domestic appliances and rational design theory masculinized the kitchen, yet these developments did not pave the way for increased male participation in household chores. Indeed, as Susan Reid has highlighted, rather than make the kitchen a more appealing space for the Soviet man, the introduction of modern equipment and ideas only served to underline the distinct gendering of domestic labor as "both the discourse of modern Soviet living and the actual, built form of housing in the Khrushchev era, reconfirmed the individual family home as a site of reproductive labor, and the housewife as its isolated, unpaid workforce."[10]

Drawing on readers' letters to the women's magazines *Rabotnitsa* and *Krest'ianka*, Lynne Attwood has also drawn attention to the continuation of "traditional" gendered divisions of labor within the home during the Khrushchev era. While some correspondents hinted at an increased willingness on the part of their husbands to participate in the drudgery of housework, others reported that their spouse's efforts were met with ridicule from neighbors and friends. As one woman commented:

> Seeing my husband bustle around the kitchen, some of our male neighbors have begun to mock him, saying he does "women's work," which they say is unseemly for a man. [...] I think that if a man sometimes prepares food, this does him proud. [...] We do not laugh at women if they do what is seen to be male work. [...] We respect her for it. So why is it shameful for a man to help his wife with housework and childcare?[11]

Even so, despite the exasperation of some contributors regarding the persistence of the "double burden," the rhetoric was geared toward getting men to help with household duties, rather than take on their fair share of the responsibility; the tasks of taking out rubbish or fetching water were often presented as suitably masculine, while a man who cooked or cleaned warranted special praise.[12] The debate regarding men and the home was not just confined to the pages of women's magazines either: in a poll carried out by *Komsomol'skaia pravda* in December 1961 entitled "Emancipate Whom: Men or Women?," one male respondent retorted that "it seems to me that it will soon be necessary to speak of the 'emancipation' of men. [...] The husband takes the child to the kindergarten and brings him home, he goes to the store and minds the child. [...] In my opinion, it is time to stop shouting about helping women."[13] One of the questions posed as part of this survey was "which of the following would be the most important in eliminating the vestiges of woman's inferior position in everyday life?" with one of the possible responses being "participation of husband and children in the management of the household": this was not seen as a solution by any of the respondents whose comments were published in the paper in the coming days, with male involvement in household tasks being seen as of minor importance when compared to government initiatives.[14]

Given the lack of clarity and consensus that abounded regarding what role the man should play within the home, it should not come as a surprise to discover that representations of the Soviet male participating in household chores were very rare indeed. During the Stalin era, aside from one or two photographs that showed the man of the house carrying out simple DIY tasks such as hanging pictures, in practically every image—whether that be photograph, painting, poster, or illustration—the man within the domestic space was not shown to be an active constructor of the home in terms of making it aesthetically pleasing, comfortable, or even just keeping it clean and tidy; rather, he was there solely as a father. Little changed after 1953: the only genre that grappled with the issue of male participation in housework was the cartoon, both those published in the mainstream press and those found on the pages of the satirical magazine *Krokodil*. Still, even though this was a new development in the 1950s, such images were not commonplace, largely appearing around International Women's Day (March 8), and were consistently based on the supposition that the combination of men and housework was a recipe for disaster.

The template for these cartoons was quickly established with a multi-paneled image depicting a husband attempting to do the laundry and only succeeding in filling the apartment with suds, published in *Sovetskaia zhenshchina* in 1958, being one of the first to exploit this new area of humor.[15] With a slightly different premise, in another cartoon from March 1965, a group of men are shown marching in formation through the street bedecked in a uniform of floral aprons and wielding an array of household appliances, as the women watch on from a dais in a parody of the military marches that took place on Red Square. Here male participation in household duties is endowed with a certain sense of heroism, as if these men were off to face their mortal enemy rather than a bit of dust and some dirty dishes![16] Still, like the cartoons that played upon male incompetence, the idea is clearly articulated that this was an aberration, an event that was not part of the normal rhythms of family life. This notion that the Soviet man was like a fish out of water when it came to housework is a sentiment echoed in the short stories and feuilletons these magazines also published, which repeatedly presented the Soviet man as "powerless over the domestic space—set up by women and crammed with 'feminine' objects or new-fangled furnishings that either suffocate or befuddle them."[17] Interestingly, though, while grown men tended to be shown failing miserably at even the most basic task, young boys excelling at housework can be found in a couple of posters—such as in N. Vigilianskaia and F. Kachelaev's image from 1957 in which a boy is shown drying dishes with his mother and sister in the kitchen[18]—and are representative of the idea espoused in pedagogical literature of the period that stated children's participation in chores was essential for teaching them independence and a solid work ethic.[19]

With regard to the representation of men and housekeeping, one other set of images is worth considering, and that is the portrayal of men carrying out domestic chores outside of the domestic space. In the interviews Attwood conducted as part of her investigation into the gender confusion of the Thaw period, a mother of eleven spoke of how her boys were mocked by friends for doing laundry, and in response to this taunting, the boys questioned their pals' self-sufficiency, retorting that the partisans had done their own laundry during the War.[20] Thus what could be dismissed as "women's work" was given a new, almost heroic, status when being performed by men outside of the home and linked to ideas of survival. While not as extreme as the hardships of war, this idea of having to survive in harsh conditions and without the comforts of home was one that was once again pertinent in the days of resettlement in the uncultivated regions of Kazakhstan and Siberia, as can be seen in Raisa Galitskii's *Love Is Not a Potato* (*Liubov'—ne kartoshka*, 1954) and Igor Kabanov's *Young Life* (*Zhizn' molodaia*, [1955–59?]), two paintings that depict a couple in the process of making a meal together.[21] Unlike the cartoons where men were derided for their shortcomings in this area—which usually resulted in smoke-filled kitchens and burnt pots—in these works the task of preparing food, in the fresh air and on a primitive stove, is portrayed as part of the exciting pioneer way of life on the Virgin Lands and as such is largely stripped of gendered connotations.[22]

While the emergence of cartoons that at least jokingly acknowledged many men's inadequate participation in housekeeping and the few representations of Virgin Landers involved in domestic chores are significant developments in their own right, there can be no denying that the artistic vision for the man within the home was very limited. As it had been during the late Stalin era, then, the primary role for the Soviet man in the home was as a father: the difference would be that during the Thaw the father would be portrayed with a frequency, range, and potency that was unprecedented.

## DE-STALINIZING PATERNITY

The idea of the paternalistic state was on shaky ground after the revelations of Khrushchev's speech in 1956, and the Thaw period's concern with a return to Leninist ideals can in many ways be seen as symptomatic of this: in denouncing the Stalinist "deviation," the fraternal values of the revolutionary period once more became the basis of Soviet society. And yet, with the rejection of the symbolic father, it would appear that the space was created for a more polyvalent vision of real paternity to be established, one that extended beyond the limited parameters of the immediate postwar period, which at last included the emotional dimension that had to date been largely absent from Soviet conceptualizations of fatherhood.

In her work on private life and morality under Khrushchev, Deborah Field situates the increased emphasis on the parental role that emerged after the death of Stalin within the new populist approach to politics formulated after 1953, arguing that this form of government "required hardworking, disciplined, active citizens [and that] mothers and fathers, taking on the distinct responsibilities deemed appropriate to each gender, had a major role in producing these citizens."[23] The years between 1954 and 1956 saw a wide-ranging public debate on the reform of the 1944 Family Code, which culminated in the re-legalization of abortion and the abolition of the "bachelor tax," the higher rate of taxation paid by all single men and any childless couple. The pragmatic 1944 code, devised at a time of war and expected demographic crisis, had further disengaged men from the family unit through the fact that they were no longer financially responsible for any illegitimate offspring, while the paternal state bestowed numerous honors on fecund mothers, regardless of their marital status. However, by the mid-1950s a discourse had emerged that centered upon the rights of unmarried mothers, fatherless children, and the morality of eliminating alimony for children born out of wedlock. The existing family code came to be perceived as at odds with the values of marital stability and a stumbling block in achieving the full liberation of women.[24] Seen as part of a wider return to Leninist values, the rhetoric surrounding the reform of the existing legislation repeatedly asserted an equal responsibility for child-raising between two parents,[25] although this desired ideal of domestic harmony was one that was sorely tested by a 270 percent increase in divorce rates in the years between 1955 and 1965.[26]

With the partial reform of the Family Code and the announcement of an expansion of the boarding school system at the Twenty-First Party Conference, the debates over the role of parents versus the state in children's upbringing and the idea of the communist family continued to rage on the pages of the Soviet press. The opposing views propounded in the work of the academician Stanislav Strumilin and that of sociologist Anatolii Kharchev during the early 1960s were demonstrative of the continuing lack of consensus as to the perfect blend between the private and public when it came to family life. Strumilin's controversial article "The Worker's Everyday Life and Communism," which was published in *Novyi Mir* in 1960, echoed many older revolutionary ideals about the benefits of communal child-raising and the evils of the bourgeois institution of marriage:

> Communal forms of upbringing have an unquestionable superiority over all others. [...] Every Soviet citizen, upon leaving the maternity home, will be sent to a nursery, from there to a kindergarten maintained day and night. [...] The former family is reduced to the married couple [...] and when these contracted families recognize that it is not sensible to expend so much work on maintaining an independent household just for two people, the family [...] will dissolve within the context of the future social commune ...[27]

In contrast, Kharchev extolled the unique virtues of the parent/child relationship, a view that seemed to be in line with the majority of public opinion, not least of all that of the Soviet leadership; as Khrushchev explained in his report to the party in 1961, "The family will grow stronger under communism [...] family relations will become pure and lasting."[28]

The year 1961 marked the apotheosis of the state's concern over parenting and the inculcation of a new morality, with the introduction of the *Moral Code of the Builder of Communism* at the Twenty-Second Party Congress. This was a code that intertwined private and public responsibilities, was founded upon correct personal conduct and the obligation to the collective, and stated there should exist a "mutual respect in the family and concern for the upbringing of children."[29] Although it was made clear, then, that both parents had a role to play in the raising and socialization of children, at the same time these roles were distinct and definitely not interchangeable. Mothers were responsible for caring and nurturing in the early years and, later, for the more social aspects of *kul'turnost'*, such as manners and etiquette, while fathers were granted no role in the initial phase of an infant's life but were to be in charge of discipline and the intellectual and cultural elements of *kul'turnost'* once the child reached an appropriate age. In one description of these perfect family dynamics, the father was hardworking and socially engaged while still finding the time to participate in household activities and to teach his son woodwork, thus creating the ideal blend between his private and his public obligations, which were after all both geared toward the same end of strengthening the Soviet collective. Generally, though, while advice for concerned mothers proliferated, when it came to outlining the obligations and responsibilities of a good father, the emphasis was on his duty not to be a workaholic, alcoholic, or physically abusive, rather than paternity being constructed in more positive terms.[30]

For all the Soviet man might have been an infrequent presence in scenes of family life up until the 1940s, when it came to representing the father, there was an important precedent that had been set in the 1920s, and that was his use in the anti-alcohol campaigns of the era. The link between alcohol abuse and the family in a Russian context was by no means a Soviet invention, as one can see from Vladimir Makovskii's painting *Don't Go!* (*Ne pushchu!*, 1892), which depicted a desperate woman and her child trying to prevent their breadwinner entering a tavern and which was reproduced in *Ogonek* in late 1953 accompanied by a review from the great nineteenth-century art critic Vladimir Stasov, who referred to the scene as a "frightful and terrible tragedy."[31] Similarly, in the posters produced during the 1920s, it was the family and especially the children who were seen to be the victims of a man's drunkenness, whether this was through the frittering away of wages on drink, the exposure of young children to alcohol, or the threat of physical abuse.[32] It was a motif that still found expression in the 1950s, as can be seen in Iraklii Toidze's poster from 1956 *A Drunken Father Is the Grief of the Family* (*P'ianyi otets—gore sem'i*), which was reproduced in the parenting journal *Sem'ia i shkola* later that year,[33] and less explicitly in Sergei Grigorev's painting *He's Come Back* (*Vernulsia*, 1954), which depicted the return of an alcoholic man to the family home.[34] In contrast to the repeated association of poor fathers with drink, it would not be until the 1960s that images that dealt with other negative behaviors, such as physical violence or being too often absent from the home, began to appear, and even then they were confined to the cartoons of *Krokodil* and were few and far between.[35]

In the main, then, according to contemporary pedagogues, aside from avoiding harmful behaviors that would impact upon the health and well-being of a child, a father's primary responsibilities were to keep order and to help his offspring develop intellectually.[36] This, of course, was not a rhetoric that was new in the 1950s: as part of the renewed focus on the family during the 1930s, the father had come to be seen as instrumental in the education and cultural development of the next generation, as for the first time being a good father became intrinsically tied to being a good Soviet citizen. While this ideal did not find an outlet in visual culture before the War, after 1945 with the huge development in the representation of the Soviet father, there was one genre that repeatedly drew upon this ideal, and that was photography. Unlike paintings, which continued to be rather emotionally one-dimensional and focused on the wartime context, the photographs published in these popular magazines often depicted proactive fathers engaging with their children—teaching them how to play the piano or how to ski, reading to them, or partaking in a spot of gardening together. While the frequency with which such photographs appeared should not be overstated—as was discussed in the previous chapter, one is dealing with fairly small numbers even though that is a great deal more than what had gone before—they do present a different vision of fatherhood from what can be found in more traditional artistic formats, and that was one rooted in this idea of passing on skills, of educating, and of inculcating a suitable socialist morality in the youth of the nation. As the subtext of the War was not explicit in such images, we also find many more depictions of fathers interacting with their daughters, as opposed to the father-son bond that tended to be held above all others in the more war-themed works. Of course, the postwar context cannot be discounted altogether for, while these men may not be wearing the uniforms of the fathers in the paintings, each photograph was implicitly based on the premise that these men who had served their country had returned to resume family life unaltered by their experience. Still, although the fathers that populated the photographs of the era were more dynamic and varied than their painted counterparts, even here men were not shown to have an independent relationship with their infant children, as emphasis was placed on the family unit as a whole, often with the interaction between mother and child taking center stage.

However, the years immediately following the death of Stalin saw two important changes in how the father was depicted visually. First of all, the image of the proactive and engaged father broke free from the confines of photography to become a legitimate subject for a whole range of media, including painting, and secondly, this active father became a presence in the life of his child right from birth. Why there was such a shift in how men and their relationship with their children was portrayed around 1955 is open to interpretation, as the essence of that relationship was relevant to a whole range of issues that were at the heart of Khrushchevite society—family sta- bility, new life, reconstruction, and resettlement in the Virgin Lands to name but a few. But anxieties over high divorce rates, what really went on behind closed doors, the morality of the next generation, and the achievement of socialism were hardly products of the Thaw, and yet this was the first time that these concerns found expression through the bond between a father and his child. As such we are left with the question of why now—what change had occurred that prompted the Soviet father to emerge as such a powerful visual presence during the Khrushchev era? Given the fact that this shift occurred prior to any changes in family policy or the introduction of any of the grand schemes—such as the housing construction project or the cultivation of the Virgin Lands—that would subsequently impact how family life was presented visually, it is hard to attribute this change to anything other than the death of Stalin. No longer shackled by the symbolic paternal power of the state, it would appear that after 1953 biological paternity was liberated, allowing the Soviet father to be represented in ways and with a frequency that was entirely unprecedented.

Given this, it is rather ironic that one of the genres that embodied this shift toward an emotionally accessible and active father figure came in the form of the resurrected Leninist leader cult. The only character with enough weight to counteract the paternalistic personality cult of Stalin, the cult around Lenin was revived with an enthusiasm and energy that had been lacking in the original, rather funereal, movement, epitomized by the move in January 1955 from commemorating Lenin's death to celebrating his birth.[37] With this shift came a pronounced change in presentation of the relationship between Lenin and the Soviet child, a relationship that had been an integral part of the cult since its inception in the years after 1924.[38] This new version of the cult drew upon a more explicitly paternalistic discourse, in which illustrations of Lenin found in the popular press depicted him sledging, listening to chil- dren read, or, in photographic form, walking hand in hand with his nephew

Viktor through the estate at Gorki.[39] However, the first artistic representations of this new relationship between the leader and child actually predates the death of Stalin, appearing in the form of pencil sketches by N. N. Zhukov in 1953's New Year edition of *Ogonek*.[40] These simple images show Lenin and Krupskaia with children around a Christmas tree and are representative of the very different presentation of the bond between Lenin and the youngest generation than those that had come before: no longer a godlike figure to be emulated and adored from on high, Lenin was presented in these sketches as a tangible presence in the lives of children, an affectionate and surprisingly human character. Zhukov's sketches may have been produced in the Stalin era, but their new paternalistic portrayal of Lenin proved to be enduring: aside from appearing in *Ogonek* in 1953, they were also published in the January edition of *Rabotnitsa* that same year and would go on to be used to mark the ninetieth anniversary of his birth in 1960 by once again being reproduced in *Ogonek*, this time as the back cover, and also by being turned into a stamp. To mark the start of the new year in 1970, Zhukov's sketches would take pride of place on the front cover of *Ogonek*, demonstrating both the longevity of their appeal and the centrality of the Lenin-child relationship in this new revived version of his cult.[41]

Running alongside such representations of the Soviet leaders, paternity also emerged as a key strand in the construction of the all-Soviet hero. As with the use of paternalism in the cult of Lenin (and to a much lesser extent in that of Khrushchev), this was not a rebranding of what had existed under Stalin, in which the father-child relationship had taken on a more metaphorical quality; rather, this was the actual biologically grounded paternity of the Soviet hero. Not just defined by their public persona, these men now frequented the pages of magazines in the role of an active and engaged father, as typified by the numerous spreads on Yuri Gagarin in the years after 1961. While he was undoubtedly the greatest hero of the Khrushchev era, Gagarin was not alone in being portrayed as a father as well as intrepid explorer of the final frontier, as other cosmonauts such as Valerii Bykovskii, and celebrities such as world record high-jumper Valerii Brumel' and, slightly earlier, the Olympic swimmer Petr Skripchenkov were also featured alongside their children.[42] Given his status within society, it is not surprising that photographs of Gagarin were published with some regularity in the short period between his historic flight in April 1961 and his untimely death in March 1968; what is perhaps surprising is the number of times these photographs prioritized his role as a family man rather than emphasizing his exploits in space.

While he was often pictured with his one or both of his daughters—as is seen on the front cover of *Sovetskaia zhenshchina* in June 1961, in the anniversary edition of *Ogonek* from April 1962, and in *Rodina*'s feature on the cosmonaut from April 1964, for example—it is the coverage following his death that is particularly revelatory when it comes to assessing the status of the father in post-Stalinist society.[43] In April 1968, in the same issue that gave extensive

FIGURE 5.1. Yurii Gagarin and His Daughters, *Rodina* 2, 1966. Reproduced courtesy of Sputnik.

coverage to his funeral, *Ogonek* published Gagarin's last interview, given just three days before his death, in a spread that was full of candid images of the family, some of which had been taken by Gagarin himself. Of all the images that could have been chosen to celebrate this man's life and achievements, it was a full-page black-and-white photograph of Gagarin and his daughters that closed both the piece and the issue as a whole.[44] Meanwhile in May 1968, *Rabotnitsa* marked Gagarin's death by publishing an article he had written on the cosmonaut Valentina Tereshkova, but rather than include any images of the first woman in space herself, it was a sweet snap of Gagarin being kissed on the cheeks by Elena and Galina that illustrated the feature.[45] What one sees in the visual presentation of Gagarin, and on a much smaller scale with other Soviet celebrities, is how his portrayal as a good family man, and especially as a caring and attentive father, only served to elevate his already stratospheric status: despite his public commitments, here was a man who still had time to read to his children, to play games with them, and to be involved in their lives. Crucially, with its balance between the public and the private, the image of Gagarin provided a model of fatherhood that was, at least in theory, achievable by all men and was a world away from the distant, mythical paternal heroes of the Stalinist past.

## "HELPS YOU WORK, REST AND PLAY": PARTICIPATORY PATERNITY, 1955–64

In December 1961, in a double-page spread showcasing some of the works at that year's All-Union Art Exhibition, *Ogonek* reproduced two paintings that presented two very different images of Soviet masculinity: Stanislav Shinkarenko's swarthy furnace workers and Anatolii Levitin's young father whose peace had been disturbed by his playful son.[46] As early representations of the Soviet father in the immediate postwar period had, by and large, retained a wartime subtext, while they were groundbreaking in their own right, they were still very limited in terms of the vision of fatherhood that they presented. In contrast, during the late Stalin years, photography offered a more interactive and diverse view of fathers' relationships with their children, but still these images were almost exclusively focused on interactions that could be collectively thought of as developing a child's *kul'turnost'*—in true Soviet style, the focus was very much on things that were productive. It is not until after 1953, then, that we begin to find fathers presented in visual culture who are engaged in activities other than educating their offspring. This is not to say that the idea of the father as an integral aspect in the development of a child's morality and behavior lost its resonance in the early years of the Thaw; indeed, works such as Dmitrii Mochal'skii's *New Settlers* (*Novosel'*, 1957), which depicted a father reading to his small child in their new home on the Virgin Lands, drew explicitly on the educational role of the father, as it became a subject area for painters as well as photographers.[47] The main difference is that, in addition to these more traditional and developmental activities, after 1953 we also begin to find images of men across a range of genres presented as doing little more than spending time with their children.

In the poll about the emancipation of the sexes that *Komsomol'skaia pravda* carried out in December 1961, one young female respondent offered the following opinion:

> The most miserable spectacle is the bored young father sitting in the garden on Sunday with his children in his arms. He is twenty-two or twenty-three and he would like to be hiking with geologists along the Angara [River] with a knapsack on his back, or else he would like to go to the library or skating rink, but instead he sits sweating as he performs the duties of an exemplary father.[48]

For this woman, fatherhood was something that stifled men rather than enriching their lives, as in her view the New Soviet Man should be off exploring nature or pursuing intellectual inquiries, not constrained by the monotony of childcare. While for this correspondent the sight of men out and about with their children was a cause for dismay, the fact that the relationship between father and child was no longer centered on the home was one of the defining features of portrayals of paternity in the Khrushchev years, as fathers and their children were presented as enjoying time at the beach, in the park, or at public events. Levitin's painting is a case in point: here is a work that is completely devoid of any idea of productive leisure time or *kul'turnost'* but rather represents a family relaxing together. With a play in the title *They Need Peace*, a common slogan from the antiwar movement in the early 1950s, Levitin depicts the parental desire for quiet in contrast to their young son's desire for fun and games with his father, while at a time of heightened Cold War tensions also offers a meditation on the potential impact of war on families such as this. In a brief review published in *Iskusstvo* a few years later, N. Volkov had little to say about the subject of the painting, other than it depicted "young, strong [and] beautiful people," and instead was more concerned about the artist's use of light and the application of the paint to capture the greenness of a meadow and the real weight of a man's body.[49] This concern with the true representation of nature and the artistic use of light was typical for the period and can be seen as a reaction against the stultifying constraints and artifice of Stalinist Socialist Realism.[50] But while an obsession with the outdoors was part of Khrushchevite culture, and while such representations of fathers could be viewed as part of this wider trend, the fact that the father was now a focus for works that explored the realm beyond the home arguably has a greater significance than merely being characteristic of a momentary artistic interest. The range and frequency of what can be found in visual culture from this period is also too great to be attributed to developments in the fine art world alone, but rather is suggestive of a much greater shift in the status of the father within Soviet society and also the place of paternity within the model of the New Soviet Man.[51]

As part of their *Family* triptych, Aleksei and Sergei Tkachev produced two paintings that took the father-child relationship as their central theme. In *In Peaceful Fields* (*Na mirnykh poliakh*, 1964), the father and the child on his shoulders are the central figures in a depiction of a family (husband, wife, child, and grandparents), whereas the other work, *Father* (*Otets*, 1964), portrays a man in the process of constructing his family's new home, alone with his two small children.[52] In his article in *Iskusstvo*, after praising the vibrancy

FIGURE 5.2. Aleksandr & Sergei Tkachev, *Father*, 1964.

of the Tkachevs' work, Vladislav Zimenko then briefly turned his attention to the narrative of *Father*. The key question for the critic was what had caused the young man's daughter to grab hold of him so fiercely and why the father looked so concerned—was it because he was separated from his wife, was it a general fear for the peace of the world, or was he thinking about the future happiness and well-being of his children?[53] Zimenko could be accused of being overly pessimistic in his interpretation of this work—what he describes as a haggard face weighed down by serious thought appears to be the face of a man gently smiling because of the affection he is receiving from his child, and the view that he and his wife may be separated is surely undermined by the fact that he is in the process of building a new home. However, as with Levitin's earlier work, the idea that the father and child relationship offered a poignant reminder of the cost of war for Zimenko demonstrates how embedded that motif had become in the years since 1945.

While the narrative of the piece may be open to interpretation, it is clear to any viewer of this work by the Tkachevs that the man at the center of it is in fine physical condition, something that is typical of many of the paintings from this period that included the father. Of course, right from the early days of the Revolution, the Soviet man was presented as a perfect physical specimen, but the physicality of specifically the father figure had been of negligible significance in his early representations in the domestic space; underneath the bulk of a uniform, it was something that was insinuated, rather than health and fitness being an explicit part of how the male body was presented in these scenarios. As the portrayal of the Soviet father moved from being based on the soldier to being based on the worker, there was a new emphasis on the corporeality of the Soviet man, as demonstrated by the toned physique of Levitin's father and the strong arms of the protagonists of the Tkachevs', Valentina Shebasheva's, and Andrei Tutunov's work (discussed below). Whether at home, at leisure, or in some cases still engaged in manual labor, these paintings seem to underline the idea that had influenced Soviet rhetoric on women and work since the early days of the Revolution—it was possible to be a worker, a provider, and a caring and attentive parent.

It is at this point, for the first time since the introduction of the father into the domestic space after 1945, that the conceptualization of the Soviet father in fine art and that presented in photography, cartoons, and illustrations were finally in synchrony, as across the range of media Soviet fathers came to be consistently represented as active, accessible, and present at each stage of their child's life. Nothing illustrates this alignment more clearly than two editions of *Sovetskaia zhenshchina* published in the middle of 1956: in the space of these two months, the magazine published Anatolii Lutsenko's *The Firstborn of the*

*New Settlers* (*Pervenets u novoselov*, 1955) and Gelii Korzhev's early work *On Leave from the Construction Site* (*So stroiki v otpusk*, [1956?]), which showed a young father returning home and embracing his small child, and featured a short story, "Ordinary Guys" ("Obyknovennye rebiata"), which told the tale of Iurii Sablin and the birth of his son Mishka. Illustrated by Petr Pinkisevich, the final image of the story was the proud new father, out with his friends, pushing his newborn son in a pram.[54] From paintings created by some of the country's leading artists to simple illustrations, by the mid-1950s the idea that the father was a real presence in the family home, with an emotional connection to his children that went beyond the inculcation of *kul'turnost'*, was firmly established. It was a trend that would only flourish as the decade progressed.

While published photographs of fathers and their children in the years of Stalinism could almost be counted on one hand, after 1955, in both women's magazines and those aimed at a mixed readership alike, the image of a man interacting with his child was a regular aspect of the Soviet popular press. As if one needed any more indication that fathers were important in Khrushchevite society, in August 1960 the most widely read magazine in the whole country published a photograph of a father with his child on its front cover for the very first time.[55] Images of real men and their children it would seem were everywhere—from the photographs of Soviet celebrities discussed earlier, to those that showed average men playing sports, lounging on the beach, or just relaxing in the company of their baby outside of the home.[56] As with painting, it was not just the number of photographs that were being published at this point, but the range of scenarios they depicted that is most telling: unlike the photographs from the Stalin era, in the main there was often nothing particularly special about what they presented as they were not dominated by the rites of passage such as the birth of a child, moving into a new apartment, or returning from war, as many had been previously, but showed far more normal and often mundane interactions. The representation of the father had stopped being based on the exceptional and, in this idealized vision of the Soviet family, had become an integral part of everyday life.

In addition to this veritable wealth of paintings and photographs, the mid-1950s also saw the development of the portrayal of the father in one other significant genre, and that was the cartoon. As we saw earlier, cartoons were used from about 1958 onward to ridicule male incompetence when it came to housework—although they can hardly be seen as a rallying cry for greater equality between the sexes when it came to domestic labor—and it is around the same time that the figure of the father also emerged as a regular feature of these sketches. There is an important distinction to draw here, though, between the lighthearted cartoons of mainstream magazines and the far more acerbic images of fathers that were published in *Krokodil*. On the pages of *Krokodil* in the late 1950s, negative images of fathers proliferated, mainly as part of the growing public discourse about the "youth problem," which for many was seen to be rooted in poor parenting.[57] The focus would change in the early 1960s as parents came to be portrayed as victims, rather than the perpetrators, of their offspring's lazy and unproductive lifestyle, but generally throughout this whole period, the focus was on problematic parental interactions with adolescents, while humorous but broadly positive cartoons featuring fathers and their younger children were absent. This is different from what is found elsewhere, as the cartoons on the humor pages of *Ogonek*, and those published far less frequently in other magazines, were not as willing to broach the negative family dynamics examined in *Krokodil*; although figures such as the *stiliagi* were ridiculed for their love of fashion and their style of dancing, this was very rarely attributed to overindulgent parenting.[58] Instead the focus remained on fathers' relationships with their young children, as can be seen in cartoons such as that of a child handing over his poor school report to his father at the end of a fishing rod or the pair standing in front of Vasnetsov's *Bogatyri*, with the small boy asking his father if the painting was about cosmonauts.[59] Another earlier cartoon, this time published in *Sovetskii sport*, was a series of six images that told the story of a father who goes out for a hike, leaving his wife and son behind. Later, after struggling to carry his rucksack, he opens it up to find his son hidden away inside it; the final cartoon in the strip shows the father and son striding off purposefully together through the countryside.[60]

Across a whole range of genres, in the years after 1955 the image of the father that is most consistently presented in print culture is one that is proactive, participatory, and out in the public space with his child, although the domestic space was, of course, still important in portrayals of family life. As the context of the War continued to recede, so the range of both scenarios and media diversified, giving rise to a visual conceptualization of paternity that was very different from that which had emerged in the immediate aftermath of 1945. Given that issues to do with homecoming and a return to normality were longer as pertinent in the late 1950s as they had been a decade ago, this does raise questions as to why the figure of the father outlasted these concerns, which had been so fundamental to his earlier representation, and also whether it is correct to see the development of the depiction of the father as an organic development of the roots that had been established back in the 1940s. While it is wrong to completely divorce the portrayal of the father in the Khrushchev era from that which came before, at the same time it is also probably inaccurate to view the expansion and diversification in the representation of the Soviet father after Stalin as an inevitability. Seeing as the origins of this trend lay in the aftermath of war, it seems entirely reasonable to assume that, once the dislocation and disruption to family life caused by this had been replaced by new artistic concerns, the father would once again fade from sight: as has been demonstrated here, quite the opposite happened. As the presence of the man in the domestic space after 1945 became a convenient shorthand for articulating ideas surrounding the restoration of prewar norms and the resumption of family life, so the relationship between man and child in the Khrushchev era was intimately linked to the prevailing concerns of the period—new life, happy childhoods, Soviet morality, and strong family units.

## THE NEW SOVIET MAN AS THE NEW SOVIET FATHER

Of all the different developments already charted through the Khrushchev period in this chapter, arguably the most radical of them all was the strand in the model of participatory paternity that explored the relationship between the Soviet man and his newborn child. Writing as recently as 2012, Iryna Koshulap reiterated a widely held opinion when she stated that "nurturing, child care, and emotional attachment to a baby were never legitimate parts of Soviet hegemonic masculinity";[61] while this may have been true of the revolutionary and Stalin eras, the vision of idealized masculinity offered by visual culture during the years of the Thaw fundamentally challenges this view. In a way, it is unsurprising that images containing babies were so prominent in the visual culture of the Thaw, as after all this was a society focused on new life and regeneration, but after decades of neglect, it is remarkable just how prominently the new father featured in such images. One of the earliest places where this shift in focus is noticeable is in the photo-essays that women's magazines published at regular intervals on the maternity home, the kind of feature that had been a staple of such publications since at least the 1930s.[62] While earlier versions of such articles would focus on health care and technological advancements designed to help women at this stage in their lives, by the mid-1950s such pieces had taken on a more human quality and were now based on interpersonal relationships, both between the child and its parents and between the new parents themselves. Despite being published in magazines designed for female consumption and on a topic seen as central to the female experience, time and again the final image of these spreads was the baby in the father's arms leaving the clinic or coming home to a beautifully decorated and well-appointed apartment, as can be seen in the full-page photograph of the new Shuvalov family arriving at their "bright and comfortable" apartment with baby Viktor, which appeared in *Sovetskaia zhenshchina* in 1954.[63]

But the image of the new father was not confined to either women's publications or just to photographs: the image of the couple leaving the maternity home was also the subject of a number of paintings, such as Boris Lavrenko's *In the Maternity Home* (1954) and, later, Nikolai Ovchennikov's *The Firstborn* (*Pervenets*, 1963), although neither of these works found a place in magazines of the era.[64] However, Anatolii Lutsenko's *The Firstborn of the New Settlers* appeared in both *Ogonek* and *Sovetskaia zhenshchina* in color within a year of its production;[65] a painting that focuses on the congratulatory back-slapping and gift-giving of the men and relegates the women to the background and encapsulated two key concerns of the Khrushchev years—that of new family life and that of new homes. Although, as one sees from works such as that of Lavrenko, and also Valentina Shebasheva's charming *At Home* (1955), which portrayed a young father waking his tiny son in order to bathe him, canvases that centered on the father-infant relationship were being produced in the early post-Stalin era, yet it was not until the housing boom was underway a few years later that reproductions of paintings depicting the father with his baby became more prominent in print culture, and a number of those that were reproduced, like Lutsenko's, blended these two very Khrushchevite preoccupations.

Unlike the earlier works focused on the maternity home, the paintings that juxtaposed new life with new homes drew upon a very familiar model of Soviet masculinity, and that was one that placed the man's status as a worker right at the heart of the image. The association of work with the father was not new of course; it was a motif that was present in the early postwar works such as Plastov's *Threshing on the Collective Farm* (1949) and had formed the narrative basis of paintings such as Korzhev's *On Leave from the Construction Site* a few years later. It is also at the heart of one of the most endearing depictions of the father-child relationship in this period, Andrei Tutunov's 1959 painting *First Steps* (*Pervye shagi*): still wearing his enormous worker's boots, his bare arms muscular, Tutunov's young father is shown helping his small son to take his first steps across a bare wooden floor.[66] Completely devoid of background detail, the canvas is comprised only of these two figures, the solid worker-father, with his feet planted firmly either side of his son's tiny and unsteady body, as Tutunov beautifully juxtaposes the physical strength of the father with the emotional strength of his bond with his child.

*Toward a New Life* (*K novoi zhizni*, 1963) was Aleksandr Basanets's diploma piece from the Kiev State Art Institute, and it was as part of an overview of graduate work from 1963 that his work appeared in both *Ogonek* in June 1964 and in *Iskusstvo* a month earlier.[67] In a manner that is frustratingly typical of the criticism found of such pieces, Koniakhin's review in the journal made no mention of the father in Basanets's painting, focusing only on the rendering of the mother and child, which in his view gave the work a "special lyrical mood."[68] While of course the inclusion of the mother and child was a central part of Basanets's narrative, it is only in examining the relationship between mother, baby, *and* father that we get a sense of the picture as a whole. Standing bare-chested, legs apart, clutching an axe in one hand and a plank of wood in the other, this young man is the epitome of rugged masculinity, shown in a characteristically Thaw-era pose of taking a momentary break from labor, which in this instance gives him the opportunity to gaze upon his newborn child in the arms of his wife who is seated on the timbers of their future home. Another contemporaneous work, Muscovite artist Nikita Novikov's *In the New Home* (*V novom dome*, 1961), which was shown at that year's All-Union Exhibition, similarly combines the romantic and somewhat primitive manliness of manual work and the ability to provide for one's family, in which building a new home was the linchpin that brought these two ideals together.[69] The Tkachevs' *Father* produced a few years later would also be based on the same premise.

As we saw in chapter 1, the Thaw years saw artists from across the Soviet Union turn their attention to the theme of man's struggle with nature—and, of course, man's eventual victory in this battle—and in a way one can see the works of Basanets, Novikov, and the Tkachevs as complementary to the hypermasculine canvases of Agapov, Popkov, and Iltner. Although transferred to a highly domesticated setting, the notion that the land could be, and was being, transformed through Soviet labor was a theme common to both genres, underlined by these men's use of natural building materials and manual labor in a time of prefabrication, cement, and towering cranes. In addition to the theme of the transformative power of labor, it is also possible to view this focus on construction as congruent with the idea that the socialist project was reaching completion. Alongside the works of Basanets, Novikov, and the Tkachevs, Iurii Anokhin's *Spring Is Coming. A Village Is Being Built* (*Vesna idet. Derevna stroitsia*, 1959), Indulis Zarin's *We Have Reached the Rafters* (*U nas uzhe stropila*, 1960), and Nikita Fedosov's *The Construction of a Village on the River Dvina* (*Stroitel'stvo poselka*, 1964) are exemplary of how popular the motif of construction, in particular house building, was during the Thaw period, and are all works that have been interpreted through the lens of completing the building of socialism.[70] However, although the progression toward communism provides a perfectly acceptable interpretation of works such as these, the less metaphorical elements of the resettlement on the Virgin Lands and the replenishment of the Soviet housing stock were also clearly factors that inspired this focus.

When it comes to the representation of the father, though, the Virgin Lands provides an interesting aberration: it would be easy to assume that with its focus on new life and new homes, the Virgin Lands project would provide fertile ground for the representation of the Soviet family, especially considering how it captured the artistic imagination, even after the project itself had proven to be an abject failure. Yet the movement of thousands of young citizens to work and start families in Kazakhstan did not translate into countless scenes of family life on the periphery. While domesticity had a key part to play in how the settlements were presented, the focus of the vast majority of the works that dealt with this aspect of the project focused on the collective experience rather than on the nuclear family. Scenes of groups of young men and women eating together and socializing together, in addition to working together on these new lands, proliferated. In contrast, this research has uncovered only two images—Dmitrii Mochal'skii's *New Settlers* and Boris Vaks's *On Virgin Lands* (*Na tseline*, 1961)—that represented the family, and only Vaks's image of a father and child asleep in a field while the mother watches over them was reproduced in contemporary popular print, albeit on a number of occasions.[71] Similarly, while numerous works showed towns in the process of being built, it would not be until Dmitrii Zhilinskii's triptych *On New Lands* (*Na novykh zemliakh*, 1967) that the link between family life, construction, and the Virgin Lands was made artistically.[72]

Yet, to contain our analysis to the fine art of the Thaw would be to underestimate just how prevalent this motif of the new father and his baby was in the visual culture of the era. In contrast to some of the other genres, photography did not engage with the father-infant relationship quite as much, largely because the focus tended to be on scenes of fathers and children being active together, something that is much harder when dealing with a very small child. Still, in representations of the heroes of the era—Gagarin, Bykovskii, and Brumel', for example—and in representations of average Soviet men, the father and baby relationship was depicted in a manner that was quite different from those early photographs centered on the maternity home. A couple of images showed the father and mother working together to care for their child, as in the celebratory article "Two Hundred Newlyweds!" published in *Ogonek* at the end of 1960, which depicted a young couple attempting to bathe their squirmy baby, and the earlier front covers both of *Rabotnitsa* and *Ogonek*, which presented the young family all together but with the father enjoying the most interaction with his infant.[73] However, what is really telling is that there are photographs that show a father and baby alone, something that we

FIGURE 5.3. Father Pushing Pram in Novorossiisk, *Ogonek* 22, 1964. Reproduced courtesy of Kommersant.

only see in painting in Tutunov's charming little scene. What is also striking is how incidental these photographs seem to be, as they were more often than not candid shots of everyday life rather than the more staged photographs that were also included in such publications; typical examples are a father pushing a pram along a street in a spread on Novorossiisk, an entire page of photographs from Moscow, and the photograph of a man reading a book with his child in a bassinet beside him that was published on the back cover of *Sovetskaia zhenshchina* in March 1965 as part of its 'The World in Which We Live' feature.[74] It was a trend that would continue beyond the Khrushchev years, as in 1970 on the final pages of its number thirty-seven issue, *Ogonek* published eight photographs under the heading "Fathers and Children," which showed men and their children simply going about their lives together.[75] While the depiction of the independent father and infant relationship in photography happened a little later than the general representation of the father-child relationship in becoming commonplace, certainly by the middle of the 1960s visual culture across the board was reinforcing the idea that a father was indeed capable of looking after his young child outside of the home.

When it came to what went on inside the home, though, that was a very different story. In both photographs and many of the paintings of the era, it was uncommon to depict the father as being solely responsible for childcare within the domestic space, and certainly in photographic representations the raison d'être behind such features tended to be either a celebration of a known individual or an event such as moving house, scenarios that by their nature tended to focus on the family as a whole. However, through the cartoons of the era, it is possible to gain insight into perceptions of fathers as primary caregivers to their infant children, and evidence would suggest that while a father being involved in the raising of a child, and certainly partaking in leisure activities together, was viewed as a key part in that child's development, the idea that he would be the one taking care of that child within the home was still a source of amusement. As was discussed earlier, the late 1950s saw the introduction of the man into the home through cartoons that demonstrated his inadequacies, if good intentions, when it came to housework, and in many respects the cartoons that drew upon the father-baby relationship played upon the same premise, which was after all ripe for humorous exploitation.

So we find images such as those of a father attempting to learn how to change a diaper from watching his daughter fasten one on her doll; a father contemplating drying the tears of his screaming child with a laundry mangle; a husband calling his wife in desperation because baby has not eaten the caviar he has tried to feed it; a father trying to placate his screaming child while his wife is at the cinema, and failing miserably; and a father who has been beaten black and blue while trying to feed his feisty son.[76] Although far more common on the humor pages of *Ogonek* generally, it was also in the mid-1960s that the first representation of a father as a primary caregiver appeared in *Krokodil*, and on the front page of the magazine no less. From the state of the apartment, it would appear that this was also the first time that this particular father had been given such a responsibility: pans bubble over on the stove, the lampshades on the ceiling swing back and forth, and the floor is littered with discarded toys, broken crockery, and half-eaten bits of food, and in the middle of this disorder sits the man with his baby in his arms, both of them plaintively calling out "Ma-a-ama!," hoping to hurry the return of the wife and mother still at work.[77] The message of these cartoons was clear: leaving a small child in the care of a man was bound to cause chaos. Interestingly, though, there were a couple of earlier cartoons that depicted the father looking after a child as a negative comment on the attitude of the mother: one that was published in *Krokodil* in 1960 in which the wife berates her husband on International Women's Day for not having lunch ready, while he is shown up to his elbows in soap suds, with laundry hanging from the ceiling, smoke billowing from the pans on the hob, and his son sitting crying on the floor, and another from 1957 in which a father feeding his baby asks him whether he loves mommy or daddy more as the wife, her back turned away from her family, puts the finishing touches to her fashionable outfit, presumably in order to hit the town.[78]

The incompetency of men when it came to childcare within the home is not only in contrast to the overwhelmingly positive representations we find of fathers caring for children outside of the home in other genres, but also stands in contrast to the few cartoons that also situated fathers and their children in the wider world. Although these were scarcer than their domestic counterparts, the cartoon of the father and baby outside the home often rested on notions of pride, rather than inadequate parenting skills, and the motif of the pram-pushing man was the most common way of expressing this. In one such image from a 1964 issue of *Ogonek*, the man's face quite literally radiates as he pushes his triplets in a rocket-shaped contraption, while in the same publication a year later, a cartoon entitled *A Novice* depicts a beaming new father pushing a pram adorned with a giant warning triangle.[79] As this was the only genre to really deal with a man's parental responsibility within the home, cartoons offer a unique insight into the visual construction of paternity during the years of the Thaw. Although there is the added complication of comparing very different kinds of visual culture—primarily because the purpose of a cartoon is to be humorous and by its very nature tends to exaggerate and push the boundaries of reality—what is striking is the ease with which fathers functioned in the public space, playing sports, going to the beach, taking walks, and in some cases taking a break from labor, when compared to the disarray and chaos caused by their attempts at childcare in the private space. That Tutunov's representation of the father and his infant son stands alone as a painted depiction of that relationship within the home underlines just how publicly oriented the vision of paternity was during this time. In contrast to those very early depictions of fathers, which were almost exclusively centered around the domestic space, the fathers of the Thaw were a part of broader society, as fathering was depicted across all genres as a fact of everyday life, not something that was based on a disruption to the norm as had been the case prior to 1953. Yet, while being an active, engaged, and emotionally accessible father was now a key part in what it meant to be a real Soviet man, what images that focused on the domestic space seem to suggest is that when it came to dealing with the more practical aspects of childcare, such as diaper-changing, feeding, and bathing, it was still a case of mother knowing best.[80]

## PATERNITY ON THE PERIPHERY? REPRESENTING FATHERHOOD AFTER 1964

Although 1965 does not hold the same resonance for images of the father as it does for those that took the War as their central concern, after the end of the Khrushchev era there was a distinct change in the way fathers were depicted, particularly in fine art: gone were the optimistic representations of happy families and new life, and in their stead came a series of introspective and melancholic works. This is not to say that the shattering of the myth of a perfect and happy family life was a development of the Brezhnev era: the tensions that could exist within families had found an outlet in painting since the mid-1950s, as epitomized by Grigorev's *He's Come Back*. Sitting beside a toy tea set, where his young daughter had previously been playing, the presence of this man evokes a range of responses from his family, from the palpable resignation of his wife to the anger of his older son, to the fear of his daughter, who hides behind a chair clutching her teddy bear.[81] Similarly, Gelii Korzhev's *They've Gone . . . (Uekhali . . .*, 1955) explored the pain of abandonment felt by a young father, who had been left with little more than a small plastic duck to remind him of his family.[82] Nor did contemporary popular commentary shy away from these less-than-positive works, with *He's Come Back* featuring as a double-page color spread in an April 1954 edition of *Ogonek*, which included reference to some of the comments left by recent visitors to the exhibition where the work was being displayed. From the brief overview offered, these comments seem to be extremely positive, with one visitor calling it "an intelligent and necessary picture" and another from Kiev ending their rhapsodic assessment of the piece with the simple statement "I love this painting." Even V. Klimashin, the author of the piece, felt that "no Soviet viewer will pass indifferently by this acute painting," whose "educational merits [... are] undeniable."[83]

In a different context, the other place where we can find a less-than-ideal vision of the Soviet family is in the cartoons of *Krokodil*. As we saw earlier, cartoons that lambasted the slothful existence of some Soviet youth appeared with a degree of regularity throughout the mid-1950s and into the 1960s, with many of the earlier representations drawing on the notion that bad parenting lay behind these adolescents' lack of productivity and obsession with frivolous things, as can be seen in cartoons such as *At Their Father's Bosom* (*U ottsa za pazukhoi*, 1957), which showed a young man quaffing wine and a young woman applying makeup while cosseted in their father's jacket pockets.[84] This rhetoric would change over the coming years as fathers came to be seen as victims of their children's excesses, as in the case of Shcheglov's cartoon that appeared on the front cover of the magazine in 1965, which showed two young adults holding their father upside down in an effort to empty his pockets of cash. However, the image of the bad father did not disappear completely from these satirical comments on family life. Although nowhere near as common as those cartoons that dealt with the interaction between the "Golden Youth" and their parents, drawings that portrayed the father as physically abusive, disengaged from his child's upbringing, or as a poor disciplinarian all found a place on the pages of this publication.[85]

The depiction of the father in the late 1960s was slightly different from what is found in these negative cartoons: it was not that he was portrayed as a "bad" father per se, but rather that he became a more distant and removed figure, but tellingly still a part of the visual representation of family life. The painting *Family*, also known as *By the Sea* (*Sem'ia*, 1964) is an early example of this trend. Along with Korzhev, Dmitrii Zhilinskii was one of the great artists of the 1960s, and although their style and subject matter is very different, both men demonstrate a concern with the interior life of the Soviet person, bringing a psychological dimension to Socialist Realism that, as we have seen time and again, could often be lacking. Deeply influenced by Renaissance fresco and icon painters, Zhilinskii's work is characterized by its flatness and distinctive use of perspective, and its usually matte coloring, a style that according to the critic Zimenko endowed his paintings with "a polished smoothness and elegance ... a simple but sonorous harmony of tones [... giving] gravity to even modest lyric scenes of everyday life."[86] The protagonists in *Family* are actually Zhilinskii himself, along with his wife, Nina Ivanova Zhilinskaia, and their two children, Dmitrii and Olga, and the scene before us is one of this young family enjoying a day at the coast, along with the numerous other families who populate the jetty behind them. Yet while the painting represents the whole family, Zhilinskii quite literally places the father/himself on a different plane of existence from his wife and children, separated by his position in the water, with his family above on the concrete boardwalk. This is not just a physical distance; the fact that his gaze is out toward the viewer, rather than directed toward his son, who is trying to grab hold of the fish his father has caught, also creates a sense of emotional distance from his wife and children. What appears to be a happy scene of a family on holiday is transformed into a melancholic and lonely scene when viewed through the eyes of the father: indeed, now hanging on the walls of the Tretyakov Gallery, Zhilinskii's painting is described as representing the "disassociation even between people who are close to one another . . . and the tortuous loneliness of modern man."[87]

It would appear that Zhilinskii was not alone in choosing to explore these themes of isolation and displacement through the figure of the father: Viktor Ivanov's *The Birth of Man* (*Rodilsia chelovek*, 1964–69),[88] Andrei Tutunov's *A Fisherman and His Sick Son* (1964),[89] T. Konovalova-Kovrigina's *Morning* (*Utro*, 1967),[90] and Viktor Popkov's *A Family in July* (1969)[91] are all strikingly similar in their tone and compositional techniques, although only Konovalova-Kovrigina's work seems to be have been reproduced at the time. While the father stares blankly out of the canvas in Konovalova-Kovrigina's, Popkov's, and Zhilinskii's paintings, in Tutunov's and Ivanov's canvases, the father is shown with his back turned to the viewer, depriving the onlooker of establishing any real emotional connection with these men. In Ivanov's work, this disconnection is not just with the viewer, as the separation between the man, who sits reading the paper at the table, and his wife, who is completely consumed with breastfeeding her newborn, is at the heart of the piece. In contrast, like his earlier *First Steps*, Tutunov's work appears to show paternal care, although as was highlighted by P. Nikiforov in his critique of the piece, the fact that the father has his back turned from the viewer, and that the child makes no attempt to interact with his father, creates a lack of clarity surrounding the relationship: he wrote, "Does he [the artist] really see humanity in this ill-defined unease, this insecurity, is this how he understands the beauty of the spiritual world of our people?"[92]

In some respects there is nothing extraordinary about works such as those by Zhilinskii and Tutunov: one only needs to look at Korzhev's *Scorched* series, Nikonov's reviled *Geologists*, or the harsh representations of military comradeship that were explored previously to see a significant number of Socialist Realist paintings from this time that offered a very different view from the confident progression of the Soviet man that predominated just a few years earlier. What is interesting in this particular context, then, is not so much that this shift occurred—although of course the significance of this should in and of itself not be underestimated—but that one of the motifs that was repeatedly used by some of the most prominent artists of the era to explore these feelings of uncertainty, isolation, and pessimism was the figure of the father. For some, the emergence of this melancholic father figure is representative of the general atmosphere of the Brezhnev era, one that has come to be defined by economic stagnation and gerontocracy: in her assessment of the representation of paternity in Soviet and post-Soviet film, Helena Goscilo argued that "the impotence of these geriatric leaders [...] surely accounts for the disappearance of virile, influential fathers in various cultural genres from the mid-1950s to the 1990s."[93] As has repeatedly been shown here, the picture painted by visual culture would certainly challenge Goscilo's assessment that the death of Stalin witnessed the end of the positive and vivacious father figure. What is more, it would also appear that the pessimism and uncertainty that one tends to associate with "stagnation" were actually beginning to infiltrate visual culture right at the start of the Brezhnev era—years still traditionally viewed as part of the Thaw—as is evident in the distant fathers of Zhilinskii and his contemporaries. Yet again, through the figure of the introspective father, one can see that the traditional concept of the "Thaw" does not satisfactorily align with the shift in representation we find, nor do the trends evident in visual culture map onto those found in other forms. Like his military counterpart, then, the representation of the father in Soviet visual culture raises broader questions concerning both our traditional periodization and characterization of the Soviet past, and how we think about the uniformity of Soviet cultural production in approaching themes that were resonant across contemporary society.

In our consideration of the visual construction of paternity after Stalin, there is one final set of works to examine, and they take us right back to the place where this book began, to the legacy of the Great Patriotic War. Even the visual culture found in the pages of these popular magazines, which represents only a small proportion of what was produced nationwide, leaves us in no doubt that the events of the War, its social and emotional cost, and issues to do with its remembrance, were a consistent artistic concern, although trends waxed and waned and the brutal honesty of the cost of victory was broached only some years later. At the heart of how visual culture examined the consequences of war were the Soviet people themselves—their experiences at the front and behind the lines, the joy of homecoming, the pain of loss, the physical scars, and the emotional wounds that for some never healed—and for this reason it is entirely logical that the most common motif for exploring this whole gamut of experience was that microcosm of society, the family. When it came to the link between the War and the father after 1953, however, works for the most part were few and far between during the optimistic days of the Thaw, as the inclusion of the father tended to go hand in hand with a focus on new life and new beginnings. The exception to this rule was the emergence of a fairly small number of works that dealt with the theme of leaving for war, which in the late 1950s found expression through the father-child relationship, but by the 1960s had shifted to focus on the pain of separation between husband and wife.[94] The lack of the wartime context and the highly positive portrayals of the father-child relationship in visual culture, though, stands in contrast to contemporary cinema, in which the father was mainly noticeable by his absence. Unlike art, films during the Thaw often retained the War as a subtext for exploring the father-child relationship, as the loss of the father during the conflict was presented as either an explanation for a son's troubled youth and later criminality, or as a motivation for the child's dedication to the Soviet cause.[95] Aleksandr Prokhorov interprets this trend as being intrinsically tied to the process of de-Stalinization, a way to resurrect the heroic memory of lost fathers and divest them of association with Stalin's crimes; as their fathers had given their lives for the state that Lenin had brought into being, so the sons would honor this legacy by completing the socialist project.[96] Alternatively, fathers of Thaw-era cinema were surrogate figures, taking on the responsibility for raising a child that was not theirs— usually one orphaned by the War—and in the process securing that child's future happiness and finding their own redemption, seen most famously in Bondarchuk's *The Fate of a Man*.[97]

By the late 1960s, though, the legacy of the War also began to infiltrate fine art as a new genre emerged that explored the relationship between the different generations and in which the experience of the older generation in the War was the underlying narrative. However, rather than being articulated through the relationship between a father and child, such works took the relationship between the veteran-grandfather and grandchild as their central focus. Why it had taken so long for the War to be conceptualized in generational terms lies in the scale of the conflict. As Stephen Lovell has highlighted, because so many men were called into service, it was not until the ranks of veterans had thinned considerably in the 1970s that it was possible to speak of a "war generation," and it is at this same point that these kinds of paintings begin to be produced.[98] Like so many other works from this era that dealt with the legacy of the War, these representations of grandfathers and grandchildren are full of pathos; this is not a celebration of the freedoms these children now enjoy because of their grandparents' sacrifice, but are often a meditation on the gulf that exists between members of the same family as a result of the war experience, and the weight of memory that the older generation endures. Originally destined for inclusion in his *Scorched by the Fire of War* series, Korzhev's *Anxiety* (*Trevoga*, 1965–68) is typical of such paintings: based on the artist's own daughter and father, here Korzhev depicts a young girl gazing out of the canvas optimistically, while her grandfather, standing behind her still in uniform, looks warily to the west, both seemingly remembering what he saw there and contemplating the possibility of a new conflict on the horizon.[99]

Two decades later in 1985, Korzhev's wounded soldier along with a new work that also included a disabled veteran, entitled *The Clouds of 1945* (*Oblaka 1945 goda*, 1980–85), were shown at a major exhibition in Leningrad to mark the fortieth anniversary of the end of the War. This was an exhibition that brought together old pieces from the war years—such as those of the Kukryniksy, Krivonogov, and Mochal'skii's famous representation of victory on the steps of the Reichstag—with other war-themed work from the intervening years, as well as new works from both established and upcoming artists. Artists who had produced paintings with fathers as their central theme during the 1950s and 1960s, such as Boris Lavrenko, Anatolii Levitin, and the Tkachevs, all had work displayed here—many of them had seen military service and some, like Sergei Tkachev, had returned home with severe injuries. If there was any one motif that characterized the more recent work shown at the exhibition, it was the gulf between the generations as a result of the War, articulated primarily through the relationship between grandfather and child. No fewer than a dozen works displayed at this exhibition conceptualized the War in generational terms, with the vast majority of these using the family to examine the memory and legacy of those terrible years.[100] We have already seen how issues to do with mourning and the lasting emotional consequences of war found expression during the course of the 1960s; in these late Soviet works the link between the family and the war experience that had been a consistent part of visual culture since 1945 reached its logical conclusion as memory, mourning, and triumph found expression, not through the figure of the soldier, but through the Soviet family man.

## SUMMARY

The Great Patriotic War might have brought the Soviet man into the domestic space, but it was in the years of the Thaw that he really flourished. There is no doubt that the 1940s marked a watershed in how the Soviet man was represented, both within the domestic space generally and particularly as a father, but the shadow of the War in the fine art of the day meant that the range of images that were produced was very limited, with the vast majority either drawing on the war experience directly or referencing the father's military service in some way. All of this served to underline the restoration of normality immediately after May 1945: victory was secured, peace had been established, fathers were home, and normal life could resume once again. It is only in the paintings produced by the likes of Fedor Reshetnikov and Aleksandr Laktionov that excluded the father, or in the range of visual material that included Stalin, that we get some sense of the ongoing demographic—if not emotional—consequences of the War. While the events of 1941–45 and their aftermath continued to be of great concern to a significant number of artists during the Khrushchev era, the father, by and large, stopped being a conduit for examining the difficulties of the past and instead was reconfigured to be a positive symbol of new life, regeneration, and the happiness of the next generation of Soviet children. As the specter of the War receded, the range of images that were produced, along with the genres that produced them and the frequency with which they were published, increased dramatically. The fact that this reconfiguration also occurred around the same time as the destruction of the paternalistic personality cult is surely not coincidental: no longer a challenge to the paternal power of the state, with the death of Stalin, real biological paternity could emerge as a potent symbol of the strength of the Soviet family and, with it, Soviet society as a whole.

Perhaps the most significant development with regard to this massive expansion of the visual depiction of the father-child relationship was that it was so frequently taken outside of the domestic space. While this is something that one sees in fine art, it was more prominent in the photographs found in print culture, as the representation of a father spending time with his child shifted from something that was based on an exceptional set of circumstances to simply being part of how one spent one's leisure time. This depiction of the quotidian aspects of parenting—whether this be bathing the child, taking it for a walk, or playing football in the park—can be seen as part of the wider development in post-Stalinist visual culture, in which Socialist Realism moved closer to depicting the realities of Soviet life. Although for the most part visual culture was still very much focused on the ideal and the positive, the willingness to broach some of the more problematic aspects of parenthood through satirical cartoons, and just a handful of paintings, also brought a new dimension to the portrayal of the father-child relationship, as conflict was no longer denied, as it had been in the *Zhdanovshchina*, but found a place amidst the ever-diversifying vision of modern family life.

The Khrushchev era is one that has come to be defined by fatherlessness: the search for new identities among those too young to have fought in the War, the disruption to the dynastic power of the state caused by Khrushchev's denunciation, and the subsequent questions raised about fathers' complicity in the crimes of the state have all been analyzed through the lens of symbolic paternity.[101] This was also a time when many families were still dealing with the far less symbolic destruction of the father, and this combination loss and repudiation of paternal authority is seen to characterize the years of the Thaw. While these issues may have found an outlet in the film and literature of the era, visual culture shows us something very different: it shows us a society populated by men who are present and engaged in their children's upbringing, it shows us strong family units, and it shows us a vision of masculinity in which being a loving and accessible father was absolutely integral to being a New Soviet Man.

# CONCLUSION

May 9, 2015, marked the seventieth anniversary of Victory Day, and it brought with it the largest military parade ever held in Red Square. In addition to the events in Moscow, an estimated twelve million people across the country also took part in the so-called March of the Immortal Regiment, and commemorations and cultural events were hosted by Russian embassies from Addis Ababa to Yangon.[1] The significance of the Great Patriotic War for contemporary Russia is undeniable, and its status in society has only increased in recent years, as it has been co-opted by the Putin regime in an effort to foster a new sense of Russian patriotism, to mobilize the nation's youth, and to bolster the president's own standing, whose biography now places heavy emphasis on his family's suffering during the Leningrad Blockade.[2] It has become, in the words of Olga Kucherenko, a "traumatic experience [that] is passed from generation to generation, [and] every new cohort is implanted with a feeling of guilt and irredeemable debt to their forefathers."[3] Today, as it was in the late Soviet era, the memory of the War is presented as a heady combination of grief, sacrifice, heroism, and the nation's greatest-ever achievement.

For all that the gloss of normalization pervaded the rhetoric of the Stalinist state after 1945, it is undeniable that Soviet society was fundamentally changed by the experience of war, and no amount of vigorous assertions to the contrary could mask this fact. While many people in reality were permanently affected—physically, mentally, and emotionally—by what they had endured during the War, those years also profoundly impacted upon the ideal of the New Soviet Man. In the immediate aftermath of war, this change is seen most pronouncedly in two interrelated genres—the representation of the Soviet soldier at the front and his depiction upon his return home. Scenes of front-line exploits remained a regular part of visual culture even after the War was over, but unlike those produced during the War itself, it was a rarity for any actual fighting to be represented in these post-1945 works as the Soviet soldier moved from being a battle-hardened warrior to a good-natured comrade. The need to celebrate the heroism of the Soviet military man yet not present him as in any way brutalized by war, or indeed a threat to the stability of society now that the fighting was over, was a tricky balance to strike; in the case of the art of the late Stalinist era, it resulted in a vision of military masculinity that was highly romanticized and divested of any suggestion of violence. It was a conceptualization that would outlast Stalin himself, as this overtly sentimental vision of life at the front continued to heavily influence visual culture until those crucial years of the mid-1960s, despite a handful of artists attempting to bring more psychological depth and complexity to how they presented the physical and emotional cost of war after 1953.

Although the challenge that the War posed to the militaristic model of idealized masculinity should not be underestimated, the introduction of the man into the domestic space in the guise of the returning veteran was arguably the most significant development in the visual presentation of the Soviet man. The years of revolution had prioritized the public role of the male in society, which, combined with the paternalistic outlook of the state, had left men completely marginalized when it came to domestic and family life. This started to change in the late 1930s with an increased discourse—if not increased representation—concerning the importance of the father to the Soviet family and flourished with the patriotic rhetoric developed during the War, which cast the Soviet man as fighting to protect those he loved; not just his mother, as is commonly thought, but also his wife and children.

It was not until the War was over, though, that the Soviet man came to be a real and regular presence in the home. Although initially this presence was largely confined to images that depicted the moment of reunion or in some way referenced the father's recent military service, the introduction of the man into the domestic space in the late 1940s fundamentally altered the portrayal of the male social role, as for the first time the notion that the Soviet man had a private as well as public function found visual expression.

In relation to both the representation of the soldier and the returning veteran, however, there can be no denying that the trauma, dislocation, and horrors of the war experience, both at the front and behind the lines, were entirely expunged. At the same time, it would be inaccurate to dismiss the more problematic legacies of the war years as being completely overlooked by the visual culture of this period: limited as they might have been, works that depicted the grief of mothers over lost sons, families where the father was notably absent, and children who found a paternal substitute in the country's leaders all suggest that in some small way the impact of the War on the Soviet people was a part of the visual representation of contemporary society, even though it was often suffused with notions of heroic sacrifice or postwar optimism of new life and material security. In this respect, while the artificial distinction between the War and the domestic space that had been established during the conflict perpetuated in the years that followed, and although these families continued to enjoy private and spacious apartments or cozy family homes, the absence of fathers in some of the most popular works of the period shattered the illusion of lives untouched by the fire of war.

The extremely limited acknowledgment of the cost of war that is found in Stalinist visual culture is in no way surprising: that the artwork of the period is not filled with disabled veterans, destroyed homes, and families teetering on the brink of survival hardly comes as a shocking revelation. What is more surprising is the fact that the hardships of life both during and immediately after the War and the physical and emotional legacy of the war years do not dominate how those years were treated in the art of the Thaw. While a good number of artists—and especially those associated with the Severe Style, such as Gelii Korzhev or Pavel Nikonov—were enthusiastically stripping away the varnished reality that had characterized Socialist Realism to date, this attempt to inject more honesty and truthfulness into the representation of Soviet life by and large did not impact on how the War or its legacies were depicted. In recent years scholars have done great work in highlighting the waves of thaw and freeze and the inconsistencies, continuities, and changes that mark the decade or so proceeding 1953 in a manner that has fundamentally altered how we think of the Khrushchev period and thrown the very idea of the Thaw itself into doubt. The way that the War was handled in the visual culture of this period is entirely congruent with this more complex and contradictory picture that has been painted of the years of de-Stalinization, as time and again across a whole range of war-related genres we find the rearticulation of old and tired Stalinist clichés and only fleeting glimpses of anything approaching a more accurate portrayal of the impact of those devastating years.

Nowhere is this seen more clearly than when it comes to the depiction of the bodily cost of war, as in the intervening years between 1945 and the creation of Korzhev's astonishing *Wounded* in 1964, the way in which the injured or disabled body was represented, and what that representation signified, changed remarkably little. The damaged body was repeatedly equated with ultimate dedication and a willingness to sacrifice for the good of the nation, and it would take almost two decades for this to be challenged by alternative views of what that sacrifice entailed for those who returned rather than dying heroically on the battlefield. There is no doubt that the 1950s saw some important changes in the art world, with many artists demonstrating an increasing desire to tackle the conflict present in everyday life, to portray characters with depth and complexity, and the move away from that high-gloss coating of the visual world that was so typical of Stalinist art. However, at the same time it must also be recognized that when it came to dealing with some of the more profound aspects of the War, such as disablement, bereavement, homelessness, or mental anguish, for the most part the art of the Thaw demonstrates a similar degree of hesitancy in openly addressing such issues as does its Stalinist counterpart. Beyond the implications of this for the representation of the Soviet man, this visual continuity in terms of motifs, themes, and omissions points to the fact that it is impossible to speak of one homogeneous way in which Soviet culture responded to the events of the early 1940s. While literature and film explored some of the more troubling legacies of the war years with a degree of regularity and profundity throughout the Thaw, the same simply cannot be said for visual culture, either in what was being produced generally, or what was being circulated in popular print. This disparity has been attributed here to the differing nature of the respective media and their ability to handle the complexity of the "correct" narrative, which usually ran from desperation to eventual triumph, whether this be redemption through work, the return home, or overcoming physical injury to resume normal life.

Although the way in which the War was depicted was patchy and inconsistent, the years of the mid-1950s did bring about a hugely significant shift in the portrayal of idealized masculinity with the figure of the father emerging as a crucial element in the new de-Stalinized model of what it meant to be a New Soviet Man. While the introduction of the father into the family home—which paralleled real-life demobilization—was a watershed moment for how Soviet men were visually represented, it is undeniable that the range of images that were produced at this time were quite limited, despite their unprecedented nature. The focus on the War or on recent military service created a vision of fatherhood that was still based on the exceptional, rather than being rooted in the everyday and the ordinary rhythms of family life. In contrast, the representation of the father during the mid-1950s became quite banal, and it is this that makes it extraordinary: the fact that the father was a presence in the home and an active participant in the upbringing of children was now no longer rooted in the dislocation and separation as a consequence of war, but something that was completely normalized and expected. It is also at this time that one sees a diversification in the range of genres that featured the father-child relationship, with photography, illustrations, cartoons, and fine art all turning to this theme with a really incredible degree of regularity; a trend that was, as we saw in the last chapter, coupled with a diversification in how the role of the father was perceived, particularly in relation to his involvement in the care of his very young children.

While scholars have repeatedly pointed to the continual marginalization of the father in Soviet society and reaffirmed the belief that fatherhood—beyond basic economic provision—was never viewed by the state as an integral part of the masculine model,[4] it is apparent from the range and number of images found in this period, that the vision of the New Soviet Man of the Thaw simply does not align with this view. Thus, the evidence from visual and print culture would suggest that we need to reevaluate current thinking on the significance of paternity when it comes to understanding the construction of Soviet men's social role. Although rhetoric and legislation throughout the period may indicate that motherhood was still seen as essential and paternal input peripheral, there is no denying the fact that visually men—both real and imagined—were repeatedly shown taking an interest in their child's development and having an emotional bond with that child in a manner that was without precedence in Soviet culture. The case has been made in regard to other nations that experienced the collective traumas of the Second World War that the idea of what constituted a "good" father after this time shifted from the distant Victorian model to a more accessible and emotionally engaged ideal:[5] drawing on the evidence presented on the pages of magazines such as *Ogonek*, arguably the Soviet Union had more in common with its Western and capitalist counterparts in this respect than has previously been acknowledged.

Across the two main and interrelated male identities that have been the focus of this book—the soldier and the father—what we return to time and again is the significance of the years around 1965. Whether it is the emergence of a whole range of images that evoke the pain of loss, the more profound treatment of injury, or the exploration of fractured interpersonal relationships as a consequence of war, these years marked a radical change in the way that the memory of the War was broached and represented visually. These changes cannot be readily aligned with shifts in official policy in the cultural sphere, nor can they be attributed to a change of guard within the art world, as those artists who had painted or served at the front and those who only knew the War through the stories of others alike began to produce works that were more brutal, introspective, and honest than almost anything that had gone before. As such, these pieces of fine art, along with the photographs of the newly constructed war memorials and other commemorations throughout the decade, challenge the prevailing understanding of the nature of the war cult in the early Brezhnev period—a movement that is traditionally characterized by a rhetoric of unremitting glory and displays of bombast. While the experiences of many continued to be marginalized or overlooked entirely, at the same time it must be recognized that the physical and emotional scars of those terrible years *were* addressed by official visual culture and, what is more, were an integral part of the way in which the War, and its memory, was presented to the Soviet public through print media.

The validity of the received wisdom that the Brezhnev era witnessed a retrenchment and a return to more conservative values after the dynamism of the Thaw is one that is yet to receive extensive scrutiny: certainly when issues surrounding the representation of the War and its legacies are examined across these two supposedly contrasting decades, what becomes immediately apparent is that the Thaw years did not bring about the artistic reconceptualization of this experience in a way that is perhaps expected, nor did the early Brezhnev era see the obfuscation of the horrors of those years. On the contrary, it is during the period that is still associated with stagnation, and for some re-Stalinization, that the most interesting developments in the visual depiction of both life at the front and the long-term consequences of war occur. Events in contemporary Russia would seem to support Nina Tumarkin's assessment that the Great Patriotic War was a reservoir of patriotic sentiment that was waiting to be tapped and mobilized for the benefit of the state,[6] but the emotion, complexity, and increasing willingness to broach issues that had been entirely ignored for the previous two decades in the visual culture of the day raises serious questions about whether it is correct to view the creation of the war myth under Brezhnev as little more than a way to bolster a state needing to reaffirm its political legitimacy. The fact that so many paintings and photographs found in the print media reference the War underlines its ongoing significance for the nation-state; but what is more, the fact that issues to do with grief, trauma, and loss are repeatedly a part of the narrative of such works demands a more nuanced way of thinking about the official memory of the War and its function in late Soviet society that moves beyond its political motivations and takes into consideration its emotional, even cathartic, function during the 1960s and beyond.

In terms of the implications of this changing depiction of the War and its aftermath for notions of idealized masculinity, as images that finally broached the issue of male grief are completely congruent with the changes seen in other war-themed genres, it is probably erroneous to see this depiction of male emotion as evidence of the looming crisis of masculinity that would, according to some, engulf Soviet men during the course of the Brezhnev era.[7] Of course, works that had a more introspective dimension became relatively common at this time, and while such paintings can be situated within this broader trend, the fact that war-themed works in the mid- to late-1960s began to address issues that had previously gone completely unexplored, such as male bereavement, the destruction of families, the violence of death, and the lasting emotional damage inflicted on individuals as a consequence of their experience, points to a broader reevaluation of the War and its significance for contemporary society that goes beyond a passing artistic trend. Still, even if we confine our analysis to the art world alone, that this more polyvalent vision of acceptable male behaviors might be viewed as somehow representative of a crisis of masculinity is both reductive and based upon the premise that up until the period of *zastoi*, the model of the New Soviet Man had been cocooned from the harsh realities of Soviet life—an assumption that simply does not hold up to scrutiny based on the evidence presented here.

On May 9, 1965, the front cover of *Krokodil* featured a cartoon by Ivan Semenov entitled *Twenty Years Later (Dvadtsat' let spustia)*, which was a pastiche of the incredibly popular painting by Iurii Neprintsev, *Rest after Battle* (1951). In his original work, Neprintsev had depicted a group of young soldiers being regaled by the stories of their charismatic comrade, and while the painting removed any insinuation of the battle that these men had just faced, it was made clear that these were real Soviet men, courageous, physically strong, and patriotic, who reveled in comradeship and found joy in collective success. Semenov's later cartoon was likewise founded upon a sense of collectivism, but rather than a group of soldiers, men from all walks of Soviet life were shown listening to Terkin's tales—from furnace workers to filmmakers, from miners to musicians, from astronauts to artists—and rather than the guns of the original painting, each man now carried a tool of his trade; even Terkin, while retaining his soldier's overcoat, had his weapon removed. In Semenov's lighthearted scene we can find a distillation of the changes that the model of the new man had undergone since the end of the War, as the experience of conflict fundamentally challenged the militaristic model of masculinity that had been so celebrated during the 1930s. With this, the vision of masculine behaviors offered by visual culture became increasingly pluralistic, allowing for the expression of emotion and the exploration of experiences that had previously been entirely absent. Such changes did not happen overnight, but in the twenty years that separated Neprintsev's painting from Semenov's cartoon, visual culture inched closer to representing life as it was in the Soviet Union: a world where the traumas of war were not miraculously solved with the advent of peace, where not everyone lived happily ever after, and where even Soviet men were no longer simply the labor machines envisaged by early Bolshevik theorists, but fathers with real and meaningful relationships with their children. What the images discussed in this book clearly demonstrate then is that, even in its idealized form, the Soviet model of masculinity was not an unchanging constant, impervious to social and political change, or completely indifferent to the experiences of real Soviet men.

# Notes

## Introduction

1. Mikhail Sholokhov, *The Fate of a Man: Sud'ba cheloveka* (Moscow, 1984), 67.

2. Denise Youngblood, *On the Cinema Front: Russian War Films, 1914–2005* (Lawrence, KS: 2007), 124. For more on the importance of the film, see Elena Baraban, "'The Fate of a Man' by Sergei Bondarchuk and the Soviet Cinema of Trauma," *The Slavic and East European Journal* 51, no. 3 (2007): 514–34.

3. *Iskusstvo* 6 (1965): 51; *Ogonek* 9 (1960): 7; *Ogonek* 20 (1965): 32–33. The Petrovs' illustration would be reproduced again just two years later in *Iskusstvo* 5 (1967): 2.

4. Mikhail Sholokhov, *Sud'ba cheloveka* (Moscow, 1964).

5. L. Petrov and V. Petrova, "Konkurs na luchshie illiustratsii k proizvedeniiam: Shekspira, Brekhta, Sholokova, Marshaka: Mikhail Sholokhov," *Sud'ba cheloveka*', *Iskusstvo* 6 (1965): 51.

6. Just a small sample of such scholarship includes work by various academics published in the edited collections B. Clements, R. Friedman, and D. Healey, eds., *Russian Masculinities in History and Culture* (Basingstoke, 2001); and Serguei Oushakine, ed., *O Muzhe(n)stvennosti* (Moscow, 2002); see also Sergei Kukhterin, "Fathers and Patriarchs in Communist and Post-Communist Russia," in *Gender, State and Society in Soviet and Post-Soviet Russia*, ed. Sarah Ashwin (London, 2000), 71–89; Dan Healey, *Homosexual Desire in Revolutionary Russia: The Regulation of Sexual and Gender Dissent* (London, 2001); Mark Edele, "Strange Young Men in Stalin's Moscow: The Birth and Life of the Stiliagi, 1945–1953," *Jahrbücher für Geschichte Osteuropas* 50 (2002): 37–61; I. N. Tartakovskaia, "'Nesostoiavshchaiasia maskulinnost' kak tip povedeniia na rynke truda," in *Gendernye otnosheniia v sovremennoi Rossii: issledovaniia 1990-kh godov. Sbornik nauchnykh statei*, ed. L. N. Popkova and I. N. Tartakovskaia (Samara, 2003), 42–71; Zh. Chernova, "'Muzhskaia rabota': analiz media-reprezentatsii," in *Gendernye otnosheniia v sovremennoi Rossii: issledovaniia 1990-kh godov. Sbornik nauchnykh statei*, ed. L. N. Popkova and I. N. Tartakovskaia (Samara, 2003), 276–94; O. Khasbulatova, *Rossiiskaia gendernaia politika v XX stoletii: mify i realii* (Ivanovo, 2005); Elena Prokhorova, "The Post-Utopian Body Politic: Masculinity and the Crisis of National Identity in Brezhnev-Era TV Miniseries," in *Gender and National Identity in Twentieth-Century Russian Culture*, ed. Helena Goscilo and Andrea Lanoux (DeKalb, IL: 2006), 131–50; Deborah A. Field, *Private Life and Communist Morality in Khrushchev's Russia* (New York, 2007); Greta Bucher, "Stalinist Families: Motherhood, Fatherhood, and Building the New Soviet Person," in *The Making of Russian History: Society, Culture, and the Politics of Modern Russia*, ed. John Steinberg and Rex Wade (Bloomington, IN: 2009), 129–52; Ethan Pollock, "Real Men Go to the Bania: Postwar Soviet Masculinities and the Bathhouse," *Kritika* 11, no. 1 (2010): 47–76; Tetyana Bureychak, "Masculinity in Soviet and Post-Soviet Ukraine: Models and Their Implications," in *Gender, Politics, and Society in Ukraine*, ed. Olena Hankivsky and Anastasiya Salnykova (Toronto, 2012), 325–61; and N. Lebina, *Muzhchina i zhenshchina: telo, moda, kul'tura. SSSR—ottepel'* (Moscow, 2014). Cinema is the cultural field where masculinity has received the most attention. See for example John Haynes, *New Soviet Man: Gender and Masculinity in Stalinist Soviet Cinema* (Manchester, 2003); Lilya Kaganovsky, *How the Soviet Man Was Unmade: Cultural Fantasy and Male Subjectivity under Stalin* (Pittsburgh, PA: 2008); and H. Goscilo and Y. Hashamova, eds., *Cinepaternity: Fathers and Sons in Soviet and Post-Soviet Film* (Bloomington, IN: 2010).

7. For more on the pre-Soviet ideal of the New Man in a Russian context, see the writings of Chernyshevskii, Dobroliubov, and Pisarev, for example N. A. Dobrolyubov, "The Organic Development

of Man in Connection with His Mental and Moral Activities," in *Selected Philosophical Essays*, ed. N. A. Dobrolyubov, trans. J. Fineberg (Moscow, 1956), 69–101; and N. G. Chernyshevskii, "The General Character of the Elements That Promote Progress," in *Selected Philosophical Essays*, ed. N. G. Chernyshevsky (Honolulu, HI: 2002), 256–70. See also Irina Paperno, *Chernyshevsky and the Age of Realism: A Study in the Semiotics of Behavior* (Stanford, CA: 1988); Beatrice Glatzer Rosenthal, *Dmitri Sergeevich Merezhkovsky and the Silver Age: The Development of a Revolutionary Mentality* (The Hague, 1975); Rosenthal, *Nietzsche in Russia* (Princeton, NJ: 1986); Barry P. Scherr, "God-Building or God-Seeking? Gorky's Confession as Confession," *The Slavic and East European Journal* 44 (2000): 448–69; Edith Clowes, *The Revolution of Moral Consciousness: Nietzsche in Russian Literature, 1890–1914* (DeKalb, IL: 1988); Douglas Weiner, "Man of Plastic: Gor'kii's Visions of Humans in Nature," *The Soviet and Post-Soviet Review* 22 (1995): 65–88; John Garrard, "The Original Manuscript of Forever Flowing: Grossman's Autopsy of the New Soviet Man," *The Slavic and East European Journal* 38, no. 2 (1994): 271–89; Jochen Hellbeck, *Laboratories of the Soviet Self: Diaries from the Stalin Era* (Ann Arbor, MI: 2003); and Alexander Etkind, "Psychological Culture," in *Russian Culture at the Crossroads: Paradoxes of Postcommunist Consciousness*, ed. Dmitrii Shalin (Oxford, 1996), 99–127.

8. Barbara Evans Clements, "Introduction," in *Russian Masculinities in History and Culture*, ed. Barbara Evans Clements, Rebecca Friedman, and Dan Healey (Basingstoke, 2001), 1–2.

9. R. W. Connell, "The Big Picture: Masculinities in Recent World History," *Theory and Society* 22 (1993): 611.

10. Nikolai Bukharin cited Kendall E. Bailes, "Alexei Gastev and the Soviet Controversy over Taylorism, 1918–24," *Soviet Studies* 29, no. 3 (1977): 387.

11. Yevgeny Zamyatin, *We*, trans. Natasha Randall (London, 2007), 12.

12. Maurizia Boscagli, *Eye on the Flesh: Fashions of Masculinity in the Early Twentieth Century* (Boulder, CO: 1996), 129.

13. Boscagli, *Eye on the Flesh*, 129.

14. For a discussion of physical health and fitness that touches on ideas of masculinity, see Julie Gilmour and Barbara Clements, "If You Want to Be Like Me, Train! The Contradictions of Soviet Masculinity," in *Russian Masculinities in History and Culture*, ed. B. Clements, R. Friedman, and D. Healey (Basingstoke, 2001), 210–22; Tricia Starks, *The Body Soviet: Propaganda, Hygiene, and the Revolutionary State* (Madison, WI: 2008); and Susan Grant, *Physical Culture and Sport in Soviet Society: Propaganda, Acculturation and Transformation in the 1920s and 1930s* (London, 2014).

15. Thomas Schrand, "Socialism in One Gender: Masculine Values in the Stalin Revolution," in *Russian Masculinities in History and Culture*, ed. B. Clements, R. Friedman, and D. Healey (Basingstoke, 2001), 203.

16. For more on the link between militarism, heroism, and celebrations, see Karen Petrone, *Life Has Become More Joyous, Comrades: Celebrations in the Time of Stalin* (Bloomington, IN: 2000).

17. Katerina Clark, *The Soviet Novel: History As Ritual*, 3rd ed. (Bloomington, IN: 2000), 114–35. More detailed discussion of Stalin as a paternal figure can be found in the work of Catriona Kelly; see for example Kelly, "Riding the Magic Carpet: Children and Leader Cult in the Stalin Era," *The Slavic and East European Journal* 49, no. 2 (2005): 199–224; Kelly, "A Joyful Soviet Childhood: Licensed Happiness for Little Ones," in *Petrified Utopia: Happiness Soviet Style*, ed. Marina Balina and Evgeny Dobrenko (London, 2012), 3–18; Kelly, "Grandpa Lenin and Uncle Stalin: Soviet Leader Cult for Little Children," in *The Leader Cult in Communist Dictatorships: Stalin and the Eastern Bloc*, ed. Balazs Apor, Jan C. Behrends, Polly Jones, and E. A. Rees (2004), 102–22. This issue is also discussed in more detail in chapter 4.

18. Just a few of the works that advocate this view include Sergei Kukhterin, "Fathers and Patriarchs in Communist and Post-Communist Russia," in *Gender, State and Society in Soviet and Post-Soviet Russia*, ed. Sarah Ashwin (London, 2000), 71–89; Greta Bucher, "Stalinist Families: Motherhood, Fatherhood, and Building the New Soviet Person," in *The Making of Russian History: Society, Culture, and the Politics of Modern Russia*, ed. John Steinberg and Rex Wade (Bloomington, IN: 2009), 129–52; Iryna Koshulap, "Cash and/or Care: Current Discourses and Practices of Fatherhood in Ukraine," in *Gender, Politics, and Society in Ukraine*, ed. Olena Hankivsky and Anastasiya Salnykova (Toronto,

2012), 362–63; Zh. Chernova, "The Model of Soviet 'Fatherhood,'" *Russian Studies in History* 51, no. 2 (2012): 35–62, originally published in E. Zdravomyslova and A. Temkina, *Rossiiskii gendernyi poryadok: sotsiologicheskii podkhod* (St. Petersburg, 2007).

19. For a sample of such scholarship, see for example Julie Hessler, "A Postwar Perestroika? Toward a History of Private Enterprise in the USSR," *Slavic Review* 57, no. 3 (1998): 516–42; Elena Zubkova, *Russia after the War: Hopes, Illusions, and Disappointments, 1945-1957*, trans. Hugh Ragsdale (New York, 1998); Zubkova, *Poslevoennoe sovetskoe obshchestvo: politika i povsednevnost', 1945–53* (Moscow, 1999); Donald Filtzer, *Soviet Workers and Late Stalinism: Labour and the Restoration of the Stalinist System after World War II* (Oxford, 2002); Mark Edele, "Strange Young Men in Stalin's Moscow: The Birth and Life of the Stiliagi, 1945–1953," *Jahrbücher für Geschichte Osteuropas* 50 (2002): 37–61; Ethan Pollock, *Stalin and the Soviet Science Wars* (Princeton, NJ: 2006); and Juliane Fürst, *Stalin's Last Generation: Soviet Post-War Youth and the Emergence of Mature Socialism* (Oxford, 2011). See also the collection of essays in *Late Stalinist Russia: Society between Reconstruction and Reinvention*, ed. Juliane Fürst (Oxford, 2006).

20. Polly Jones, *Myth, Memory, Trauma: Rethinking the Stalinist Past in the Soviet Union, 1953–70* (London, 2013); Miriam Dobson, *Khrushchev's Cold Summer: Gulag Returnees, Crime, and the Fate of Reform after Stalin* (Ithaca, NY: 2009); Stephen Bittner, *The Many Lives of Khrushchev's Thaw: Experience and Memory in Moscow's Arbat* (Ithaca, NY: 2008). See also Iurii Aksiutin, *Khrushchevskaia "ottepel'" i obshchestvennye nastroeniia v SSSR v 1953-1964 gg.* (Moscow, 2004); Denis Kozlov, *The Readers of Novyi Mir: Coming to Terms with the Stalinist Past* (Cambridge, MA: 2013); and the essays in the collected volume, Polly Jones, ed., *The Dilemmas of De-Stalinization: Negotiating Cultural and Social Change in the Khrushchev Era* (New York, 2006).

21. The experimentation of the revolutionary period is discussed in the following works: John Bowlt, ed., *Russian Art of the Avant-Garde: Theory and Criticism 1902-1934* (New York, 1976); S. Barron and M. Tuchman, eds., *The Avant Garde in Russia, 1910–1930* (London, 1980); Christine Lodder, *Russian Constructivism* (London, 1983); Camilla Gray, *The Russian Experiment in Art, 1863–1922*, revised ed. (London, 1986); David Elliot, *New Worlds: Russian Art and Society 1900–1937* (London, 1986); V. Leniashin, *Soviet Art 1920s–1930s: Russian Museum, Leningrad* (Moscow, 1988); William Rosenberg, ed., *Bolshevik Visions: First Phase of the Cultural Revolution in Soviet Russia, Part II: Creating Soviet Cultural Forms: Art, Architecture, Music, Film and the New Tasks of Education*, 2nd ed. (Ann Arbor, MI: 1990); L. N. Vostretova, *Zhivopis' 20–30 kh. godov* (St. Petersburg, 1991); Brandon Taylor, *Art and Literature under the Bolsheviks*, vol. 1: *The Crisis of Renewal, 1917-1924* (London, 1991); Taylor, *Art and Literature under the Bolsheviks*, vol. 2: *Authority and Revolution, 1924-1932* (London, 1992); Stedelijk Museum Amsterdam: *De Grote Utopie: De Russische Avant-Garde 1915-1932* (Amsterdam, 1992); Boris Groys, *The Total Art of Stalinism: Avant-Garde, Aesthetic Dictatorship, and Beyond* (Oxford, 1992); Christine Lodder, *Russian Painting of the Avant Garde, 1906-1924* (Edinburgh, 1993); J. Bowlt and O. Mitich, *Laboratory of Dreams: The Russian Avant-Garde and Cultural Experiment* (Stanford, CA: 1996); The State Hermitage Museum, *Circling the Square: Avant-Garde Porcelain from Revolutionary Russia* (London, 2004); and Christina Kiaer, *Imagine No Possessions: The Socialist Objects of Russian Constructivism* (Cambridge, MA: 2005).

22. Socialist Realist art, particularly from the 1930s, has received a great deal of attention in both popular and academic circles. A small sample of such work includes A. B. Liubimova, *Agitatsiia za schast'e: sovetskoe iskusstvo stalinskoi epokhi* (Moscow, 1985); Hans Gunther, ed., *The Culture of the Stalin Period* (London, 1990); Matthew Cullerne Bown, *Art under Stalin* (Oxford, 1991); Regine Robin, *Socialist Realism: An Impossible Aesthetic* (Stanford, CA: 1992); Boris Groys, *The Total Art of Stalinism: Avant-Garde, Aesthetic Dictatorship, and Beyond* (Oxford, 1992); Matthew Cullerne Bown and Brandon Taylor, eds., *Art of the Soviets: Painting, Sculpture and Architecture in a One-Party State, 1917-1992* (Manchester, 1993); Institute for Contemporary Art, P.S. 1 Museum, *The Aesthetic Arsenal: Socialist Realism under Stalin* (New York, 1993); Gleb Prokhorov, *Art under Socialist Realism: Soviet Painting, 1930-1950* (Roseville East, NSW: 1995); A. Efimova, "To Touch on the Raw: The Aesthetic Affections of Socialist Realism," *Art Journal* 56, no. 1, *Aesthetics and the Body Politic* (1997): 72–80; Susan Reid, "Stalin's Women: Gender and Power in Soviet Art of the 1930s," *Slavic Review* 57, no. 1

(1998): 133–73; Reid, "Socialist Realism in the Stalinist Terror: The Industry of Socialist Art Exhibition 1935–41," *Russian Review* 60, no. 2 (2001): 153–84; Boris Groys et al., eds., *Traumfabrik Kommunismus: Die Visuelle Kultur der Stalinzeit = Dream Factory Communism: The Visual Culture of the Stalin Era* (Frankfurt, 2003); Christina Kiaer, "Was Socialist Realism Forced Labour? The Case of Aleksandr Deineka in the 1930s," *Oxford Art Journal* 28, no. 3 (2005): 321–45; V. S. Manin, *Iskusstvo i vlast': Bor'ba techenii v sovetskom izobraziteľnom isskustve 1917–1941 godov* (St. Petersburg, 2008); Oliver Johnson, "'A Premonition of Victory': A Letter from the Front," *Russian Review* 68, no. 3 (2009): 408–28; and Johnson, "The Stalin Prize and the Soviet Artist: Status Symbol or Stigma?," *Slavic Review* 70, no. 4 (2011): 819–43.

23. See for example Clark, *The Soviet Novel*; Susan Reid, "All Stalin's Women: Gender and Power in Soviet Art of the 1930s," *Slavic Review* 57, no. 1 (1998): 133–73; Reid, "Masters of the Earth: Gender and Destalinisation in the Soviet Reformist Painting of the Khrushchev Thaw," *Gender and History* 11, no. 2 (1999); Reid, "Socialist Realism in the Stalinist Terror: The Industry of Socialist Art Exhibition 1935–41," *Russian Review* 60 no 2 (2001): 153–84; Reid, "Modernizing Socialist Realism in the Khrushchev Thaw: The Struggle for a 'Contemporary Style' in Soviet Art," in *The Dilemmas of De-Stalinization: Negotiating Cultural and Social Change in the Khrushchev Era*, ed. P. Jones (New York, 2006), 209–30; and Denise Youngblood, *On the Cinema Front: Russian War Films, 1914–2005* (Lawrence, KS: 2007).

24. For a detailed account of the work of Simonov and how literature responded to the traumas of the Stalin era more generally during the Thaw, see Jones, *Myth, Memory, Trauma*, esp. 173–211.

25. Kamenskii cited in Aleksandr Sidorov, "The Thaw: Painting of the Khrushchev Era," in The Museum of Modern Art, Oxford, *Soviet Socialist Realist Painting 1930s-1960s: Paintings from Russia, the Ukraine, Belorussia, Uzbekistan, Kirgizia, Georgia, Armenia, Azerbaijan and Moldova Selected in the USSR by Matthew Cullerne Bown* (Oxford, 1992), 34.

26. Jørn Guldberg, "Socialist Realism as Institutional Practice: Observations of the Interpretation of Works of Art in the Stalin Period," in *The Culture of the Stalin Period*, ed. H. Günther (London, 1990), 150.

27. Jones, *Myth, Memory, Trauma*, 212–58.

28. Mark Edele, *Soviet Veterans of the Second World War: A Popular Movement in an Authoritarian Society, 1941–1991* (Oxford, 2008), 185–214.

29. See especially Nina Tumarkin, *The Living & the Dead: The Rise and Fall of the Cult of World War II in Russia* (New York, 1994).

30. Lynne Attwood, *Creating the New Soviet Woman: Women's Magazines as Engineers of Female Identity, 1922–53* (Basingstoke, 1999), 2.

31. This assumption is based on the fact that it was very common for these reading materials to be circulated within families and distributed through the workplace, workers' clubs, libraries, and other communal centers. For more on the origins of the reading habits of the Soviet population, see Jeffrey Brooks, *When Russia Learned to Read: Literacy and Popular Literature, 1861–1917* (Princeton, NJ: 1985).

32. This figure is based on statistics published in the *Concise Encyclopaedia of Russia*, which gives the circulation of *Ogonek* at 1 million per issue for 1955. The total circulation figure given for journals and magazines published in 1958 is 637 million; S. V. Utechin, *Everyman's Concise Encyclopaedia of Russia* (London, 1961), 436.

33. For a more theoretical discussion of the reproduction of fine art, see Pierre Bourdieu, *Distinction: A Social Critique of the Judgement of Taste*, trans. Richard Nice (Padstow, 1994); and Walter Benjamin "The Work of Art in the Age of Mechanical Reproduction" (1936), reproduced at Marxist Internet Archive, https://www.marxists.org/reference/subject/philosophy/works/ge/benjamin.htm, accessed April 30, 2017.

34. For more on the evolution of photography in *Ogonek* through the 1950s and 1960s, see Jessica Werneke, "Photography in the Late Soviet Period: Ogonek, the SSOD, and Official Photo Exchanges," *Vestnik, The Journal of Russian and Asian Studies* (August 2015), http://www.sras.org/photography_late_soviet_period, accessed April 30, 2017.

35. See for example N. Konchalovskaia, "Zateriannaia v tolpe," *Ogonek* 21 (1961): 16–17 with color supplement; "Risunki V. Vasnetsova k 110-letshiuiu so dnia rozhdeniia," *Ogonek* 20 (1958): 16–17 with color supplement; M. Nikitin, "Khudozhnik mstiashchei kisti," *Ogonek* 25 (1957): 16–17 with color supplement; and G. Gluzman, "Velikii zhivopisets," *Sovetskaia zhenshchina* 1 (1965), 33–35.

36. "Repin i russkaia natsional'naia zhivopis," *Pravda,* August 5, 1944; V. Iakolev, "Velikii russkii khudozhnik," *Krasnaia zvezda,* August 5, 1944; "K 100-letiiu so dnia rozhdeniia I. E. Repina," *Izvestiia,* August 5, 1944; N. Sokolova, "Velikii russkii khudozhnik," *Izvestiia,* August 5, 1944.

37. Solov'ev, *Pochtovye marki Rossii i SSSR,* 107. This painting was reproduced numerous times during this period. See for example *Ogonek* 48 (1953): between 16–17; and *Ogonek* 33 (1961): between 16–17.

38. The influence of nineteenth-century realist art on Socialist Realism is something that has not received much attention in its own right, although it is often referred to in discussions of the latter. One notable exception to this is Aleksandr I. Morozov, *Sotsrealizm i realizm* (Moscow, 2007).

39. Dmitrii Stonov, "Sunday at the Tretyakov Art Gallery," *Soviet News,* April 15, 1946, 4.

## Chapter 1

1. V. Pavlovskii, "A Soldier and a Half," reproduced in *Soviet War News,* March 29, 1945, 7–8.

2. Eric Naiman, *Sex in Public: The Incarnation of Early Soviet Ideology* (Princeton, NJ: 1997), esp. 250–88; Eliot Borenstein, *Men without Women: Masculinity and Revolution in Russian Fiction, 1917–1929* (London, 2000); Catherine Merridale, *Ivan's War: The Red Army 1939–1945* (London, 2005); Svetozar Rajak, *Yugoslavia and the Soviet Union in the Early Cold War: Reconciliation, Comradeship, Confrontation, 1953–1957* (London, 2011).

3. For a very useful history of comradeship in Russia prior to 1917, see Borenstein, *Men without Women,* 23–31.

4. Although he does not discuss this in a Soviet context, these ideas are taken from J. Glenn Gray, *The Warriors: Reflections on Men in Battle* (London, 1998), 89–90.

5. The seminal work on the militarization of Bolshevik society and culture is Sheila Fitzpatrick, "The Civil War as a Formative Experience," in *Bolshevik Culture: Experiment and Order in the Russian Revolution,* ed. Abbot Gleason and Richard Stites (Bloomington, IN: 1985), 57–76.

6. Katerina Clark, "Little Heroes and Big Deeds: Literature Responds to the First Five-Year Plan," in *Cultural Revolution in Russia, 1928–1931,* ed. Sheila Fitzpatrick (London, 1978), 191. See also her groundbreaking work *The Soviet Novel: History As Ritual, 3rd Edition* (Bloomington, IN: 2000).

7. For more on Gorky's theories of the New Man and the recreation of humanity, see for example Barry Scherr, "God-Building or God-Seeking? Gorky's Confession as Confession," *The Slavic and East European Journal* 44 (2000): 448–69; and Douglas Weiner, "Man of Plastic: Gor'kii's Visions of Humans in Nature," *The Soviet and Post-Soviet Review* 22 (1995): 65–88.

8. For more detailed discussion, see for example Victoria Bonnell, *Iconography of Power: Soviet Political Posters under Lenin and Stalin* (Berkeley, CA: 1999); John McCannon, *Red Arctic: Polar Exploration and the Myth of the North in the Soviet Union, 1932–1939* (New York, 1998); and Jay Bergman, "Valerii Chkalov: Soviet Pilot as New Soviet Man," *Journal of Contemporary History* 33, no. 1 (1998): 132–54.

9. See for example S. Gerasimov, *Mat' partizana,* 1943; V. Ivanov, *Za rodunu, za chest', za svobodu,* 1941; and Vladimir Koretskii and Vera Gitsevich, *Partizany, beite vraga bez poshchady!,* 1941.

10. P. Suzdalev, "Kartina A. Deineki 'Oborona Sevastopolia'" *Iskusstvo* 2 (1967): 21; Tretyakov Gallery http://www.tretyakovgallery.ru/en/museum/history/gallery/1941_1945/, accessed April 30, 2017.

11. For one of the earliest postwar discussions of the work and detailed reproductions, see R. Kaufman, "O batal'noi zhivopisi ody Velikoi Otechestvennoi voiny," *Tvorchestvo* 1 (1947): 2–8. For later reproductions in the popular press, see for example *Ogonek* 35 (1961) and *Rabotnitsa* 5 (1965). A reproduction of the stamp can be found in V. Iu. Solov'ev, *Pochtovye marki Rossii i SSSR 1857–1991*

(Moscow, 1998), 194. Deineka's painting was used again in 1968 in a series of stamps issued to celebrate the Russian Museum; Solov'ev, *Pochtovye marki Rossii i SSSR*, 229.

12. Early reproductions include *Iskusstvo* 2 (1952): 5; *Ogonek* 2 (1952): between 16–17; and *Rabotnitsa* 2 (1952): 8.

13. *Iskusstvo* 5 (1965): 5.

14. *Iskusstvo* 3 (1955): between 24–25.

15. *Iskusstvo* 3 (1950): between 6–7.

16. Nina Tumarkin, *The Living & the Dead: The Rise and Fall of the Cult of World War II in Russia* (New York, 1994), 103–5; Merridale, *Ivan's War* (London, 2005), 313.

17. Juliane Fürst, "Introduction: Late Stalinist Society: History, Policies and People," in *Late Stalinist Russia: Society between Reconstruction and Reinvention*, ed. Juliane Fürst (Oxford, 2006), 5.

18. Elena Zubkova, *Russia after the War: Hopes, Illusions, and Disappointments 1945–1957*, trans. Hugh Ragsdale (London, 1998), 27; Mark Edele, "More Than Just Stalinists: The Political Sentiments of Victors 1945–53," in *Late Stalinist Russia: Society between Reconstruction and Reinvention*, ed. Juliane Fürst (Oxford, 2006), 167–91.

19. Mark Edele, *Soviet Veterans of the Second World War: A Popular Movement in an Authoritarian Society 1945–1991* (Oxford, 2008), 11.

20. Eric Leeds, *No Man's Land: Combat and Identity in World War I* (Cambridge, 1979), 195.

21. Zubkova, *Russia after the War*, 24–27; Edele, *Soviet Veterans*, 60.

22. Just a small sample from articles that ran in *Sovetskaia zhenshchina* in 1951 alone include "Za mir, za schast'e i druzhbu narodov!" (1); "Pesni mira" (2); "Za pakt mira" (5); "Vo imia mira i zhizn'" (5); and "Znamia oktiabria—znamia mira!" (6).

23. Fedor Reshetnikov, *Za mir!*, *Sovetskaia zhenshchina* 3 (1951); Vera Mukhina et al. *Trebuem mira!*, *Sovetskaia zhenshchina* 3 (1951).

24. As no testimony has been found from the artist, it is impossible to establish whether this global view of the scene was intended, or whether it was actually meant to be a specific comment on the supposedly peaceful and positive interaction between the greater Soviet Union and the Latvian people.

25. V. Mukhina "Sovetskie khudozhniki v bor'be za mir," *Sovetskaia zhenshchina* 2 (1951): 19–20; O. Sopotsinskii, "Sovetskie khudozhniki v bor'be za mir," *Iskusstvo* 2 (1951): 33.

26. Nikolai Gogol's *Taras Bulba* (1835); Leo Tolstoy, *The Cossacks* (1863). For more on literary representations, see Judith Deutsch Kornblatt, *The Cossack Hero in Russian Literature: A Study in Cultural Mythology* (London, 1992). Kriuchkov's exploits would be reproduced many times in poster form, and he became the central character in satirical works in the early war years; see for example D. Moor, *Bogatyrskoe delo Koz'my Kriuchkova* (1914), Hoover Institution Poster Collection RU/SU 134 (henceforth RU/SU); I. Gorskii, *Bred' Vil'gel'ma* (1914), RU/SU 479; A. F. Postnov, *Khrabryi nash kazak Kriuchkov* (1914), RU/SU 83; and Unknown artist, *Podvig kazaka Kriuchkova* (1914), RU/SU 15. The death of Kriuchkov on August 12, 1919, while fighting for the Whites also warranted the production of a *lubok* (Otdel izdanii, Rossiiskaia Gosudarstvennaia Biblioteka [henceforth RGB]; item XIV 7g 28237). The legacy of the Cossacks under the tsarist regime and the subsequent process of de-Cossackization during the Civil War would put an end to the Cossack as a heroic figure within a Soviet context, although appeals were made during those early years to get the Cossacks to join the Soviet cause. See for example D. Moor, *Kazak u tebia odna doroga—s trudovoi rossiei* (1919), RGB VI.4ж 1846, which was styled on Viktor Vasnetsov's *Vitiaz' na rasput'e* (1882); and Unknown artist, *Kazak ty s kem? S nami ili s nimi?* (1918), RGB VI.4ж 817, which actually used Kriuchkov as its embodiment of the Cossack. The real-life exploits of Kriuchkov and his subsequent place in Russian culture are examined in Karen Petrone, *The Great War in Russian Memory* (Bloomington, IN: 2011).

27. "Vse ottenkhi smekha . . ." *Ogonek* 33 (1961): 16–17 with color supplement.

28. Iu. Neprintsev, "Kak ia rabotal nad kartinoi 'Otdykh posle boia,'" *Iskusstvo* 4 (1952): 17.

29. Ibid.

30. Katherine Hodgson, *Written with the Bayonet: Soviet Poetry of the Second World War* (Liverpool, 1996), 194–45.

31. For more detail, see for example Karel C. Berkhoff, *Motherland in Danger: Soviet Propaganda during World War II* (New York, 2012); Kevin Platt and David Brandenberger, *Epic Revisionism: Russian History and Literature as Stalinist Propaganda* (Madison, WI: 2005); Stephen Norris, *A War of Images: Russian Popular Prints, Wartime Culture, and National Identity, 1812–1945* (Chicago, 2006); and Maureen Perrie, *The Cult of Ivan the Terrible in Stalin's Russia* (Basingstoke, 2002).

32. Hodgson, *Written with the Bayonet*, 197.

33. Susan Reid, "Masters of the Earth: Gender and Destalinisation in the Soviet Reformist Painting of the Khrushchev Thaw," *Gender and History* 11, no. 2 (1999): 290.

34. Examples include Mikhail Samsonov, *Sestritsa* (1950), *Iskusstvo* 8 (1964):34; and V. Khimachin, "Kavalier trekh ordenov slavy, medsestra Motia Nechiporchkova," *Ogonek* 7 (1946): between 34–35. See also the posters of Viktor Koretskii and Vera Gitsevich, *Vstavai v riady frontovykh podrug, druzhinnitsa—boitsu pomoshchnik i drug!* (1941) and Viktor Koretskii, *Druzhinnitsy Krasnogo kresta! Ne ostovim na pole boia . . .* (1942). For discussion of the participation of women in the armed forces, see Anna Krylova, *Soviet Women in Combat: A History of Violence on the Eastern Front* (Cambridge, 2010); Roger Markwick, *Soviet Women on the Frontline in the Second World War* (Basingstoke, 2012); and Reina Pennington, *Wings, Women, and War: Soviet Airwomen in World War II Combat* (Lawrence, KS: 2007).

35. The earliest non-photographic representations of *official* women fighters that have been found are I. M. Baldina's portrait, *Geroinia Stalingradskoi bitvy Natasha Kachuevskaia* (1984) and Anatolii Levitin, *Soldatskoe gore* (1985). Both paintings were part of the 1985 exhibition *Mir otstoiali, mir sokhranim*. Reproduced in S. N. Levandovskii, *Mir otstoiali, mir sokhranim* (Leningrad, 1985), pls. 19, 84. Representations of women taking part in the partisan movement can be found much earlier; see for example I. Stasevich, *Kliatva* (1965–67), *Iskusstvo* 5 (1968): 11, as well as works such as that by the Kukryniksy, *Tania: Podvig Zoia Kosmodem'ianskoi* (1947) that depicted the death of probably the most well-known female partisan figure.

36. *Sovetskaia zhenshchina* 5 (1955): 16 (fragment); *Rabotnitsa* 2 (1952): 19. Reproduced as part of E. Polishchuk's review of the 1951 All-Union Exhibition, "Tvorcheskie uspekhi khudozhnikov," 17–19.

37. V. Shvedova, "Novye raboty khudozhnikov leningrada," *Iskusstvo* 5 (1954): 24.

38. For more on Soviet notions of hygiene, see Tricia Starks, *The Body Soviet: Propaganda, Hygiene, and the Revolutionary State* (Madison, WI: 2008).

39. See for example S. M. Muzharskii, *13 maia 14 zhertvuite na knigu soldatu* (1916) issued by Komitet' kniga soldatu.

40. This motif was particularly common in representations of Franz Joseph of Austria. See for example S. Ivanov, *Avstro-prusskii tseppelin'* (1914); and A. Postnov, *Gliadite zdes', smotrite tam . . .* (1914).

41. Unknown artist, *Chto delaiut gruppy zdorov'ia v krasnoi armii . . .* [1917–22] and Unknown artist, *Chistota pobezhdaet sypnoi i vozvratnyi tify* (1921).

42. A. Deineka, *After Battle*, 1944, reproduced in Matthew Cullerne Bown, *Art under Stalin* (Oxford, 1991), pl. 113.

43. See also N. Ponomarev, *V kotlovane 'Zharko'* (1951), *Iskusstvo* 2 (1952): 42, from his Volga-Don series, which showed workmates showering each other with a hose while on a construction site.

44. Alexander Tvardovsky, *Vasilii Tyorkin: A Book about a Soldier* (Moscow, 1975), 359.

45. For more on the masculinity of the *bania* throughout the postwar period, see Ethan Pollock, "Real Men Go to the Bania: Postwar Soviet Masculinities and the Bathhouse," *Kritika: Explorations in Russian and Eurasian History* 11, no. 1 (2010): 47–76. For the role of the bania in Soviet homosexual culture, see Dan Healey, *Homosexual Desire in Revolutionary Russia: The Regulation of Sexual and Gender Dissent* (London, 2001), esp. 26–36.

46. Shvedova, "Novye raboty khudozhnikov leningrada," 24; Tvardovsky, *Vassili Tyorkin*, 361.

47. Tvardovsky, *Vassili Tyorkin*, 355.

48. Catriona Kelly, "The Education of the Will: Advice Literature, *Zakal* and Manliness in Early Twentieth-Century Russia," in *Russian Masculinities in History and Culture*, ed. B. Clements, R. Friedman, and D. Healey (Basingstoke, 2001), 131.

49. For more detail on a range of issues raised by the process of de-Stalinization, see P. Jones, ed., *The Dilemmas of De-Stalinization: Negotiating Cultural and Social Change in the Khrushchev Era* (New York, 2006).

50. For full details of the exhibition, see B. V. Ioganson, *Vsesoiuznaia iubileinaia khudozhestven-naia vystavka 1957 goda* (Moscow, 1958). Popular coverage includes "V masterskikh khudozhnikov," *Ogonek* 43 (1957): 30–31; and "Vsesoiuznaia khudozhestvennaia vystavka," *Sovetskaia zhenshchina* 2 (1958), 20. Works from the exhibition can be found in numerous issues of *Ogonek* including 50 (1957), 6 (1958), and 19 (1958).

51. E. Polishchuk, "Sovetskaia armiia v proizvedeniiakh zhivopisi," *Iskusstvo* 1 (1958): 43.

52. *Iskusstvo* 1 (1958): 45.

53. Other significant examples of this attempt to incorporate psychological depth into works that dealt with the War include Gelii Korzhev, *Vliublennye* (1959), and Edgar Iltner, *Muzh'ia vozvrash-chaiutsia* (1957). See chapter 2 for further discussion of these works.

54. *Iskusstvo* 1 (1958): 46; *Iskusstvo* 3 (1955): 45. The scene also bears a resemblance to that described by Isaak Babel, in *My First Goose* (c. 1923) of a group of Civil War soldiers sleeping in a deserted hayloft; "Six of us slept there, warming each other with our bodies, our legs tangled together"; Isaac Babel, *Collected Stories*, trans. David McDuff (Harmondsworth, 1994), 123.

55. Given the prominence of Loskutov, it is entirely probable that Oboznenko would have been aware of his work. The photograph was itself reproduced in *Sovetskaia zhenshchina* 5 (1965): 47, as part of the commemoration of the twentieth anniversary of victory.

56. Polishchuk, "Sovetskaia armiia v proizvedeniiakh zhivopisi," 48.

57. Other reproductions around this time include *Ogonek* 7 (1958): between 24–25; and *Ogonek* 25 (1961): between 24–25.

58. Matthew Cullerne Bown, *Socialist Realist Painting* (London, 1998), 367.

59. *Iskusstvo* 12 (1961): 6; V. Knyzhov, *Zashchitniki Sevastopolia* (1963) *Iskusstvo* 5 (1964): 8.

60. *Ogonek* 38 (1960): between 16–17; *Iskusstvo* 2 (1958): 16.

61. *Iskusstvo* 12 (1961): 7.

62. *Iskusstvo* 8 (1960): 9.

63. *Iskusstvo* 1 (1958): 42; *Ogonek* 5 (1958): between 16–17.

64. *Iskusstvo* 11 (1967): 18.

65. For a detailed discussion of Nikonov's work, see Susan Reid, *De-Stalinization and the Remodernization of Soviet Art: The Search for a Contemporary Realism, 1953–1963* (PhD dissertation, University of Pennsylvania, 1996), 291–300.

66. Korzhev's triptych comprised three of the most popular works of the day, although the *Raising of the Banner* was probably the one that was reproduced most frequently. See *Ogonek* 23 (1960) for the first reproduction of this triptych, which formed part of the magazine's coverage of the Soviet Russia Exhibition. All three works are reproduced in color, with *Raising of the Banner* warranting a double-page spread, and there is a short write-up following the images. *Homer*, one of the other pieces from the series, would later be turned into a stamp as part of a series issued to celebrate the Russian Museum; Solov'ev, *Pochtovye marki Rossii i SSSR*, 229.

67. A. Kantor, "Cherty novogo," *Tvorchesto* 2 (1958): 8

68. Borenstein, *Men without Women*, 4, 3.

69. Edward Said, *The World, the Text and the Critic* (London, 1991), 16–24, 20.

70. These changes were enacted by the catchily titled Decree on the Prohibition of Abortions, the Improvement of Material Aid to Women in Childbirth, the Establishment of State Assistance to Parents of Large Families, and the Extension of the Network of Lying-in Homes, Nursery Schools and Kindergartens, the Tightening-up of Criminal Punishment for the Non-payment of Alimony, and on Certain Modifications in Divorce Legislation (June 28, 1936), reproduced in J. Meisel and E. S. Kozera, eds., *Materials for the Study of the Soviet System* (Ann Arbor, MI: 1953), 229–30.

71. For more, see for example Wendy Webster, "Domesticating the Frontier: Gender, Empire and Adventure Landscapes in British Cinema, 1945–59," *Gender and History* 15, no. 1 (2003): 85–107; Graham Dawson, "The Blonde Bedouin: Lawrence of Arabia, Imperial Adventure and the Imagining of English-British Masculinity," in *Manful Assertions: Masculinities in Britain since 1800*, ed. Michael Roper and John Tosh (Basingstoke, 1991), 113–44.

72. Uta Poiger, "A New, 'Western' Hero? Reconstructing German Masculinity in the 1950s," *Signs* 24, no. 1 (1998): 158.

73. Steven Cohen, *Masked Men: Masculinity and the Movies in the Fifties* (Bloomington, IN: 1997), 209.

74. S. G. Prociuk, "The Manpower Problem in Siberia," *Soviet Studies* 19, no. 2 (1967): 194.

75. Prociuk, "The Manpower Problem in Siberia," 191. Emphasis my own.

76. This transformation resembles the shift in the conceptualization of Siberia that occurred in the nineteenth century, which combined the physical hardship of the climate with the promise of material wealth and the exile of those who had been involved in the Decembrist plot. For more, see Mark Bassin, "Inventing Siberia: Visions of the Russian East in the Early Nineteenth Century," *American Historical Review* 96, no. 3 (1991): 763–94; Bassin, "Russia between Europe and Asia: The Ideological Construction of Geographical Space," *Slavic Review* 50, no. 1 (1991): 1–17; Bassin, *Imperial Visions: Nationalist Imaginations and Geographical Expansion in the Russian Far East 1840–1865* (Cambridge, 1999); and Janet Hartley, *Siberia: A History of the People* (New Haven, CT: 2014).

77. G. M. Malenkov in *Otchetnyi doklad XIX s'ezdu partii o rabote TSK VKP(b), 5 oktiabria 1952 g.* (Moscow, 1952), 73. For a discussion of the problem of conflict in art, see E. Polishchuk, "Problema konflikta v Sovetskoi siuzhetnoi kartine," *Iskusstvo* 1 (1954): 26–30.

78. "Khrushchev's Speech in New Virgin Land Territory," *Pravda,* March 19, 1961, translated in *Current Digest of the Soviet Press* 13, no. 11 (1961): 18–19.

79. See for example E. Shulman, "Soviet Maidens for the Socialist Fortress: The Ketagurovite Campaign to Settle the Far East 1937–1939," *Russian Review* 62, no. 3 (2003): 387–410; Shulman, *Stalinism on the Frontier of Empire: Women and State Formation in the Soviet Far East* (Cambridge, 2008); and Shulman, "'Those Who Hurry to the Far East': Readers, Dreamers and Volunteers," in *Peopling the Russian Periphery: Borderland Colonization in Eurasian History*, ed. Nicholas Breyfogle, Abby Schrader, and Willard Sunderland (London, 2007), 213–37.

80. See for example D. Mochal'skii, *Ukha zhery* (1957), *Iskusstvo* 5 (1962): 9; *Molodozheny tselinniki* (1959–61), reproduced in O. I. Sopotsinskii, *Sovetskoe izobrazitel'noe iskusstvo* (Moscow, 1962), pl. 185; and B. Vaks, *Na tseline* (1961), *Ogonek* 15 (1962): between 8–9.

81. M. Pohl, "Women and Girls on the Virgin Lands," in *Women in the Khrushchev Era*, ed. M. Ilic, S. Reid, and L. Attwood (Basingstoke, 2004), esp. 54–56.

82. For example F. Maleav, *Podniataia tselina* (1954), *Iskusstvo* 3 (1955), 21; N. Lomakin and G. Pesis, *Na mirnoi zemle* [1955–61?], *Ogonek* 42 (1961): between 24–25; and L. Chegarovskii, *Kommunisty na poliakh. Seiat' pora!* [1955–61?], *Ogonek* 45 (1961): between 16–17.

83. *Iskusstvo* 3 (1955): 20; *Ogonek* 4 (1959): between 8–9.

84. *Ogonek* 26 (1960): between 16–17. This painting was based on one of Basov's earlier works, *Portret traktorista I. Zinenko*, 1954, which is reproduced in *Iskusstvo* 3 (1955): 21.

85. *Ogonek* 22 (1959): between 24–25; *Ogonek* 10 (1966): between 8–9. Basov was a participant in *Sovetskaia rossiia* (1960), and Oreshnikov's work was shown at *Nash Sovremennik* (1959).

86. B. Berezovskii, M. Solov'ev, and I. Shagin, *Pod voditel'stvom velikogo Stalina—vpered k kommunizmu!*, RU/SU 2237. Reproduction information also taken from the Hoover Institute's poster database. *Sovetskaia zhenshchina* 1 (1951): 1–2.

87. For other posters that link the construction of hydroelectric dams with Stalinist power, see Viktor Koretskii's *Mir Pobedit!* (1950), RU/SU 2234, and the Czech poster by an unknown artist, *Za Mír* (1951), RU/SU 2235. Interestingly, Koretskii's work would be translated into Czech but, like *Za Mír*, still only referenced works that were being undertaken in the Soviet Union—those at Kuibyshev, Stalingrad, and in Turkmenistan. Reproduced in Galerie U Křižovníků, *Moc Obrazů Obrazy Moci: Power of Images, Images of Power: Politický Plakát a Propaganda: The Political Poster and Propaganda* (Prague,

2005), 176. See also the earlier work by Iraklii Toidze, *Tovarishch Stalin na Riongese* (1931), *Iskusstvo* 6 (1937): 58, which was also turned into a postcard, reproduced in M. Chapkina, *Khudozhestvennaia Otkrytka* (Moscow, 1993), pl. 378. More obliquely, see Toidze's painting *Ilich's Lightbulb* (1927), which was a comment on the electrification project begun under Lenin and showed a small child on his mother's knee reaching for a lightbulb that was being dangled above his head. In the background is Zemo-Avchali GES, which opened in Georgia in 1927. Reproduced in Matthew Cullerne Bown, "Painting in the Non-Russian Republics," in *Art of the Soviets: Painting, Sculpture and Architecture in a One-Party State, 1917–1992*, ed. M. Cullerne Bown and B. Taylor (Manchester, 1993), 144.

88. M Volodin, V. Sokolov, L. Naroditskii, N. Tolkunov, Sokolov-Skalia, and A. Plotnov, *Iskusstvo* 2 (1952): between 44–45; *Rabotnitsa* 2 (1952): 19.

89. For more, see John McCannon, "Positive Heroes at the Pole: Celebrity Status, Socialist-Realist Ideal and the Soviet Myth of the Arctic, 1932–39," *Russian Review* 56, no. 3 (1997): 249. See also McCannon, *Red Arctic: Polar Exploration and the Myth of the North in the Soviet Union, 1932–39* (New York, 1998); and McCannon, "Tabula Rasa in the North: The Soviet Arctic and Mythic Landscape in Stalinist Popular Culture," in *The Landscape of Stalinism: The Art and Ideology of Soviet Space*, ed. E. Dobrenko and E. Naiman (London, 2003), 241–60. For representation in culture, see Emma Widdis, *Visions of a New Land: Soviet Film from the Revolution to the Second World War* (London, 2003).

90. Cullerne Bown, *Socialist Realist Painting*, 389–95; Susan Reid, "Modernizing Socialist Realism in the Khrushchev Thaw: The Struggle for a 'Contemporary Style' in Soviet Art," in *The Dilemmas of De-Stalinization: Negotiating Cultural and Social Change in the Khrushchev Era*, ed. Polly Jones (New York, 2006), 164–65; V. Maslenikov, "Sotsialisticheskii realizm i uslovnost'," *Iskusstvo* 1 (1961): 38–41.

91. A. Sidorov, "The Thaw: Painting of the Khrushchev Era," in The Museum of Modern Art, Oxford, *Soviet Socialist Realist Painting 1930s-1960s: Paintings from Russia, the Ukraine, Belorussia, Uzbekistan, Kirgizia, Georgia, Armenia, Azerbaijan and Moldova Selected in the USSR by Matthew Cullerne Bown* (Oxford, 1992), 35.

92. "Prizyvy TsK KPSS k 46-i godovshchine Velikoi Oktiabr'skoi sotsialisticheskoi revoliutsii," *Pravda*, October 1963.

93. Fragment reproduced in *Iskusstvo* 2 (1963): 6; full image reproduced in *Iskusstvo* 7 (1965): 26.

94. Susan Reid, "The Art of Memory: Retrospectivism in Soviet Painting of the Brezhnev Era," in *Art of the Soviets: Painting, Sculpture and Architecture in a One-Party State, 1917–1992*, ed. M. Cullerne Bown and B. Taylor (Manchester, 1993), 165.

95. See for example A. I. Morozov, "Traditsii nravstvennosti," *Tvorchestvo* 4 (1979): 9, 18.

96. "Khrushchev on Modern Art," *Encounter* (April 1963), reproduced in P. Johnson, ed., *Khrushchev and the Arts: The Politics of Soviet Culture, 1962–64* (Cambridge, MA: 1965), 102–3. For more on the public debate surrounding works shown at the Manezh, see Susan Reid, "In the Name of the People: The Manège Affair Revisited," *Kritika* 6, no. 4 (2005): 673–716.

97. Anon., "Za ideinuiu chistotu sovetskogo izobrazitel'nogo iskusstva," *Iskusstvo* 2 (1963): 7.

98. For other works featuring the heroic geologists that were much better received, see B. Korneev, *Geologi*, 1961, reproduced in *Iskusstvo* 12 (1961): 9 and *Ogonek* 28 (1963): between 24–25; and Oleg Gadalov, *Geologi* (1963), reproduced in *Iskusstvo* 5 (1964): 9 and *Ogonek* 12 (1964): between 16–17. Both artists also received a brief review of their work to accompany the *Ogonek* reproductions. See also Iurii Aleksandrov's sculpture *N. Doinikov, Geolog* (1961), *Iskusstvo* 3 (1962): 15. Compare the hardships one sees in these paintings to S. Frolov's *Sovetskie geologi* (1951), reproduced in *Ogonek* 1 (1959): between 16–17.

99. For details of the written campaign that followed Manezh, see Reid, "In the Name of the People," 673n1.

100. See for example A. Golikov, "Girliandnaia GES," *Ogonek* 21 (1961): 11; Anon., "... Plius electrifikatsiia," *Sovetskaia zhenshchina* 11 (1961): 19–21; and N. Bukov, "Sozvezdie bratska," *Ogonek* 36 (1963): 16–17 with color supplement.

101. *Iskusstvo* 9 (1961): 23. Published under the title *Sibir' v stroike* in *Khudozhnik* 2 (1963); it is likely that this is an editorial mistake as this was the title of another Agapov painting from 1959. This in itself is an interesting work, depicting two muscular men in a Promethean struggle with a faltering heavy goods vehicle, although it was heavily criticized for lacking depth of characterization. Reproduced in *Iskusstvo* 5 (1961): 8.

102. This was a very popular painting and was reproduced numerous times between 1945 and 1965. See for example *Rabotnitsa* 7 (1951): 9; and *Ogonek* 20 (1958): between 16–17.

103. V. Zimenko, "Trudnosti rosta," *Iskusstvo* 9 (1961): 23.

104. Reid, "Masters of the Earth," 303. Other works that feature the construction of hydroelectric power stations and draw upon the same hypermasculine tropes include Nadir Abdurakhmanov, *Stroitel'stvo Ali-Bairamlinskoi GES* (1961), *Iskusstvo* 4 (1962): 12; and V. Vassiltsev, *Na strontel'stve GES* (1960), *Iskusstvo* 2 (1961): 7. See V. Trifonov's diploma work *Zapadno-Sibirskaia neft'* (1965), *Khudozhnik* 5 (1966): 10 for a further work that places an all-male group of workers in Siberia, and also Gunar Mitrevits, *Novyi most* (1960), *Ogonek* 2 (1962): between 24–25. Unlike these examples from the 1960s, two earlier works of note also on the GES theme contain women: Iurii Podliaskii *Oni nachinali Bratskuiu GES* (1957–60), *Iskusstvo* 5 (1960): 2; and Nikolai Andronov, *Kuibyshevskaia GES* (1957), *Iskusstvo* 9 (1958): 32. Another landmark piece of art, Andronov's work received a great deal of critical attention when it was displayed at the Fourth Moscow Youth Exhibition in 1958. For more, see Reid, "Modernizing Socialist Realism in the Khrushchev Thaw," 218–21.

105. Kharitonov's work was reproduced in *Iskusstvo* 1 (1960): 6, and twice in *Ogonek* within the space of nine months, both times in color and once as a double-page image; *Ogonek* 1 and 37 (1960); Chekaniuk's work can be found in *Iskusstvo* 11 (1963): 7, and *Ogonek* 45 (1964): between 16–17.

106. *Iskusstvo* 9 (1961): 25. See also Igor' Simonov, *V tsekhovoi laboratorii* (1961), *Ogonek* 44 (1961): between 8–9, which juxtaposes the delicacy and fragility of the female body surrounded by glass flasks with the looming presence of two giant workers. Simonov's later works would continue to depict the Soviet superman and were greatly influenced by both the Thaw interest in the relationship between the land and man and the contemporary style. See for example *Moi geroi* (1964), reproduced in A. G. Fedotova, *Obraz zhizni-sovetskii: Proizvedeniia khudozhnikov Rossiiskoi federatsii* (Leningrad, 1986); *Na poliarnom* (1966), *Khudozhnik* 2 (1967): 3; and *Taezhnye kilometry* (1967), *Khudozhnik* 3 (1968): between 10–11.

107. Zimenko, "Trudnosti rosta," 23.

108. *Iskusstvo* 6 (1960): 14.

109. Zimenko, "Trudnosti rosta," 23.

110. Reid, *De-Stalinization and the Remodernization of Soviet Art*, 505–6. The painting and its reception is discussed at length in Reid's work, see esp. 495–505.

111. *Iskusstvo* 10 (1960): 6; *Ogonek* 14 (1963): between 16–17. For more detail on the anxiety of female involvement in heavy industry, see Reid, "Masters of the Earth," 293.

112. See for example E. Popova, "Podskazano kaspiem," *Ogonek* 14 (1963): 16; N. Tomskii, "Liubite prekrasnoe!," *Ogonek* 10 (1966): 8; and E. Belashova, "Khudozhnik. Vremia. Zhizn," *Ogonek* 10 (1967): 16.

113. L. Akimova, "Tair Salakhov i ego geroi," *Iskusstvo* 3 (1966): 40.

114. Cullerne Bown, *Socialist Realist Painting*, 397.

115. Reid, "Masters of the Earth," 304.

116. *Iskusstvo* 1 (1961): 12; *Ogonek* 9 (1967): between 16–17.

117. Reid, "Masters of the Earth," 301.

118. Ibid., 303–4.

119. Polishchuk, "Sovetskaia armiia v proizvedeniiakh zhivopisi," 46–47.

120. One notable exception to this is the sculpture by Semen Loik, *S pobedoi synok!* (1958), which continued the earlier trend of examining homecoming through human relations; *Iskusstvo* 1 (1959): 28.

121. For more detail on late imperial depictions of landscape, see Christopher Ely, *This Meager Nature: Landscape and National Identity in Imperial Russia* (DeKalb: IL, 2002); and Jane Costlow, *Heart-Pine Russia: Walking and Writing the Nineteenth-Century Forest* (New York, 2012).

122. *Iskusstvo* 4 (1958): 23; reproduced in color in *Sovetskaia zhenshchina* 6 (1961): between 24–25.

123. *Iskusstvo* 10 (1958): 10.

124. *Ogonek* 9 (1958): between 16–17; *Ogonek* 8 (1961): between 16–17.

125. See also the later paintings Grigorii Bulgakov's *Back Home* (1964), reproduced in Vern Grosvenor Swanson, *Soviet Impressionism* (Woodbridge, 2001), pl. 137; and Mikhail Kugach, *Vozvrashchenie* (1969), reproduced in K. Suzdalev, *9.V.45—9.V.75: Podvigu 30 let* (Moscow, 1975), pl. 132. See also Ilya Repin's *"Na rodinu." Geroi minuvshei voiny* (1878) for a *Peredvizhniki*-era representation of homecoming in which the landscape was prominent.

126. Afsaneh Najmabadi, "The Erotic Vatan [Homeland] as Beloved and Mother: To Love, to Possess and to Protect," *Comparative Studies in Society and History* 39, no. 3 (1997): 442. See also Lynn Hunt, *The Family Romance of the French Revolution* (Berkeley, CA: 1992); and Eve Kosofsky Sedgwick, *Between Men: English Literature and Male Homosocial Desire* (New York, 1985). For more on the idea of Mother Russia, see Joanne Hubbs, *Mother Russia: The Feminine Myth in Russian Culture* (Indianapolis, IN: 1993); and Linda Edmundson, "Putting Mother Russia in a European Context," in *Art, Nation and Gender: Ethnic Landscapes, Myths and Mother Figures*, ed. Tricia Cusack and Signle Bhreathnach-Lynch (Aldershot, 2003), 53–65.

127. See Victoria Bonnell, "The Peasant Woman in Stalinist Political Art of the 1930s," *The American Historical Review* 98 (1993): 55–82, for more on Stalin-era representations of peasant women. For female-led disturbances during collectivization, see Lynne Viola, "Bab'i Bunty and Peasant Women's Protest during Collectivisation," *Russian Review* 45 no 1 (1986): 23–42; William Husband, "Mythical Communities and the New Soviet Woman: Bolshevik Anti-Religious *Chastushki*, 1917– 1932," *Russian Review* 63, no. 1 (2004): 89–106; and Tracy McDonald, "A Peasant Rebellion in Stalinist Russia: The Pitelinskii Uprising, Riazan, 1930," in *Contending with Stalinism*, ed. L. Viola (New York, 2002), 84–108.

128. See for example P. Krivonogov, *Komissar kretsosti* (1966), and N. But, *Vo imia zhizn'* (1965), both of which can be found in Oleg Sopotsinskii, *Velikaia Otechestvennaia voina v proizvedeniiakh sovetskikh khudozhnikov: zhivopis', skul'ptura, grafika* (Moscow, 1979).

129. Cullerne Bown, *Socialist Realist Painting,* 418.

130. Examples include Gelii Korzhev, *Starye rany* (1967) and *Trevoga* (1965–68); and M. I. Likachev, *Pamiat'* (1974).

131. Reproduced in V. I. Gapeeva, V. A. Gusev, and A. V. Tsvetov, *Izobrazitel'noe iskusstvo Leningrada: vystavka proizvedenii Leningradskikh khudozhnikov, Moskva, Noiabr' 1976—Ianvar' 1977* (Leningrad, 1981), unpaged. It has not been possible to establish whether this work was exhibited prior to this.

132. All three of these works can be found in A. A. Iuferova, *Velikaia Otechestvennaia voina v proizvedeniiakh sovetskikh khudozhnikov* (Moscow, 1985), pls. 152, 174, 151. Like Oboznenko's earlier work, *Night of the Nightingales*, the inspiration behind Ianke's image would appear to be a photograph taken in 1943 after the Battle of Kursk Arc, which depicted a soldier, head in hands, sitting beside the wreckage of a gun carriage and the body of a comrade. See also Safronov's later work *Boevoe znamia* (1985), reproduced in S. N. Levandovskii, *Mir otstoiali, mir sokhranim* (Leningrad, 1985), pl. 17.

133. V. Kramov, "Ottsu posviashchaetsia," *Ogonek* 7 (1968): 16.

134. *Iskusstvo* 3 (1969): 14; see chapter 3 for further discussion of this painting.

135. Reproduced in Suzdalev, *9.V.45–9.V.75: Podvigu 30 let*, pl. 152. Savitskii's work was clearly an inspiration behind other later works that expressed the ferocity of war, as seen for example in Shalva Bedoev, *Proryv* (1985), which was highly reminiscent of Savitskii's painting in both its conceptualization of the soldier and its composition and palette. Reproduced in Levandovskii, *Mir otstoiali, mir sokhranim*, pl. 35.

136. Iurii Neprintsev, *Vot soldaty idut* (1973), reproduced in Suzdalev, *9.V.45–9.V.75: Podvigu 30 let,* pl. 140.

## Chapter 2

1. Fedor Gladkov, *Cement,* trans. A. S Arthur and C. Ashleigh (London, 1929), 68.

2. Alexander Tvardovsky, *Vassili Tyorkin: A Book about a Soldier,* trans. Alex Miller (Moscow, 1975), 351. The sentiments expressed by Gladkov and Tvardovskii with regard to the scars of war-inflicted wounds were not unique to Soviet culture. For example, William Shakespeare in his *Henry V* (1594–99) wrote that a man who had taken part in the Battle of Agincourt, years after the event would "strip his sleeve and show his scars, / And say 'These wounds I had on Crispin's day'" (act 4, scene 3). Two centuries later, Jacques-Louis David in a speech to the National Convention (July 11, 1794) proclaimed that "The scars of the heroes of liberty are the richest dowry and the most durable ornament"; cited in Alex Potts, "Beautiful Bodies and Dying Heroes: Images of Ideal Manhood in the French Revolution," *History Workshop Journal* 30, no. 1 (1990): 15. For more on authenticity, the exposure of scars, and the bania, see Ethan Pollock, "Real Men Go to the Bania: Postwar Soviet Masculinities and the Bathhouse," *Kritika: Explorations in Russian and Eurasian History* 11, no. 1 (2010): 47–76.

3. See especially Lilya Kaganovsky, *How the Soviet Man Was Unmade: Cultural Fantasy and Male Subjectivity under Stalin* (Pittsburgh, PA: 2008).

4. For more on the transgressive body, see Mikhail Bakhtin, *Rabelais and His World,* (Cambridge, MA: 1968); and Julia Kristeva, *Powers of Horror: An Essay on Abjection,* trans. Leon S. Roudiez (New York, 1982).

5. RU/SU 1066. For more on the issue of masculinity and war trauma in the early twentieth century, see Laura L. Phillips, "Gendered Dis/ability: Perspectives from the Treatment of Psychiatric Casualties in Russia's Early Twentieth Century Wars," *Social History of Medicine* 20, no. 2 (2007): 333–50.

6. Pasternak cited in Nina Baburina, *Russkii plakat Pervoi mirovoi voiny* (Moscow, 1992), 7–8. Emphasis in original.

7. Examples include E. E. Sporius, *Na dom invalidov* (1914), RGB XIV 7b 10946; Unknown artist, *Pochta, telegraf, telefon 21, 22, 23, aprelia organizuiut sbor na ustroistvo zdravnits i podarki voinam* (1916), RGB XIV 7b 65646; and S. A. Vinogradov, *Na pomoshch' zhertvam' voiny* (1914), RGB XIV. 7b 18420. For further discussion of the representation of the disabled in the posters of the First World War, see Karen Petrone, *The Great War in Russian Memory* (Bloomington, IN: 2011), esp. 89–93.

8. *Harold M. Fleming Papers, 1917–71,* New York Public Library Digital Gallery, Image ID 416744, www.digitalgallery.nypl.org, accessed April 30, 2017. Apsit, *Den' ranenogo krasnoarmeitsa,* found at GARF *Otdel izdanii,* uncatalogued. There are a couple of other examples of posters depicting the wounded soldier that date from the Civil War, but they were aimed at the recruitment of nurses rather than expressing explicit concerns over the welfare of the invalided or injured soldier. For example, Anon., *Ranenyi krasnoarmeets naidet sebe Mat' i sestru v kazhdoi trudiashchesia zhenshchine* [1917–22?], RU/SU 1243; and Anon., *Tovarishchi rabotnitsy idite v riady krasnykh sester miloserdiia* [1917–22?], RU/SU 1244.

9. Matthew Cullerne Bown, *Socialist Realist Painting* (London, 1998), 95.

10. For an interesting discussion of the work of Grosz, Dix, and their contemporaries, see Sabine Rewald, ed., *Glitter and Doom: German Portraits from the 1920s* (New York, 2007).

11. Aranovich cited in Cullerne Bown, *Socialist Realist Painting,* 95.

12. The disabled veteran was a consistent feature of Dix's work. See also his triptych *Grosstadt* (1927–28) and *Die Streichholzhaendler* (1920).

13. Beate Fieseler, "Work as the Overall Remedy to Reconstruct Disabled Soldiers' Bodies in the Post-War Soviet Union," unpublished conference paper, *American Association for the Advancement of Slavic Studies,* Philadelphia, November 2008.

14. Kaganovsky, *How the Soviet Man Was Unmade,* 3.

15. *Iskusstvo* 2 (*1950*): 79; *Tvorchestvo* 1 (1947): 6; published under the title *Starshii leitenant A. S. Buryi* in *Khudozhnik* 2 (1963), 2.

16. For a broader discussion of some of the issues raised by the Soviet war poster, see Mark Edele, "Paper Soldiers: The World of the Soldier Hero according to Soviet Wartime Posters," *Jahrbücher für Geschichte Osteuropas 47* (1999), 89–108; Helena Goscilo, "History and Metahistory in Soviet World War II Posters," in *Recalling the Past, (Re)Constructing the Past: Collective and Individual Memory of World War II in Russia and Germany*, ed. W. Bonner and A. Rosenholm (Jyväskylä, 2008), 221–29.

17. Rossiiskaia gosudarstvennaia biblioteka, *Plakaty voiny i pobedy, 1941–1945* (Moscow, 2005), 98.

18. See for example A. F. Postnov, *Shar zemnoi pokryl ty krov'iu, Ne morgnuv pri etom brov'iu* (1914), RU/SU 81; D. Moor, *Kak chort ogorod gorodil* (1914), RU/SU 371; and E. F. Chelnakov, *Prussaki* (1914), RU/SU 377.

19. Examples of posters include A. Kokorekin, *Ubei Ego!* (1945), RU/SU 2132; and B. Efimov, *Chelovekoliubivyi Gitler* [1944–45?], RU/SU 2463; cartoons in the press include Kukryniksy, "Unichtozhit' nemetskoe chudovishche!," *Pravda*, August 6, 1942, which shows a gorilla in a Nazi uniform rampaging through a village while holding the body of a dead woman; Kukryniksy, "Liudoedy 'Vysshei rasy,'" *Pravda*, August 11, 1942, which shows Hitler, Goering, Goebbels, and Himmler chewing on bones and wearing loincloths made up of human skulls; Kukryniksy, Untitled, *Pravda*, April 29, 1942, which depicts Hitler and Goering as ferocious, spiky beasts feeding off the bodies of dead women and children; and Kukryniksy, "Fashistskaia dzhaz-banda," *Pravda*, May 8, 1942, which again shows the Nazi leadership this time playing musical instruments made out of body parts or bloody axes, with Hitler conducting to the tune of "*Mein Kampf.*"

20. *Plakaty voiny i pobedy*, 20.

21. *Plakaty voiny i pobedy*, 142.

22. RU/SU 2094.

23. Kukryniksy, "Godovoi itog," *Pravda*, February 24, 1944. Other examples include Boris Efimov, "Skoraia pomoshch," *Pravda*, January 31, 1943; and Unknown artist, "Zima i letom odnim tsvetom," *Pravda*, July 25, 1943. Similar images can also be found in *Krokodil*, such as I. Semenov, "Opasnaia igra," in *Krokodil* 29 (1943).

24. G. F. Krivosheev, *Soviet Casualties and Combat Losses in the Twentieth Century*, trans. John Erickson (London, 1997), 89–91.

25. Ibid., 95.

26. Catherine Merridale, *Ivan's War: The Red Army 1939–1945* (London, 2005), 314. For more on the treatment of disabled veterans after the War, see Mark Edele, *Soviet Veterans of the Second World War: A Popular Movement in an Authoritarian Society, 1941–1991* (Oxford, 2008); Beate Fieseler, "Stimmen aus dem gesellschaftlichen Abseits: Die sowjetrussischen Kriegsinvaliden im 'Tauwetter' der fünfziger Jahre," *Osteuropa* 52, no. 7 (2002): 945–62; Fieseler, "'Nishchie pobediteli': Invalidy Velikoi Otechestvennoi voiny v Sovetskom Soiuze," *Neprikosnovenyi zapas* 40–41, no. 2–3, available at http://magazines.russ.ru/nz/2005/2/fi33.html, accessed April 30, 2017; Fieseler, "The Bitter Legacy of the Great Patriotic War: Red Army Disabled Soldiers under Late-Stalinism," in Fürst, *Late Stalinist Russia*, 46–61; and Ekaterina Tchueva, "Mir posle voiny': Zhaloby kak instrument regulirovaniia otnoshenii mezhdy gosudarstvom i invalidami Velikoi Otechestvennoi Voiny," in *Sovetskaia Sotsial'naia Politika: Stseny i deistvuiushchie litsa, 1940–1985*, ed. Elena Iarskaia-Smirnova and Pavel Romanov (Moscow, 2005), 96–120. See also Sarah D. Phillips, "'There Are No Invalids in the USSR!': A Missing Soviet Chapter in the New Disability History," *Disability Studies Quarterly* 29, no. 3 (2009): unpaginated, http://dsq-sds.org/article/view/936/1111, accessed April 30, 2017.

27. Robert Dale, "The Varlaam Myth and the Fate of Leningrad's Disabled Veterans," *Russian Review* 72, no. 2 (2013): 260–84.

28. Edele, *Soviet Veterans of the Second World War*, 94. See also Elena Zubkova, "S protianutoi rukoi nishchie i nishchenstvo v poslevoennom SSSR," *Cahiers de Monde russe* 2, no. 49 (2008), 441–74.

29. For detailed figures on this urban clearing, see Dale, "The Varlaam Myth and the Fate of Leningrad's Disabled Veterans," 268–73.

30. A. Sukhov, "What We Do for Disabled Ex-Servicemen," *Soviet News*, May 4, 1946, 1. Sukhov's figures are disputed by Fieseler ["The Bitter Legacy of the Great Patriotic War," 53–54].

31. "Prizyvy TsK VKP(b) k 1 maia 1946 goda," *Pravda*, April 24, 1946.

32. Fieseler, "The Bitter Legacy of the Great Patriotic War," 48–52.

33. "Letter to the Editor: On Poor Artificial Limbs," *Pravda*, September 14, 1949, translated in *Current Digest of the Soviet Press* 1, no. 38 (1949): 63.

34. The degree to which this idea of "overcoming" disability through work was a distinctly Soviet attitude should not be overemphasized. As well as being a rhetoric that was found in other countries after 1945, in a Russian context it appears to have its roots at least in the First World War as demonstrated by charity posters such as that by an unknown artist, *Labor Will Return Life and Happiness to You* (1916), which depicted a one-legged man, somewhat ironically, at a workbench mending shoes [RGB XIV. 7b 10457]. For the idea of overcoming disability in other national contexts, see for example David Gerber, "Disabled Veterans, the State, and the Experience of Disability in Western Societies, 1914–1950," *Journal of Social History* 36, no. 4 (2003): 899–916; and Carol Poore, "Who Belongs: Disability and the German Nation in Postwar Literature and Film," *German Studies Review* 26, no. 1 (2003): 21–42.

35. The notion that 1948 represented a watershed moment for other aspects of postwar society has been put forward by a number of historians. See for example Elena Zubkova, *Russia after the War: Hopes, Illusions, and Disappointments*, trans. H. Ragsdale (London, 1998), 102; and Donald Filtzer, *Soviet Workers and Late Stalinism: Labour and the Restoration of the Stalinist System after World War II* (Cambridge, 2002), 258. March 1948 also saw the last wave of demobilization [Edele, *Soviet Veterans of the Second World War*, 23].

36. *Ogonek* 7 (1946): between 34–35; *Sovetskaia zhenshchina* 6 (1947), 51. Orlova's image was actually reproduced as part of a rare feature on art and the female war experience: E. Braginskii, "Ikh podvig: mastera izobraziteľnogo iskusstva o zhenshchinakh-geroiniakh otchestvennoi voiny," 48–51.

37. For more on Obryn'ba's own personal experience of the War, see his memoir, published in English as *Red Partisan: The Memoirs of a Soviet Resistance Fighter on the Eastern Front* (Barnsley, 2006).

38. *Iskusstvo* 3 (1948): 13; *Iskusstvo* 5 (1948): 9.

39. Aleksandr Laktionov cited in Oliver Johnson, "'A Premonition of Victory': A Letter from the Front," *Russian Review* 68 no 3 (2009), 408–28 (410).

40. Image reproduced in the program for an evening with Laktionov, *Doklad o tvorcheskoi deiateľnosti A. I. Laktionova, 6 iiunia 1960, Akademii khudozhestv SSSR*. I am grateful to Oliver Johnson for sharing this information with me.

41. Johnson, "A Premonition of Victory," 418.

42. *Sovetskaia zhenshchina* 4 (1948), 33.

43. Vladimir Solov'ev, *Pochtovye marki Rossii i SSSR 1857–1991* (Moscow, 2003), 251.

44. For more, see Anna Krylova, *Soviet Women in Combat: A History of Violence on the Eastern Front* (Cambridge, 2010).

45. For more, see Vera Dunham, "Images of the Disabled, Especially the War Wounded in Soviet Literature," in *The Disabled in the Soviet Union: Past and Present, Theory and Practice*, ed. L. Siegelbaum and W. McCragg (Pittsburgh, PA: 1989), 151–65. For a detailed discussion of the treatment of the damaged man in wartime Soviet literature, see Krylova, "Healers of Wounded Souls." The issues of subjectivity and disability are discussed in relation to blinded war veterans in Maria Christina Galmarini, "Turning Defects into Advantages: The Discourse of Labour in the Autobiographies of Soviet Blinded Second World War Veterans," *European History Quarterly* 44, no. 4 (2014): 651–77.

46. Dunham, "Images of the Disabled, Especially the War Wounded in Soviet Literature," 153.

47. Anna Krylova, "'Healers of the Wounded Souls': The Crisis of Private Life in Soviet Literature, 1944–1946," *The Journal of Modern History* 73 (2001): 310.

48. Krylova, "Healers of the Wounded Souls," 324.

49. Katherine Hodgson, *Written with the Bayonet: Soviet Poetry of the Second World War* (Liverpool, 1996), 114–15.

50. M. Lukonin, "I'll Come to You," in *Land of the Soviets in Verse and Prose Vol. 1*, ed. Vladimir Tsybin (Moscow, 1982), 257–58.

51. Cited in Hodgson, *Written with the Bayonet*, 115. Information about Orlov's own injuries taken from Valentina Polukhina, *Brodsky through the Eyes of His Contemporaries Vol. II* (Brighton, MA: 1992), 96.

52. Boris Polevoi, *A Story about A Real Man* (Amsterdam, 2002, reprint of 1949 edition), 165.

53. N. N. Zhukov, *Iz illiustratsii k 'Povest' o nastoiashchem cheloveke' B. Polovogo: Razreshite poproshchat'sia, tovarishch polkovoi komissar!* and *Poshel!* (1950), *Ogonek* 11 (1951): between 8–9.

54. S. Iutkevich, "Zrelost' talenta," *Ogonek* 50 (1948): 27.

55. A. Tarasenkov, "Living Heroes of Literature," *Soviet Union: Illustrated Monthly* 7 (1950), 35.

56. Kaganovsky, *How the Soviet Man Was Unmade*, 122.

57. *Iskusstvo* 8 (1959): 30; *Ogonek* 26 (1959): between 16–17.

58. For further discussion, see Susan Reid, "Masters of the Earth: Gender and Destalinisation in the Soviet Reformist Painting of the Khrushchev Thaw," *Gender and History* 11, no. 2 (1999): 290–92.

59. D. Bezrukova, "Uroki odnoi vystavki," *Isskustvo* 8 (1959): 33. This appreciation of more emotional honesty in Soviet visual culture can be seen to have parallels to the responses of readers to the novels of Konstantin Simonov in the early 1960s. See Polly Jones, *Myth, Memory, Trauma: Rethinking the Stalinist Past in the Soviet Union, 1952–70* (New Haven, CT: 2013), 183–93.

60. B. V. Ioganson, *Vsesoiuznaia iubileinaia khudozhestvennaia vystavka 1957 goda* (Moscow, 1958), 7.

61. Both *Decree* paintings are reproduced in *Ogonek* 50 (1957): between 16–17. *Waiting for the Signal* can be found in *Iskusstvo* 5 (1958): 5.

62. *Iskusstvo* 10 (1958): 5; *Iskusstvo* 2 (1959): 26; *Ogonek* 4 (1959): between 8–9. See also V. V. Sokolov, *Kostry pokhodnye* (1957), reproduced in V. I. Gapeeva, V. A. Gusev, and A. V. Tsvetov, *Izobrazitel'noe iskusstvo Leningrada: vystavka proizvedenii leningradskikh khudozhnikov, Moskva, Noiabr' 1976—Ianvar' 1977* (Leningrad, 1981), unpaged.

63. Other examples include G. P. Sorogin, *Bylye pokhody*, 1956; and V. V. Sokolov, *Kostry pokhodnye*, 1957.

64. *Iskusstvo* 2 (1950): between 80–81; also published as a double-page color spread in *Ogonek* 9 (1950): between 16–17.

65. *Iskusstvo* 1 (1952): 21.

66. B. Polevoi, "Groznoe oruzhie," *Ogonek* 47 (1955): 11–13; Solov'ev, *Pochtovye marki Rossii i SSSR*, 190.

67. *Iskusstvo* 4 (1958): 22; *Ogonek* 25 (1961): between 24–25.

68. *Ogonek* 22 (1960): between 24–25.

69. Alex Potts, "Beautiful Bodies and Dying Heroes: Images of Ideal Manhood in the French Revolution," *History Workshop Journal* 30, no. 1 (1990): 11.

70. Alex Potts, *Flesh and the Ideal: Winckelmann and the Origins of Art History* (Singapore, 2000), 59.

71. John Berger, *Art and Revolution: Ernst Neizvestny, Endurance and the Role of Art* (New York, 1969), 99.

72. Albert Leong, *Centaur: The Life and Art of Ernst Neizvestny* (Oxford, 2002), 94.

73. S. S. Valerius cited in Leong, *Centaur*, 91.

74. Khrushchev is said to have referred to Neizvestnyi's work as "dog shit" at the Thirty Years of Moscow Art Exhibition in 1962. According to James von Geldern, Neizvestnyi was so enraged at Khrushchev's comments that he removed his shirt to show the scars of his body, mementos of injuries sustained during the Great Patriotic War. This action provoked an hour-long debate between the two men, which, although it did not end with agreement, did end with some kind of mutual respect. Of course, at the former leader's own request, it was Neizvestnyi who went on to design Khrushchev's tombstone upon his death in 1971. http://soviethistory.msu.edu/1961–2/khrushchev-on-the-arts/, accessed April 30, 2017.

75. Susan Reid, *De-Stalinization and the Remodernization of Soviet Art: The Search for a Contemporary Realism, 1953-1963*, unpublished PhD, University of Pennsylvania, 1996, 361, fig. 7.7.

76. Susan Reid, "Modernizing Socialist Realism in the Khrushchev Thaw: The Struggle for a 'Contemporary Style' in Soviet Art," in *The Dilemmas of De-Stalinization: Negotiating Cultural and Social Change in the Khrushchev Era*, ed. Polly Jones (New York, 2006), 218.

77. Ibid., 221.

78. See in particular Josephine Woll, *Real Images: Soviet Cinema and the Thaw* (London, 2000), 74-79; and Denise Youngblood, *On the Cinema Front: Russian War Films, 1914-2005* (Lawrence, KS: 2007).

79. Aleksandr Sidorov, "The Thaw: Painting of the Khrushchev Era," in The Museum of Modern Art, Oxford, *Soviet Socialist Realist Painting 1930s-1960s* (Oxford, 1992), 39-40.

80. Bezrukova, "Uroki odnoi vystavki," 32-33.

81. Vladimir Serov, "Truth of Life and Innovation," *Izvestiia*, January 16, 1964, translated in *Current Digest of the Soviet Press* 15, no. 4 (1964): 34-36.

82. Krylova, "Healers of the Wounded Souls," 315.

83. Nina Tumarkin, *The Living & the Dead: The Rise and Fall of the Cult of World War II in Russia* (New York, 1994), 133.

84. Jones, *Myth, Memory, Trauma*, 212-57.

85. Stephen Lovell, *The Shadow of the War: Russia and the USSR, 1941 to the Present* (Oxford 2010), 9. As Lovell himself points out, Denise Youngblood has shown that some of the profound themes found in Thaw-era cinema also perpetuated in a few cases into the late 1960s and the 1970s; Youngblood, *On the Cinema Front: Russian War Films*, chps. 6 and 7.

86. *Iskusstvo* 2 (1965): 9.

87. V. Zimenko, "Iskusstvo, vedushchee v glubiny zhizn'," *Iskusstvo* 12 (1967): 45.

88. V. Zimenko, "Ozarennye ognem zhizni," *Iskusstvo* 5 (1965): 14. The language of the war experience being an unhealed wound is also prominent in literary discussions of those years. See Jones, *Myth, Memory, Trauma*, esp. 173-211.

89. V. Gavrilov, "Tseleustremlennost' tvorchestva," *Khudozhnik* 5 (1968): 8-9.

90. *Iskusstvo* 12 (1967): 47.

91. Alexander Tvardovsky, *Selected Poetry* (Moscow, 1981), 433.

92. *Iskusstvo* 5 (1963): 27.

93. See also Korzhev's later work, *Oblaka 1945 goda* (1980-85). The attitude toward *baian* players and beggar veterans in real life is discussed in Galmarini, "Turning Defects into Advantages," 667-69.

94. Anon., "Za kazhdoi kartinoi—zhizn'," *Rabotnitsa* 2 (1968): 16.

95. The first reproduction of this triptych can be found in *Ogonek* 23 (1960): where it was reproduced in color and each painting was reproduced as a full-page image. The painting *Gomer* from this series was also used on a stamp in 1968; Solov'ev, *Pochtovye marki Rossii i SSSR*, 229.

96. See for example Iu. Bychkov and V. Voronov, "Mera khudozhnika," *Ogonek* 11 (1963): 8-9; N. Tomskii, "Liubite prekrasnoe," *Ogonek* 10 (1966): 8; and E. Belashova, "Khudozhnik, vremia, zhizn'," *Ogonek* 10 (1967): 16.

97. The exhibition that received the most coverage in *Ogonek* during the 1960s was the 1962 Thirty Years of Moscow show at the Manezh; material from this exhibition and comment upon it can be found in the first dozen issues of the magazine from 1963.

98. V. Voronov, "Za krasotu v otvete," *Ogonek* 12 (1965): 15-18 with color supplement.

99. See for example P. Krivonogov, *Komissar kretsosti* (1966), and N. But, *Vo imia zhizn'* (1965), both of which can be found in Oleg Sopotsinskii, *Velikaia Otechestvennaia voina v proizvedeniiakh sovetskikh khudozhnikov: zhivopis', skul'ptura, grafika* (Moscow, 1979).

100. *Ogonek* 50 (1967): between 16-17.

101. V. Rostovshchikov, "Ia dralsia za tebia, ne znaia strakha" *Rabotnitsa* 5 (1970): 4-5.

102. P. I. Pinkisevich, *V zapadnoi germanii* (1952), *Ogonek* 3 (1953): 12.

103. *Sovetskaia zhenshchina* 2 (1951); 6 (1952); 11 (1954).

104. "Mir, a ne mech!," *Ogonek* 49 (1960): 7; "Iaponskie zarisovski," *Ogonek* 23 (1961): 19; M. Abramov, *Pobeditel' i pobezhdennye* (1961), *Ogonek* 37 (1963): between 24–25. For a very early representation, see L. Brodat, "Tochno vypolneno," *Krokodil* 20 (1944).

105. See for example Iurii Pimenov, *Doloi voini* (1929), which depicts two disabled veterans, one, a double amputee, on a *telezhka*, begging on the streets while being ignored by the bourgeoisie who pass them by. It is likely, however, that this was not set in the Soviet Union but rather somewhere in the unspecified West. Reproduced in A. A. Sidorov, *Iurii Pimenov* (Moscow, 1986), pl. 2. Also Fedor Bogorodskii, *Invalidy voiny* (1930), which again is not set in the Soviet Union. Reproduced in S. V. Razumovskaia and I. G. Miiamlin, *Fedor Bogorodskii: Vospominaniia, stat'i, vystupleniia, pis'ma* (Leningrad, 1987), 157.

106. The depiction of emotion in photographs taken at war memorials is discussed in greater detail in Chapter 3.

107. "Rodina pomnit i slavit," *Ogonek* 40 (1971): 27–28. In his work on the renowned photographer Dmitrii Baltermants, Theodore von Laue claimed that Baltermants's image *Once There Was a War*, taken at the Victory Day parade in 1965 and appearing in *Ogonek* in 1971, was the first photograph to be published that featured a Soviet war amputee. This research is unable to support von Laue's assertion, as Baltermants's photograph has not been found in any edition of *Ogonek* up until the mid-1970s. See Theodore H. Von Laue and Angela Von Laue, *Faces of a Nation: The Rise and Fall of the Soviet Union, 1917–1991*, (Denver, CO: 1996), 187.

108. Scott Palmer, "How Memory Was Made: The Construction of the Memorial to the Heroes of the Battle of Stalingrad," *Russian Review* 68 no 3 (2009): 378.

109. Anatolii Sofronov, "Vse oni byli prostymi smertnymi," *Ogonek* 44 (1965): 10–13.

110. *Komsomol'skaia pravda*, October 17, 1967, 1; *Ogonek* 46 (1967): between 8–9.


## Chapter 3

1. A. Grechko, "Great Victory," *Pravda*, May 9, 1967, translated in *Current Digest of the Soviet Press* 19, no. 19 (1967): 20. Visual coverage of the lighting of the flame can be found in *Ogonek* 20 (1967): 2–3.

2. See for example Daniel Rancour-Laferriere, *The Slave Soul of Russia: Moral Masochism and the Cult of Suffering* (London, 1995).

3. For more, see Catherine Merridale, "War, Death and Remembrance in Soviet Russia," in *War and Remembrance in the Twentieth Century*, ed. Jay Winter and Emmanuel Sivan (Cambridge, 2010), esp. 70–73.

4. Catherine Merridale, *Ivan's War: The Red Army 1939–1945* (London, 2005), 306.

5. Karel C. Berkhoff, *Motherland in Danger: Soviet Propaganda during World War II* (London, 2012), 122–31.

6. "Chudovishchnoe prestuplenie gitlerovtsev v khutore Vertiachem," *Pravda*, December 21, 1942, 3; "Chudovishchnoe prestuplenie gitlerovtsev v khutore Vertiachem," *Krasnaia zvezda*, December 22, 1942, 3.

7. "Zverstva nemetsko-fashistskikh liudoedov v Rostove na Donu," *Pravda*, March 13, 1943, 3; "Zverstva nemetsko-fashistskikh liudoedov v Rostove na Donu," *Izvestiia*, March 13, 1943, 3.

8. For more on the coverage of the Jewish aspects of this atrocity, see David Shneer, *Through Soviet Jewish Eyes: Photography, War, and the Holocaust* (London, 2011), 100–108.

9. http://www.tretyakovgallery.ru/en/museum/history/gallery/1941_1945/, accessed April 30, 2017.

10. Matthew Cullerne Bown, *Socialist Realist Painting* (London, 1998), 209

11. In addition to being represented by the Kukryniksy, and later by Nikolai Zhukov, the hanging of Zoia was also covered in the press, which repeatedly featured a photograph of her corpse lying in the snow with the rope still around her neck. See for example "Tania," *Pravda*, January 27, 1942, 3. For more on the construction and deconstruction of the reputation of Zoia, see A. Livshiz, "Children's

Lives after Zoia's Death: Order, Emotions and Heroism in Children's Lives and Literature in the Post-War Soviet Union," in *Late Stalinist Russia: Society between Reconstruction and Reinvention*, ed. J. Fürst (Oxford, 2006), 192–208; and R. Sartorti, "On Making Heroes, Heroines, and Saints," in *Culture and Entertainment in Wartime Russia*, ed. Richard Stites (Bloomington, IN: 1995), 157–93.

12. *Iskusstvo* 12 (1964): 43.

13. *Sovetskaia zhenshchina* 6 (1961), between 24–25.

14. *Sovetskaia zhenshchina* 6 (1947), 50.

15. *Iskusstvo* 2 (1947).

16. It should be remembered that at this point the official death toll from the War stood at around 7 million. It was not until the Khrushchev era that the figure rose to 20 million, much closer to modern estimates of around 27 million, 9 million of which were military.

17. "Vstrecha s ottsom," *Ogonek* 19 (1965): 27.

18. I am indebted to my dear friend and fellow travel enthusiast Phil Bradford for first bringing this sculpture to my attention. Reproduced in *Ogonek* 8 (1949): 3, and *Iskusstvo* 4 (1961): 45. The monument was also used as a stamp to mark the fifteenth anniversary of the Czechoslovak Republic in 1960.

19. See for example N. N. Zhukov, *My zavoevali mir dlia narodov—My ego otstoim!* (1950); D. Gabitashvilii *et al.*, *Molodozh' mira! Za mir!* (1951), *Iskusstvo* 1 (1954): 71; the front cover of *Krokodil* 13 (1950); the back cover of *Krokodil* 13 (1957); the front cover of *Sovetskaia zhenshchina* 2 (1958); and the back cover of *Ogonek* 19 (1970).

20. *Ogonek* 43 (1959). More details about the publication can be found in Arup Banerjee, *Writing History in the Soviet Union: Making the Past Work* (New Delhi, 2008), 77–78.

21. V. Iu. Solov'ev, *Pochtovye marki Rossii i SSSR 1857–1991* (Moscow, 1998), 141, 167, 190, 225, 236.

22. At the very least it was used as a 60h stamp in Czechoslovakia in 1956 and as a stamp in the GDR in 1955, 1967, 1973, and 1975.

23. N. Lapunova, "Monument pobedy," *Pravda*, March 11, 1963, 4.

24. For a discussion of the post-Soviet legacy of this site, see Paul Stangl, "The Soviet War Memorial in Treptow, Berlin," *Geographical Review* 93 (April 2003): 213–36. For more on the development of the Moscow memorial site, see Nurit Schleifman, "Moscow's Victory Park: A Monumental Change," *History and Memory* 13 (Fall/Winter 2001), 5–34.

25. While not quite emulating her more iconic counterpart, the grieving mother statue was also used on a stamp in the GDR in 1970.

26. M. Bugeyeva, "A Monument to Eternal Glory," *Soviet Union: Illustrated Monthly* 3 (1950): 8–9.

27. Julia Kristeva, *Black Sun: Depression and Melancholia*, trans. Leon S. Roudiez (New York, 1989), 256. See also Daniel J. Sherman, "Monuments, Mourning and Masculinity in France after World War I," *Gender and History* 8, no. 1 (1996): 82–107.

28. For more on differing European presentations of the motherland, see Linda Edmondson, "Putting Mother Russia in a European Context," in *Art, Nation and Gender: Ethnic Landscapes, Myths and Mother Figures*, ed. Tricia Cusack and Signle Breathach-Lynch (Aldershot, 2003), 53–62; Marina Warner, *Monuments and Maidens: The Allegory of the Female Form* (London, 1985); and Maurice Aughlon, *Marianne into Battle: Republican Imagery and Symbolism in France 1789–1880* (Cambridge, 1981).

29. See also S. M. Orlov, *Mat'* (1941–43), reproduced in A. A. Iuferova, *Velikaia Otechestvennaia voina v proizvedeniiakh sovetskikh khudozhnikov* (Moscow, 1985), pl. 97; E. A. Zaitsev, *Pokhorony geroia* (1945), reproduced in P. M. Sysoev, *225 let Akademii khudozhestv SSSR: katalog vystavki: zhivopis', skul'ptura, arkhitektura, grafika, teatral'no-dekoratsionnoe iskusstvo, dekorativno-prikladnoe iskusstvo, dokumenty, izdaniia* (Moscow, 1985), pl. 157; D. Shmarinov, *Mat'* (1942), reproduced in Oleg Sopotsinskii, *Sovetskoe iskusstvo 1917–1957: zhivopis', skul'ptura, grafika* (Moscow, 1957), pl. 260.

30. See for example *Ogonek* 1 (1946): between 16–17; *Tvorchestvo 1*, (1947), color supplement; *Ogonek* 23 (1965): between 24–25; and *Iskusstvo* 4 (1969): 44.

31. Solov'ev, *Pochtovye marki Rossii i SSSR 1857–1991*, 211.

32. I. Kirikova, "O F. Bogorodskom i D. Shvartse," *Iskusstvo* 4 (1969): 44. The inscription on the canvas reads "Svetloi pamiati syna moego Vasiliia posviashchaiu Fedor Bogorodskii, 1945."

33. *Iskusstvo* 3 (1949): 18; *Ogonek* 16 (1949): between 16–17. See chapter 4 for a more detailed discussion of this work.

34. *Iskusstvo* 5 (1965): 9. See also S. Gorno, *Poplavskii, Mat' Beloianisa* (1953), *Iskusstvo* 5 (1959): 16; and Ivan Kirkov, *Pietà* (1964), *Tvorchestvo* 9 (1969): 17. Korzhev would later return to this theme of the grieving mother in his 1998 painting *V teni kresta*, which depicts a mourning Mary sitting alongside the deceased body of Christ. Reproduced in A. I. Morozov, *Sotsrealizm i realizm* (Moscow, 2007), pl. 250. See also Korzhev's *Blagovshchenie* (1987–90), which also explored female grief in a religious context, reproduced in Morozov, *Sotsrealizm*, pl. 251.

35. V. Zimenko, "Iskusstvo, vedushchee v glubuny zhizn," *Iskusstvo* 12 (1967): 47.

36. *Sovetskaia zhenshchina* 5 (1948): 53.

37. *Iskusstvo* 3 (1967): 8; published under the title *Vospominanie* in L. Sharafutdinova et al., *Istoriia iskusstva narodov SSSR, Tom 9: Iskusstvo narodov SSSR, 1960–1977 godov* (Moscow, 1984), pl. 91.

38. G. Pletneva, "Ob'ektivnoe i sub'ektivnoe v rabote nad kartinoi," *Iskusstvo* 3 (1967): 12.

39. See also Aleksei Eremin, *Ottsy i synov'ia* (1973–75), reproduced in S. N. Levandovskii, *Mir otstoiali, mir sokhranim* (Leningrad, 1985), pl. 87.

40. I. Leonova, "Novella o boitse," *Khudozhnik* 12 (1963): 7. While the finished piece was not published, it was shown in 1965 at the Leningrad Regional Exhibition.

41. Pavel Antokolskii, "Son," in *Land of the Soviets in Verse and Prose Vol. 1*, ed. Vladimir Tsybin (Moscow, 1982), 229. When imagining the death of his son, Antokolskii wrote, "Mother earth took him in her embrace; He pressed to her with all his tired body [. . .] He whispered, not with his lips, but with all his being; With his extinct existence: 'Motherland.'"

42. Mikhail Sholokhov, *The Fate of a Man: Sud'ba cheloveka* (Moscow, 1984), 277.

43. Mikhail Isakovskii, "The Nazis Burnt His House to Ashes," in Tsybin, *Land of the Soviets*, 167.

44. Alexander Tvardovsky, *Vassili Tyorkin: A Book about A Soldier* (Moscow, 1975), 329.

45. In contrast, in literature works such as Konstantin Simonov's *The Living and the Dead* (1959) did tackle the mass death and trauma of the early days of the War. For a detailed discussion of this work and the reception of the Soviet public to this new de-Stalinized vision of the War, see Polly Jones, *Myth, Memory, Trauma: Rethinking the Stalinist Past in the Soviet Union, 1953–70* (London, 2013), esp. 173–211.

46. *Iskusstvo* 5 (1968): 11; *Iskusstvo* 5 (1967): 23; *Tvorchestvo* 11 (1967): 10.

47. *Iskusstvo* 7 (1966): 16; *Iskusstvo* 7 (1967): 7.

48. For one such attempt, see Alice Förster and Birgit Beck, "Post-Traumatic Stress Disorder and World War II: Can a Psychiatric Concept Help Understand Postwar Society?" in *Life after Death: Approaches to a Cultural and Social History of Europe during the 1940s and 1950s*, ed. Richard Bessle and Dirk Schumann (Cambridge, 2003), 15–35.

49. Catherine Merridale, "The Collective Mind: Trauma and Shell-Shock in Twentieth Century Russia," *Journal of Contemporary History* 35, no. 1, Special Issue: *Shell-Shock* (2000), 39–55; Robert Dale, "Coming Home: Demobilization, Trauma and Postwar Readjustment in Late Stalinist Leningrad," in *Special Issue Psychische Versehrungen im Zeitalter der Weltkriege*, ed. G. Gahlen, W. Meteling, and C. Nübel (May 2015).

50. Catherine Merridale, *Night of Stone: Death and Memory in Russia* (London, 2000), 20–23. For a discussion of trauma in the context of the Chechen War but with reference to the legacy of the Great Patriotic War, see Serguei A. Oushakine, *The Patriotism of Despair: National, War, and Loss in Russia* (London, 2009). See also the special issue on war trauma in *Journal of Power Institutions in Post-Soviet Society* 14/15 (2013). See Serguei A. Oushakine and Elena Trubina, eds., *Travma: Punkty* (Moscow, 2009), for a wider discussion of issues related to trauma in both a Russian and non-Russian context.

51. Förster and Beck, "Post-Traumatic Stress Disorder and World War II," 17.

52. Zimenko, "Iskusstvo, vedushchee v glubuny zhizn," 49.

53. *Sovetskaia Rossiia: Vtoraia Respublikanskaia khudozhestvennaia vystavka 6 fevralia–11 aprelia 1965 goda: katalog.* (Moscow, 1965), 21.

54. It is interesting to note that these paintings started to be produced around the same time as the discussion of trauma was beginning to be shut down by those involved in literary production. See Jones, *Myth, Memory, Trauma*, 216–25.

55. Cited in Nina Tumarkin, "The Great Patriotic War as Myth and Memory," *European Review* 11, no. 4 (2003): 599.

56. Tumarkin, "The Great Patriotic War as Myth and Memory," 600–601.

57. For more on masculinity and dying heroes of the French Revolution, see Alex Potts, "Beautiful Bodies and Dying Heroes: Images of Ideal Manhood in the French Revolution," *History Workshop Journal* 30, no. 1 (1990): 1–21.

58. The scene for the diorama was published as a range of individual sketches in *Iskusstvo* 6 (1961): 40–46.

59. *Ogonek* 11 (1947): between 4–5.

60. J. Glenn Gray, *The Warriors: Reflections on Men in Battle* (London, 1998), 116.

61. Nina Tumarkin, *The Living & the Dead: The Rise and Fall of the Cult of World War II in Russia* (New York, 1994), 112–13.

62. See Marino Madzakurati, *Poverzhennyi partizan* (1955), *Iskusstvo* 8 (1956): 58; and Gunar Mitrevits, *Latgal'skie partizany* (1958), *Iskusstvo* 1 (1959): 9.

63. Boris Nemenskii, "The Power of Truth and Light," *Galereia* 2 (2015): http://www.tretyakov-gallerymagazine.com/articles/2-2015-47/power-truth-and-light, accessed April 30, 2017.

64. Cullerne Bown, *Socialist Realist Painting*, 408. Unfortunately, Cullerne Bown failed to provide any references to support this claim, and so the veracity of his argument cannot be verified in contemporary sources.

65. Nemenskii, "The Power of Truth and Light."

66. *Iskusstvo* 3 (1969): 14.

67. *Iskusstvo* 10 (1968): 44.

68. E. Vostokov, "Podvig naroda," *Iskusstvo* 5 (1970): 7. Taken from Orlov's "Ego zaryli v shar zemnoi" (1944).

69. Michael Ignatieff, "Soviet War Memorials," *History Workshop* 17 (1984): 158.

70. "Surovyi i spokoinyi," *Ogonek* 5 (1964): 16; *Rabotnitsa* 12 (1966). For more on the development of Leningrad's memorials, see Lisa Kirschenbaum, *The Legacy of the Siege of Leningrad: Myth, Memories and Monuments* (Cambridge, 2006), 186–228.

71. Scott Palmer, "How Memory Was Made: The Construction of the Memorial to the Heroes of the Battle of Stalingrad," *Russian Review* 68 no 3 (2009): 380–82.

72. Ia. Ostrovskii, "Geroiam Stalingrada," *Iskusstvo* 8 (1958): 10–14.

73. Ostrovskii, "Geroiam Stalingrada," 14.

74. *Ogonek* 6 (1963).

75. Anatolii Sofronov, "Vse oni byli prostymi smertnymi," *Ogonek* 44 (1965): 4–8.

76. Palmer, "How Memory Was Made," 389.

77. Palmer, "How Memory Was Made," 388.

78. A. Fedorov, "Geroiam velikoi bitvy," *Iskusstvo* 10 (1967): 44.

79. "Po zovet serdtsa," *Rodina* 2 (1966): 24; A. Fedorov, "Geroiam velikoi bitvy," *Iskusstvo* 10 (1967): 42; "Monumenty bessmertiiu," *Tvorchestvo* 6 (1968): 5; Solov'ev, *Pochtovye marki Rossii i SSSR*, 249.

80. The first photographs found of *Rodina-mat' zovet!* in the popular press are in *Ogonek* 43 (1967) and accompany coverage of the opening of the site. This was quickly followed by other photographs in *Ogonek* 46 (1967): between 8–9, as part of the fiftieth anniversary of the Revolution commemorations, and *Ogonek* 10 (1968): between 16 and 17, in a feature on the work of Evgenii Vuchetich.

For the controversy and problems that surrounded the creation of the Motherland statue, see Palmer, "How Memory Was Made," esp. 390–99.

81. *Ogonek* 46 (1963); *Ogonek* 32 (1963). See also *Rodina* 2 (1966): 24; and *Rabotnitsa* 2 (1968): 8.

82. See for example Kirschenbaum, *The Legacy of the Siege of Leningrad*, 5–17. For a discussion of the interplay between personal and official narratives in the context of the memorialization of the Terror, see Alexander Etkind, *Warped Mourning: Stories of the Undead in the Land of the Unburied* (Stanford, CA: 2013).

83. Although the monument was not officially unveiled until the following year, the body of the soldier was reinterred in December 1966 to mark the twenty-fifth anniversary of the Battle of Moscow.

84. Anatolii Sofronov, "Vse oni byli prostymi smertnymi," *Ogonek* 44 (1965): 4; "25 let spustia," *Ogonek* 5 (1968); "Surovyi i spokoinyi," *Ogonek* 5 (1964): 16; "Moskva. U mogily Neizvestnogo soldata," *Ogonek* 50 (1966); "Rodina pomnit i slavit," *Ogonek* 40 (1971): 28.

85. L. Lesnia, "Mesto prestupleniia—Koriukovka," *Ogonek* 5 (1962): 8–9.

86. "Ognennoe slovo politruka," *Ogonek* 47 (1971): 28–29. For work that explores some of the controversy surrounding the Panfilov Division, see Alexander Statiev, "'La Garde meurt mais ne se rend pas!': Once Again on the 28 Panfilov Heroes," *Kritika: Explorations in Russian and Eurasian History* 13, no. 4 (2012): 769–98; and Denis Kozlov, *The Readers of Novyi Mir: Coming to Terms with the Stalinist Past* (Cambridge, MA: 2013), 265–68.

87. *Ogonek* 16 (1965): 19; *Ogonek* 19 (1970): 13.

88. "Nikogda ne zabudem!" *Ogonek* 5 (1965). Shneer believes it is possible that Baltermants himself wrote this caption in his new capacity as photo editor for the magazine; Shneer, *Through Soviet Jewish Eyes*, 225.

89. Shneer, *Through Soviet Jewish Eyes*, 100–108, 224.

90. Shneer, *Through Soviet Jewish Eyes*, 224.

91. For Baltermants's own recollections of this photograph and the glossing over of its Jewish subject matter in the 1960s, see Shneer, *Through Soviet Jewish Eyes*, 224–26.

92. T. G. Ashplant, Graham Dawson, and Michael Roper, "The Politics of War Memory and Commemoration: Contexts, Structures and Dynamics," in *The Politics of War Memory and Commemoration*, ed. Ashplant, Dawson, and Roper (New York, 2000), 9. Emphasis in the original.

93. For a particularly damning indictment of the motivations of the Brezhnev regime, see Tumarkin, *The Living & the Dead*, 129–33.

## Chapter 4

1. John Steinbeck, *A Russian Journal* (Harmondsworth, 2000), 119–20.

2. Elena Zubkova, *Russia after the War: Hopes, Illusions, and Disappointments,* trans. Hugh Ragsdale (London, 1998), 20.

3. See for example Wendy Z. Goldman, *Women, The State and Revolution; Soviet Family Policy and Social Life 1917–1936* (Cambridge, 1993); Melanie Ilic, ed., *Women in the Stalin Era* (Basingstoke, 2001); Richard Stites, *The Women's Liberation Movement in Russia: Feminism, Nihilism, and Bolshevism, 1860–1930* (Princeton, NJ: 1990); and Elizabeth Wood, *The Baba and the Comrade: Gender and Politics in Revolutionary Russia* (Indianapolis, IN: 1997).

4. Sergei Kukhterin, "Fathers and Patriarchs in Communist and Post-Communist Russia," in *Gender, State and Society in Soviet and Post-Soviet Russia*, ed. Sarah Ashwin (London, 2000), 74.

5. See David Hoffmann, *Stalinist Values: The Cultural Norms of Soviet Modernity, 1917–1941* (Ithaca, NY: 2003), 88–117.

6. Katerina Clark, *The Soviet Novel: History As Ritual, 3rd Edition* (Bloomington, IN: 2000), 114–35.

7. See Vladim Volkov, "The Concept of *Kul'turnost'*: Notes on the Stalinist Civilising Process" in Sheila Fitzpatrick, ed., *Stalinism: New Directions* (London, 2000), 210–30; and Catriona Kelly,

"*Kul'turnost'* in the Soviet Union: Ideal and Reality," in *Reinterpreting Russia*, ed. G. Hosking and R. Service (London, 1999), 198–213.

8. Clark, *The Soviet Novel*, 114–15.

9. Ibid., 119.

10. See Catriona Kelly, "Riding the Magic Carpet: Children and Leader Cult in the Stalin Era," *The Slavic and East European Journal* 49, no. 2 (2005): 199–224; and Kelly, "Grandpa Lenin and Uncle Stalin: Soviet Leader Cult for Little Children," in *The Leader Cult in Communist Dictatorships: Stalin and the Eastern Bloc*, ed. Balazs Apor, Jan C. Behrends, Polly Jones, and E. A. Rees (Basingstoke, 2004), 102–22.

11. Clark, *The Soviet Novel*, 120.

12. Jay Bergman, "Valerii Chkalov: Soviet Pilot as New Soviet Man," *Journal of Contemporary History* 33, no. 1 (1998): 132–54.

13. Cited in Bergman, "Valerii Chkalov: Soviet Pilot as New Soviet Man," 141.

14. Bergman, "Valerii Chkalov: Soviet Pilot as New Soviet Man," 146–47.

15. Chkalov cited in Bergman, "Valerii Chkalov," 148.

16. V. Chkalov, "Nash Otets," *Izvestiia*, August 18, 1938.

17. *Iskusstvo* 4 (1935): 51.

18. See also the poster by Konstantin Zotov, *Liuboi krest'ianin, kolkhoznik ili edinolichnik imeet teper' vozmozhnost' zhit' po-chelovecheski* (1934). The loving father can also be seen in V. Govorkov, *Za radostnoe tsvetushchee detstvo* (1936), although this poster does not have a domestic setting.

19. D. Hoffmann, "Mothers in the Motherland: Stalinist Pronatalism in Its Pan-European Context," *Journal of Social History* 34 (2000): 35–53; Elizabeth Waters, "The Modernisation of Russian Motherhood, 1917–1937," *Soviet Studies* 44 (1992): 123–35.

20. *Pravda*, June 9, 1936, published in Rudolf Schlesinger, ed., *Changing Attitudes in Soviet Russia: The Family in the USSR, Documents and Readings* (London, 1949), 266–69.

21. V. Svetlov, "Socialist Society and the Family" (1936), published in Schlesinger, *The Family in the USSR*, 336.

22. Lisa Kirschenbaum, "'Our City, Our Hearths, Our Families': Local Loyalties and Private Life in Soviet World War II Propaganda," *Slavic Review* 59, no. 4 (2000): 825.

23. Just a few of the many examples include Viktor Koretskii, *Bud' geroem!* (1941), pl. 2; Iosif Serebrianyi, *Bei krepche, synok!* (1941), pl. 18; and Fedor Antonov, *Syn Moi!* (1942), pl. 90, all reproduced in Rossiiskaia Gosudarstvennaia Biblioteka (henceforth RGB), *Plakaty voiny i pobedy* (Moscow, 2005).

24. Jeffrey Brooks, *Thank You, Comrade Stalin!: Soviet Public Culture from Revolution to Cold War* (Princeton, NJ: 1999), 161–87; John Barber, "The Image of Stalin in Soviet Propaganda and Public Opinion during World War 2," in *World War 2 and the Soviet People: 4th World Congress for Soviet and East European Studies: Selected papers*, ed. John Garrard and Carol Garrard (London, 1993), 43.

25. Kirschenbaum draws the same conclusion through analysis of *Komsomol'skaia pravda* and *Pravda*, focusing on written rather than visual propaganda. See Kirschenbaum, "Local Loyalties and Private Life," 826n5. Visual examples include Iraklii Toidze, *Za Rodinu-mat'!* (1943), RU/SU 2108; Antonov, *Synok rodimyi moi!* (1943), pl. 115; Viktor Ivanov, *Msti za gore naroda!* (1943), pl. 117; Viktor Koretskii, *Novymi pobedami proslavim nashi boevye znamena* (1944), pl. 149; and Viktor Ivanov, *Osvobozhdennye sovetskie liudi* (1945), pl. 176; all reproduced in RGB, *Plakaty voiny i pobedy*.

26. RU/SU 1921.10; RGB, *Plakaty voiny i pobedy*, pl. 94.

27. RU/SU 2254.

28. The poster also has visual parallels with Dmitrii Moor's iconic Civil War poster *Ty zapisal-sia dobrovol'tsem?* (1920). Other examples of the use of the spousal or parental role include Aleksei Kokorekin, *Ubei ego!* (1945), RU/SU 2132; Viktor Ivanov and Ol'ga Burova, *Boets Krasnoi Armii!* (1942), pl. 89; Dementii Shmarinov, *Otomsti!* (1942), pl. 88; Leonid Golovanov, *Spasem sovetskikh rebiat nemtsev!* (1943), pl. 114; Dementii Shmarinov, *Smert' nemtsam-dushegubam!* (1944), pl. 151; Viktor Ivanov, *Ty budesh' zhit' schastlivo!* (1944), pl. 152; and Vladimir Ladiagin, *Ia zhdal tebia, voin-os-voboditel'* (1945), pl. 179; all reproduced in RGB, *Plakaty voiny i pobedy*.

29. See for example Viktor Govorkov, *Slavna bogatyriami zemlia nasha* (1941), pl. 17, and Viktor Ivanov, *Bei, koli, goni, beri v polon!* (1942), pl. 74, reproduced in RGB, *Plakaty voiny i pobedy*; and Iraklii Toidze, *Vo imia Rodiny: vpered, bogatyri!* (1943), RU/SU 2145. The quote of Stalin's *"Pust' vdokhnovliaet vas v etoi voine muzhestvennyi obraz nashikh velikikh predkov!"* was used for a series of works by Viktor Ivanov and Ol'ga Burova in 1942, which aligned the heroics in the Great Patriotic War and other great historic battles. See also the triptych by Pavel Korin, *Aleksandr Nevskii* (1942), *Iskusstvo* 7 (1962): 12; and Mikhail Avilov's *Poedinok na Kulikovom pole. Edinoborstvo Peresveta s Uelubeem* (1943), *Ogonek* 8 (1952): between 16–17, for examples of works that invoke the mythologized Russian past away from the war poster.

30. For example, Mikhail Mal'tsev, *Krasnoarmeets, bud' dostoin bogatyrskoi slavy tvoego naroda!* (1943), which depicts a Soviet airman, a soldier, and a tank driver shadowed by Vasnetsov's three medieval heroes. Reproduced in RGB, *Plakaty voiny i pobedy*, pl. 121. Also Dementii Shmarinov's *V bogatyrskikh podvigakh vnuchat vizhu dedovskuiu slavy!* (1943), RU/SU 2142, whose protagonist was based on Vasnetsov's central hero. For a discussion of how Vasnetsov's work has been used in the post-Soviet era, see Helena Goscilo, "Viktor Vasnetsov's Bogatyrs: Mythic Heroes and Sacrosanct Borders Go to Market," in *Picturing Russia: Explorations in Visual Culture*, ed. Joan Neuberger and Valerie Kivelson (New York, 2008), 248–53.

31. RU/SU 2175.

32. Kirschenbaum, "Local Loyalties, Private Life," 837–38. This was by no means an invention of the Soviet state as demonstrated, for example, by Lawson Wood's 1914 British war posters "A Chip off the Old Block" and "The Veteran's Farewell," both of which depict the British Tommy going off to war being wished well by his hero-veteran father.

33. RU/SU 2251. Other examples include Koretskii, "Nasha armiia eto armiia osvobozhdeniia trudishchikhsia" (1940), RU/SU 2331; and M. Solov'ev's front cover of Okna Tass 1044, *Slava osvoboditeliam kishineva* (1945), RU/SU 2420.

34. "Vstrecha moskvichei pobeditelei," *Pravda*, July 16, 1945, 3.

35. Mark Edele, *Soviet Veterans of the Second World War: A Popular Movement in an Authoritarian Society, 1941–1991* (Oxford, 2008), 21–34.

36. In its first year alone it was published in *Iskusstvo* 1 (1948): 13; *Sovetskaia zhenshchina* 1 (1948): 23; and *Ogonek* 8 (1948): 24–25.

37. G. Portnov, "Shtrikhi portreta: khudozhnik V. Kostetskii," *Iskusstvo* 2 (1968): 27. *The Return of the Prodigal Son* work was included in a spread on Rembrandt published in *Ogonek* 40 (1949): 26–27.

38. Anon., "Vozvrashchenie. Khudozhnik V. Kostetskii," *Sovetskaia zhenshchina* 1 (1948): 23.

39. Portnov, "Shtrikhi portreta: khudozhnik V. Kostetskii," 27.

40. See for example *Iskusstvo* 3 (1947); *Ogonek* 19 (1949); *Sovetskaia zhenshchina* 5 (1950); and *Rabotnitsa* 5 (1956).

41. David Jackson, *The Russian Vision: The Art of Ilya Repin* (Schoten, 2006), 155. See also Repin's lesser-known work, *Vozvrashchenie s voiny* (1877), which depicted a wounded soldier returned home from the Russo-Turkish War regaling his friends with his tales of war. Reproduced in *Iskusstvo* 1 (1958): 55.

42. Ibid., 153.

43. Reproduced in P. K. Suzdalev, *9.V.45—9.V.75: Podvigu 30 let* (Moscow, 1975), pl. 19.

44. *Ogonek* 19 (1955): between 16–17.

45. *Iskusstvo* 2 (1950): 65; *Ogonek* 28 (1947): between 8–9. See also L. Abdullaev, *Vstrecha geroia* (1947), *Iskusstvo* 5 (1949): 17; and A. M. Orlov, *Vozvrashchenie partizan* (1945), *Sovetskaia zhenshchina* 6 (1947): 51.

46. A. Avdeenko, "Vera, Nadezhda, Liubov'," *Ogonek* 18 (1946): 23; Nina Vatolina, *Ty khrabro voeval s vragom—voidi, khoziain, v novyi dom!* (1945), and Maria Nesterova-Berzina, *Dozhdalis'*, both reproduced in RGB, *Plakaty voiny i pobedy*, pls. 201, 203.

47. *Iskusstvo* 3 (1950): 12.

48. *Ogonek* 1 (1955): between 16–17.

49. See for example Larisa Pis'mennaia, "Otets," *Sovetskaia zhenshchina* 3 (1952), 41–43; and "Ikh liubot, rastit i leleet strana," *Ogonek* 27 (1949).

50. *Iskusstvo* 2 (1953): 18.

51. N. Dmitrieva, "Vsesoiuznaia khudozhestvennaia vystavka 1952 goda," *Iskusstvo* 2 (1953): 18.

52. These figures are based on a survey of *Ogonek* between 1945 and 1953 and on photographs that depicted direct father-child contact and do not include other, far more numerous, images that presented the father as present in a general family scene, or representations of grandfathers and grandchildren. A detailed survey of publications aimed at a female audience would possibly yield different results; for example, the first postwar photograph of a father and his child did not appear in *Sovetskaia zhenshchina* until the final issue of 1951.

53. V. Dunham, *In Stalin's Time: Middleclass Values in Soviet Fiction* (Cambridge, 1976), 91.

54. Ibid., 91–96, 24.

55. Ibid., 13.

56. *Iskusstvo* 3 (1949): 18; *Ogonek* 16 (1949): between 16–17.

57. "Khudozhniki Rossiiskoi Federatskii," *Ogonek* 16 (1949): 17.

58. Anon., "Torzhestvo sotsialisticheskogo realizma," *Iskusstvo* 2 (1949): 6.

59. *Iskusstvo* 2 (1949): 5; *Ogonek* 1 (1949). For the work being referenced by others, see Iu. Pimenov, *S novym godom* (1957); Reshetnikov even referenced himself in *Opiat' dvoika!* in which the painting was transformed into a calendar. The fact that the painting was turned into a sewing pattern can be found in Susan Reid, *De-Stalinization and the Remodernization of Soviet Art: The Search for a Contemporary Realism, 1953–1963* (PhD dissertation, University of Pennsylvania, 1996), 146. Reshetnikov was an extremely popular artist and one of only a handful that warranted a number of articles solely based on their own work; see for example "Pevets detskoi ulybki," *Sovetskaia zhenshchina* 1 (1956), and O. Knorring, "Poisk vsegda . . . ," *Ogonek* 37 (1966): 8–9.

60. *Iskusstvo* 1 (1953): 9; *Ogonek* 17 (1953): between 24–25. Like his earlier painting, *Opiat' dvoika* was also referenced extensively in other images, most commonly in cartoons found in both *Ogonek* and *Krokodil,* such as those published in *Ogonek* 20 (1957), *Krokodil* 12 (1955), and *Krokodil* 9 (1965). The title "Opiat' dvoika" was even used in *Komsomol'skaia pravda* to comment on the achievements of renowned gymnast Larissa Latynina at the World Championships in Sofia. The article on the event starts with a specific reference to Reshetnikov's work (May 25, 1965).

61. Catriona Kelly, *Children's World: Growing Up in Russia, 1890–1991* (London, 2007), 127. As Reshetnikov would make clear in a later work, *Pereekzamenovka* (1954), *Ogonek* 2 (1955): between 8–9, discipline was enforced on this errant young lad, as he was forced to work while his friends, gathered outside his bedroom window, try to tempt him out to play.

62. Dmitrieva, "Vsesoiuznaia khudozhestvennaia vystavka 1952 goda," 18, 21.

63. Anon., "Torzhestvo sotsialisticheskogo realizma," *Iskusstvo* 2 (1949): 6.

64. A. Kamenskii, "Vsesoiuznaia khudozhestvennaia vystavka 1952 goda," *Ogonek* 3 (1953): 10.

65. Jan Plamper, "Abolishing Ambiguity: Soviet Censorship Practices in the 1930s," *Russian Review* 60, no. 4 (2001): 526–44.

66. For a detailed discussion of Laktionov's work and its reception, see Oliver Johnson, "'A Premonition of Victory': *A Letter from the Front,*" *Russian Review* 68 no 3 (2009), 408–28; and Susan Reid, "In the Name of the People: The Manège Affair Revisited," *Kritika* 6, no. 4 (2005): 697–706.

67. Matthew Cullerne Bown, *Socialist Realist Painting* (London, 1998), 259–61.

68. Ibid., 261.

69. For more, see Oliver Johnson, "Assailing the Monolith: Popular Responses to the 1952 All Union Exhibition," *Art History and Criticism*, vol. 3: *Art and Politics: Case Studies from Eastern Europe* (2007): 45–51.

70. Dunham, *In Stalin's Time*, esp. 91–96; Susan Reid, "Women in the Home," in *Women in the Khrushchev Era*, ed. M. Ilic, S. Reid, and L. Attwood (Basingstoke, 2004), 151.

71. Lynne Attwood, *Gender and Housing in Soviet Russia* (Manchester, 2010), 146.

72. Attwood, *Gender and Housing*, 147–48; Mark Smith, "Individual Forms of Ownership in the Urban Housing Fund of the USSR, 1944–64," *Slavonic and East European Review* 86, no. 2 The Relaunch of the Soviet Project, 1945–64 (2008): 290–92. For a later discussion of the use of war experience in relation to housing and the concept of home, see Christina Varga-Harris, "Forging Citizenship on the Home Front: Reviving the Socialist Contract and Constructing Soviet Identity during the Thaw," in *The Dilemmas of De-Stalinization: Negotiating Cultural and Social Change in the Khrushchev Era*, ed. P. Jones (New York, 2006), 101–17.

73. Attwood, *Gender and Housing*, 149–59.

74. *Khudozhnik* 12 (1963): 7.

75. *Ogonek* 25 (1966): between 16–17.

76. Later works that connect grief with the home include V. A. Safronov, *Proshchanie* (1985), reproduced in Levandovskii, *Mir otstoiali, mir sokhranim*, pl. 22; and S. M. Muradian, *Ne dozhdalis'* (1985), reproduced in P. M. Sysoev, *225 let Akademii khudozhestv SSSR: katalog vystavki: zhivopis', skul'ptura, arkhitektura, grafika, teatral'no-dekoratsionnoe iskusstvo, dekorativno-prikladnoe iskusstvo, dokumenty, izdaniia* (Moscow, 1985), 201.

77. See the special issue *Journal of Contemporary History* 40, no. 2: *Domestic Dreamworlds: Notions of Home in Post-1945 Europe* (2005).

78. Some notable exceptions include Edgar Iltner, *Muzh'ia vozvrashchaiutsia* (1957), and Gelii Korzhev, *Vliublennye* (1959).

79. Dmitrieva, "Vsesoiuznaia khudozhestvennaia vystavka 1952 goda," 22.

80. *Iskusstvo* 1 (1953): 8; *Iskusstvo* 2 (1953): 19. Other early reproductions include *Ogonek* 24 (1953): between 24–25.

81. Reid, "Women in the Home," 149.

82. Jørn Guldberg, "Socialist Realism as Institutional Practice: Observations on the Interpretation of the Works of Art of the Stalin Period," in *The Culture of the Stalin Period*, ed. Hans Günther (London, 1990), 169.

83. Clark, *The Soviet Novel*, 114–35; Günther, "Wise Father Stalin and His Family in Soviet Cinema," 178–90; Kelly, "Riding the Magic Carpet," 199–224; Jan Plamper, *The Stalin Cult: A Study in the Alchemy of Power* (London, 2012).

84. Maria Enzensberger, "'We Were Born to Turn a Fairy Tale into Reality': Grigori Alexandrov's *The Radiant Path*," in *Stalinism and Soviet Cinema*, ed. Richard Taylor and Derek Spring (London, 1993), 99; Haynes, *New Soviet Man: Gender and Masculinity in Stalinist Soviet Cinema* (Manchester, 2003), 61.

85. *Sovetskaia zhenshchina* 5 (1951): 21.

86. E. Kostenko, *Future Builders* (1952), reproduced in Vern Grosvenor Swanson, *Soviet Impressionism* (Woodbridge, 2001), 321. Gelia shot to fame after a photograph of her embracing Stalin was published on the front page of *Pravda* in June 1936; it would become one of the most enduring images of the period and probably the most famous depiction of Stalin's interaction with the Soviet child. Gelia's father was executed in 1938 on charges of being a Japanese spy; her mother died shortly afterward while the family was living in exile in Kazakhstan. Despite this, the image of Gelia and Stalin was used up until 1953.

87. Reproduced in Gleb Prokhorov, *Art under Socialist Realism: Soviet Painting, 1930–1950* (Roseville East, NSW: 1995), pl. 45.

88. *Ogonek* 5 (1952); *Ogonek* 1 (1951).

89. Zhukov's poster was shown on the wall of a children's home in a photograph published in *Ogonek* 42 (1949).

90. *Rabotnitsa* 8 (1951): 8; *Rabotnitsa* 6 (1953): 12.

91. *Ogonek* 6 (1951): frontispiece.

92. Plamper, *The Stalin Cult*, 33–35; 127–35.

93. Mie Nakachi, "Population, Politics and Reproduction: Late Stalinism and Its Legacy," in *Late Stalinist Russia: Society between Reconstruction and Reinvention*, ed. Juliane Fürst (Oxford, 2006), 37.

94. Such works are numerous; see for example the sculpture by G. Stolbova and V. Bogatyrev, "Spasibo Tovarishchu Stalinu za schastlivoe detstvo," *Ogonek* 6 (1952): 6; N. N. Zhukov, "Pervoe slovo," *Ogonek* 22 (1950): frontispiece; F. Antonov, "Schast'e iunostyi," *Sovetskaia zhenshchina* 3 (1951): frontispiece; the series of sketches by N. N. Zhukov that showed Lenin with children around Christmas, *Ogonek* 3 (1953): between 16–17, and *Rabotnitsa* 1 (1953): between 8–9; A. Varlanov, *V. I. Lenin s detvoroi* (1950), *Iskusstvo* 1 (1951): 20; the photograph of a young girl kissing Stalin on the cheek, *Rabotnitsa* 6 (1952): frontispiece; and *Ogonek* 18 (1952): frontispiece, to name but a few of the works reproduced in the popular press at this time.

95. Plamper, *The Stalin Cult*, 86.

96. *Iskusstvo* 2 (1948): 2–3; *Rabotnitsa* 5 (1952).

97. This was on August 3, 1935; Plamper, *The Stalin Cult*, 44.

98. Krylova, "Healers of the Wounded Souls," 315.

## Chapter 5

1. "Izvestiia in the Family Circle," *Izvestiia*, December 11, 1960, translated in *Current Digest of the Soviet Press* 12, no. 50 (1960): 30.

2. Victor Buchli, *An Archaeology of Socialism* (Oxford, 1999), 138.

3. *Khrushchoba* is a neologism based on the combination of Khrushchev and *trushchoba*, meaning slum.

4. For more, see Susan Reid, "Destalinisation and Taste, 1953–63," *Journal of Design History* 10, no. 2 (1997): 177–202; Reid, "Cold War in the Kitchen: Gender and the Destalinization of Consumer Taste under Khrushchev," *Slavic Review* 61, no. 2 (2002): 211–52; and Christine Varga-Harris, "Homemaking and the Aesthetic and Moral Perimeters of the Soviet Home during the Khrushchev Era," *Journal of Social History* 41, no. 3 (2008): 561–89.

5. Varga-Harris, "Homemaking and the Aesthetic and Moral Perimeters of the Soviet Home during the Khrushchev Era," 568.

6. Blair A. Ruble, "From Khrushcheby to Korobki," in *Russian Housing in the Modern Age: Design and Social History*, ed. W. Brumfield and B. Ruble (Cambridge, 1993), 232.

7. *Ogonek* 15 (1962): between 8–9.

8. The exception to this are the illustrations found in DIY manuals, which often portrayed men carrying out skilled maintenance, such as electrical repairs; Aleksandr Vysokovskii, "Will Domesticity Return?" trans. Carl Sandstrom, in *Russian Housing in the Modern Age: Design and Social History*, ed. W. Brumfield and B. Ruble (Cambridge, 1993), 284.

9. Susan Reid, "The Khrushchev Kitchen: Domesticating the Scientific-Technological Revolution," *Journal of Contemporary History* 40, no. 2: *Domestic Dreamworlds: Notions of Home in Post-1945 Europe* (2005): 289–316.

10. Ibid., 293.

11. Lynne Attwood, "Celebrating the 'Frail-Figured Welder': Gender Confusion in Women's Magazines of the Khrushchev Era," *Slavonica* 8, no. 2 (2002): 166.

12. Ibid., 167–69.

13. "Emancipate Whom: Men or Women?," *Komsomol'skaia pravda*, December 17, 1961, translated in *Current Digest of the Soviet Press* 14, no 9 (1962): 17.

14. "What Do You Think of the Young Family?" *Komsomol'skaia pravda*, December 17, 1961, translated in *Current Digest of the Soviet Press* 14, no. 9 (1962): 17.

15. I. Semenov, "Iz samykh lushikh pobuzhdenii . . . ," *Sovetskaia zhenshchina* 3 (1958). See also I. Lisogors, "V den' 8 marta," *Krokodil* 7 (1960); G. and V. Karaveav, "Dorogoi, ty opiat' zabyl chto 8 Marta ia delaiu vse sama," *Ogonek* 10 (1961); and the page of cartoons "Prazdnik zhenshchin v raznye epokhi," *Krokodil* 6 (1963). For a more detailed discussion of the satirical representation of men in the home, see Claire E. McCallum "Man about the House: Male Domesticity and Fatherhood in

Soviet Visual Satire aunder Khrushchev," in *The Palgrave Handbook of Women and Gender in Twentieth Century Russia and the Soviet Union*, ed. Melanie Ilic (London, 2018), 331–47.

16. S. Aleksandrov, Untitled, *Krokodil* 6 (1965).

17. Varga-Harris, "Homemaking and the Aesthetic and Moral Perimeters of the Soviet Home during the Khrushchev Era," 571.

18. N. Vigilianskaia and F. Kachelaev, *Vse umeem delat' sami, pomogaem nashei mame!* (1957); see also S. Nizovaia, *Ne zhdi, chtob dobryi diadia vse sdelal za tebia* (1960). See also the earlier poster by Nizovaia, *Ty truda drugogo uvazhai. . . .* All reproduced in A. Snopkov, P. Snopkov, and A. Skliaruk, *Shest'sot plakatov* (Moscow, 2004), pls. 485, 486, 480.

19. Deborah Field, "Mothers and Fathers and the Problem of Selfishness in the Khrushchev Period," in *Women in the Khrushchev Era*, ed. M. Ilic, S. Reid, and L. Attwood (Basingstoke, 2004), 100.

20. Attwood, "Celebrating the 'Frail-Figured Welder,'" 169.

21. *Iskusstvo* 3 (1955): 20; *Ogonek* 4 (1959): between 8–9.

22. In a different context, see also G. Ogorodnikov, "Schastlivy novosel'e," *Krokodil* 24 (1966), for a later representation of a man involved in food preparation outside the home.

23. Deborah A. Field, *Private Life and Communist Morality in Khrushchev's Russia* (New York, 2007), 83–84.

24. Helene Carlbäck, "Lone Mothers and Fatherless Children: Public Discourse on Marriage and Family Law," in *Soviet State and Society under Nikita Khrushchev, eds.* Melanie Ilic and Jeremy Smith (London, 2008), 87–88. See also Carlbäck, "Lone Motherhood in Soviet Russia in the Mid-20th Century—In a European Context," 25–46; and Elena Zhidkova, "Family, Divorce and Comrades' Courts: Soviet Family and Public Organizations during the Thaw," 47–64, both in H. Carlbäck, Y. Gradskova, and Zh. Kravchenko, eds., *And They Lived Happily Ever After: Norms and Everyday Practices of Family in Russia and Eastern Europe* (Budapest, 2012).

25. Carlbäck, "Lone Mothers and Fatherless Children," 94.

26. Field, *Private Life and Communist Morality*, 67.

27. S. G. Strumilin, "Rabochii byt i kommunism," cited in Urie Bronfenbrenner, "The Changing Soviet Family," in *The Role and Status of Women in the Soviet Union*, ed. D. R. Brown (New York, 1968), 112–13.

28. A. Kharchev, "O roli sem'i v kommunisticheskom vospitanii," and N. S. Khrushchev, "O programme kommunisticheskoi partii sovetskogo soiuza," citied in Bronfenbrenner, "The Changing Soviet Family," 115.

29. Charlotte Sakowski and Leo Gruliow, *Current Soviet Politics IV: Documentary Record of the 22nd Party Congress of the Communist Party of the Soviet Union* (London, 1962), 28.

30. Field, "Mothers and Fathers and the Problem of Selfishness in the Khrushchev Period," 101–2.

31. *Ogonek* 38 (1953): 6.

32. See for example D. Bulanov, *Papa, ne pei!* (1929), RU/SU 1988; I. Fedorova, *Stoi!* (1929), RU/SU 523; Unknown artist, *Posledstviia alkogolizma* (1930), RU/SU 616; Unknown artist, *Kak boriatsia deti s alkogolizmom* (1930), RU/SU 617; Unknown artist, *Alkogol' uroduet semeinyi byt* [1917–25?], RU/SU 1199.6; Unknown artist, *Na bor'bu s samoganom!* [1917–25?], RU/SU 1795; and Unknown artist, *Gde den'gi? A sem'e?* [1920–30?], RU/SU 1926.

33. *Sem'ia i shkola* (December 1956), 17.

34. *Iskusstvo* 3 (1954): 5; *Ogonek* 14 (1954): between 16–17.

35. See A. Kanevskii, "Protivorechiia vospitaniia," *Krokodil* 17 (1961); V. Goriaev, "S bozh'ei pomoshch'iu," *Krokodil* 8 (1964); and A. Tsvetkov, "Eto tvoi papa. U nego mnogo obshchestvennykh nagruzok. No kogda on poidet v otpusk, ty ego uvidish," *Krokodil* 6 (1965).

36. Field, *Private Life and Communist Morality*, 88.

37. Nina Tumarkin, *Lenin Lives! The Lenin Cult in Soviet Russia*, enlarged edition (London, 1997), 257.

38. Catriona Kelly, "Grandpa Lenin and Uncle Stalin: Soviet Leader Cult for Little Children," in *The Leader Cult in Communist Dictatorships: Stalin and the Eastern Bloc*, ed. Balazs Apor, Jan C. Behrends, Polly Jones, and E. A. Rees (Basingstoke, 2004), 102.

39. See for example N. Zhukov, *Lenin i deti, Rabotnitsa* 4 (1960): (reading); V. Bulankin, *Snegiri, Rabotnitsa* 5 (1960): (sledging); and *Ogonek* 17 (1955), for one of the earliest reproductions of a photograph of Lenin and Viktor; other versions of this photograph can be found in *Ogonek* 16 (1960) and *Ogonek* 16 (1970). See also the illustration by I. Il'inskii for the book *Rasskazam o Lenine* by A. Kononova (1957), which showed Lenin taking part in a game of blindman's bluff. Reproduced in Dmitrii Bisti, *Knizhnoe iskusstvo SSSR* (Moscow, 1983), pl. 183.

40. *Ogonek* 1 (1953): between 24–25.

41. *Rabotnitsa* 1 (1953); *Ogonek* 16 (1960); *Ogonek* 1 (1970). The stamp to commemorate the 90th anniversary of Lenin's birth can be found in V. Solov'ev, *Pochtovye markii Rossii i SSSR, 1857–1991* (Moscow, 1998), 166.

42. *Ogonek* 13 (1964): frontispiece; *Ogonek* 14 (1964): front cover; *Ogonek* 22 (1955).

43. *Sovetskaia zhenshchina* 6 (1961); *Ogonek* 16 (1961): frontispiece; *Rodina* 2 (1964), 8.

44. "24 Marta 1968 goda: Poslednee interv'iu," *Ogonek* 15 (1968): 30–33.

45. Iu. Gagarin, "Khorosho, 'Chaechka'!," *Rabotnitsa* 5 (1968): 8–9. Gagarin's views in this article are in contrast to the views he supposedly expressed elsewhere regarding female cosmonauts, who according to the memoirs of Valentina Ponomareva, he called "little tarts." For more, see Andrew Jenks, *The Cosmonaut Who Couldn't Stop Smiling: The Life and Legend of Yuri Gagarin* (DeKalb, IL: 2012), 187–89. See also Sue Bridger, "The Cold War and the Cosmos: Valentina Tereshova and the First Woman's Space Flight," in *Women in the Khrushchev Era*, ed. M. Ilic, S. Reid, and L. Attwood (Basingstoke, 2004), 222–36.

46. S. Shinkarenko, *Liudi kommunisticheskogo truda* (1961); A. Levitin, *Im nuzhen mir* (1961), *Ogonek* 50 (1961): between 24–25.

47. Reproduced in R. Abolina, *50 let sovetskogo iskusstvo* (Moscow, 1967), pl. 347.

48. "Love and the Passage of Time," *Komsomol'skaia pravda*, December 24, 1961, translated in *Current Digest of the Soviet Press* 14, no. 9 (1962): 18.

49. N. Volkov, "O zhivopisnoi kul'ture," *Iskusstvo* 5 (1963): 26.

50. See for example E. Tabakova, *V chas otdykha* [1960–61?], *Ogonek* 42 (1961): between 16–17; P. Fattakhov, *Utro sekretaria raikoma* [1960–61?], *Ogonek* 44 (1961): between 8–9; and R. Valnere, *Na rabotu* (1961), *Iskusstvo* 3 (1962): 26.

51. See also D. Shmarinov, *The Family* (1957), A. S. Mikhailov, *On Holiday* (1964), and A. D. Dashkevich, *On the Beach* (1960), all of which feature the father and child in a setting outside of the home. Unfortunately, none of these works have been found in contemporary print culture, but they are reproduced in Vern Grosvenor Swanson, *Soviet Impressionism* (Woodbridge, 2001), pls. 238, 124, 114.

52. *Iskusstvo* 5 (1965): 13; *Khudozhnik* 1 (1965): 24. The final image in the triptych is *Vera Petrovna Paketova s vnukom*.

53. V. Zimenko, "Ozarennye ognem zhizni," *Iskusstvo* 5 (1965): 13.

54. *Sovetskaia zhenshchina* 7 (1956): 30; Korzhev and the short story appeared on consecutive pages of *Sovetskaia zhenshchina* 5 (1956): 6, 7–10.

55. *Ogonek* 33 (1960). Sketches of fathers with their children had appeared prior to this in *Ogonek* 18 (1955), but this was the first photographic front cover that contained only the father and his child.

56. In terms of photographs of "average" men, see for example G. V. Kolesnikov and his sons reading, *Ogonek* 13 (1955): between 16–17; father and son on the beach, *Ogonek* 33 (1960): between 16–17; father and son playing football, *Ogonek* 44 (1960): back cover; and Miklosha Vokhanek "Otets," *Sovetskaia zhenshchina* 3 (1965), back cover.

57. "O ser'eznykh nedostatkakh v vospitanii detei," August 24, 1955, in *Prezidium TSK KPSS 1954-1964: chernovye protokol'nye zapisi zasedanii, stenogrammy, postanovleniia: v 3 tomakh, Tom 2 1954-58* (Moscow, 2003), 114–22. For more on the link between "bad" parenting and juvenile delinquency, see Ann Livschiz, "Destalinising Soviet Childhood: The Quest for Moral Rebirth, 1953–58," in *The Dilemmas of Destalinization: Negotiating Cultural and Social Change in the Khrushchev Era*, ed. P. Jones (New York, 2006), 116–25.

58. Examples include L. Samoilov, "Podonki," *Ogonek* 42 (1960), and "Ploshchadka stil'nogo molodniaka," *Ogonek* 43 (1961).

59. A. Grunin, "Paposhka, podpishi dnevnik . . . ," *Ogonek* 5 (1962); Iu. Cherepanov, "Papa, eto pro kosmonavtov?" *Ogonek* 43 (1964).

60. "Sluchai s turistom," *Sovetskii sport* 7 (July 1956): 4. I am indebted to the article by Julie Gilmour and Barbara Evans Clements, "If You Want to Be Like Me, Train! The Contradictions of Soviet Masculinity," in *Russian Masculinities in History and Culture*, ed. B. Clements, R. Friedman, and D. Healey (Basingstoke, 2001), which brought these images to my attention.

61. Iryna Koshulap, "Cash and/or Care: Current Discourses and Practices of Fatherhood in Ukraine," in *Gender, Politics, and Society in Ukraine*, ed. Olena Hankivsky and Anastasiya Salnykova (Toronto, 2012), 362–63.

62. See for example N. Mar, "Deti rozhdaiutsia dlia schast'ia," *Sovetskaia zhenshchina* 3 (1951): 13–14.

63. *Sovetskaia zhenshchina* 1 (1954). See also the photograph of nurse M. M. Balandina strolling the grounds of the maternity home with baby Sergei and his father in *Sovetskaia zhenshchina* 6 (1953) and the spread E. Mikulinov, "Rozhdenie syna," *Sovetskaia zhenshchina* 3 (1954): 41.

64. For a slightly later work on the same theme that was reproduced, see Irina Shevandronova, *V roddome* (1964), *Iskusstvo* 7 (1965): 30. See also the cartoon "Ottsy i deti," which shows men desperately trying to get a glimpse of their newborn outside the maternity home, *Krokodil* 1 (1966).

65. *Ogonek* 19 (1955): between 16–17; *Sovetskaia zhenshchina* 7 (1956): 30.

66. *Iskusstvo* 5 (1961): 40.

67. *Ogonek* 21 (1964): between 24–25; G. Koniakhin, "Diplomanty khudozhestvennykh buzov," *Iskusstvo* 5 (1964): 6–14.

68. Koniakhin, "Diplomanty khudozhestvennykh buzov," 12.

69. *Ogonek* 15 (1962): between 24–25.

70. *Ogonek* 38 (1960): between 16–17 (published under the title *Pylaiushchii vecher* in *Khudozhnik* 6 [1966]); *Iskusstvo* 12 (1961): 12; *Iskusstvo* 5 (1964): 9. See also Zarin's *Kakaia vysota!* (1958), *Iskusstvo* 4 (1967): 12; V. Arakelo, *Strontel'stvo* (1960), *Iskusstvo* 7 (1960): 8; and Aleksandr Deineka, *Mirnye stroiki* (1960), *Iskusstvo* 7 (1960): 9.

71. The first of these was in *Ogonek* 15 (1962): between 8–9. Mochal'skii's work can be found in R. Abolina, *50 let sovetskogo Iskusstvo* (Moscow, 1967), pl. 347.

72. *Iskusstvo* 12 (1968): 28.

73. Ts. Solodar', "Dvesti molodozheno," *Ogonek* 52 (1960): 2; *Rabotnitsa* 10 (1955); *Ogonek* 3 (1956).

74. "Novorossiiskie kuranty," *Ogonek* 22 (1964); "Moskva," *Ogonek* 32 (1964); Miklosha Vokhanek, "Otets," *Sovetskaia zhenshchina* 3 (1965), back cover.

75. *Ogonek* 37 (1970).

76. *Zhenskii den'*, *Ogonek* 10 (1968); G. and V. Karavaev, "Eshche raz prostirnu i budu sushit," *Ogonek* 10 (1966); V. Tamaev, "Vozvrashchaisia skoree, on ne p'et, ne est," *Ogonek* 10 (1966); Iu. Uzbiakov, "Mama ushla v kino," *Ogonek* 10 (1955); Iu. Cherepanov, "Nakonets-to s mannoi kashei my pokonchili!," *Ogonek* 50 (1965).

77. V. Chizhikov, "Zhena zaderzhalas' na rabote . . . ," *Krokodil* 5, 1964.

78. N. Lisogorskii, "V den' 8 Marta," *Krokodil* 7 (1960); Iu. Cherepov, "Kogo ty bol'she liubish': papu ili mamu?," *Ogonek* 11 (1957).

79. Iu. Cherepanov, Untitled, *Ogonek* 43 (1964); V. Zharinov, "Novichok," *Ogonek* 50 (1965). For an earlier representation of the pram-pushing man, see Iuzbykov, Bogatyr. For the only painted representation found of this motif, see Iu. Kugach, *Prazdnichnoe utro* (1969), *Ogonek* 7 (1970): between 24–25.

80. For further discussion of these issues see Claire E. McCallum "Man about the House: Male Domesticity and Fatherhood in Soviet Visual Satire under Khrushchev," in *The Palgrave Handbook of Women and Gender in Twentieth Century Russia and the Soviet Union*, ed. Melanie Ilic (London, 2018), 331–47.

81. *Iskusstvo* 3 (1954): 5; *Ogonek* 14 (1954): between 16–17.

82. *Iskusstvo* 4 (1956): 42. Other works such as Mikhail Strizhenov's *Chuzhie* (1951–54), *Ogonek* 24 (1954): between 16–17; and Samuil M. Khinskii, *The Return (Will She Forgive Him?)* (1957), reproduced in Cullerne Bown, *Socialist Realist Painting,* pl. 324, explored marital conflict but without any explicit reference to children.

83. *Ogonek* 14 (1954): between 16–17. For other negative representations of family life, see the two works by Aleksei Burak, *K synu za pomoshch'iu* (1954), *Ogonek* 14 (1955): between 16–17; and *Progliadeli,* [1958–60?], *Ogonek* 13 (1960): between 16–17.

84. V. Konovalov, "U ottsa za pazukhoi," *Krokodil* 22 (1957). See also E. Shcheglov, "Iz goda v god," *Krokodil* 21 (1955); B. Leo, "Odnazhdy on zabralsia ottsu na sheiu … da tak i ne slez," *Krokodil* 32 (1955); A. Kanevskii, "So vsemi udobstvami," *Krokodil* 8 (1958); and A. Kanevskii. "Ruki zaniaty," *Krokodil* 35 (1958).

85. See for example A. Kanevskii, "Protivorechiia vospitaniia," *Krokodil* 17 (1961); V. Goriaev, "S bozh'ei pomoshch'iu," *Krokodil* 8 (1964); V. Goriaev, "Papa, chto takoe blagorodstvo? … ," *Krokodil* 24 (1962); and G. Andrianov, "Vash syn?—Da. No zaidite s nim v drugoi raz, zheny net doma," *Krokodil* 6 (1965).

86. Vladislav Zimenko, "Ozarennye ognem zhizni," *Iskusstvo* 5 (1965): 12.

87. The Tretyakov Gallery, "Zhilinsky, Dmitri Dmitriyevich, *By the Sea. Family,*" http://www. tretyakovgallery.ru/en/collection/_show/image/_id/2192, accessed April 30, 2017.

88. Reproduced in Vladimir Sysoev, *Viktor Ivanov* (Moscow, 2002), 26.

89. The Museum of Modern Art, Oxford, *Soviet Socialist Realist Painting 1930s–1960s: Paintings from Russia, the Ukraine, Belorussia, Uzbekistan, Kirgizia, Georgia, Armenia, Azerbaijan and Moldova Selected in the USSR by Matthew Cullerne Bown* (Oxford, 1992), pl. LVII.

90. *Khudozhnik* 3 (1969): 12.

91. The Museum of Modern Art, *Soviet Socialist Realist Painting 1930s–1960s,* pl. LV. See also Popkov's *Sem'ia Bolotovykh* (1969), reproduced in G. Pletneva, "Tema, obraz, stil' v proizvedeniiakh Viktora Popkova," in *Sovetskoe izobrazitel'noe iskusstvo i arkhitektura 60–70kh godov,* ed. V. E. Khazanova (Moscow, 1979), 104; and V. Gavrilov, *Dmitrii Fedorovich s priemnym synom* (1969), reproduced in L. Sharafutdinova et al., *Istoriia iskusstva narodov SSSR, Tom 9: Iskusstvo narodov SSSR 1960–1977 godov, Kniga pervaia* (Moscow, 1982), pl. 27.

92. Springfield Museum of Art, "The Fisherman and His Sick Son," http://www.smofa.org/collections/browse.html?x=art&art_id=1654&name=Fisherman_and_his_Sick_Son, accessed April 30, 2017.

93. Helena Goscilo, "Cinepaternity: The Psyche and Its Heritage," in *Cinepaternity: Fathers and Sons in Soviet and Post-Soviet Film,* ed. H. Goscilo and Y. Hashamova (Bloomington, IN: 2010), 9–10.

94. See for example D. Cherniaev's *1942-god* (1958), *Iskusstvo* 2 (1959): 28; and N. Kormashov, *Proshchanie* (1958), *Iskusstvo* 1 (1959): 15. Later husband/wife-focused works include Gelii Korzhev, *Provody* (1967), *Iskusstvo* 12 (1967): 45; A. Eremenko, *Proshchanie* (1967), *Khudozhnik* 10 (1967): 13; and Fiviski's synonymous sculpture of the same year in *Iskusstvo* 12 (1967): 45. In the latter years of the Soviet Union, particularly in the years preceding the fortieth anniversary of the War, the Tkachev brothers became the leading exponents of representations of both wartime homecoming and leaving. Although they would turn to the familiar trope of the mother and son in works such as *Mat'* (1982–85), which depicted the heartbreak of an elderly woman as her sons leave for the front, most commonly these themes were explored through the representation of the Soviet soldier as a family man. See for example *V dni voiny* (1979), *Mai 1945* (1979–81), and *Vesna, 1945 goda* (1980–85). This last work and *Mat'* are reproduced in S. N. Levandovskii, *Mir otstoiali, mir sokhranim* (Leningrad, 1985), pls. 9, 93; all other works can be found in I. A. Krugli, *Brat'ia Tkachevy* (Moscow, 1985), pls. 199, 225. See also Akhmat Lutfullin's *Proshchanie. 1941g.* (1973), reproduced in V. E. Khazanova, *Sovetskoe izobrazitel'noe iskusstvo i arkhitektura 60–70-kh godov* (Moscow, 1979); and A. A. Mul'nikov, *Proshchanie* (1975), reproduced in A. A. Iuferova, *Velikaia Otechestvennaia voina v proizvedeniiakh sovetskikh khudozhnikov* (Moscow, 1985), pl. 139. For a pre-Soviet representation of the emotional distress caused by leaving for war, see Konstantin Savitskii, *Na voinu* (1888), which depicted the chaotic scenes at a train

station as the troops prepare to board, which was reproduced as a double-page color image in *Ogonek* 31 (1949): between 2–3, and again in *Iskusstvo* 3 (1955): 51. A mention should also go to S. Loik's emotive sculpture, *S pobedoi synok!* from 1958, which encapsulated the joy and relief of a man returning home to his child and which stood alone amidst the other Thaw-era representations of homecoming that focused upon the landscape and which were discussed in chapter 1; *Iskusstvo* 1 (1959): 28.

95. Alexander Prokhorov, "The Myth of the 'Great Family' in Marlen Khutsiev's *Lenin's Guard* and Mark Osep'ian's *Three Days of Viktor Chernyshev*," in *Cinepaternity: Fathers and Sons in Soviet and Post-Soviet Film*, ed. H. Goscilo and Y. Hashamova (Bloomington, IN: 2010), 30.

96. Prokhorov, "The Myth of the 'Great Family,'" 30.

97. Josephine Woll, *Real Images: Soviet Cinema and the Thaw* (London, 2000), 112–24.

98. Stephen Lovell, "Soviet Russia's Older Generation," in *Generations in Twentieth Century Europe*, ed.–S. Lovell (Basingstoke, 2007), especially 209–21.

99. Reproduced in The Museum of Modern Art, Oxford, *Soviet Socialist Realist Painting 1930s–1960s*, pl. LVI. See also A. Vychutzhanin, *Portret kommunista I. V. Eustrolova (1967)*, *Khudozhnik* 5 (1968): 12.

100. This includes A. P. and S. P. Tkachev, *Deti mira* (1982–85); N. P. Karacharskov, *Pobediteli 9 mai v Iangorchino* (1984–85); A. I. Korentsov, *Vnuchka iz serii "Soldaty"* (1983–84); A. G. Eremin, *Otsy i synov'ia* (1973–75); R. N. Ermolin, *Nikto ne zabyt* (1984); A. P. Kholmogorov, *V Den' Pobedy* (1984); M. Iu. Kugach, *Ded i vnuk* (1984); and L. N. Vinogradov, *V rodnoi derevne* (1984). See also the cartoon published in *Ogonek* 45 (1971) by Iu. Chereponov, "Vystree, poka dedushka ne vidit . . ." (inside back cover), which shows two young children wearing their grandfather's medal-covered jacket while another takes their photograph.

101. Mark Edele, "Strange Young Men in Stalin's Moscow: The Birth and Life of the Stiliagi, 1945–1953," *Jahrbücher für Geschichte Osteuropas* 50 (2002), 37–61; Nancy Condee, "Cultural Codes of the Thaw," in *Nikita Khrushchev*, ed. William Taubman, Sergei Khrushchev, and Abbott Gleason (Chelsea, MI: 2000), 160–76; Dina Spechler, *Permitted Dissent in the USSR: Novyi Mir and the Soviet Regime* (New York, 1982), 121–22. The link between new forms of expression and fatherlessness was first made by socio-psychologist Alexander Mitscherlind in his *Society without the Father: A Contribution to Social Psychology*, trans. Eric Mosbacher (London, 1969).

## Conclusion

1. The Diplomatic Society, "The Long Way to Victory," http://www.thediplomaticsociety.co.za/archive/archive/1354-the-long-way-to-victory, accessed April 30, 2017; Russian behind the Headlines, "Yangon hosts WW2 photo exhibition to mark Victory Day," http://rbth.co.uk/news/2015/05/08/yangon_hosts_ww2_photo_exhibition_to_mark_victory_day_45815.html, accessed April 30, 2017.

2. For more on the Putin government's use of the War, see Elizabeth A. Woods, "Performing Memory: Vladimir Putin and the Celebration of World War II in Russia," *The Soviet and Post-Soviet Review* 38, no. 2 (2011): 172–200; and L. Gudkov, "'Pamiat' o voine i massovaia identichnost' rossiian," Neprikosnovennyi Zapas, vols. 2–3 (2005), http://magazines.russ.ru/nz/2005/2/gu5.html, accessed April 30, 2017. Olga Kucherenko, "'That'll Teach'em to Love Their Motherland!': Russian Youth Revisit the Battles of World War II," *The Journal of Power Institutions in Post-Soviet Societies* 12 (2011), http://pipss.revues.org/3866, accessed April 30, 2017.

3. Kucherenko, "That'll Teach'em to Love Their Motherland!"

4. Sergei Kukhterin, "Fathers and Patriarchs in Communist and Post-Communist Russia," in *Gender, State and Society in Soviet and Post-Soviet Russia*, ed. Sarah Ashwin (London, 2000), 71–89; Greta Bucher, "Stalinist Families: Motherhood, Fatherhood, and Building the New Soviet Person," in *The Making of Russian History: Society, Culture, and the Politics of Modern Russia*, ed. John Steinberg and Rex Wade (Bloomington, IN: 2009), 129–52; Iryna Koshulap, "Cash and/or Care: Current Discourses and Practices of Fatherhood in Ukraine," in *Gender, Politics, and Society in Ukraine*, ed. Olena Hankivsky and Anastasiya Salnykova (Toronto, 2012), 362–63; Zh. Chernova, "The Model of Soviet 'Fatherhood,'"

*Russian Studies in History* 51, no. 2 (2012): 35–62; originally published in E. Zdravomyslova and A. Temkina, *Rossiiskii gendernyi poryadok: sotsiologicheskii podkhod* (St. Petersburg, 2007).

5. One of the most recent and detailed studies of fatherhood that also recognizes the Second World War as bringing about an important shift in the paternal model is Laura King, *Family Men: Fatherhood and Masculinity in Britain, 1914–1960* (Oxford, 2015).

6. Nina Tumarkin, *The Living & the Dead: The Rise and Fall of the Cult of World War II in Russia* (New York, 1994), esp. 129–33.

7. Discussion of the notion of a crisis in masculinity can be found in E. Zdravomyslova and A. Temkina, "Krizis masculinnosti v pozdnesovetskom diskurse," in *O Muzhe(n)stvennosti*, ed. Serguei Oushakine (Moscow, 2002), 432–51; Susan Larsen, "National Identity, Cultural Authority and the Post-Soviet Blockbuster: Nikita Mikhalov and Aleksei Balabanov," *Slavic Review* 62, no. 3 (2003): 491–511; Sarah Ashwin and Tatyana Lytkina, "Men in Crisis in Russia: The Role of Domestic Marginalisation," *Gender and Society* 18, no. 2 (2004): 189–206; Rebecca Kay, *Men in Contemporary Russia: The Fallen Heroes of Post-Soviet Change?* (London, 2006); Elena Prokhorova, "The Post-Utopian Body Politic: Masculinity and the Crisis of National Identity in Brezhnev-Era TV Miniseries," in *Gender and National Identity in Twentieth-Century Russian Culture*, ed. Helena Goscilo and Andrea Lanoux (DeKalb, IL: 2006), 130–36; and Dawn Seckler, "Engendering Genre: The Contemporary Russian Buddy Film" (PhD dissertation, University of Pittsburgh, 2010).

# Bibliography

## ARCHIVAL POSTER COLLECTIONS:

British Library, London
Gosudarstvennyi arkhiv Rossiiskoi Federatsii, Moscow
Hoover Institution, Stanford University, California
National Library of Finland, Helsinki
Otdel izoizdanii, Rossiiskaia Gosudarstvennaia Biblioteka, Moscow

## PERIODICALS AND NEWSPAPERS:

*Current Digest of the Soviet Press*
*Iskusstvo*
*Izvestiia*
*Khudozhnik*
*Komsomol'skaia pravda*
*Krasnaia zvezda*
*Krasnyi sport*
*Krokodil*
*Ogonek*
*Pioneer: Detskii zhurnal*
*Pravda*
*Rabotnitsa*
*Rodina*
*Sem'ia i shkola*
*Sovetskaia zhenshchina*
*Sovetskii sport*
*Soviet News*
*Soviet Union: Illustrated Monthly*
*Soviet War News*
*Tvorchestvo*
*The USSR under Construction*

## PUBLISHED ART COLLECTIONS AND EXHIBITION CATALOGUES

Abolina, R. *50 let sovetskogo iskusstvo*. Moscow, 1967.
Akimova, L. I. *Iskusstvo RSFSR*. Leningrad, 1972.
Aleshina, L. S. *Russkoe iskusstvo XIX–nachala XX veka*. Moscow, 1972.
Antonova, V. I. *Gosudarstvennaia Tret'iakovskaia galereia*. Moscow, 1968.
Art Council of Great Britain and the Ministry of Culture of the USSR. *Art in Revolution: Soviet Art and Design since 1917*. London, 1971.
Baburina, N. I. *Russia in the Twentieth Century: A History of the Country in Poster*. Moscow, 2000.

——. *Russkii platkat Pervoi mirovoi voiny.* Moscow, 1992.

——. *Sovetskii zrelishchnyi plakat teatr, tsirk, balet, kino.* Moscow, 1990.

——. Sovetskii politicheskii plakat 1917–1980. Moscow, 1985.

Barabanov, E. *Vremia peremen: iskusstvo 1960–1985 v sovetskom soiuze.* St. Petersburg, 2006.

Barkhatova, E. *Konstruktivism v sovetskom plakate.* Moscow, 2005.

Bisti, D. *Knizhnoe iskusstvo SSSR.* Moscow, 1983.

Bruk, Ia. V. *Gosudarstvennaia Tret'iakovskaia Galereia: istoriia i kolloktsii.* Moscow, 1986.

Bulanova, M. *Soviet Dis-Union: Socialist Realist and Non-Conformist Art.* Minneapolis: MN, 2006.

Burdin, V. *Plakaty strany sovetov.* Moscow, 1982.

Butnik-Siversky, B. S. *Sovetskii plakat epokhi grazhdanskoi voiny 1918–1921.* Moscow, 1960.

Chapkina, M. *Khudozhestvennaia otkrytka.* Moscow, 1993.

Elliot, D., and V. Dudakov, eds. *One Hundred Years of Russian Art: From Private Collections in the USSR.* Oxford, 1989.

Fedotova, A. G. *Obraz zhizn-sovetskii: cherty sovetskogo obraza zhizni v proizvedeniia khudozhnikov Rossiikoi Federatsii.* Leningrad, 1986.

Galerie U Křižovníků. *Moc Obrazů, Obrazy Moci: Power of Images, Images of Power: Politický Plakát a Propaganda: The Political Poster and Propaganda.* Prague, 2005.

Gankina, E. Z. *Russkie khudozhniki detskoi kniga.* Moscow, 1963.

Gapeeva, V. I., V. A. Gusev, and A. V. Tsvetov. *Izobraziteľnoe iskusstvo Leningrada: vystavka proizvedenii leningradskikh khudozhnikov, Moskva, Noiabr' 1976—Ianvar' 1977.* Leningrad, 1981.

Glushko, N. N. *Velikaia pobeda i vozrozhdenie moskvy.* Moscow, 2005.

Gosudarstvennaia Tret'iakovskaia Galereia. *Ot avangarda do postmodernizma mastera XX veka.* Moscow, 2006.

——. *Sovetskoe iskusstvo.* Moscow, 1970.

——. *Sovetskoe iskusstvo v Gosudarstvennoi Tret'iakovskoi galeree 1917–1957.* Moscow, 1959.

——. *Sovetskaia skul'ptura, 1917–1952.* Moscow, 1953.

Gosudarstvennyi tsentraľnyi muzei sovremennoi istorii Rossii. *Lybochnaia kartinka i plakat perioda Pervoi mirovoi voiny 1914–1918gg., chast' I.* Moscow, 2005.

Gosudarstvennyi tsentraľnyi muzei sovremennoi istorii Rossii. *Lybochnaia kartinka i plakat perioda Pervoi mirovoi voiny 1914–1918gg., chast' II.* Moscow, 2005.

Guggenheim Museum. *Russia! Nine Hundred Years of Masterpieces and Master Collections.* New York, 2005.

*Historiia Belaruskaha mastatstva v shasti tamakh, 1941–1960.* Minsk, 1992.

Institute for Contemporary Art, P.S.1 Museum. *The Aesthetic Arsenal: Socialist Realism under Stalin.* New York, 1993.

Institut Istorii Iskusstv Ministerstva Kultury SSSR. *Iskusstvo i byt.* Moscow, 1959.

Ioganson, B. V. *Vsesoiuznaia iubileinaia khudozhestvennaia vystavka 1957 goda.* Moscow, 1958.

Iuferova, A. A. *Velikaia Otechestvennaia voina v proizvedeniiakh sovetskikh khudozhnikov.* Moscow, 1985.

Khazanova, V. E. *Sovetskoe izobraziteľnoe iskusstvo i arkhitektura 60–70-kh godov.* Moscow, 1979.

Krugli, I. A. *Brat'ia Tkachevy.* Moscow, 1985.

Lace, R. *Edgars Iltners.* Riga, 1992.

Lafont, M. *Soviet Posters: The Sego Grigorian Collection.* New York, 2007.

Leniashin, V. *Soviet Art 1920s–1930s: Russian Museum, Leningrad.* Moscow, 1988.

Levandovskii, S. N. *Mir otstoiali, mir sokhranim.* Leningrad, 1985.

Liubimova, A. B. *Agitatsiia za schast'e: sovetskoe iskusstvo stalinskoi epokhi.* Moscow, 1985.

Malakhov, M. I. *Sotsialisticheskii realizm i modernizm.* Moscow, 1970.

Mochaľskii, N. *Dmitrii Mochaľskii.* Moscow, 2008.

Morozov, A. I. *Sotsrealizm i realizm.* Moscow, 2007.

——. *Dniu pobedy: sovetskoe iskusstvo perioda Velikoi Otechestvennoi voiny.* Moscow, 2005.

Mozhukhovskaia, E. V. *Poiu moe otechestvo, respubliku moiu.* Leningrad, 1987.

Museum of Modern Art, Oxford. *Soviet Socialist Realist Painting 1930s–1960s: Paintings from Russia, the Ukraine, Belorussia, Uzbekistan, Kirgizia, Georgia, Armenia, Azerbaijan and Moldova Selected in the USSR by Matthew Cullerne Bown.* Oxford, 1992.

Nefedova, I. *Mastera sovetskogo iskusstva: E. Iltner*. Moscow, 1988.

Nemenskaia, L. *Boris Nemenskii*. Moscow, 2005.

Nikiforov, B. M. *Arkadii Aleksandrovich Plastov*. Moscow, 1972.

Nikolaeva, E. V. *Aleksandr Ivanovich Laktionov*. Leningrad, 1978.

Nurmukhammedov, N. B. *Iskusstvo Kazazhstana*. Moscow, 1970.

Orlova, M. A. *Iskusstvo sovetskoi Belorussi: zhivopis, skul'ptura, grafika*. Moscow, 1980.

Ovsiannikov, Iu. M. *Russkoe iskusstvo: illiustrirovannaia entsiklopediia: arkhitektura, grafika, zhivopis, skul'ptura, khudozhniki teatre*. Moscow, 2001.

Pankratova, V. N. *Iskusstvo, proverennoe, vremenem: agitplakat 1919, 1941, 1956*. Moscow, 1974.

Polikarov, V. P. *Soiuz iskusstvo i truda: Liudi truda v sovetskom izobraziteľnoe iskusstve*. Moscow, 1982.

Razumovskaia, S. V., and I. G Miiamlin. *Fedor Bogorodskii: Vospominaniia, stat'i, vystupleniia, pis'ma*. Leningrad, 1987.

Roginskai, F. C. *Peredvizhniki*. Moscow, 1997.

Rossiiskaia Gosudarstvennaia Biblioteka. *Plakaty voiny i pobedy, 1941–1945*. Moscow, 2005.

Sidorov, A. A. *Iurii Pimenov*. Moscow, 1986.

———. *Russkaia grafika nachala XX veka: ocherki istorii i teorii*. Moscow, 1969.

Snopkov, A., P. Snopkov, and A. Skliaruk. *Shest'sot plakatov*. Moscow, 2004.

Sokolnikov, M. P. *A. M. Gerasimov: zhizn' i tvorchestvo*. Moscow, 1954.

Solov'ev, V. Iu. *Pochtovye marki Rossii i SSSR 1857–1991*. Moscow, 1998.

Sopotsinskii, O. I. *Velikaia Otechestvennaiia voina v proizvedeniiakh sovetskikh khudozhnikov: zhivopis', skul'ptura, grafika*. Moscow, 1979.

———. *Art in the Soviet Union: Painting, Sculpture and Graphic Arts*. Leningrad, 1978.

———. *Iskusstvo narodov SSSR 1917–1970 g.* Leningrad, 1977.

———. *Sovetskoe izobraziteľnoe iskusstvo*. Moscow, 1962.

———. *Sovetskoe iskusstvo 1917–1957: zhivopis', skul'ptura, grafika*. Moscow, 1957.

*Sovetskaia Rossiia: Vtoraia Respublikanskaia khudozhestvennaia vystavka 6 fevralia—11 aprelia 1965 goda: katalog*. Moscow, 1965.

State Russian Museum. *The Russian Museum: A Centennial Celebration of a National Treasure*. St. Petersburg, 1998.

Suzdalev, P. K. *Podvigu 30 let: 9 V 1945–9 V 1975*. Moscow, 1975.

Svetlov, I. E. *O sovetskoi skul'ptura 1960–1980*. Moscow, 1984.

Sviridova, I. A. *Sovetskii politicheskii plakat*. Moscow, 1975.

Sysoev, P. M. *225 let Akademii khudozhestv SSSR: katalog vystavki: zhivopis', skul'ptura, arkhitektura, grafika, teatral'no-dekoratsionnoe iskusstvo, dekorativno-prikladnoe iskusstvo, dokumenty, izdaniia*. Moscow, 1985.

Sysoev, P. M., and V. A. Shivarikov. *Mastera sovetskogo izobraziteľnogo iskusstva*. Moscow, 1981.

Sysoev, V. P. *Viktor Ivanov*. Moscow, 2002.

———. *Aleksandr Deineka, zhizn', iskusstvo, vremia*. Leningrad, 1974.

Udre, A. *Tevijas kara impresijas: Impressii Velikoi Otechestvennoi*. Riga, 1982.

Veimarn, B. V. *Istoriia iskusstvo narodov SSSR, Tom 7*. Moscow, 1977.

Vishniakov, B. *Fedor Reshetnikov*. Moscow, 1982.

Voronov, N. V. *Sovetskaia monumentalnaia skul'ptura 1960–1980*. Moscow, 1984.

Vostretova, L. N. *Zhivopis' 1920–30 kh. godov*. St. Petersburg, 1991.

Zaitsev, E. V. *Khudozhestvennaia letopis' Velikoi Otechestvennoi: k 40-letiiu pobedy v Velikoi Otechestvennoi voine, 1941–1945*. Moscow, 1986.

## SELECTED ADDITIONAL PRIMARY MATERIAL:

Alexeyeva, L., and P. Goldberg. *The Thaw Generation: Coming of Age in the Post-Stalin Era*. Pittsburgh, PA: 1990.

*Ballada o soldate*; directed by G. Chukhrai, 1959.

Ehrenburgh, I. *The Thaw*, trans. M. Harari. London, 1955.

Gladkov, F. *Cement,* trans. A. S Arthur and C. Ashleigh. London, 1929.

Gruliow, L., ed. *Current Soviet Policies II: The Documentary Record of the 20th Communist Party Congress and Its Aftermath.* New York, 1956.

Johnson, P. *Khrushchev and the Arts: The Politics of Soviet Culture 1962-1964.* Cambridge, MA: 1965.

Khrushchev, N. S. *The Great Mission of Literature and Art.* Moscow, 1964.

*Letiat zhuravli;* directed by M. Kalatozov, 1957.

Ostrovskii, N. *How the Steel Was Tempered,* trans. R. Prokofieva. Moscow, 1959.

Polevoi, B. *Povest' o nastoiashchem cheloveka.* Moscow, 1955.

———. *A Story about a Real Man.* Amsterdam, 2002; reprint of 1949 edition.

*Povest' o nastoiashchem cheloveka;* directed by Aleksandr Stolper, 1948.

Sakowski, C., and L. Gruliow. *Current Soviet Politics IV: Documentary Record of the 22nd Party Congress of the Communist Party of the Soviet Union.* London, 1962.

Schlesinger, R., ed. *Changing Attitudes in Soviet Russia: The Family in the USSR, Documents and Readings.* London, 1949.

Sholokhov, M. *The Fate of a Man: Sud'ba cheloveka.* Moscow, 1984.

———. *Sud'ba cheloveka.* Moscow, 1964.

Steinbeck, J. *A Russian Journal.* Harmondsworth, 2000.

Tsybin V., ed. *Land of the Soviets in Verse and Prose Vol. 1.* Moscow, 1982.

———. *Land of the Soviets in Verse and Prose Vol. 2.* Moscow, 1982.

Tvardovsky, A. *Selected Poetry.* Moscow, 1981.

———. *Vasilii Tyorkin: A Book about a Soldier.* Moscow, 1975.

Weissbort, D. *Twentieth Century Russian Poetry: Selected with an Introduction by Yevgenii Yevtushenko.* London, 1993.

Werth, A. *Russia, The Post-War Years.* London, 1971.

———. *The Khrushchev Phase: The Soviet Union Enters the "Decisive" Sixties.* London, 1961.

## SELECTED SECONDARY MATERIAL

Aksiutin, Iu. *Khrushchevskaia "ottepel'" i obshchestvennye nastroeniia v SSSR v 1953-1964 gg.* Moscow, 2004.

Apor, B., J. C. Behrends, P. Jones, and E. A. Rees, eds. *The Leader Cult in Communist Dictatorships: Stalin and the Eastern Bloc.* Basingstoke, 2004.

Ashplant, T. G., G. Dawson, and M. Roper. "The Politics of War Memory and Commemoration: Contexts, Structures and Dynamics." In *The Politics of War Memory and Commemoration,* edited by T. G. Ashplant, G. Dawson, and M. Roper, 3-85. New York, 2000.

Ashwin, S., ed. *Gender, State and Society in Soviet and Post-Soviet Russia.* London, 2000.

Ashwin, S., and T. Lytkina. "Men in Crisis in Russia: The Role of Domestic Marginalisation." *Gender and Society* 18, no. 2 (2004): 189-206.

Attwood, L. *Gender and Housing in Soviet Russia: Private Life as Public Space.* Manchester, 2010.

———. "Housing in the Khrushchev Era." In *Women in the Khrushchev Era,* edited by M. Ilic, S. Reid, and L. Attwood, 177-202. Basingstoke, 2004.

———. "Celebrating the 'Frail-Figured Welder': Gender Confusion in Women's Magazines of the Khrushchev Era," *Slavonica* 8, no. 2 (2002): 159-77.

———. *Creating the New Soviet Woman: Women's Magazines as Engineers of Female Identity 1922-1953.* Basingstoke, 1999.

———. *Red Women on the Silver Screen: Soviet Women and Cinema from the Beginning to the End of the Communist Era.* London, 1993.

———. *The New Soviet Man and Woman: Sex-Role Socialization in the USSR.* Bloomington, IN: 1990.

Aulich, J., and M. Sylvestrová. *Political Posters in Central and Eastern Europe, 1945-1995: Signs of the Times.* Manchester, 2000.

Bailes, K. "Alexei Gastev and the Soviet Controversy over Taylorism, 1918–24." *Soviet Studies* 29, no. 3 (1977): 373–94.

Baliana, M. "It's Grand to Be an Orphan: Crafting Happy Citizens in Soviet Children's Literature of the 1920s." In *Petrified Utopia: Happiness Soviet Style*, edited by M. Baliana and E. Dobrenko, 99–114. London, 2011.

Baliana, M., and E. Dobrenko, eds. *Petrified Utopia: Happiness Soviet Style*. London, 2011.

Baraban, E. "'The Fate of a Man' by Sergei Bondarchuk and the Soviet Cinema of Trauma." *The Slavic and East European Journal* 51, no. 3 (Fall, 2007): 514–34.

Bartov, O. *Murder in Our Midst: The Holocaust, Industrial Killing, and Representation*. Oxford, 1996.

Berger, J. *Art and Revolution: Ernst Neizvestny, Endurance, and the Role of Art*. New York, 1997.

Bergman "Valerii Chkalov: Soviet Pilot as New Soviet Man." *Journal of Contemporary History* 33, no. 1 (1998): 132–54.

———. "The Idea of Individual Liberation in Bolshevik Visions of the New Soviet Man." *European History Quarterly* 21, no. 1 (1997): 57–92.

Berkhoff, K. C. *Motherland in Danger: Soviet Propaganda during World War II*. New York, 2012.

Bernstein, F. L. "Prosthetic Promise and Potemkin Limbs in Late-Stalinist Russia." In *Disability in Eastern Europe and the Former Soviet Union: History, Policy, and Everyday Life*, edited by M. Rassell and E. Iarskaia-Smirnova, 42–66. London, 2014.

———. "Envisioning Health in Revolutionary Russia: The Politics of Gender in Sexual-Enlightenment Posters of the 1920s." *The Russian Review* 57 no 2 (1998): 191–217.

Betts, P., and D. Crowley. "Introduction." *Journal of Contemporary History* 40, no. 2, *Domestic Dreamworlds: Notions of Home in Post-1945 Europe* (2005): 213–36.

Biess, F. "Men of Reconstruction—The Reconstruction of Men: Returning POWs in East and West Germany, 1945–55." In *Home/Front: The Military, War and Gender in Twentieth Century Germany*, edited by K. Hagemann and S. Schüler-Springorum, 335–58. Oxford, 2002.

Bittner, S. *The Many Lives of Khrushchev's Thaw: Experience and Memory in Moscow's Arbat*. Ithaca, NY: 2008.

Black, C. E., ed. *The Transformation of Russian Society: Aspects of Social Change since 1861*. Cambridge, MA: 1967.

Bohm-Duchen, M. *Art and the Second World War*. Farnham, 2013.

Bonnell, V. *Iconography of Power: Soviet Political Posters under Lenin and Stalin*. Los Angeles, 1999.

———. "The Peasant Woman in Stalinist Political Art of the 1930s." *The American Historical Review* 98, no. 1 (1993): 55–82.

———. "The Representation of Women in Early Soviet Political Art." *The Russian Review* 50, no. 3 (1991): 267–88.

Borenstein, E. *Men without Women: Masculinity and Revolution in Russian Fiction, 1917–1929*. London, 2000.

Boscagli, M. *Eye on the Flesh: Fashions of Masculinity in the Early Twentieth Century*. Boulder, CO: 1996.

Bourdieu, P. *Masculine Domination*. Translated by R. Nice. Cambridge, 2001.

———. *Distinction: A Social Critique of the Judgement of Taste*. Translated by R. Nice. London, 1986.

Bourke, J. "Effeminacy, Ethnicity and the End of Trauma: The Sufferings of 'Shell-Shocked' Men in Great Britain and Ireland, 1914–1939." *Journal of Contemporary History* 35, no. 1, Special Issue: Shell Shock (2000): 57–69.

———. *Dismembering the Male: Male Bodies, Britain and the Great War*. London, 1999.

Bowlt, J. *The Silver Age: Russian Art in the Early Twentieth Century and the World of Art Group*. Newtonville, MA: 1979.

Bowlt, J., ed. *Russian Art of the Avant-Garde: Theory and Criticism 1902–1934*. New York, 1976.

Bowlt, J., and O. Mitich. *Laboratory of Dreams: The Russian Avant-Garde and Cultural Experiment*. Stanford, CA: 1996.

Boym, S. *Common Places: Mythologies of Everyday Life in Russia*. London, 1994.

Brandenberger, D. *National Bolshevism: Stalinist Mass Culture and the Formation of Modern Russia.* London, 2002.

Braudy, L. *From Chivalry to Terrorism: War and the Changing Nature of Masculinity.* New York, 2005.

Brooks, J. *Thank You, Comrade Stalin! Soviet Public Culture from Revolution to Cold War.* Princeton, NJ: 1999.

———. *When Russia Learned to Read: Literacy and Popular Literature, 1861–1917.* Princeton, NJ: 1985.

Broughton, T., and H. Rogers, eds. *Gender and Fatherhood in the Nineteenth Century.* Basingstoke, 2007.

Brumfield, W. *A History of Russian Architecture.* Cambridge, 1993.

Brumfield W., and B. Ruble, eds. *Russian Housing in the Modern Age: Design and Social History.* Cambridge, 1993.

Bucher, G. "Stalinist Families: Motherhood, Fatherhood, and Building the New Soviet Person." In *The Making of Russian History: Society, Culture, and the Politics of Modern Russia,* edited by J. Steinberg and R. Wade, 129–52. Bloomington, IN: 2009.

Buchli, V. *An Archaeology of Socialism.* Oxford, 1999.

Buckley, M. *Mobilizing Soviet Peasants: Heroines and Heroes of Stalin's Field.* Lanham, 2006.

———. *Women and Ideology in the Soviet Union.* Hemel Hempstead, 1989.

Bureychak, T. "Masculinity in Soviet and Post-Soviet Ukraine: Models and Their Implications." In *Gender, Politics, and Society in Ukraine,* edited by O. Hankivsky and A. Salnykova, 325–61. Toronto, 2012.

Bushnell, J. "The 'New Soviet Man' Turns Pessimist." In *The Soviet Union since Stalin,* edited by S. Cohen, A. Rabinowitch, and R. Sharlet, 179–99. Bloomington, IN: 1980.

Carlbäck, H. "Lone Motherhood in Soviet Russia in the Mid-20th Century—In a European Context." In *And They Lived Happily Ever After: Norms and Everyday Practices of Family in Russia and Eastern Europe,* edited by H. Carlbäck, Y. Gradskova, and Zh. Kravchenko, 25–46. Budapest, 2012.

———. "Lone Mothers and Fatherless Children: Public Discourse on Marriage and Family Law." In *Soviet State and Society under Nikita Khrushchev,* edited by M. Ilic and J. Smith, 86–103. London, 2008.

Chernova, Zh. "The Model of Soviet 'Fatherhood.'" *Russian Studies in History* 51, no. 2 (2012): 35–62.

———. "'Muzhskaia rabota': analiz media-reprezentatsii." In *Gendernye otnosheniia v sovremennoi Rossii: issledovaniia 1990-kh godov. Sbornik nauchnykh statei,* edited by L. N. Popkova and I. N. Tartakovskaia, 276–94. Samara, 2003.

Clark, K. *Moscow, The Fourth Rome: Stalinism, Cosmopolitanism, and the Evolution of Soviet Culture, 1931–1941.* Oxford, 2012.

———. *The Soviet Novel: History as Ritual,* 3rd Edition. Bloomington, IN: 2000.

———. "Little Heroes and Big Deeds: Literature Responds to the Five-Year Plan." In *Cultural Revolution in Russia, 1928–1931,* edited by S. Fitzpatrick, 189–206. Bloomington, IN: 1978.

Clark, K., and E. Dobrenko, eds. *Soviet Culture and Power: A History in Documents 1917–1953.* London, 2007.

Clark, T. *Art and Propaganda in the Twentieth Century: The Political Image in the Age of Mass Culture.* London, 1997.

———. "The 'New Man's' Body: A Motif in Early Soviet Culture." In *Art of the Soviets: Painting, Sculpture and Architecture in a One-Party State, 1917–1992,* edited by M. C. Bown and B. Taylor, 33–50. Manchester, 1993.

Clements, B., R. Friedman, and D. Healey, eds. *Russian Masculinities in History and Culture.* Basingstoke, 2001.

Cohen, E. "Sex and the Married Communist: Family Troubles, Marital Infidelity, and Party Discipline in the Postwar USSR, 1945–64." *The Russian Review* 68, no. 3 (2009): 429–50.

Cohen S. *Masked Men, Masculinity and the Movies in the Fifties.* Bloomington, IN: 1997.

Condee, N. "Cultural Codes of the Thaw." In *Nikita Khrushchev,* edited by W. Taubman, S. Khrushchev, and A. Gleason, 160–76. Chelsea, MI: 2000.

Condee, N., ed. *Soviet Hieroglyphics: Visual Culture in Late Twentieth-Century Russia.* Bloomington, IN: 1995.

Connell, R. W. "The History of Masculinity." In *The Masculinity Studies Reader,* edited by R. Adams and D. Savran, 245–61. Oxford, 2002.

———. *The Men and the Boys.* Cambridge, 2000.

———. *Masculinities.* Cambridge, 1995.

———. *Gender and Power: Society, the Person and Sexual Politics.* Cambridge, 1987.

Cox, R. "All This Can Be Yours! Soviet Commercial Advertising and the Social Construction of Space, 1928–1956." In *The Landscape of Stalinism: The Art and Ideology of Soviet Space,* edited by E. Dobrenko and E. Naiman, 125–62. London, 2003.

Crowley, D., and S. E. Reid, eds. *Style and Socialism: Modernity and Material Culture in Post-War Eastern Europe.* Oxford, 2000.

Cullerne Bown, M. *Socialist Realist Painting.* London, 1998.

———.. *Art under Stalin.* Oxford, 1991.

Cullern Bown, M., and B. Taylor, eds. *Art of the Soviets: Painting, Sculpture and Architecture in a One-Party State, 1917–1992.* Manchester, 1993.

Cuordileone, K. A. "Politics in an Age of Anxiety: Cold War, Political Culture and the Crisis in American Masculinity 1949–1960." *Journal of American History* 87, no. 2 (2000): 515–45.

Dale, *Demobilized Veterans in Late Stalinist Leningrad.* London, 2015.

———. "Coming Home: Demobilization, Trauma and Postwar Readjustment in Late Stalinist Leningrad." In *Special Issue Psychische Versehrungen im Zeitalter der Weltkriege,* edited by G. Gahlen, W. Meteling, and C. Nübel. May 2015.

———. "The Varlaam Myth and the Fate of Leningrad's Disabled Veterans." *The Russian Review* 72, no. 2 (2013): 260–84.

Davies, S. *Popular Opinion in Stalin's Russia: Terror, Propaganda and Dissent 1934–1941.* Cambridge, 1997.

Davies, S., and J. Harris, eds. *Stalin: A New History.* Cambridge, 2005.

Davis, R., ed. *The Fictional Father: Lacanian Reading of the Text.* Amherst, MA: 1981.

Dawson, G. *Soldier Heroes: British Adventure, Empire and the Imagining of Masculinities.* London, 1994.

———. "The Blonde Bedouin: Lawrence of Arabia, Imperial Adventure and the Imagining of an English-British Masculinity." In *Manful Assertions: Masculinities in Britain since 1800,* edited by M. Roper and J. Tosh, 113–44. London, 1991,.

Deak, I. *The Politics of Retribution in Europe: World War II and Its Aftermath.* Princeton, NJ: 2000.

De Baecque, A. *The Body Politic: Corporeal Metaphor in Revolutionary France 1770–1800.* Stanford, CA: 1997.

DeGraffenried, J. *Sacrificing Childhood: Children and the Soviet State in the Great Patriotic War.* Lawrence, KS: 2014.

Demetriou, D. "Connell's Concept of Hegemonic Masculinity: A Critique." *Theory and Society* 30 (2001): 337–61.

Dobrenko, E., and E. Naiman, eds. *The Landscape of Stalinism: The Art and Ideology of Soviet Space.* London, 2003.

Dobson, M. *Khrushchev's Cold Summer: Gulag Returnees, Crime, and the Fate of Reform after Stalin.* Ithaca, NY: 2009.

Dower, J. *War without Mercy: Race and Power in the Pacific.* London, 1986.

Dudink, S. "Cuts and Bruises and Democratic Contestation: Male Bodies, History and Politics." *European Journal of Cultural Studies* 4, no. 2 (2001): 153–70.

Dudink, S., K. Hagemann, and A. Clark, eds. *Representing Masculinity: Male Citizenship in Modern Western Culture.* Basingstoke, 2007.

Dudink, S., K. Hagemann, and J. Tosh, eds. *Masculinities in Politics and War.* Manchester, 2004.

Dunham, V. S. "Images of the Disabled, Especially the War Wounded in Soviet Literature." In *The Disabled in the Soviet Union: Past and Present, Theory and Practice,* edited by L. Siegelbaum and W. McCragg, 151–65. Pittsburgh, PA: 1989.

———. *In Stalin's Time: Middleclass Values in Soviet Fiction*. Cambridge, 1976.

Dunn, E. "Disabled Russian War Veterans: Surviving the Collapse of the Soviet Union." In *Disabled Veterans in History*, edited by D. Gerber, 251–71. Ann Arbor, MI: 2000.

Dunn, S., and E. Dunn. "Soviet Attitudes and Achievements in Disability and Rehabilitation." *University of California Center for Slavic Studies, Berkeley*. December 1968.

Edele, M. *Soviet Veterans of the Second World War: A Popular Movement in an Authoritarian Society, 1941–1991*. Oxford, 2008.

———. "More Than Just Stalinists: The Political Sentiments of Victors 1945–53." In *Late Stalinist Russia: Society between Reconstruction and Reinvention*, edited by J. Fürst, 167–91. Oxford, 2006.

———. "Strange Young Men in Stalin's Moscow: The Birth and Life of the Stiliagi, 1945–1953." *Jahrbücher für Geschichte Osteuropas* 50 (2002): 37–61.

———. "Paper Soldiers: The World of the Soldier Hero according to Soviet Wartime Posters." *Jahrbücher für Geschichte Osteuropas* 47 (1999): 89–108.

Edmondson, L. "Putting Mother Russia in a European Context." In *Art, Nation and Gender: Ethnic Landscapes, Myths and Mother Figures*, edited by T. Cusack and S. Bhreathnach-Lynch, 53–62. Aldershot, 2003.

Edmondson, L., ed. *Women and Society in Russia and the Soviet Union*. Cambridge, 1992.

Efimova, A., and L. Manovich, eds. *Tekstura: Russian Essays on Visual Culture*. London, 1993.

Ely, C. *This Meagre Nature: Landscape and National Identity in Imperial Russia*. DeKalb, IL: 2002.

Ermeeva, A. N. "Women and Violence in Artistic Discourse of the Russian Revolution and Civil War, 1917–1922." Translated by D. Healey. *Gender and History* 16 (2004): 726–43.

Etkind, A. *Warped Mourning: Stories of the Undead in the Land of the Unburied*. Stanford, CA: 2013.

Fainsod, M. "Soviet Youth and the Problem of the Generations." *Proceedings of the American Philosophical Society* 108, no. 5 (1964): 429–36.

Field, D. A. *Private Life and Communist Morality in Khrushchev's Russia*. New York, 2007.

———. "Mothers and Fathers and the Problem of Selfishness in the Khrushchev Period." In *Women in the Khrushchev Era*, edited by M. Ilic, S. Reid, and L. Attwood, 96–113. Basingstoke, 2004.

———. "Irreconcilable Differences: Divorce and Conceptions of Private Life in the Khrushchev Era." *The Russian Review* 57, no. 4 (1998): 599–613.

Fieseler, B. "Soviet-style Welfare. The Disabled Soldiers of the Great Patriotic War." In *Disability in Eastern Europe and the Former Soviet Union: History, Policy, and Everyday Life*, edited by M. Rassell and E. Iarskaia-Smirnova, 18–41. London, 2014.

———. "The Bitter Legacy of the Great Patriotic War: Red Army Disabled Soldiers under Late-Stalinism." In *Late Stalinist Russia: Society between Reconstruction and Reinvention*, edited by J. Fürst, 46–61. Oxford, 2006.

———. "'Nishchie pobediteli': Invalidy Velikoi Otechestvennoi voiny v Sovetskom Soiuze." *Neprikosnovenyi zapas* 40–41, nos. 2–3 (2005): 1, accessed April 30, 2017, http://magazines.russ.ru/nz/2005/2/fi33.htm.

———. "Stimmen aus dem gesellschaftlichen Abseits: Die sowjetrussischen Kriegsinvaliden im 'Tauwetter' der fünfziger Jahre." *Osteuropa* 52, no. 7 (2002): 945–62.

Fitzpatrick, S., ed. *Stalinism: New Directions*. London, 2000.

———, ed. *Cultural Revolution in Russia, 1928–1931*. Bloomington, IN: 1978.

Fitzpatrick, S. "Social Parasites: How Tramps, Idle Youth and Busy Entrepreneurs Impeded the Soviet March to Communism." *Cahiers du Monde Russe* 47, nos. 1–2 (2006): 377–408.

———. *The Cultural Front: Power and Culture in Revolutionary Russia*. New York, 1992.

———. "Postwar Soviet Society: The 'Return to Normalcy', 1945–1953." In *The Impact of World War II on the Soviet Union*, edited by S. Linz, 129–55. Totowa, NJ: 1985.

Forest, B., and J. Johnson. "Unraveling the Threads of History: Soviet-Era Monuments and Post-Soviet National Identity in Moscow." *Annals of the Association of American Geographers* 92, no. 3 (2002): 524–47.

Förster A., and B. Beck. "Post-Traumatic Stress Disorder and World War II: Can a Psychiatric Concept Help Understand Postwar Society?" In *Life after Death: Approaches to a Cultural and Social*

*History of Europe during the 1940s and 1950s,* edited by R. Bessle and D. Schumann, 15–35. Cambridge, 2003.

Forth, C. *Masculinity and the Modern West: Gender, Civilisation and the Body.* Basingstoke, 2008.

Francis, M. "A Flight from Commitment? Domesticity, Adventure and the Masculine Imaginary in Britain after the Second World War." *Gender and History* 19, no. 1 (2007): 163–85.

Frantzen, A. *Bloody Good: Chivalry, Sacrifice, and the Great War.* London, 2004.

Friedman, R. *Masculinity, Autocracy and the Russian University, 1804–1863.* Basingstoke, 2005.

Fürst, J. *Stalin's Last Generation: Soviet Post-War Youth and the Emergence of Mature Socialism.* Oxford, 2011.

———. "Between Salvation and Liquidation: Homeless and Vagrant Children and the Reconstruction of Soviet Society." *Slavonic and East European Review* 86, no. 2 The Relaunch of the Soviet Project, 1945–64 (2008): 232–58.

———. "The Arrival of Spring? Changes and Continuities in Soviet Youth Culture and Policy between Stalin and Khrushchev." In *The Dilemmas of De-Stalinization: Negotiating Cultural and Social Change in the Khrushchev Era,* edited by P. Jones, 135–53. New York, 2006.

———. "The Importance of Being Stylish: Youth, Culture and Identity in Late Stalinism." In *Late Stalinist Russia: Society between Reconstruction and Reinvention,* edited by J. Fürst, 209–30. Oxford, 2006.

———. "Prisoners of the Soviet Self? Political Youth Opposition in Late Stalinism." *Europe-Asia Studies* 54 (2002): 353–75.

Fürst, J., ed. *Late Stalinist Russia: Society between Reconstruction and Reinvention.* Oxford, 2006.

Galmarini, M. C. "Turning Defects into Advantages: The Discourse of Labour in the Autobiographies of Soviet Blinded Second World War Veterans." *European History Quarterly* 44, no. 4 (2014): 651–77.

Garrard, J., ed. *World War 2 and the Soviet People, 4th World Congress for Soviet and East European studies: Selected papers.* London, 1993.

Gerber, D. "Disabled Veterans, the State, and the Experience of Disability in Western Societies, 1914–1950." *Journal of Social History* 36, no. 4 (2003): 899–916.

Gilmour, J., and B. Clements. "If You Want to Be Like Me, Train! The Contradictions of Soviet Masculinity." In *Russian Masculinities in History and Culture,* edited by B. Clements, R. Friedman, and D. Healey, 210–22. Basingstoke, 2001.

Golomstock, I. *Totalitarian Art: In the Soviet Union, the Third Reich, Fascist Italy and the People's Republic of China.* London, 1990.

Goscilo H. "Cinepaternity: The Psyche and Its Heritage." In *Cinepaternity: Fathers and Sons in Soviet and Post-Soviet Film,* edited by H. Goscilo and Y. Hashamova, 1–28. Bloomington, IN: 2010.

———. "Viktor Vasnetsov's Bogatyrs: Mythic Heroes and Sacrosanct Borders Go to Market." In *Picturing Russia: Explorations in Visual Culture,* edited by J. Neuberger and V. Kivelson, 248–53. New York, 2008.

———. "History and Metahistory in Soviet World War II Posters." In *Recalling the Past— (Re)Constructing the Past: Collective and Individual Memory of World War II in Russia and Germany,* edited by W. Bonner and A. Rosenholm, 221–29. Jyväskylä, 2008.

Goscilo, H., and Y. Hashamova, eds. *Cinepaternity: Fathers and Sons in Soviet and Post-Soviet Film.* Bloomington, IN: 2010.

Grant, S. *Physical Culture and Sport in Soviet Society: Propaganda, Acculturation and Transformation in the 1920s and 1930s.* London, 2014.

Gray, J. G. *The Warriors: Reflections on Men in Battle.* London, 1998.

Groys, B. "The Art of Totality." In *The Landscape of Stalinism: The Art and Ideology of Soviet Space,* edited by E. Dobrenko and E. Naiman, 96–124. London, 2003.

———. *The Total Art of Stalinism: Avant-Garde, Aesthetic Dictatorship, and Beyond.* Oxford, 1992.

Groys, B. et al., eds. *Traumfabrik Kommunismus: Die Visuelle Kultur der Stalinzeit = Dream Factory Communism: The Visual Culture of the Stalin Era.* Frankfurt, 2003.

Gudkov, L. "'Pamiat" o voine i massovaia identichnost' rossiian." *Neprikosnovennyi Zapas* vols. 2–3 (2005), accessed April 30, 2017, http://magazines.russ.ru/nz/2005/2/gu5.html.

Guerin, F., and R. Hallis. *The Image and the Witness: Trauma, Memory and Visual Culture.* London, 2007.

Guldberg, J. "Socialist Realism as Institutional Practice: Observations of the Interpretation of Works of Art in the Stalin Period." In *The Culture of the Stalin Period*, edited by H. Günther, 149–77. London, 1990.

Günther, H. "Wise Father Stalin and His Family in Soviet Cinema." In *Socialist Realism without Shores*, edited by T. Lahusen and E. Dobrenko, 178–90. London, 1997.

———. ed. *The Culture of the Stalin Period.* London, 1990.

Gutkin, I. *The Cultural Origins of the Socialist Realist Aesthetic, 1890–1934.* Evanston, IL: 1999.

Hagemann, K., and S. Schüler-Springorum, eds. *Home/Front: The Military, War and Gender in Twentieth-Century Germany.* Oxford, 2002.

Harris, S. *Communism on Tomorrow Street: Mass Housing and Everyday Life after Stalin.* Baltimore, MD: 2013.

———. "I Know All the Secrets of My Neighbors": The Quest for Privacy in the Era of the Separate Apartment." In *Borders of Socialism: Private Sphere of Soviet Russia*, edited by L. Siegelbaum, 171–90. New York, 2006.

Haynes, J. "Reconstruction or Reproduction? Mothers and the Great Soviet Family in Cinema after Stalin." In *Women in the Khrushchev Era*, edited by M. Ilic, S. Reid, and L. Attwood, 114–30. Basingstoke, 2004.

———. *New Soviet Man: Gender and Masculinity in Stalinist Soviet Cinema.* Manchester, 2003.

———. "Brothers in Arms: The Changing Face of the Soviet Soldier in Stalinist Cinema." *The Modern Language Review* 95 (2000), 154–67.

Healey, D. *Homosexual Desire in Revolutionary Russia: The Regulation of Sexual and Gender Dissent.* London, 2001.

Hellebust, R. "Aleksei Gastev and the Metallisation of the Revolutionary Body." *Slavic Review* 56, no. 3 (1997): 500–518.

———.. *Flesh to Metal: Soviet Literature and the Alchemy of Revolution.* London, 2003.

Hixson, W. L. *Parting the Curtain: Propaganda, Culture, and the Cold War, 1945–1961.* Basingstoke, 1997.

Hobsbawm E., and T. Ranger, eds. *The Invention of Tradition.* Cambridge, 1992.

Hodgson, K. *Written with the Bayonet: Soviet Poetry of the Second World War.* Liverpool, 1996.

Hoffmann, D. *Stalinist Values: The Cultural Norms of Soviet Modernity, 1917–1941.* Ithaca, NY: 2003.

———. "Mothers in the Motherland: Stalinist Pronatalism in Its Pan-European Context." *Journal of Social History* 34 (2000): 35–53.

———., ed. *Stalinism: The Essential Readings.* Oxford, 2003.

Horne, J. "Masculinity in Politics and War in the Age of Nation-States and World Wars, 1850–1950." In *Masculinity in Politics and War: Gendering Modern History*, edited by S. Dudink, K. Hagemann, and J. Tosh, 22–40. Manchester, 2004.

Hubbs, J. *Mother Russia: The Feminine Myth in Russian Culture.* Bloomington, IN: 1988.

Hudson, H. D. *Blueprints and Blood: The Stalinization of Soviet Architecture, 1917–1937.* London, 1994.

Ignatieff, M. "Soviet War Memorials." *History Workshop* 17 (1984): 157–63.

Ilic, M., ed. *Women in the Stalin Era.* Basingstoke, 2001.

———. "Women in the Khrushchev Era: An Overview." In *Women in the Khrushchev Era*, edited by M. Ilic, S. Reid, and L. Attwood, 5–28. Basingstoke, 2004.

Ilic, M, S. Reid, and L. Attwood, eds. *Women in the Khrushchev Era.* Basingstoke, 2004.

Ilic, M., and J. Smith, eds. *Soviet State and Society under Nikita Khrushchev.* London, 2008.

Jahn, H. *Patriotic Culture in Russia during World War One.* New York, 1998.

Jarvis, C. *The Male Body at War: American Masculinity during World War II.* DeKalb, IL: 2004.

Jenks, A. *The Cosmonaut Who Couldn't Stop Smiling: The Life and Legend of Yuri Gagarin.* DeKalb, IL: 2012.

Johnson, O. "The Stalin Prize and the Soviet Artist: Status Symbol or Stigma?" *Slavic Review* 70, no. 4 (2011): 819–43.

———. "'A Premonition of Victory': *A Letter from the Front*." *The Russian Review* 68 no 3 (2009): 408–28.

———. *Aleksandr Laktionov: A Soviet Artist*. PhD dissertation, University of Sheffield, 2008.

———. "Assailing the Monolith: Popular Responses to the 1952 All Union Exhibition." *Art History and Criticism*, vol. 3: *Art and Politics: Case Studies from Eastern Europe* (2007): 45–51.

Johnston, T. *Being Soviet: Identity, Rumour and Everyday Life under Stalin*. Oxford, 2011.

———. "Peace or Pacifism? The Soviet 'Struggle for Peace in All the World,' 1948–1954." *Slavonic and East European Review* 86, no. 2 The Relaunch of the Soviet Project, 1945–64 (2008): 257–82.

Jones, J. *Everyday Life and the "Reconstruction" of Soviet Russia during and after the Great Patriotic War, 1943–1948*. Bloomington, IL: 2008.

Jones, P. *Myth, Memory, Trauma: Rethinking the Stalinist Past in the Soviet Union, 1953–70*. London, 2013.

———. "Memories of Terror or Terrorizing Memories? Terror, Trauma and Survival in Soviet Culture of the Thaw." *Slavonic and East European Review* 86 no 2 The Relaunch of the Soviet Project, 1945–64 (2008): 346–71.

———. "From the Secret Speech to the Burial of Stalin: Real and Ideal Responses to de-Stalinization." In *The Dilemmas of De-Stalinization: Negotiating Cultural and Social Change in the Khrushchev Era,* edited by P. Jones, 41–61. New York, 2006.

Jones P., ed. *The Dilemmas of De-Stalinization: Negotiating Cultural and Social Change in the Khrushchev Era*. New York, 2006.

Judt, T. *Postwar: A History of Europe since 1945*. London, 2005.

Kaganovsky, L. *How the Soviet Man Was Unmade: Cultural Fantasy and Male Subjectivity under Stalin*. Pittsburgh, PA: 2008.

Kamemski, A. "Art in the Twilight of Totalitarianism." In *Art of the Soviets: Painting, Sculpture and Architecture in a One-Party State, 1917–1992,* edited by M. Cullerne Bown and B. Taylor, 154–60. Manchester, 1993.

Kaminsky, K. "Utopian Visions of Family Life in the Stalin-Era Soviet Union." *Central European History* 44, no. 1 (2011): 63–91.

Kassimeris, G. eds. *The Barbarization of Warfare*. London, 2006.

Kassof, A. "Youth Vs the Regime: Conflict in Values." *Problems of Communism* 3, no. 6 (1957): 15–23.

Kelly, C. "A Joyful Soviet Childhood: Licensed Happiness for Little Ones." In *Petrified Utopia: Happiness Soviet Style,* edited by M. Balina and E. Dobrenko, 3–18. London, 2012.

———. *Children's World: Growing Up in Russia, 1890–1991*. London, 2007.

———. "Riding the Magic Carpet: Children and Leader Cult in the Stalin Era." *The Slavic and East European Journal* 49, no. 2 (2005): 199–224.

———. "Grandpa Lenin and Uncle Stalin: Soviet Leader Cult for Little Children." In *The Leader Cult in Communist Dictatorships: Stalin and the Eastern Bloc,* edited by B. Apor, J. C. Behrends, P. Jones, and E. A. Rees, 102–22. Basingstoke, 2004.

———. "The Education of the Will: Advice Literature, Zakal and Manliness in Early Twentieth Century Russia." In *Russian Masculinities in History and Culture,* edited by B. Clements, R. Friedman, and D. Healey, 131–51. Basingstoke, 2001.

———. "Kul'turnost' in the Soviet Union: Ideal and Reality." In *Reinterpreting Russia,* edited by G. Hosking and R. Service, 198–213. London, 1999.

Kelly, C., and D. Shepherd, eds. *Constructing Russian Culture in the Age of Revolution 1881–1940*. Oxford, 1998.

———, eds. *Russian Cultural Studies: An Introduction*. Oxford, 1998.

Kettering, K. "'Ever More Cosy and Comfortable': Stalinism and the Soviet Domestic Interior, 1928–1938." *Journal of Design History* 10, no. 2 (1997): 119–35.

Khasbulatova, O. *Rossiiskaia gendernaia politika v XX stoletii: mify i realii*. Ivanovo, 2005.

Kiaer, C. "Was Socialist Realism Forced Labour? The Case of Aleksandr Deineka in the 1930s." *Oxford Art Journal* 28, no. 3 (2005): 321–45.

Kiaer, C., and E. Naiman, eds. *Everyday Life in Early Soviet Russia: Taking the Revolution Inside.* Bloomington, IN: 2006.

Kienitz, S. "Body Damage: War Disability and Constructions of Masculinity in Weimar Germany." In *Home/Front: The Military, War and Gender in Twentieth-Century Germany,* edited by K. Hagemann and S. Schüler-Springorum, 181–203. Oxford, 2002.

Kirschenbaum, L. A. *The Legacy of the Siege of Leningrad, 1941–1995: Myth, Memories, and Monuments.* Cambridge, 2006.

———. "'Our City, Our Hearths, Our Families': Local Loyalties and Private Life in Soviet World War II Propaganda." *Slavic Review* 59, no. 4 (2000): 825–47.

Kondoyanidi, A. "The Liberating Experience: War Correspondents, Red Army Soldiers, and the Nazi Extermination Camps." *The Russian Review* 69, no. 3 (2010): 438–62.

Koshulap, I. "Cash and/or Care: Current Discourses and Practices of Fatherhood in Ukraine." In *Gender, Politics, and Society in Ukraine,* edited by O. Hankivsky and A. Salnykova, 362–63. Toronto, 2012.

Kozlov, D. *The Readers of Novyi Mir: Coming to Terms with the Stalinist Past.* Cambridge, MA: 2013.

Krivosheev, G. F. *Soviet Casualties and Combat Losses in the Twentieth Century,* translated by J. Erickson. London, 1997.

Krylova, A. "'Healers of Wounded Souls': The Crisis of Private Life in Soviet Literature, 1944–1946." *The Journal of Modern History* 73, no. 2 (2001): 307–31.

Kucherenko, O. "'That'll Teach'em to Love Their Motherland!': Russian Youth Revisit the Battles of World War II." *The Journal of Power Institutions in Post-Soviet Societies* 12 (2011), accessed April 30, 2017, http://pipss.revues.org/3866.

———. *Little Soldiers: How Soviet Children Went to War 1941–45.* Oxford, 2011.

Kudrayshov, S. "Remembering and Researching the War: The Russian and Soviet Experience." In *Experience and Memory: The Second World War in Europe,* edited by J. Echternkamp and S. Martens, 86–115. New York, 2010.

Kukhterin, S. "Fathers and Patriarchs in Communist and Post-Communist Russia." In *Gender, State and Society in Soviet and Post-Soviet Russia,* edited by S. Ashwin, 71–89. London, 2000.

Landes, J. "Republican Citizenship and Heterosocial Desire: Concepts of Masculinity in Revolutionary France." In *Masculinity in Politics and War: Gendering Modern History,* edited by S. Dudink, K. Hagemann, and J. Tosh, 96–115. Manchester, 2004.

Lapierre, B. "Making Hooliganism on a Mass Scale: The Campaign against Petty Hooliganism in the Soviet Union 1956–64." *Cahiers du Monde Russe* 47, nos. 1–2 (2006): 349–76.

Lebina, N. *Muzhchina i zhenshchina: telo, moda, kul'tura. SSSR—ottepel'.* Moscow, 2014.

Lee, C. "Visual Stalinism from the Perspective of Heroisation: Posters, Paintings and Illustrations in the 1930s." *Totalitarian Movements and Political Religions,* 8, 3–4 (2007), 503–21.

Leeds, E. *No Man's Land: Combat and Identity in World War I.* Cambridge, 1979.

Leong, A. *Centaur: The Life and Art of Ernst Neizvestny.* Oxford, 2002.

Linz, S., ed. *The Impact of World War II on the Soviet Union.* Totowa, NJ: 1985.

Lipovetsky, M. "War as the Family Value: Failing Fathers and Monstrous Sons in *My Stepbrother Frankenstein.*" In *Cinepaternity: Fathers and Sons in Soviet and Post-Soviet Film,* edited by H. Goscilo and Y. Hashamova, 114–37. Bloomington, IN: 2010.

Livshiz, A. "Children's Lives after Zoia's Death: Order, Emotions and Heroism in Children's Lives and Literature in the Post-War Soviet Union." In *Late Stalinist Russia: Society between Reconstruction and Reinvention,* edited by J. Fürst, 192–208. Oxford, 2006.

———. "De-Stalinizing Soviet Childhood: The Quest for Moral Rebirth, 1953–58." In *The Dilemmas of De-Stalinization: Negotiating Cultural and Social Change in the Khrushchev Era,* edited by P. Jones, 117–34. New York, 2006.

Lovell, S. *The Shadow of the War: Russia and the USSR, 1941 to the Present.* Oxford 2010.

———. "Soviet Russia's Older Generation." In *Generations in Twentieth-Century Europe,* edited by S. Lovell, 205–26. Basingstoke, 2007.

Lyford, A. *Surrealist Masculinities: Gender Anxiety and the Aesthetics of Post World War I Reconstructions.* Berkeley, CA: 2007.

Maksakova, L. V. *Kul'tura sovetskoi Rossii v gody Velikoi Otechestvennoi voiny.* Moscow, 1977.

Maniychuk, J. *Realizm ta sotsialistychnyy realizm v Ukrajins'komu zhyvopysu radians'kogo chasu: Realism and Socialist Realism in Ukrainian Painting of the Soviet Era.* Kiev, 1998.

Markwick, R. *Soviet Women on the Frontline in the Second World War.* Basingstoke, 2012.

Maurer, R. "Restoring the Disabled Veteran and His Family." In *The USSR in Reconstruction: A Collection of Essays,* The American-Russian Institute, 45–71. New York, 1944.

McCallum, C. E. "Man about the House: Depicting Fatherhood and Male Domesticity in Soviet Visual Satire after Stalin." In *Palgrave Handbook of Women and Gender in Twentieth-Century Russia and the Soviet Union,* edited by M. Ilic, 329–46. London, 2018

———. "Scorched by the Fire of War: Masculinity, War Wounds and Disability in Soviet Visual Culture, 1941–65." *Slavonic and East European Review* 93, no. 2 (2015): 251–85.

———. "The Return: Post-War Masculinity and the Domestic Space in Stalinist Visual Culture, 1945–53." *The Russian Review* 74, no. 1 (2015): 117–43.

McCannon, J. "Tabula Rasa in the North: The Soviet Arctic and the Mythic Landscape in Stalinist Popular Culture." In *The Landscape of Stalinism: The Art and Ideology of Soviet Space,* edited by E. Dobrenko and E. Naiman, 241–60. London, 2003.

———. *Red Arctic: Polar Exploration and the Myth of the North in the Soviet Union, 1932–1939.* New York, 1998.

———. "Positive Heroes at the Poles: Celebrity Status, Socialist-Realist Ideals and the Soviet Myth of the Arctic, 1932–39." *The Russian Review* 56, no. 3 (1997): 346–65.

Mclman, B., ed. *Borderlines: Gender and Identities in War and Peace, 1870–1930.* London, 1998.

Merridale, C. "War, Death and Remembrance in Soviet Russia." In *War and Remembrance in the Twentieth Century,* edited by J. Winter and E. Sivan. Cambridge, 2010.

———. *Ivan's War: The Red Army 1939–1945.* London, 2005.

———. "The Collective Mind: Trauma and Shell-Shock in Twentieth-Century Russia." *Journal of Contemporary History* 35:1 Special Issue: Shell-Shock (2000), 39–55.

———. *Night of Stone: Death and Memory in Russia.* London, 2000.

Mosse, G. *The Image of Man: The Creation of Modern Masculinity.* Oxford, 1998.

———. *Fallen Soldiers: Reshaping the Memory of the World Wars.* Oxford, 1990.

Nakachi, M. "Gender, Marriage and Reproduction in the Postwar Soviet Union." In *Writing the Stalin Era: Sheila Fitzpatrick and Soviet Historiography,* edited by G. Alexopoulos, J. Hessler, and K. Tomoff, 87–100. New York, 2011.

———. "Population, Politics and Reproduction: Late Stalinism and Its Legacy." In *Late Stalinist Russia: Society between Reconstruction and Reinvention,* edited by J. Fürst, 23–45. Oxford, 2006.

Norris, S. "Laughter's Weapon and Pandora's Box: Boris Efimov in the Khrushchev Era." In *Cultural Cabaret: Russian and American Essays for Richard Stites,* edited by D. Goldfrank and P. Lyssakov, 105–38. Washington, DC: 2012.

———. *A War of Images: Russian Popular Prints, Wartime Culture, and National Identity, 1812–1945.* DeKalb, IL: 2006.

Nye, R. *Masculinity and Male Codes of Honour in Modern France.* Oxford, 1993.

O'Mahony, M. *Sport in the USSR: Physical Culture, Visual Culture.* London, 2006.

Oushakine, S. A. *The Patriotism of Despair: Nation, War, and Loss in Russia.* London, 2009.

Oushakine, S. A., ed. *O Muzhe(n)stvennosti.* Moscow, 2002.

Oushakine, S. A., and E. Trubina, eds. *Travma: Punkty.* Moscow, 2009.

Palmer, S. "How Memory Was Made: The Construction of the Memorial to the Heroes of the Battle of Stalingrad." *The Russian Review* 68 no 3 (2009): 373–403.

Papernaya, N. *Podvig veka: Khudozhnik, skul'ptory, arkhitekory, iskusstvovedy v gody Velikoi Otchestvennoi voiny i blokady Leningrada: vospominaniia, dnevniki, pis'ma, ocherku, litera-turnye zapisi.* Leningrad, 1969.

Paperny, V. *Architecture in the Age of Stalin: Culture Two.* Cambridge, 2002.

Peacock, M. *Innocent Weapons: The Soviet and American Politics of Childhood in the Cold War*. Chapel Hill, NC: 2014.

Pennington, R. *Wings, Women, and War: Soviet Airwomen in World War II Combat*. Lawrence, KS: 2007.

Petrone, K. *The Great War in Russian Memory*. Bloomington, IN: 2011.

———. "Motherland Calling? National Symbols and the Mobilization for War." In *Picturing Russia: Explorations in Visual Culture*, edited by J. Neuberger and V. Kivelson, 196–200. New York, 2008.

———. "Masculinity and Heroism in Imperial and Soviet Military-Patriotic Cultures." In *Russian Masculinities in History and Culture*, edited by B. Clements, R. Friedman, and D. Healey, 172–93. Basingstoke, 2001.

———. *Life Has Become More Joyous, Comrades: Celebrations in the Time of Stalin*. Bloomington, IN: 2000.

Phillips, L. L. "Gendered Dis/ability: Perspectives from the Treatment of Psychiatric Casualties in Russia's Early Twentieth-Century Wars." *Social History of Medicine* 20, no. 2 (2007): 333–50.

Phillips, S. D. "'There Are No Invalids in the USSR!': A Missing Soviet Chapter in the New Disability History." *Disability Studies Quarterly* 29, no. 3 (2009): unpaginated, accessed April 30, 2017, http://dsq-sds.org/article/view/936/1111.

Plamper, J. *The Stalin Cult: A Study in the Alchemy of Power*. London, 2012.

———. "Fear: Soldiers and Emotion in Early Twentieth-Century Russian Military Psychology." *Slavic Review* 68, no. 2 (2009): 259–83.

———. "The Spatial Poetics of the Personality Cult: Circles around Stalin." In *The Landscape of Stalinism: The Art and Ideology of Soviet Space*, edited by E. Dobrenko and E. Naiman, 19–50. London, 2003.

———. "Abolishing Ambiguity: Soviet Censorship Practices in the 1930s." *The Russian Review* 60, no. 4 (2001): 526–44.

Plamper, J., and K. Heller, eds. *Personality Cults in Stalinism = Personen Kulte im Stalinismus*. Göttingen, 2004.

Platt, K., and D. Brandenberger. *Epic Revisionism: Russian History and Literature as Stalinist Propaganda*. Madison, WI: 2005.

Pohl, M. "Women and Girls in the Virgin Lands." In *Women in the Khrushchev Era*, edited by M. Ilic, S. Reid, and L. Attwood, 52–74. Basingstoke, 2004.

Poiger, U. "A New, 'Western' Hero? Reconstructing German Masculinity in the 1950s." *Signs* 24, no. 1 (1998): 147–62.

Pollock, E. "Real Men Go to the Bania: Postwar Soviet Masculinities and the Bathhouse." *Kritika* 11, no. 1 (2010): 47–76.

Poore, C. "Who Belongs: Disability and the German Nation in Postwar Literature and Film." *German Studies Review* 26, no. 1 (2003): 21–42.

Potts, A. "Beautiful Bodies and Dying Heroes: Images of Ideal Manhood in the French Revolution." *History Workshop Journal* 30, no. 1 (1990): 1–21.

Prokhorov, A. "The Myth of the 'Great Family' in Marlen Khutsiev's *Lenin's Guard* and Mark Osep'ian's *Three Days of Viktor Chernyshev*." In *Cinepaternity: Fathers and Sons in Soviet and Post-Soviet Film*, edited by H. Goscilo and Y. Hashamova, 29–50. Bloomington, IN: 2010.

Prokhorov, G. *Art under Socialist Realism: Soviet Painting, 1930–1950*. Roseville East, NSW: 1995.

Prokhorova, E. "Mending the Rupture: The War Trope and the Return of the Imperial Father in 1970s Cinema." In *Cinepaternity: Fathers and Sons in Soviet and Post-Soviet Film*, edited by H. Goscilo and Y. Hashamova, 51–88. Bloomington, IN: 2010.

———. "The Post-Utopian Body Politic: Masculinity and the Crisis of National Identity in Brezhnev-Era TV Miniseries." In *Gender and National Identity in Twentieth-Century Russian Culture*, edited by H. Goscilo and A. Lanoux, 130–36. DeKalb, IL: 2006.

Reese, R. *Stalin's Reluctant Soldiers: A Social History of the Red Army, 1925–1941*. Lawrence, KS: 1996.

Reid, S. E. "Communist Comfort: Socialist Modernism and the Making of Cosy Homes in the Khrushchev Era." *Gender and History* 21, no. 3 (2009): 465–98.

———. "Modernizing Socialist Realism in the Khrushchev Thaw: The Struggle for a 'Contemporary Style' in Soviet Art." In *The Dilemmas of De-Stalinization: Negotiating Cultural and Social Change in the Khrushchev Era,* edited by P. Jones, 209–30. New York, 2006.

———. "The Meaning of Home: 'The Only Bit of the World You Can Have to Yourself.'" In *Borders of Socialism: Private Sphere of Soviet Russia,* edited by L. Siegelbaum, 145–70. New York, 2006.

———. "In the Name of the People: The Manège Affair Revisited." *Kritika* 6, no. 4 (2005): 673–716.

———. "The Khrushchev Kitchen: Domesticating the Scientific-Technological Revolution." *Journal of Contemporary History* 40, no. 2: *Domestic Dreamworlds: Notions of Home in Post-1945 Europe* (2005): 289–316.

———. "Two Russian Sculptors of the Twentieth Century." *The Russian Review* 64 no 1 (2005): 105–11.

———. "Women in the Home." In *Women in the Khrushchev Era,* edited by M. Ilic, S. Reid, and L. Attwood, 149–76. Basingstoke, 2004.

———. "Cold War in the Kitchen: Gender and the De-Stalinization of Consumer Taste under Khrushchev." *Slavic Review* 61, no. 2 (2002): 211–52.

———. "Socialist Realism in the Stalinist Terror: The Industry of Socialist Art Exhibition 1935–41." *The Russian Review* 60 no 2 (2001): 153–84.

———. "Masters of the Earth: Gender and Destalinisation in the Soviet Reformist Painting of the Khrushchev Thaw." *Gender and History* 11, no. 2 (1999): 276–312.

———. "All Stalin's Women: Gender and Power in Soviet Art of the 1930s." *Slavic Review* 57, no. 1 (1998): 133–73.

———. "Destalinisation and Taste, 1953–63." *Journal of Design History* 10, no. 2 (1997): 177–202.

———. *De-Stalinization and the Remodernization of Soviet Art: The Search for a Contemporary Realism, 1953–1963.* PhD dissertation, University of Pennsylvania, 1996.

———. "The 'Art of Memory': Retrospectivism in Soviet Painting of the Brezhnev Era." In *Art of the Soviets: Painting, Sculpture and Architecture in a One-Party State, 1917–1992,* edited by M. Cullerne Bown and B. Taylor, 161–87. Manchester, 1993.

Rosenfeld, A., ed. *Defining Russian Graphic Arts: From Diaghilev to Stalin, 1898–1934.* London, 1999.

Ruble, B. "From Khrushcheby to Korobki." In *Russian Housing in the Modern Age: Design and Social History,* edited by W. Brumfield and B. Ruble, 232–70. Cambridge, 1993.

Sanborn, J. A. *Drafting the Russian Nation: Military Conscription, Total War, and Mass Politics, 1905–1925.* DeKalb, IL: 2003.

Sandomirsky, V. "Sex in the Soviet Union." *The Russian Review* 10, no. 3 (1951): 199–202.

Sartorti, R. "On Making Heroes, Heroines, and Saints." In *Culture and Entertainment in Wartime Russia,* edited by R. Stites, 157–93. Bloomington, IN: 1995.

Schivelbusch, W. *The Culture of Defeat: On National Trauma, Mourning, and Recovery.* New York, 2003.

Schleifman, N. "Moscow's Victory Park: A Monumental Change." *History and Memory* 13 (Fall/Winter, 2001): 5–34.

Schoeberlein, J. S. "Doubtful Dead Fathers and Musical Corpses: What to Do with the Dead Stalin, Lenin and Tsar Nicholas?" In *Death of the Father: An Anthropology of the End in Political Authority,* edited by J. Borneman, 201–19. Oxford, 2004.

Schrand, T. "Socialism in One Gender: Masculine Values in the Stalin Revolution." In *Russian Masculinities in History and Culture,* edited by B. Clements, R. Friedman, and D. Healey, 194–209. Basingstoke, 2001.

Seckler, D. *Engendering Genre: The Contemporary Russian Buddy Film.* PhD dissertation, University of Pittsburgh, 2010.

Seniavkaia, E. S. *1941–1945. Frontovoe pokolenie. Istoriko-psikhologicheskoe issledovanie.* Moscow, 1995.

Sherman, D. J. "Monuments, Mourning and Masculinity in France after World War I." *Gender and History* 8, no. 1 (1996): 82–107.

Sherman, G. "Soviet Youth: Myth and Reality." *Daedelus* 91, no. 1: *Youth: Change and Challenge* (1962): 216–37.

Shneer, D. *Through Soviet Jewish Eyes: Photography, War, and the Holocaust.* London, 2011.

Shoemaker, R., and M. Vincent, eds. *Gender and History in Western Europe.* Oxford, 1998.

Sidorov, A. "The Thaw: Painting of the Khrushchev Era." In *Soviet Socialist Realist Painting 1930s–1960s: Paintings from Russia, the Ukraine, Belorussia, Uzbekistan, Kirgizia, Georgia, Armenia, Azerbaijan and Moldova Selected in the USSR by Matthew Cullerne Bown,* The Museum of Modern Art, Oxford, 30–40. Oxford, 1992.

Smith, M. *Property of Communists: The Urban Housing Program from Stalin to Khrushchev.* DeKalb, IL: 2010.

———. "Individual Forms of Ownership in the Urban Housing Fund of the USSR, 1944–64." *Slavonic and East European Review* 86, no. 2 The Relaunch of the Soviet Project, 1945–64 (2008), 285–305.

Smorodinskaia, T. "The Fathers' War through the Sons' Lens." In *Cinepaternity: Fathers and Sons in Soviet and Post-Soviet Film,* edited by H. Goscilo and Y. Hashamova, 89–113. Bloomington, IN: 2010.

Sokolova, N. I., V. F. Rynbin, and B. I. Volkov. *Khdozhniki teatra.* Moscow, 1969.

Solomon-Godeau, A. *Male Trouble: A Crisis in Representation.* London, 1997.

Sontag, S. *Regarding the Pain of Others.* New York, 2003.

Stangl, P. "The Soviet War Memorial in Treptow, Berlin." *Geographical Review* 93 (April 2003): 213–36.

Starks, T. *The Body Soviet: Propaganda, Hygiene, and the Revolutionary State.* Madison, WI: 2008.

Statiev, Alexander, "'La Garde meurt mais ne se rend pas!': Once Again on the 28 Panfilov Heroes." *Kritika: Explorations in Russian and Eurasian History* 13, no. 4 (2012): 769–98.

Stites, R. *Russian Popular Culture: Entertainment and Society since 1900.* Cambridge, 1993.

Stites, R., ed. *Culture and Entertainment in Wartime Russia.* Bloomington, IN: 1995.

Swanson, V. G. *Soviet Impressionism.* Woodbridge, 2001.

Tartakovskaia, I. N. "'Nesostoiavshchaiasia maskulinnost' kak tip povedeniia na rynke truda." In *Gendernye otnosheniia v sovremennoi Rossii: issledovaniia 1990-kh godov. Sbornik nauchnykh statei,* edited by L. N. Popkova and I. N. Tartakovskaia, 42–71. Samara, 2003.

Taubman, W., ed. *Khrushchev: The Man and His Era.* London, 2003.

Taubman, W., S. Khrushchev, and A. Gleason, eds. *Nikita Khrushchev.* London, 2000.

Taylor, B., and M. Cullerne Bown, eds. *Art of the Soviets: Painting, Sculpture and Architecture in a One Party State, 1917–1992.* Manchester, 2003.

Tchueva, E. "'Mir posle voiny': Zhaloby kak instrument regulirovaniia otnoshenii mezhdy gosudarstvom i invalidami Velikoi Otechestvennoi Voiny." In *Sovetskaia Sotsial'naia Politika: Stseny i deistvuiushchie litsa, 1940–1985,* edited by E. Iarskaia-Smirnova and P. Romanov, 96–120. Moscow, 2005.

Thurston, R., ed. *The People's War: Responses to World War II in the Soviet Union.* Chicago, 2000.

Tumarkin, N. "The Great Patriotic War as Myth and Memory." *European Review* 11, no. 4 (2003): 595–611.

———. *Lenin Lives! The Lenin Cult in Soviet Russia,* Enlarged Edition. London, 1997.

———. *The Living and the Dead: The Rise and Fall of the Cult of World War II in Russia.* New York, 1994.

Valkenier, E. K. *Ilya Repin and the World of Russian Art.* New York, 1990.

———. *Russian Realist Art: The State and Society: The Peredvizhniki and Their Tradition.* New York, 1989.

Valkenier, E. K., ed. *The Wanderers: Masters of 19th-Century Russian Painting: An Exhibition from the Soviet Union.* Dallas, TX: 1990.

Varga-Harris, "Homemaking and the Aesthetic and Moral Perimeters of the Soviet Home during the Khrushchev Era." *Journal of Social History* 41, no. 3 (2008): 561–89.

———. "Forging Citizenship on the Home Front: Reviving the Socialist Contract and Constructing Soviet Identity during the Thaw." In *The Dilemmas of De-Stalinization: Negotiating Cultural and Social Change in the Khrushchev Era,* edited by P. Jones, 101–17. New York, 2006.

Volkov, V. "The Concept of Kul'turnost': Notes on the Stalinist Civilising Process." In *Stalinism: New Directions,* edited by Sheila Fitzpatrick, 210–30. London, 2000.

Von Laue, T. H., and A. Von Laue. *Faces of a Nation: The Rise and Fall of the Soviet Union, 1917–1991.* Denver, CO: 1996.

Vysokovskii, A. "Will Domesticity Return?", translated by C. Sandstrom. In *Russian Housing in the Modern Age: Design and Social History,* edited by W. Brumfield and B. Ruble, 271–308. Cambridge, 1993.

Waterlow, J. "Sanctioning Laughter in Stalin's Soviet Union." *History Workshop Journal* 79, no. 1 (2015): 198–214.

Weiner, A. *Making Sense of War: The Second World War and the Fate of the Bolshevik Revolution.* Oxford, 2001.

——. "Saving Private Ivan: From What, Why, and How?" *Kritika* 1 (2000): 303–36.

——. "Nature, Nurture and Memory in a Socialist Utopia: Delineating the Soviet Socio-Ethnic Body in the Age of Socialism." *American Historical Review* 104, no. 4 (1999): 1114–55.

——. "The Making of the Dominant Myth: The Second World War and the Construction of Political Identities within the Soviet Polity." *The Russian Review* 55, no. 4 (1996): 638–60.

White, S. *The Bolshevik Poster,* 3rd Edition. Ljubljana, 1998.

Wingfield, N., and M. Bucur, eds. *Gender and War in Twentieth-Century Eastern Europe.* Bloomington, IL: 2006.

Woll, J. *Real Images: Soviet Cinema and the Thaw.* London, 2000.

Woods, E. "Performing Memory: Vladimir Putin and the Celebration of World War II in Russia." *The Soviet and Post-Soviet Review* 38, no. 2 (2011): 172–200.

Youngblood, D. *On the Cinema Front: Russian War Films, 1914–2005.* Lawrence, KS: 2007.

——. "A War Remembered: Soviet Films of the Great Patriotic War." *The American Historical Review* 106, no. 3 (2001): 839–56.

Yurchak, A. *Everything Was Forever until It Was No More: The Last Soviet Generation.* Princeton, NJ: 2006.

Zdravomyslova, E., and A. Temkina. "Krizis masculinnosti v pozdnesovetskom diskurse." In *O Muzhe(n)stvennosti,* edited by S. Oushakine, 432–51. Moscow, 2002.

Zdravomyslova, E., and A. Temkina, eds. *Rossiiskii gendernyi poriadok: sotsiologicheskii podkhod.* St. Petersburg, 2007.

Zegers, P., and D. Druick, eds. *Windows on the War: Soviet TASS Posters at Home and Abroad, 1941–1945.* Chicago, 2011.

Zhidkova, E. "Family, Divorce and Comrades' Courts: Soviet Family and Public Organizations during the Thaw." In *And They Lived Happily Ever After: Norms and Everyday Practices of Family in Russia and Eastern Europe,* edited by H. Carlbäck, Y. Gradskova, and Zh. Kravchenko, 47–64. Budapest, 2012.

Zubkova, E. "S protianutoi rukoi nishchie i nishchenstvo v poslevoennom SSSR." *Cahiers de Monde Russe* 2, no. 49 (2008): 441–74.

——. *Russia after the War: Hopes, Illusions, and Disappointments, 1945–1957,* translated by H. Ragsdale. New York, 1998.

——. *Obshchestvo i reformy.* Moscow, 1993.

# Index

*Page numbers for illustrations are in boldface.*